HUMAN SOCIETY AT THE CROSSROADS

About the Foundation

The volume has been produced by **Dr. L.M. Singhvi Foundation**. The trust is headed by **Smt. Kamala Singhvi** and managed by **Dr. Abhishek Manu Singhvi**. The Advisory Council is chaired by Dr. Karan Singh. The Foundation is a registered Public Charitable Trust. It seeks to promote schemes and activities in the realm of public life, law, politics, human rights, diaspora, education, literature, art, poetry, inter-faith movement and Indian history and culture, without reference to caste, creed or religion. All these areas were dear to the Late Dr. L.M. Singhvi, in each of which he made significant contributions.

About the Editor

Dr. S.R. Mohnot, Executive/Chairman, Centre for Industrial and Economic Research. He has served as United Nations Industrial Economist and Team Leader and as consultant to a number of governments, governmental institutions, such as the Asian Development Bank. He is President Emeritus, Indian Society for Training and Development and was honoured as Fellow. He has headed and associated with several professional institutions. He has authored or edited some widely acclaimed books including path-breaking • *Concise Encyclopaedia of Management and Economic Sciences (2000-09)* • *Concentration of Economic Power* • *Market Forecast and Indicators (2010-2020)* • *Reinventing the Public Sector (2003)* • *Towards a New Global Order (1993)*.

DR. L. M. SINGHVI
COMMEMORATION VOLUME

HUMAN SOCIETY AT THE CROSSROADS

IN SEARCH OF A NEW VISION

Edited by
Dr. S.R. Mohnot

Concept
Since 1974

Concept Publishing Company Pvt. Ltd.
New Delhi-110059

ISBN-13: 978-81-8069-837-8

First Published 2012

Published and Printed by

Concept Publishing Company Pvt. Ltd.
A/15-16, Commercial Block, Mohan Garden
New Delhi-110059 (India)
T : 25351460, 25351794, *F* : 091-11-25357109
E: publishing@conceptpub.com, W: www.conceptpub.com
Editorial Office: H-13, Bali Nagar, New Delhi-110 015, India.

Cataloging in Publication Data--*Courtesy:* D.K. Agencies (P) Ltd. <docinfo@dkagencies.com>

Human society at the crossroads : in search of a new vision : Dr. L.M. Singhvi commemoration volume/ edited by S.R. Mohnot.
p. cm.
Includes bibliographical references and index.
ISBN 9788180698378

1. India—Social conditions. 2. India—Politics and government. 3. India—Economic conditions. I. Singhvi, L. M. (Laxmi Mall), 1931-2007. II. Mohnot, Sohan Raj.

DDC 306.0954 23

The Prologue

The world is passing today through a turbulent phase in human history. It has become a conundrum of extremes leading to unprecedented complexities. Accelerated speed of advancement in science, technology and knowledge and human care, are juxtaposed with deepening concerns for human misery and the worst of criminal behaviour culminating in mindless and meaningless animosities. The phase is too complex to earn a single identity of its own. We experiment with one as expressed in the title of this commemorative volume, **Human Society at the Crossroads**.

The turbulent world of today needs the balm of wisdom, compassion and nobility of some unique personality like the Late Dr. L.M. Singhvi. One has only to span through scores of his writings, speeches and social and cultural initiatives, let alone rewarding actions, to comprehend how one could contribute to the stupendous and challenging tasks that have emerged for the present and future generations. It is this global scenario which has prompted us to include in this volume a few selected writings and addresses of Dr. Singhvi while being fully conscious of the fact that it is a volume to commemorate his memory.

Dr. Singhvi's concerns, always positively expressed, are too many to be included comprehensively. He had chaired and mentored literally over a thousand institutions engaged in social, legal, literary, philanthropic, and scientific work benefiting divergent segments of the society in India and around the world.

The volume represents a wide spectrum of issues, social concerns, human values, positive thoughts and advances which were not only dear to Dr. Singhvi but on which he devoted immense dedication and commitment. The essays and discourses are penned by luminaries in the respective areas of their rich work and contributions.

The volume is divided into four modules. The first attempts to analyse basic societal dynamics, all geared to the central theme of the volume. The second module focuses on specific themes, highlighting basic issues confronting the contemporary society. Economic and business dimensions are covered in the third module considering the growing dominance of economic and business developments.

The fourth module presents in his own scholastic and erudite manner selected thoughts and concerns of Dr. Singhvi. It represents a small basket of great thoughts providing a quick but thought-provoking bird's eye view.

Dr. L.M. Singhvi Foundation expresses a deep sense of gratitude to the erudite contributors who have spared their very valuable time from the outstanding work they are doing in different walks of life. It is their great regard for Dr. L.M. Singhvi and their own dedication to express their views on vital issues confronting the present and future generations of human society, which have prompted their contributions. Several other outstanding thinkers, artists, littérateurs, professsionals, social scientists and public figures have expressed their desire to join but we thought it would be better to reserve their contributions for another volume in the series.

This volume has been personally inspired, conceived and supported by Smt. Kamala Singhvi and Dr. Abhishek Manu Singhvi. It is their continued contribution, especially in preserving Dr. L.M. Singhvi's and other leading contributions included in this volume, that has made the venture successful.

We have been keen to name the leading authors for their thoughtful and scholarly contributions but when we attempted this, it meant that we will have to name almost all authors. Rather than repeating their most distinguished names, it would be preferable to refer to the contents. We have appended brief profiles of all the authors at the end of the volume although it appears that their contributions to the society are so well known that it would be sufficient and revealing to know their names only.

The primary object of the volume is to spur debate on each of the issues highlighted here. We are fully conscious that a lot more incisive probing could be devoted to unfold the intricacies of human society.

We acknowledge with immense appreciation the painstaking editorial assistance provided by Shri Harish Barthwal, Shri K.L. Kaul and Shri Ankur, besides others. These include the computer secretarial assistance extended by Shri Abhay Kumar and Shri P.G.M. Tharakan.

S. R. Mohnot

Contents

MODULE II

FOCUSED THEMES: ON CULTURE, GOVERNANCE & JUDICIARY

MODULE III

ECONOMIC AND BUSINESS DIMENSIONS

MODULE IV

SELECTED THOUGHTS AND CONCERNS OF DR. L.M. SINGHVI

Module I

Basic Societal Dynamics

CHAPTER 1

Approaching the Twenty-first Century*

JUSTICE A.S. ANAND

The Role of Judiciary in Society

As we stand on the threshold of the new millennium, it is time for us to reflect on what the future holds in store for us and review what we have achieved so far. As a nation much has been accomplished and yet so much more remains to be done. The world is changing in numerous ways—technology has become a central force—national borders are dissolving and economies are wedded together in ways scarcely imaginable a decade ago. Yet certain basic aims of every society remain the same. The aim of securing a just society is one such aim that has been with us long before the Christian calendar began. The institution that I will reflect on during the course of this discourse, lies today at the centre of the endeavour of securing a just society.

As an institution the Indian judiciary has always commanded considerable respect from the people of this country. The roots of this high regard lie in the impartiality, independence and integrity of the members of the judiciary. Respect for the judiciary is part of the common man's aspirations for maintaining Rule of Law and building a just society. The deeper aim of law is creation of a good society. Chanakya said "Law and morality sustain the world", which morality stems from ethical values. The real source of strength of the judiciary lies in public confidence in the institution. Today it is because of the public perception that the higher judiciary in the country occupies a position of pre-eminence among the three organs of the state. An independent judiciary is a national asset.

---

* The revised version of the Dashrath Mall Singhvi Memorial Lecture.

Expansion of Judicial Process in India

The Government of India Act, 1935 introduced the federal principle into Indian constitutional law. It also required Federal Court to decide constitutional matters. Appeals lay from the Federal Court to the Judicial Committee. Under the Constitution of India, 1950, the Supreme Court succeeded to the jurisdiction of the Federal Court and the Judicial Committee.

In a historical perspective, if we trace the path taken by the judiciary, in general, and the Supreme Court, in particular, we find that the Court has been responsive to the changes in the Indian society. The Constitution of India, with its chapters on Fundamental Rights and Directive Principles coupled with the federal system, inevitably threw new burdens on the Indian judiciary. You know the Latin maxim *bani judicis est ampliare jurisdictianem*—it is the duty of a good judge to extend the jurisdiction based as it is on the principle that law must keep pace with the society to retain its relevance. If the society moves but the law remains static, it shall be bad for both. The Indian judiciary has, during the last few decades, acted on the maxim pretty extensively in cases where protection of fundamental rights or basic human rights are concerned. I shall, however, deal a little more fully with the need of self-restraint in judge-made extensions.

The deeper aim of law is creation of a good society. Chanakya said, "Law and morality sustain the world", and morality stems from ethical values.

On January 28, 1950 at 9.50 a.m., the Supreme Court of India was inaugurated by the President of India, Babu Rajendra Prasad. Chief Justice Harilal Kania, and other judges, Fazal Ali, Patanjali Sastri, Mehr Chand Mahajan, B.K. Mukherjee and S.R. Das, and Attorney General M.C. Setalvad and Advocate Generals of different States were present. Also present were the first Prime Minister of India, Pandit Jawaharlal Nehru, his Cabinet colleagues and members of the Diplomatic Corps. On the morning of the inauguration, both Attorney General Setalvad and Chief Justice Kania, were much too conscious of the apprehensions entertained by many about the institution which they were destined to operate. They were aware of the following statement of Alladi Krishnaswamy Ayyar made in the Constituent Assembly:

> "The doctrine of independence is not to be raised to the level of a dogma so as to enable the judiciary to *function as a kind of super-legislature or super-executive*" (*Constituent Assembly Debates, Official Reports*, Volume XI, p. 837).

The following warning of Shri B.N. Rau, the then Constitutional Adviser about "arming the Supreme Court with vast powers" given in the Constituent Assembly was also present in their minds:

> "The Courts, manned by an irremovable Judiciary not so sensitive to public needs in the social or economic sphere as the representatives of a periodically elected legislature will, in effect, have a veto on legislation exercisable at any time and at the instance of any litigant"*(B.N. Rau, Constitutional Precedents, Third Series, p. 18)*.

In their address, Chief Justice Kania and Attorney General Setalvad, therefore, explained to the country the role that they and their newly born Court intended to play. They were anxious to make the institution 'noble and great'. Said Setalvad:

> "The task before us all is the building of a nation alive to its national and international duties, consisting of a strong central authority and federal units, each possessed of ample power for the diverse uses of a progressive people. In the attainment of this noble end, we hope and trust that this Court will play a great and singular role and establish itself in the consciousness of the Indian people."

Justice Kania, the Court's first Chief Justice, said that the Supreme Court would declare and interpret the law of the land, and with the tradition of the judiciary in the country, it would work in 'no spirit of formal on barren legalism'. Within the limits prescribed, the Supreme Court would be able to make a substantial contribution towards the formation of India into a great unit retaining its own civilisation, traditions and customs. He trusted that the people of India would also maintain the 'independence, honour and dignity' of the Supreme Court.

Initially, the Court followed a policy of adherence to narrow doctrine and tended to shy away from development of the law. In 1950 in *A.K. Gopalan's case,* AIR 1950 SC 27, the Supreme Court placed a rather narrow and restrictive interpretation upon Article 21 of the Constitution. By a majority, it was held in that case that ".... the procedure established by law means procedure established by a law made by the state" and the Court refused to infuse in that procedure the principles of natural justice. The Court also arrived at the conclusion that Article 21 excluded enjoyment of the freedom guaranteed under Article 19 because Article 19, according to the Court, postulated legal capacity to exercise the rights guaranteed by it. The Court appears to have been, at that time, clearly influenced by the changes made by the Drafting Committee to the original drafted article. The draft article read : "No person shall be deprived of his life and personal liberty without due process of law". The Committee appointed by the Constituent Assembly, guided by the American judges, recommended the substitution of the expression 'without due process of law' by the expression 'except according to the procedure established by law'. *Gopalan's case* was decided soon after the Constitution came into force more than 48 years ago. The judgment was mainly based on the language of the Constitution and the requirements of the particular case before the Court. "Life of law is not logic but experience". The law has not remained static. The doctrine of exclusivity of fundamental rights as evolved in *Gopalan's case* was thrown overboard by the same Court, about two decades later in *Bank Nationalisation case,* AIR 1970 SC 56, and four years later in 1974, in *Hardhan Saha's case,* AIR 1974 SC 2154. The Court judged the constitutionality of preventive detention with reference to Article 19 also.

Twenty-eight years after the judgment in *Gopalan's case* in 1978, the Supreme Court in *Maneka Gandhi's case,* AIR 1978 SC 597, pronounced that the procedure contemplated by Article 21 must be 'right, just and fair' and not arbitrary; it must pass the test of reasonableness and the procedure should be in conformity with the principles of natural justice and unless it was so, the requirement of Article 21 would not be satisfied.

This line of precedence is both dramatic and educative. The Court was obviously conscious that in human affairs, there is a constant recurring cycle of change and experiment and that a society changes as the norms acceptable to the society undergo a change. Since the progress of the society is dependant upon proper application of law to its needs, the path from *Gopalan* to *Maneka Gandhi* was covered by an attempt of the judiciary to mould and shape the law to respond to the society's desire that liberty must be effectively protected. I shall revert to the subsequent development and evolution of Article 21 a little later.

Soon after the coming into force of the Constitution, the State embarked upon various agrarian reforms. The Supreme Court felt that in the bargain the fundamental right to hold and enjoy property by the citizens under Article 31 was being sacrificed. The Supreme Court held that the method of deprivation was irrelevant and the compensation must be the market value. There, thus, arose a conflict between the ideals of fundamental rights, on the one hand, and the socialistic ideals in the Directive Principles and the policy of the

The Court was obviously conscious that in human affairs, there is a constant recurring cycle of change and experiment and that a society changes as the norms acceptable to the society undergo a change.

Congress party, on the other. Interference by the Courts in implementing agrarian reforms was seriously resented by the Executive and its view was shared by the Parliament, which had overwhelming Congress party's majority.

The Parliament felt that the Judges of the Supreme Court, in matters of land reform legislation, were trying to impose their personal philosophy on the nation rather than accepting the national philosophy. Judgments of the Supreme Court, particularly in the area of land reform, were neutralised by the Parliament by exercising its powers under Article 368 of the Constitution by amending the Constitution and removing the basis of those judgments. This was done, not in a spirit of confrontation but because the Parliament and the Executive believed that the socio-economic fabric on which the Constitution was founded was being defeated by the approach of the Supreme Court to property rights. By the amendment, the Parliament restricted the right to compensation in cases of acquisitions and requisitions for the State or State Corporations to the amount which the legislature prescribed.

The path from Gopalan to Maneka Gandhi was covered by an attempt of the judiciary to mould and shape the law to respond to the society's desire that liberty must be effectively protected.

Faced with a situation where the Parliament was amending the Constitution to neutralise judgment after judgment of the Supreme Court, in *I.C. Golaknath* v. *State of Punjab*, 1967 (2) SCR 762, the Supreme Court by a thin majority of six to five, on 27th February, 1967, ruled that Article 368 of the Constitution only provided for the procedure to amend the Constitution and was not to be construed as any independent source of power. It was opined that the amendments to the Constitution made by the Parliament could not encroach upon fundamental rights and if they did so, the amendments had to be declared void by reason of Article 13(2) of the Constitution. The Court, however, consciously adopted the principle of prospective overruling in that judgment and did not upset anything that had been done before.

The Parliament was once again quick to react and neutralise the effect of *Golaknath*. Article 368 as well as Article 13 were amended by the Constitution (Twenty-fourth Amendment) Act in 1971 with effect from November 5, 1971. Even the marginal note to Article 368 was amended. The validity of Twenty-fourth Amendment Act came up for consideration before the Supreme Court and in *Kesavananda Bharti* v. *State of Kerala*, 1973 (4) SCC 225, a 13-Judge Bench (7 : 6) rendered the judgment abridging the power of the Parliament to amend the Constitution so as to prevent uncontrolled exercise of the amendment power to abrogate or destroy the basic structure on which the very foundation of the Constitution was built. It is a part of history now that barely two days after the judgment in *Kesavananda Bharti's* case was delivered, on the retirement of the Chief Justice Sikri, the Executive struck a blow to the independence of the judiciary. It abandoned the precedent of appointing the senior most puisne judge as the Chief Justice and superseding Justice Shelat, Justice Hegde and Justice Grover, who along with Chief Justice Sikri had formed the majority, appointed the fourth senior most judge, Justice A.N. Ray, as the Chief Justice. The superseded Judges resigned.

The interpretation placed on Article 368 by the thin majority was sought to be removed by the Parliament by enacting the 42nd Amendment to the Constitution asserting parliamentary supremacy. The amendment had far reaching consequences for the judiciary. The statement of objects and reasons makes an interesting reading :

> "The democratic institutions provided in the Constitution had been subjected to considerable stresses and strains and vested interests had been trying to promote their selfish ends to the great detriment of public good."

Suspension of Constitutional Provisions and Emergency

The internal emergency was declared on 26th June, 1975. Articles 14, 19 and 21 were suspended. The fate of hundreds of political detenus came up for consideration before the Courts. While many of the High Courts in the country faced the situation rather bravely, the Supreme Court in the infamous case of ADM Jabalpur, leaving the courageous lone dissent of Justice H.R. Khanna by a majority of four, declared that the very right to life and liberty was no more available to a person detained by the State during the emergency. The consequences of independence and courage exhibited by Justice H.R. Khanna resulted in his supersession on the retirement of the Chief Justice Ray on the 27th January, 1977 and Justice M.H. Beg and not Justice H.R. Khanna was appointed the Chief Justice of India.

The Constitution (43rd Amendment) Act, 1977 omitted Article 31-D of the Constitution and amended various other Articles like Article 32A, 226, 131A and 145. After the internal emergency was lifted and there was change of political power at the centre with the Janta Party coming to power, immediate steps to neutralise 42nd Amendment by enacting Constitution (44th Amendment) Act, 1978 was taken to restore to the judiciary its lost independence. In the next stage of constitutional evolution by the judiciary, Article 21 came to protect a wider range of interests covering almost every field of human life. In *Madhav Hoskot's case,* AIR 1978 SC 1548, it was held that providing *free legal service to the poor* and needy was an essential element of the 'reasonable, fair and just procedure'. Again, in *Hussainara Khatoon's case,* AIR 1979 SC 1819, while considering the plight of the under trials in jail, *speedy trial* was held to be an integral and essential part of the 'right to life and liberty' contained in Article 21 of the Constitution of India. In *Nandini Satpathy* v. *P.L. Dani,* AIR 1978 SC 1025, the Supreme Court held that an accused has the *right to consult a lawyer* during interrogation and that the right not to make self-incriminatory statements should be widely interpreted to cover the pre-trial stage also. Again, in *Sheela Barse* v. *State of Maharashtra,* 1983 (2) *SCC* 96, the Supreme Court laid down certain *safeguards for arrested* persons. In *Bandhua Mukti Morcha's case,* AIR 1984 SC 802, the Supreme Court held that right to life guaranteed by Article 21 included the right to live with human dignity, free from exploitation. The concern of the courts for the under-privileged and the poor sections of the society was again reflected in *Bihar Legal Support Society* v. *The Chief Justice of India and others,* AIR 1987 SC 38.

Decisions on such matters as the right to protection against solitary confinement as in *Sunil Batra* v. *Delhi Admn.,* 1978 (4) SCC 494; the right not to be held in fetters as in *Charles Sobraj* v. *Supdt., Central Jail,* 1978 (4) SCC 104; the right against handcuffing as in *T.V. Vatheeswaran* v. *State of Tamil Nadu,* 1983 (2) SCC 68; the right against custodial violence as in *Nilabati Behera* v. *State of Orissa,* 1993 (2) SCC 746; the rights of the arrestee as in *D.K. Basu* v. *State of West Bengal,* 1997 (1) SCC 416; the right of the female employees not to be sexually harassed at the place of work as in the case of *Vishaka* v. *State of Rajasthan,* 1997(6) SCC 241, and *Apparel Export Promotion Council* v. *A.K. Chopra,* JT 1999 (1) SC 61, were extended by expanding the ambit and scope of Article 21 so as to include within its fold the right to live with human dignity because the dignity of man supersedes all other considerations. Realising that while human rights are necessary to promote the personality development of human beings, healthy environment is necessary to safeguard conditions conducive to such personality development, there being a natural link between environment development and human rights, this Court ruled in *Subhash Kumar* v. *State of Bihar,* 1991 (J) SCC 598, *that the right to pollution free water and air* is also a facet of Article 21. In *Doon Valley's case,* 1985 (2) SCC 431, the Court held that Article 21 includes in its sweep clean environment

Realising that while human rights are necessary to promote the personality development of human beings, healthy environment is necessary to safeguard conditions conducive to such a personality development, there being a natural link between environment development and human rights.

and that the permanent assets of mankind cannot be allowed to be exhausted. Again, with a view to minimise, if not altogether prevent, the violation of fundamental rights, award of compensation consequential upon the deprivation of fundamental right to life and liberty of a citizen, as a "palliative" for the unlawful acts of the instrumentalities of the State as in *Rudul Sah* v. *State of Bihar*, AIR 1983 SC 1086, and the line of cases following it like *Sebastian M Hongray* v. *Union of India*, AIR 1984 SC 1026 and *Bhim Singh* v. *State of J & K*, AIR 1986 SC 494, culminated in *Nilabati Behera* v. *State of Orissa*, 1993 (2) SCC 746, where this Court held :

> "The relief of monetary compensation, as exemplary damages in proceedings under Article 32 by this Court or under Article 226 by the High Courts, for established infringement of the indefeasible right guaranteed under Article 21 of the Constitution is a remedy available in public law and is based on the strict liability for contravention of the guaranteed basic and indefeasible rights of the citizen. The purpose of public law is not only to civilise public power but it is also to assure the citizen that they are under a legal system which aims to protect their interests and preserve their rights. Therefore, when the Court moulds the relief by granting compensation in proceedings under Article 32 or 226 of the Constitution seeking enforcement or protection of fundamental rights, it does so under public law by way of penalising the wrongdoer and fixing the liability for the public wrong on the State which has failed in its public duty to protect the fundamental rights of the citizen. The payment of compensation in such cases is not to be understood as it is generally understood in a civil action for damages under private law but in the broader sense of providing relief by an order of making 'monetary amends' under public law for the wrong done due to breach of public duty of not protecting the fundamental rights of the citizen."

Access to justice to protect their fundamental rights was almost illusory for the weaker sections of the Indian people due to their poverty, ignorance and illiteracy. To them, rights and benefits conferred by the Constitution meant nothing. Because of the handicap, they lacked the capacity to assert their rights. Thus, majority of the people of our country were subjected to denial of justice. The judiciary regarded it as its duty to come to the rescue of the underprivileged to help them to reap the benefits of economic and social entitlements. The strategy of Public Interest Litigation (PIL) was evolved to bring justice within the reach of the underprivileged classes.

The crucial point in the transformation of the Supreme Court was the introduction of wide ranging changes in modalities of access. The Supreme Court ruled that where judicial redress is sought in respect of a legal injury or a legal wrong suffered by persons, who by reason of their poverty or disability, are unable to approach the Court for enforcement of their fundamental rights, any member of the public, acting *bona fide*, can maintain an action for judicial redress. A large section of the people in India comprise 'have-nots' who suffer from different kinds of disabilities and are not even aware of any of their constitutional rights. Access to Courts for them has become a reality through the medium of PIL brought by social activists, not busy bodies, who are well equipped to espouse their cause. Judicial creativity of this kind has enabled realisation of the promise of socio-economic justice envisaged in the Preamble to the Constitution of India. This weapon was effectively used by the Supreme Court and the High Courts, being Constitutional courts, to a large extent in 1980s and later. The decisions of the Supreme Court in *Prem Shankar Shukla* v. *Delhi Administration*, AIR 1980 SC 1535; *Sunil Batra* v. *Delhi Administration*, AIR 1980 SC 1579; *Municipal Council, Ratlam* v. *Vardhichand*, AIR 1980 SC 1622; *Akhil Bharatiya Soshit Karamchari Sangh Railway* v. *Union of India*, AIR 1981 SC 298, and umpteen number of decisions thereafter and more particularly the decision of the Supreme Court in *S.P. Gupta's case*, AIR 1982 SC 149, represent watersheds in the development of Public Interest Litigation and liberalisation of the concept of *locus standi*.

The judiciary regarded it as its duty to come to the rescue of the under-privileged to help them to reap the benefits of economic and social entitlements.

One of the essential features of the Democratic Republic established under our Constitution is division of powers between the three important wings of the State : the Parliament and State Legislatures, the Executive and the Judiciary. These three wings have to operate in their own respective earmarked fields so that the democratic Governments both at the Centre and the States may function for the welfare of the citizens of this country. In the case of *Delhi Laws*, 1951 SCR 747, the Supreme Court noted the absence of specific provisions in the constitutional document exclusively vesting legislative powers in the legislature and judicial powers in the judiciary. Though the Judges differed widely as to the constitutional limits to delegation of legislative power but the majority opinion imported the "essence" of the doctrine of separation of powers and the doctrine of constitutional limitation and trust implicit in the constitutional scheme. In *Indira Gandhi* v. *Raj Narain* (1975), distribution and separation of power was treated as a basic structure. For the progress of the nation, however, it is imperative that all the three wings of the State function in harmony.

Power of Judicial Review

Since the Constitution divides power between different organs and prescribes limitations of the Parliament, the State Legislatures and the Executive, it also provides for an impartial umpire in the shape of an independent judiciary to resolve the inevitable disputes over the boundaries of constitutional power which arise in the processes of governance. The founding fathers entrusted this power of judicial review exclusively to the judiciary.

It is not generally appreciated that when a Court invalidates legislation, it neither approves nor condemns any legislative policy, nor is it concerned with its wisdom or expediency. It merely determines whether the legislation is in conformity with or contrary to the provisions of the Constitution. Similarly, when the Court strikes down an executive order, it does so not in a spirit of confrontation or to assert its superiority but it does in discharge of its constitutional duties and the majesty of the law. Likewise, when it upholds legislation or vindicates the executive, the Court does not play a second fiddle to the Government. In all those cases, the Court discharges its duty as a judicial sentinel, guarding the Ark of the Constitution so as to protect the integrity of the Constitution. It must, however, be borne in mind that in exercise of their power of judicial review, Courts do not decide a dispute or controversy which is purely theoretical or for which there are no judicially manageable standards available with them. The Courts, generally speaking, do not interfere with the policy matters of the executive unless the policy is either against the Constitution or some statute or is actuated by *mala fide* policy matters, fiscal or otherwise, are best left to the judgment of the executive.

The Court discharges its duty as a judicial sentinel, guarding the Ark of the Constitution so as to protect the integrity of the Constitution.

The expanded role of the judiciary has been given the title of *"Judicial Activism"* by those who are critical of this expanded role. The main thrust of the criticism is that the judiciary by its directives to the administration is usurping the functions of the legislatures and of the executive and is attempting to run the country, and according to some, even ruining it. What these critics of the judiciary overlook is that it is the tardiness of legislatures and the indifference of the executive to address itself to the complaints of the citizens about violations of their human rights and unfair treatment which provides the necessity for judicial intervention. In cases where the executive refuses to carry out the legislative will or ignores or thwarts the legislative will, it is surely legitimate for Courts to step in and ensure compliance with the legislative mandate. It must be remembered that the judiciary is always moved by an aggrieved person after traditional routes have failed. When the Court is apprised of and is satisfied about gross violations of basic human rights, it cannot fold its hands in despair and look the other way. The judiciary can neither prevaricate nor procrastinate. It MUST respond to the knock of the oppressed and the downtrodden for justice by adopting certain operational principles within the parameters of the Constitution and pass appropriate directions in order to render full and effective relief. Judicial activism generally encompasses an area of legislative vacuum in the field of human rights. In my opinion, judicial activism reinforces the strength of democracy and reaffirms the faith of the public in the Rule of Law. If the judiciary was also to shut its door to the citizen who finds the legislature as not responding and the executive is indifferent, the citizen would take to the streets and that would be bad both for the Rule of Law and democratic functioning of the State. No one can now suggest, as was done 20 years ago, that civil liberties can be deprived of by arbitrary means and all judicial interference is unwarranted so long as there is statutory authority.

What these critics of the judiciary overlook is that it is the tardiness of legislatures and the indifference of the executive to address itself to the complaints of the citizens about violations of their human rights and unfair treatment which provide the necessity for judicial intervention.

This is just a bird's eye view of the state of the Indian judiciary as we delve into the twenty-first century. So far the judiciary has acquitted itself well in its role, minor aberrations here and there, notwithstanding.

Future Challenges

(i) The Need for Restraint and Caution

Judicial activism and judicial restraint are two sides of the same coin. It is, therefore, essential to remember that judicial restraint in the exercise of its functions is of equal importance for the judiciary while discharging its judicial obligations under the Constitution. With a view to see that judicial activism does not become "judicial adventurism" and leads a Judge going in pursuits of

Judicial activism reinforces the strength of democracy and reaffirms the faith of the public in the Rule of Law.

his own notions of justice and beauty, ignoring the limits of law, the bounds of his jurisdiction and the binding precedents, the Courts must act with proper restraint and self-discipline. The Courts have to be careful to see that by their over zealousness, they do not cause any uncertainty or confusion either through their observations during the hearing of a case or through their written verdicts. If unmindful of the expected restraint, the Courts make observations orally or through written decisions, one way or the other, they may consciously or unconsciously cause uncertainty and confusion in the law. In that event, the law will not only develop along uncertain lines instead of a straight and consistent path but the judiciary's image may also, in the bargain, get tarnished and its respectability eroded. That would, indeed, be a sad day. The Courts should only create rights where they are certain that the right so created can be vindicated and the order of the Court can be enforced. The danger of the judiciary creating a multiplicity of rights without possibility of adequate enforcement is a real one. It must be guarded against. The judiciary should not become an institution of mere form bereft of substance. There are real limits to what the judicial process should attempt to accomplish and the judiciary should resist the temptation to cross those limits. The decisions of the Courts should be within the zone of juridical legitimacy. The judiciary cannot give decisions that ignore authoritative sources and are inconsistent or incoherent with the larger body of law.

The danger of the judiciary creating a multiplicity of rights without possibility of adequate enforcement is a real one.

I may, in this connection, also usefully refer to the observations of Justice V.R. Krishna Iyer, in an article on "Judicial Activism and Administrative Autonomy" published in a special issue, by the Lal Bahadur Shastri National Academy of Administration, Mussoorie 1997. The learned author said :

> "The Court cannot run the Government nor the Administration indulge in abuse of or non-use of power and get away with it. Even the Legislature has limitations and must comply with the parameters prescribed by the Constitution; and when they are breached, the Court steps in to correct. The essence or judicial review, which is a basic feature of the Constitution, is a constitutional fundamental. The radical role of the high bench (and even of the High Courts under Article 226) assigned to the Judiciary casts on it a great obligation as the sentinel in the *qui vive* to defend the values of the Constitution and the rights of Indians."

The judiciary can act only as an alarm clock and not as a time-keeper. The Courts can neither take over the functions of the Government nor allow the Administration to get away with its omissions and commissions.

Every judge must remain conscious of the limits of his jurisdiction and remember that his role is to uphold the majesty of the Rule of Law and his power is meant to be harnessed in public interest. There are certain tasks which it is not possible for the judiciary to perform. Complex problems of policy cannot be resolved with the limited data available within the confines of the judicial process. These kinds of problems are incapable of resolution by "judicially manageable standards" and the Courts must tread carefully when confronted by them. We, in the judiciary, must for ever remember the well-known saying that "absolute power corrupts absolutely". It is, therefore, the duty of the Courts to ensure that while exercising their powers, they do not overstep their permissible limits and remain within the bounds of the Constitution and the law. The greater the power—greater is the need for restraint. No civilised system of justice can permit judicial authoritarianism and, therefore, the Judges at all levels are expected to be circumspect and self-disciplined in the discharge of their judicial functions. The function of a Judge is Divine but the problem arises when the Judge starts thinking that he himself has become Divine. That is where ego takes over rationality and logic, and also rules of constitutionalism are placed on a back-burner. To retain public confidence in the institution, the Judges must guard against such pitfalls.

The judiciary should not become an institution of mere form bereft of substance. There are real limits to what the judicial process should attempt to accomplish and the judiciary should resist the temptation to cross those limits.

With a view to retain legitimacy and its efficacy, the potent weapon of PIL forged for the benefit of the weaker sections of society and those who, as a class, cannot agitate their legal problems by themselves, has to be used carefully so that it may not get blunted by wrong or overuse. It is necessary and essential that "public interest litigation" should develop on a consistent and firm path. Care has to be taken to see that PIL essentially remains public interest litigation and does not become either Political Interest Litigation or Personal Interest Litigation or Publicity Interest Litigation or used for persecution. If that happens, it would be unfortunate. PIL would lose its legitimacy and the credibility of the Courts would suffer. Finding the delicate balance and behaviour which it sets for others, and as

The function of a Judge is Divine but the problem arises when the Judge starts thinking that he himself has become Divine.

a matter of fact before laying down standards of behaviour for others the judiciary must demonstrate that the same standards apply to it and are being followed by it. Constant evaluation of the functioning of the institution needs, therefore, to be encouraged if the high esteem conferred on the judiciary is to be justified.

The societal perception of Judges as being detached and impartial referees is the greatest strength of the judiciary and every Judge must ensure that this perception does not receive a setback on any account. The Courts act for the people who have reposed confidence in them and, therefore, the greatest threat to the independence of judiciary is the erosion of credibility of the judiciary in public mind, for whatever reasons. Lord Denning who left for his heavenly abode after completing 100 years, once said: "Justice is rooted in confidence, and confidence is destroyed when right-minded go away thinking that the Judge is biased." The import of these observations is that the persons who don the robes of Judges, should, as far as practicable, be fair, just, unbiased and impartial, while engaged in the administration of justice.

Care has to be taken to see that PIL essentially remains public interest litigation and does not become either Political Interest Litigation or Personal Interest Litigation or Publicity Interest Litigation or used for persecution.

As Justice Marshall of the United States Supreme Court put it : "We must never forget that the only real source of power that we as Judges can tap is the respect of the people." The source of this respect was beautifully explained by Lord Denning :

> "They (meaning Judges) will not be diverted from their duty by any extraneous influences; nor by any hope of reward nor by the fear of penalties; nor by flattering praise nor by indignant reproach. It is the sure knowledge of this that gives the people confidence in judges."
>
> (*What next in the Law*, 1982, p. 310)

If a Judge decides wrongly out of motives of self-promotion, he is no less corrupt than a Judge who decides wrongly out of motives of financial gain. In either case the incumbent of the office is not worthy of being a Judge. His actions erode the status of the Judges. To guard against such latent dangers is, therefore, necessary.

(ii) Speedy Justice

One of the greatest challenges that stares us in the face as we advance into the new environment of the twenty-first century is the failure of judiciary to deliver justice expeditiously, which has brought about a sense of frustration amongst the litigants. Human hope has its limits and waiting endlessly is not possible in the current lifestyle.

When the judicial administration enters the twenty-first century, in not too distant a future, the first thing to be kept in view by all concerned is that the arrears of Court cases which have mounted up till now get eradicated at the earliest. This is not possible without the full and unstinted cooperation of the members of the Bar and the presiding Judges as partners in the great task of administration of justice. The consumer of justice wants unpolluted, expeditious and inexpensive justice. In absence of it, instead of taking recourse to law, he may be tempted to take law in his own hands. This is what the judicial system must guard against so that people do not take recourse to extra-judicial methods to settle scores and seek redress of their grievance. It has been noticed with dismay in recent years that often landlords do not file suits in rent courts but take help of anti-social elements to throw out the tenants by force and coercion. This is nothing else but resorting to the rule of the jungle. If this tendency proliferates, it would be a sad day for the constitutional democracy to which we are all wedded. The Bar and the Bench, have to together resolve to remedy these ills to preserve people's faith in the Rule of Law.

The high regard that people have for the judiciary often turns to dismay when faced with the working of the justice delivery system. The problem of delay on account of arrears has been a topic of discussion for decades. Many attempts at improvement of the situation have been made but there is no denying the fact that this continues to remain the central challenge facing the Indian judiciary. The lack of a speedy dispute resolution system has a direct impact on the level of lawlessness in our society. On the other hand, a peaceful society is a necessary precondition for any kind of development.

The report of the Arrears Committee 1989-90, highlighted and identified some of the causes. It was opined that unfilled vacancies in the High Courts, largely account for the accumulation of cases as loss of mandays was directly proportionate to the accumulation of cases. It is rather unfortunate that in the last fifty years, no scientific study has been undertaken to assess the needs of the number of judges needed, more particularly in the subordinate judiciary. A proper study is needed to be undertaken to work out proper requirement

The lack of a speedy dispute resolution system has a direct impact on the level of lawlessness in our society. On the other hand, a peaceful society is a necessary precondition for any kind of development.

of the infrastructure and number of Judges in the country on the basis of the pendency, rate of inflow of legal matters into the Courts and the estimated growth of litigation in the future. The ratio of Judges per million population in this country is the lowest in the world. However, it must not be forgotten that it is not merely a question of raising the strength of the Judges in the subordinate Courts and the High Courts which is the need of the day. It is crucial that the right appointments are made based on merit, suitability, ability and integrity. An unfilled vacancy may not cause that much harm as a wrongly filled vacancy. The difficulty in persuading the leading members of the Bar to accept Judgeship is real and so well known that I need not dwell on it in any greater detail.

The over flowing dockets of the Courts all over the country should, however, not be taken as a sign of failure of the system but a sign of faith in the administration of justice by those who are involved in litigation. Public resort to Court to suppress public mischief is a tribute to the justice delivery system.

Cumbersome features of the procedural law also contribute in no small measure to the delay in the disposal of cases. Too many appeals and revisions against even interim orders help vested interests to prolong litigation. These need to be curtailed. The Code of Civil Procedure was amended more than two decades ago but experience shows that cases are still adjourned for the asking either for filing written statement or documents or even for settlement of issues. No attempt is made to examine the parties at the first hearing, which may more often than not narrow down the controversy. This needs urgent attention of the Bar and the Bench.

The delay in the disposal of cases is also "Judge-made". Lack of punctuality, laxity and lack of control over the case file and Court proceedings contributes in no small measure to the delay in disposal of cases. The grant of unnecessary adjournments on the mere asking or on account of "strike call" adds to the problem. Court time is sacrosanct and no Judge has any right to waste it. The Judges of all levels must, therefore, respect the Court time and remain punctual. No laxity in that behalf is permissible. Not adhering strictly to Court timings is a serious aberration. It must be avoided at all costs. The delay in pronouncing judgments is yet another aspect which we the Judges at all levels must address. Administration of justice must resolve not to become parties to slow motion justice. To meet the challenge of delay in dispensation of justice all the three wings of the State must act without any further delay.

I believe that some of the ills with which our administration of justice is presently afflicted are capable of being cured if financial and administrative autonomy is granted to the judiciary. I have been observing and analysing the functioning of the judicial system as a citizen, as a practicing advocate and also as a Judge. The edifice of the administration of Justice rests on the shoulder of district level judiciary, as the majority of the litigants go only up to district level. The High Courts have power over the State Judiciary but they do not have any financial or administrative powers to create even one post of a subordinate Judge or of the subordinate staff, acquire or purchase any land or building for Courts, decide and implement any plan for modernisation of Court working. Chief Justices and their companion Judges of the High Court are best suited to know the requirements of the judiciary in their respective States. Their assessment and demand should receive proper consideration and not "rejected" on account of merely financial constraints. The Chief Justices of the High Courts who are high constitutional functionaries, know the needs of the judiciary of the State. They need to be given financial and administrative powers *vis-à-vis* State judiciary, by transfer of financial as well as administrative powers, from the executive to enable them to function effectively. One of the essential elements of the Rule of Law is judicial independence and every society has seen the need for it. Financial dependence on the executive, to an extent, impinges upon the independence of the judiciary when it is required to "negotiate" every time with the largest litigant—the State. Should that not be avoided to make the judiciary truly independent, vibrant and effective?

Some of the ills with which our administration of justice is presently afflicted are capable of being cured if financial and administrative autonomy is granted to the judiciary.

(iii) The Challenge of Expensive Justice

The high cost of litigation is yet another challenge which must be squarely met by the Bar and the Bench. We must admit that even after 50 years of independence, the poor, backward and weaker sections of the society do not feel that they have equal opportunities for securing justice because of their socio-economic conditions. The Government has demonstrated its *bona fide* and resolve in that behalf by enforcing and supporting Legal Services Authorities Act, which aims at providing a protective umbrella to the weaker sections of the society, against all injustices and giving it adequate funds. National Legal Services Authority is introducing various schemes to ensure speedy and inexpensive justice to the poor and downtrodden of this country. Last year the National Legal Services Authority had introduced a scheme for deputing Legal Aid Counsel in every Court of Magistrate in the country so that the poor prisoners in custody get immediate and free of cost legal assistance. The National Legal Services Authority has also initiated steps for establishing permanent and continuous Lok Adalats in all the districts in the country for providing a statutory forum to the litigants for amicable settlements of their disputes. Efforts are also on to establish such *Lok Adalats* in different government departments, statutory authorities and autonomous bodies so that the citizens' problems *vis-à-vis* these departments are settled through negotiations in the presence of Lok Adalat Judges. This experiment of alternative dispute resolution needs support of the Bar and the Bench.

Financial dependence on the executive, to an extent, impinges upon the independence of the judiciary when it is required to "negotiate" every time with the largest litigant—the State. Should that not be avoided to make the judiciary truly independent, vibrant and effective?

(iv) Administration of Criminal Justice

The administration of criminal justice in our country appears to be at crossroads. Large scale acquittals are eroding people's confidence in the effectiveness of criminal justice system. It is natural also because when people see persons accused of heinous and ghastly offences getting acquitted, they believe that either the Courts are too liberal or pro-criminal or are not functioning the way they ought to function. Unfortunately, they do not know nor do they try to know the reasons for such acquittals. I must, however, point out that most of the acquittals are on account of the fact that the witnesses produced by the prosecuting agencies do not support the prosecution cases. A very large number of acquittals are also on account of faulty, non-scientific and disoriented investigation.

Some acquittals also take place because the judicial officers, rather than carefully and properly sifting the evidence, take to the easy course of throwing out the prosecution case on account of insignificant discrepancies and narrow technicalities. They ignore human psychology and behavioural probability when assessing the testimonial potency of the evidence. It is often overlooked that justice cannot be made sterile on the spacious plea that no innocent should be punished even if many guilty escape. Indeed, innocent should not be punished but why should the guilty escape? The Courts must respond to the society's cry for justice and punish the guilty by a proper and judicious approach to assess the evidence.

CHAPTER 2

Dimensions of the Knowledge Society*

DR. A.P.J. ABDUL KALAM

My field of interest is rocketry. I have worked in Indian Space Research Organisation (ISRO) for 20 years and for an equal time in DRDO (Defence Research and Development Organisation). During my early phase of work in rocketry, I came across the book, *History of Rockets* by W. Van Braun, the designer of Saturn rocket that put astronauts on the moon and also Dr. Brown's research paper about India's ancient rocket development during the period 1750-1850. They describe it as a tiny war rocket used first in Sriranga Pattinam war to defeat the British and later, as reported, taken to Woolwick Artillery Museum at London. I also had an opportunity to visit the Woolwich Museum and was thrilled to see India's war rocket displayed from 1980s onwards. I then made up my mind that I must get India's first war rocket and also the first in the world and put it in one of my research centres at Imarat, Hyderabad. I then wrote a letter to Dr. Singhvi who was then the High Commissioner of India in UK, requesting to help. He tried his best and shared the same feelings with me. I am sure, with all his and our continuing efforts, India will get back its first rocket. That was the first interaction with Dr. Singhvi.

Another important event was when I met him during the Paramachar as Award (Kanchi Sankaracharya) function at Bhartiya Vidya Bhavan at Chennai. It was a spiritual environment where Swami Jayendra Saraswathigal, Swami Vijayendra Saraswathigal, along with Shri C. Subramaniam and Shri N.A. Pallkhivala were present. On that occasion, Dr. Singhviji gave a talk for ten minutes on connectivity in India's

*Based on Shri Dashrath Mall Singhvi Memorial Lecture delivered at India International Centre, New Delhi.

civilization and the spiritual strength of the nation. The whole audience was spell-bound as he made us feel that our civilizational strength is great knowledge and it is continuing. This should be the foundation. With technological advancement, the nation should be enriched spiritually with quality of life. Dr. Murli Manohar Joshi, in his talk on the Technology Day 2001, addresses superior society integrating science, technology and spiritual experiences. He quotes what Werner Heisenberg said in 1975, *"You know, in the west we have built a large, beautiful ship. It has all the comforts in it, but one thing is missing: it has no compass and does not know where to go. Men like Tagore and Gandhi and their spiritual forebears found the compass. Why can this compass not be put in the ship, so that both can realise their purpose?"* Hence, I have selected the topic "Dimensions of Knowledge Society", for this memorial lecture, and one of the dimensions is India's civilizational strength.

Integration of Multi-knowledge Resource

As an introduction, I would like to highlight how knowledge is multi-dimensional, based on some of our own experiences. Missile Technology Control Regime (MTCR) was clamped when I was busy in the missile programme, in 1980s. We had to necessarily indigenise a number of materials like electronic and structural material and various systems. During this phase, we needed delta ferrite free austenite stainless steel for specific applications. At that time, I had the opportunity to meet a famous cardiologist, Dr. Soma Raju, CARE Foundation, Hyderabad. I shared with him my concerns. He suggested that I must see the angiography and angioplasty process. I saw the angiography and angioplasty process in the monitor, where I witnessed two arteries blocked and two stents put through a cardiac catheter and a balloon fixed. After witnessing this process, Dr. Soma Raju told me that each cardiac stent costs around Rs. 80,000 to Rs. 100,000 depending on the specific needs. He mentioned, "missile induces pain in the heart, mind and body. But, I hope you have material that can be designed and configured as stent, so that a cost effective indigenous stent is available within the country to remove the pain". Our friendship intensified and in addition to my task, scientists at defence laboratories at Hyderabad along with Dr. Soma Raju and my friend Arun entered into the design and development of cardiac stent. The challenge was, how do you make it bio-compatible? In three months time, we succeeded in developing a cardiac stent. Of course, the stent went through animal casts and also the ethics committee clearance. It was implanted to thousands of patients under the guidance of Dr. Soma Raju. This stent was called the "KS stent" and has gone into production. This experience and knowledge is embedded in my heart because of the fact that a critical material developed for a missile can remove the pain of human hearts when medical science and material technology fused.

In this context, I would like to narrate another incident, which I experienced very recently. I have a friend, Dr. W. Selvamurthy, who is a physio-psycho-immuno expert. He highlights, how meditation, yoga or any other form of meditation normally removes the pain in an integrated treatment of meditation plus conventional medical treatment. Dr. Selvamurthy and myself were debating how insertion of stent in the artery can be avoided. But, it is a challenge. Fortunately, Global Hospital and Research Centre at Mt. Abu, headed by Dr. Pratap Midha and Defence Institute of Physiology and Allied Sciences joined together and formulated the best way of treatment to cardiac problem. When I reviewed this project two years back, about 60 people reported about their well-being. A few weeks back, I had the opportunity to visit the Global Hospital again. About 400 patients gave us a joyful presentation about their experiences during the past many years. We further discussed the performance of the new way of treatment, which is meditation plus unit on methods plus physical exercise. It was an experience of happiness to see the patients present X-ray records showing us how this new way of treatment has given great relief to their heart. The conflict between cardiology, psychology and theology still persists. But this experiment has given a new thrust for heart patients.

In the twentyfirst century, a new society is emerging where knowledge is the primary production resource and not capital and labour.

The message I would like to convey is: a knowledge system from medical science, physiology, psychology and healthcare should be integrated from a beautiful native Indian solution. This new integrated knowledge will give new dimensions to healthcare. In this integration of minds is essential.

Challenge of Change and Need for Second Vision

Since our independence in 1947, in many aspects of life, improvement in literacy, agricultural products, strategic areas, certain small and large-scale industries took place. Also, the life expectancy has increased. We are capable of producing sufficient foodgrains, cereals and milk. Today, India has the capability to design, develop and promote production of strategic systems for national development and security. Also, we have seen in the ambient conditions the growth in the Information Technology : the country is progressing in a limited way in software business and in hardware we are yet to take off. When India was clamped with economic sanctions in 1998, after the nuclear tests, by developed world, we combated successfully. The tools were food security and self-reliance in most of the strategic areas and production capability in certain sectors of industry. Now more than fifty years have gone by and we are counted as one of the hundreds of developing countries, in a distinct way from G-8 countries. We have many challenges. We are a nation of billion people. Nearly *300* million people who are below the poverty line have to join the mainstream of a good life : 100 per cent literacy, health for all, multiple industrial and agricultural productivity. Even life style with value system has to change. The question is: where do we stand in the competitive world?

Indices of World Competitiveness

One of the important needs is to understand, where we stand in the competitive world. The indices of world competitiveness are based on the global competitiveness report prepared by the World Economic Forum. The competitiveness is defined as 'the ability of a national economy to achieve sustained high rates of economic growth'. In that order of ranking Singapore is 1, USA 2, Hong Kong 3, Taiwan 4, Canada 5, UK 13, France 23, Germany 25, India 59. What decides world competitiveness? It is a combination triangle consisting of progressiveness of industry, technology push and governmental deregulation. All the three aspects have to work for achieving world competitiveness. In terms of overall GDP size, we are 12th in the world; in terms of per capita GDP we are 57th in the world. Is this status acceptable to us? Especially the young, I believe we should work for fourth or fifth position in terms of GDP as well as in terms of world competitiveness. This position should be reached by 2020 and we should aim for higher position in the later decades. I will share with you some ideas about the strategies and the tools to realise this status. That will pave the way for a developed India.

Knowledge, the Primary Production Resource

A knowledge society can be one of the foundations for such a vision of the nation: Developed India. Knowledge has many forms and it is available at many places. Knowledge has always been the prime mover of prosperity and power. The acquisition of knowledge has, therefore, been the thrust area throughout the world and sharing the experience of knowledge is a unique culture of our country. India is a nation endowed with natural and competitive advantages as also certain distinctive competencies. But these are scattered in isolated pockets and the awareness on these is inadequate. During the last century, the world has undergone a change from agricultural society, where manual labour was the critical factor, to industrial society where the management of technology, capital and labour provided the competitive advantage. Then the information era was born during the last decade, where connectivity and software products are driving the economy of a few nations. In the twenty-first century, a new society is emerging where knowledge is the primary production resource instead of capital and labour. Efficient utilisation of the existing knowledge can create wealth for the nation to improve the quality of life—in the form of better health, education, infrastructure and other social indicators. Ability to create and maintain the knowledge infrastructure, to develop knowledge workers and to enhance their productivity through creation, growth and exploitation of new knowledge, will be the key factors in deciding the prosperity of this Knowledge Society. Whether a nation has arrived at a stage of knowledge society is judged by the way the country effectively deals with knowledge creation and knowledge deployment. I am glad that a task team of the Planning Commission has taken a lead in generating a road map for transforming India to a knowledge society.

Knowledge Society Components

Knowledge Society has certain very important components driven by societal transformation and wealth generation. The societal transformation is on education, health care, agriculture and governance. These will lead to employment generation, high productivity and rural prosperity. How do we do that?

The wealth generation is a very important task for the nation, which has to be woven around national competencies. The task team has identified core areas that will spearhead our march towards knowledge society. The areas are: Information Technology (IT), bio-technology, space technology, weather forecasting, disaster management, tele-medicine and tele-education, technologies to produce native knowledge products, service sector and 'Infotainment' which is the emerging area resulting from convergence of information and entertainment. These core technologies, fortunately, can be interwoven by IT. IT took off only due to enterprising spirit of the young. Thus, there are multiple technologies and management structures that have to work together to generate knowledge society. It has to be recognised that the difference between an IT-driven society and a knowledge-driven society

Ability to create and maintain the knowledge infrastructure, to develop knowledge workers and to enhance their productivity and exploitation of new knowledge will be the key factors in deciding the prosperity of this Knowledge Society.

is in the role of multiple technology growth engines. With India carving a niche for itself in Information Technology, the country is uniquely placed to fully capitalise on the opportunity to quickly transform itself into a knowledge society.

Evolution of policy and administrative procedures, changes in regulatory methods, identification of partners and most importantly creation of young and dynamic leaders are the components to be in place. In order to generate wealth, which is the second component for establishing a knowledge society, it is essential that simultaneously a citizen-centric approach to evolution of business policy, user-driven technology generation and intensified industry-lab-academy linkages are established.

Societal Transformation

The agricultural society concentrated on producing the natural products such as grains, fruits, timber, ores and natural minerals. The industrial society added value to these products by incorporating explicit knowledge (high technology) to it. This not only added value to products but also increased the productivity. The Information Society adds further value by widely making available the explicit knowledge through electronic networking of information centres and thus making available information products worldwide. The knowledge society will be the society producing products and services that are rich in both explicit and tacit knowledge, thus creating more valuable products. It will emerge as a centre of excellence in certain institutions, which will expand to cover the entire country in a decade. The leading social group of the knowledge society will be its knowledge workers, who will have sufficient knowledge to create explicit and tacit knowledge-rich products. The society will be highly networked to create knowledge-intensive environment along with enabling process to efficiently create, share, exploit and protect the knowledge.

The IT growth in India has really highlighted that the data transformation into information is a business proposition. By 2010, India aimed at IT-enabled services consisting of human resource service, customer interaction, finance and accounting data search and integration and remote education. The wealth generation in real sense comes out of data, information, knowledge and innovation. But how fast we move India on the innovation path of business, e-business demands innovative software and hardware. As you all know, India is well placed at the dawn of the knowledge era. We should not miss this opportunity. Our culture and civilization has been enriched over the ages by great thinkers who have always taken an integrated view of life as a fusion of mind, body and intellect. Their vision of knowledge has blossomed in the form of many spiritual centres and classics. In the coming decades, the enriched young will see a confluence of civilizational and modern technological streams.

Knowledge Resource Protection

As regards the dimension of protection of knowledge there is a responsibility to design and implement an Intellectual Property Rights (IPR) system, which will protect India's vast biological and microbial wealth, the indigenous innovations and traditions of its people. For protecting wealth what we have at the present and what we were endowed with in the past, we need to look at the future opportunities, such as in genomic research. The knowledge of human genome is coming in the public domain today. Discovery and prospecting of new genes and new molecules for drug development and administration with full IPR protection is very vital. Otherwise, people of India will not benefit from this new knowledge through. Indians would have contributed in all the three niche areas—providing creative IT solutions, providing genetic material and creating leaders in pharma co-genomics for the rest of the world. We need to do value addition ourselves to generate IPR in these areas and not encash tomorrow's wealth today by just providing low cost services. With this background, let us look at the profile of second vision for the nation.

Second Vision for the Nation

The aspirations are mounting that India should become a developed country soon. This is the second vision for the nation. How we can prepare ourselves for this challenge? To become a developed India, the essential needs are:

(a) India has to be economically and commercially powerful, at least to be one of the five top nations in terms of size of the economy. Our target should be a GDP growth of 9 to 11 per cent annually and that the number of people below poverty line be reduced to a negligible level.
(b) Near self-reliance in defence needs of weapons and equipment with no umbilical attached to any outside world.
(c) India should have a right place in world forums.

Technology Vision 2020 is a pathway to realise this cherished mission. Technology Vision 2020 consisted of 17 technology packages in the core sectors such as agriculture and food, healthcare, infrastructure and strategic industries. The Task Teams formed by TIFAC with nearly 500 experts of our country worked for two years, deliberated on the national status of various branches of national development and generated 25 documents detailing the steps to be taken for creating wealth for the nation and the well-being of our people. A specialist team collated these documents into integrated strategies for development leading to the birth of India Millennium Mission 2020 (IMM 2020).

Five Mega Projects to Transform the Nation

We have identified five areas where India has a core competence for integrated action. The first is agriculture and food processing. We have to put a target of 360 million tonnes of food and agricultural production. Other areas of agriculture and agro food processing would bring prosperity to rural people and speed up the economic growth. Second, reliable and quality electric power for all parts of the country. Third, education and healthcare. We have seen, based on the experience, education and healthcare are inter-related. For example, Kerala with education and better healthcare can bring down the population growth and provide improvements in quality of life of the people. Similarly, in Tamil Nadu also, we have seen the downward growth of population resulting from a unique system of "mid-day meal" coupled with education. Studies about Andhra Pradesh also have different facets. These experiences, we feel, should be taken and spread in big States like Bihar and Uttar Pradesh. Beginning of agricultural prosperity through better yields in these States will help this process. Fourth, Information Technology. This is one of our core competence. We believe, this area can be used to promote education in remote areas and also to create national wealth. Fifth, Strategic Sectors. This area, fortunately, witnessed the growth in nuclear technology, space technology and defence technology.

These five areas are closely inter-related and lead to national, food and economic security. A strong partnership among the R&D, academia, industry, business and the community as a whole with the Government departments and agencies will be essential to accomplish the vision. The core to success is in various forms of connectivity.

The knowledge society will be the society producing products and services that are rich in both explicit and tacit knowledge, thus creating more valuable products.

We Can Do It

Freedom movement (1857-1947) was the first vision for the nation. This vision was realised in 90 years. It would have been a dream of an individual or collective groups. That dream transformed into thoughts which lead to revolutionary actions and finally resulted into freedom. Also, that period of independence move created great leaders with great actions.

Vision for a 'developed India', as discussed, is the second vision for the nation. I would like you to hear a great mind's powerful call, few thousand years ago, that would inspire actions for the second vision for the nation. Maharishi Patanjali in *Yoga Sutras* stated: *"When you are inspired by some great purpose, some extraordinary project, all your thoughts break the bounds. Your mind transcends limitations, your consciousness expands in every direction, and you find yourself in a new, great, and wonderful world. Dormant forces, faculties, and talents become alive, and you discover yourself to be a greater person by far than you ever dreamed yourself to be."*

That was a saintly saying to all of us. A nation is made great by the thoughts of its people and their action. The people in turn become important citizens of that great country. The next 20 years period, I consider, is a period of technology transformation in India. I anticipate new emerging economic situations. There is a possibility of India becoming a knowledge society with focused tool of Information Technology and entrepreneurial push. All the more, this ambience will demand our cultural and traditional value system to be embedded in our societal growth.

When I am in the midst of you, I thought of sharing with you three events that I came across. A few months back I had the opportunity to hear the talk of Nobel Laureate Prof Norman Borlaug at Vigyan Bhavan in Delhi. At the age of 87, he was unfurling the audience the vision of wheat production for the world population for the next two decades. He said that today the world population is 6 billion people. In 20 years time it will increase to 8 billion people. Food production has to double with the same available area and water or even less. Only technology and efficient management can help doubling the food production by improving the existing agricultural practices and above all efficient management of water and fertilizer, both inorganic and organic.

There is a possibility of India becoming a knowledge society with focused tool of Information Technology and entrepreneurial push. This ambience will demand our cultural and traditional value system to be embedded in our societal growth.

I had a similar experience with Shri C. Subramaniam. He was the main architect of first green revolution. I used to meet him very often at Chennai. Whenever I met him, I remember, at the age of 90 years, he was unfurling his second green revolution. This was the second event. The first green revolution was the process of seed to grain. The second green revolution that he envisaged is soil to seed to grain to food to marketing. He visualised a change of chain of not grain alone, but food processing and marketing.

Recently, I met a unique group who think different and want to travel on the untravelled road. This team (consisting of young and old) is dreaming about using advanced aerospace and energy technologies for bringing in revolution in abundant supply of fresh drinking water to the coastal cities using energy from space for desalination of seawater in a cost effective way.

The Promise

When I think of these three events and visionary thoughts, I feel confident that 'developed India' is possible in 20 years' time. As India fought for its freedom in an integrated way from 1857-1947, the young have to be responsible for a movement for transforming 'developing India' into 'developed India'. It is possible only by hard work, sweat and creativity.

The second movement for the nation will definitely result if our nation proclaims the second vision—developed India by 2020. I can see a virtual image of India, the children by 2020 will not see the high illiteracy, poverty and social differentiation. They will see a new India. Our children will sing the song of prosperous India if we sweat in this decade. Today, the Indian mind has to get ignited by the second vision for the nation. The ignited human mind is the most powerful resource on the earth, under the earth and above the earth to transform India into a developed nation with the foundation of knowledge society.

CHAPTER 3

Education for Shared Values for Inter-Cultural and Inter-Religious Understanding

DR. KARAN SINGH

Contradictions of Today's Life

Humanity stands today at a crucial and potentially decisive crossroads in its long and tortuous history on planet earth. On the one hand the twentieth century witnessed an astounding development in almost every sphere of human activity, with science and technology transforming life on this planet before our very eyes. The breaking of the space barrier, the landing on the moon, the probing of the planets and the stars beyond are a symbol of the astounding creativity of the human mind. Instant communications have now become routine, the Internet and other aspects of Information Technology have spread around the globe. For tens of millions of human beings there has been a substantial rise in living standards, and some have reached levels of affluence unknown in the past. The world has literally shrunk before our eyes and whether it is probing the majestic rhythms of cosmos or the sub-atomic dance of the neutrinos, human ingenuity has broken all barriers. We now have enough resources, if used with wisdom and compassion, to ensure for every human being on Planet Earth the material, educational and vocational inputs necessary for a decent human existence.

The breaking of the space barrier, the landing on the moon, the probing of the planets and the stars beyond are a symbol of the astounding creativity of the human mind.

On the other hand, the twentieth century has been probably the most lethal and destructive in the entire recorded history of humanity. The First and Second World Wars, and dozens of regional conflicts some of which are still raging, have killed millions of human beings—men, women and children alike—and dislocated many millions more. The rise and fall of Nazism and of Marxism-Leninism carried with them immense human suffering, death and disaster. The advent of nuclear power has introduced a new and deeply disturbing dimension into possible future conflicts. Fundamentalism, fanaticism and terrorism are on the rise in many parts of the world, and while the number of nations living in a democratic system have considerably increased, there are still grave threats to global peace and stability. Unilateralism has become a new doctrine putting in the shade the United Nations attempts to build a more democratic global society.

In this ambiguous situation, education for inter-cultural and inter-religious understanding assumes tremendous significance. The Unesco Commission for Education in the Twenty-first Century, of which I had the privilege to be a member, came out in 1996 with a report entitled *"Learning: the Treasure Within"*. I would warmly commend this report to educationists around the world as it covers in a comparatively short compass a broad gamut of educational problems and challenges. In this report we identified what we call Four Pillars of Learning : *Learning to Know, Learning to Do, Learning to Live Together and Learning to Be.* In this article I will direct my remarks at the third pillar, *Learning to Live Together.* There is an ancient Sanskrit hymn which exhorts "Let us work together, let us enjoy together, let us achieve together, may there be no hatred between us". To achieve this we need to develop at least six dimensions of value education.

The Human Values

The first dimension relates to family values. By this I do not mean a reversion to conservative or retrogressive social structures. What I speak of is the necessity for there to be harmony within the family, which after all is the first classroom and laboratory for every child. If there is constant conflict within the family, the effect upon children cannot but be negative. Family values such as respect and regard for elders, helpfulness, cooperative functioning and mutual affection can go a long way in laying the foundations for a positive mindset in the future. True, our educational system does not reach into the families,

On the other hand, the twentieth century has been probably the most lethal and destructive in the entire recorded history of humanity.

but that is where the first elements of education are inculcated, and where parent-teacher associations have an important role to play.

Here I must mention that the constant stream of horror and violence, of ultra-promiscuity and hyper *consumerism* that constantly bombard us through our television screen is surely having a negative impact upon young and impressionable minds. The frightful images that dominate our films appear as if they are rising from some bottomless pit of darkness and despair. The American obsession with death, disaster and dinosaurs is something that always astounds me. Small children are now plonked down in front of television screens even before they learn to run, so that these images become etched in their subconscious minds to fester and explode later in negative emotions and action. I am not sure what we can do about this, but I do wish to place this matter on the table so that educationists can seriously consider its implications. Certainly television is a marvellous tool for education, and programmes like the Discovery Channel and the National Geographic Channel are profoundly educative. But how do we ensure that children watch the positive rather than the negative programmes, that is the question.

The second set of values can be called societal values, which include courtesy, consideration to strangers and elders, punctuality, cleanliness and cooperation. After the family it is the school and college where these values need to be inculcated. Competition is certainly important, but in the process we must not lose the art of cooperative functioning within the educational institutions. Involving students in the proper maintenance of the campus and other activities such as catering and socially productive work is an excellent training for inter-cultural understanding. Educational institutions, wherever possible, should have an outreach to the community. In developing nations like India we have introduced the concept of Socially Productive Work (SPW) which involves students making periodic visits to slums or villages in the vicinity and assisting in projects designed to improve the standard of living, specially *vis-à-vis* health and education. This early training helps in developing a social conscience among students, and is important because it contains the seeds of what will hopefully grow into a cooperative society.

The frightful images that dominate our films appear as if they are rising from some bottomless pit of darkness and despair.

The third set of values involves environmental issues. It is now well known that the twentieth century witnessed a massive exploitation and degradation of the biosphere. Millions of acres of forest have disappeared, tens of thousands of species have vanished, the ozone layer is steadily attenuating and global warming is already upon us. If this trend continues, the long-range prospects for the very survival of the human race may itself be brought into question. It is, therefore, necessary that the students develop an awareness of the importance of preserving and improving the natural environment. All the religions of the world speak of this dimension. Almost two decades ago the historic conference at Assisi in Italy came out with Inter-religious Declarations on Man and Nature. I happened to write the Hindu Declaration. These declarations, although written from the point of view of the different religions, all stress the significance of nurturing Mother Earth, and are compiled in a WWF India publication which contains the text of these eight Declarations as well as supplementary material which could be valuable as an educational tool.

Inter-religious Understanding

The fourth set of values involves inter-religious understanding. Religion in history has had a very mixed record. On the one hand, much that is great and noble in human civilisation—art and architecture, painting and sculpture, scriptures and literature, moral codes and social organizations—can be traced back to one or other of the great religions of the world. On the other hand, more people have been massacred and burnt, tortured and persecuted in the name of religion than any other. Now that we have entered a new century where globalisation is growing rapidly, we can no longer afford the luxury of endless conflict in the name of religion. Even as I speak, fierce conflicts are raging around the world pitting one religion against the other and causing havoc and massive suffering.

The twentieth century witnessed a massive exploitation and degradation of the biosphere. Millions of acres of forest have disappeared, tens of thousands of species have vanished, the ozone layer is steadily attenuating and global warming is already upon us.

In many countries even today school textbooks are full of venom against other religions. Racism and tribal conflicts fall within the same category. In order to counteract this, an Interfaith movement has developed over the last century which seeks to bring together people of different religious persuasions in a harmonious and creative dialogue.

Between the First Parliament of the World's Religions in Chicago in 1893 and the Fourth in Barcelona earlier this year, there have been hundreds of Interfaith meetings around the globe and several major Interfaith organisations are active, including the Temple of Understanding of which I happen to be Chairman.

The key to inter-religious understanding lies in the acceptance of multiple paths to the divine. We must realise that there can be no monopoly of divine wisdom or spiritual methodology. The *Rig Veda* has a significant statement—The Truth is One, the wise call it by several names. If the divine exists, surely it cannot be monopolised by any one creed or religion. It is open to us to claim that our own religion is the most effective way to achieve the spiritual goal, but it is not acceptable that we should, therefore, persecute and terrorise people who belong to different religious tradition. Who are we, denizens of a tiny speck of dust that we call Planet Earth, to lay down that in the infinite billions of galaxies that surround us the illimitable spirit of the divine can appear only in one form or at one place or at one time. *Prima facie* this is unacceptable, and the time has now come when the great religions of the world must forgo their mutual antagonism and work together for the abolition of poverty and deprivation, hunger and malnutrition, disease and deprivation that still engulf more than half the population of our planet.

Now that we have entered a new century when globalisation is growing rapidly, we can no longer afford the luxury of endless conflict in the name of religion.

In this context, it is important that interfaith education should become part of curricula around the world. I am aware that this is a very sensitive matter, but if at least a basic introduction to the great religions of the world could be available to students, it would help to broaden their outlook, prevent extremism and further interfaith and inter-cultural understanding. I have brought out a small book entitled *Unity in Diversity* which contains extracts from the great religions of the world on a large number of topics. If even a book like this is available to students around the world as supplementary reading, it would help in the process of developing inter-religious understanding.

Spiritual Values

This brings me to the fifth set of values that I wish to speak about today, and that is spiritual values. I am making a distinction between religion and spirituality, although they are in fact closely intertwined. Religion necessarily involves a great deal of outer conformity and often mutual antagonism, whereas spirituality attempts to access the divine's power that resides within the deeper processes of our consciousness and cuts across theological and denominational differences. This is the many splendoured light mentioned in all the great religions of the world, what the Bible calls "the light that lighten every man that cometh into the world", Sufism the '*Noor i-Ilahi*'; Buddhism 'the *Bodhichitta*'; the

The key to inter-religious under standing lies in the acceptance of multiple paths to the divine. We must realise that there can be no monopoly of divine wisdom or spiritual methodology.

seers of the Hindu *Upanishads* exclaim in ecstasy "I have seen that great being shining like a thousand suns beyond the darkness". It is this inner light that we all need to access, whether through prayer, meditation, yoga, zen, tao, zikr or any other methodology. This, in the ultimate analysis, is the treasure within.

Finally, we need shared values for the emerging global society. We must have the courage to think globally, to break away from traditional paradigms and plunge boldly into the unknown. We must so mobilise our inner and outer resources that we begin consciously to build a new world based on mutually assured welfare rather than mutually assured destruction. As global citizens committed to human survival and welfare, we must use the latest array of innovative and interactive pedagogic methodologies to structure a worldwide programme of education—for children and adult alike—that would open their eyes to the reality of the dawning global age and their hearts to the cry of the oppressed and the suffering. And there is no time to be lost for, along with the emergence of the global society, the sinister forces of fundamentalism and fanaticism, of exploitation and intimidation are also active.

If these six sets of values could be incorporated into educational theory and curricula around the world, it will surely help in the process of global understanding. In addition, exchange of academics and students between different countries can help to break down barriers and negative stereotypes that have grown over the centuries, and help us move towards a sane and harmonious global society based upon inter-cultural and inter-religious understanding.

CHAPTER 4

The Cultural Foundation of Human Unity and the Growth of Multiculturalism

PROF. INDRA NATH CHOUDHURI

Cultural Foundations of Human Society

Thinking and sharing thoughts and the basic quest to find a common purpose of life is the cultural foundation of human unity. There are various ways of looking at the issue. Before that, let us start with an anecdote.

In 1973, I was ICCR Visiting Professor at the University of Bucharest. During the summer holidays, I came to London with my wife to spend our holidays. Because of my long association with the British Council, I made a visit to the British Council Headquarters in London. As I entered the office, the man at the reception asked my name in a typical King's English accent. It was 1973. In between I must have visited London several times but it was in 1997 when I was offered a job in London and I went to stay there for a period of three years. As usual I made a visit to the British Council and again the same question was repeated by the man at the reception, but this time not in the King's English accent but in a typical cockney style, what is my nyme (name)? I realised that England in the post-modernist period had shifted from mono-cultural to multicultural disposition. The way to multiculturalism in Britain became clear with the acceptance of a legislation (CRE) in 1976 against religious discrimination and incitement and subtle discrimination that replaced the explicit racism of the 1960s.

This could be defined as a social-political phenomenon of post-industrial society and also a post-modernist phenomenon to establish one's own identity and show respect for other identities. In the post-modernist era, the effort is to be natural, to be patriotic, to be nearer to the common man, to be socially conscious. In this period, writers, artists, cultural workers are showing awareness of their inheritance, complexity and uniqueness and as a result people have become conscious of their rootedness and also ethnicity and culture. Besides these twin impacts of socio-political and post-modernist phenomena the impact of modernisation and globalisation has also led both (i) the post-industrial society, as well as (ii) the newly industrialising developing society to multiculturalism arising from changes in the distribution of goods and services stemming from essential capitalist economic development. It is true that globalisation does not accept diversity. Its nature is to coopt, homogenise and appropriate all diversities for maximum gain and go for one homogeneous culture but in the process it has realised that local and regional concerns are to be protected for utmost gain and profit and hence acceptance of multi-culturalism has become a strategic necessity.

The topic assumes that the growth of multiculturalism is related to the cultural foundation of human unity. So far as the West is concerned, the question of human unity is quite problematic. West always thinks about its cultural uniqueness. It is a troublesome notion. It is rarely borne out by empirical research. It is an ideology which very often has been buttressed by nationalism, chauvinism and religious bigotry and hence the question of human unity is redundant in the West.

There is another reason. The 'other' in the West is an inalienable entity external to oneself. It is both a source of terror and an object of desire. Sartre's famous statement "Hell is the other" carries a strong echo of Hegel, who always defines one's identity as identity against the other either to be appropriated or to be destroyed. But the Western mind knows well that if he succeeds in completely subjugating the 'other' the identity of his own self becomes dubious. He wants to become whole by destroying the 'other' but without the 'other', he becomes nothing.

Herein is proclaimed the unity of the human beings in the midst of all their diversities. This is based on the concept of unity in diversity, instead of uniformity.

The whole issue of the cultural foundation of human unity is related to the concept of humanism or the concept of dignity of human beings, love and the welfare of human race. For most people in the West, humanism means the literary and aesthetic renaissance with which medievalism ended and the modern age began. The Fifteenth Century European Renaissance was dominantly characterised by (i) scientific reasoning, (ii) individual freedom, and (iii) humanism. But Christian humanism has existed long before. The voice that said: 'Sabbath is intended for man and not man for Sabbath' was a humanist's accent. Since God was known as the Father of all, the soul—as a drop of His Being—is naturally His son. As it says in John's gospel, concerning John the Baptist: 'As many as received him he gave to them the power to become the sons of God' (John 1 : 12.).

Humanism

Humanism means something different today. In renaissance, it stood for a view of life that, while devoutly accepting the existence of God, shared many of the intellectual attitudes of the ancient pagan world. It was interested in aesthetics, saw the usefulness of a knowledge of history, and was convinced that man's chief duty was to enjoy his life soberly and serve his community actively. Thus humanism restored to balance the scales which the Middle Ages had tilted with a concern for eternity. It stressed earthly fulfilment rather than preparation for paradise. It had its spiritual side but it reflected a society that was more interested in worldly matters—a society that was practical, canny, self-conscious, and ambitious. One quality that renaissance stressed was that of all-round competence, which became the hallmark of renaissance man. It was also stressed that a man's learning should be put at the disposal of others, that he should live an active civic life rather than revel privately in the delights of scholarship.

In the Middle Ages, to praise man was to praise God, for man was a creation of God. But renaissance writers praised man himself as a creator. They played down the sinfulness he was born with and emphasised his ability to think and act for himself, to produce works of art, to guide the destiny of others. They freed man from his sagged place in the medieval hierarchy, half-way between matter and spirit, and allowed him to roam at will through all the levels of being, sometimes identifying himself with the brutes, sometimes with the angels. He was seen as the ruler of nature—the Lord—although not the Lord of creation.

This new vision of man sprang from a heightened awareness of self. Medieval men had been preoccupied with searching their souls, but renaissance men were much more intrigued with exploring and, indeed parading, their own personalities. Patriarch is a perfect example. Although his serious interests centred on his work in discovering and editing ancient texts, Patriarch was also interested in himself. In his letters, designed for posterity as well as his friends, he left a record of his reactions to love affairs and friendship, to mountains and flowers in his garden. They are intellectual and emotional self-portrait, the first since antiquity.

All these lead to a cultural uniqueness and it is a troublesome notion that goes against the concept of human unity.

On the contrary, any discussion on universality reflects a political bias and smacks of racism. Fear of hegemonic homogenisation is expressed by many whenever claims like by our great books, our cultural heritage are made. Chinua Achebe, in his essay on 'Colonialist Criticism', says that in the nature of things, the work of a western writer is automatically informed by universality. It is only others who must strain to achieve it. Fredric Jameson's statement which is no doubt inadequate and slanted, describes the Third World literary works, as national allegories, which have nothing to do with universal cosmopolitanism. And so Chinua Achebe says that he should like to see the world "universal" banned altogether from the discussions on African or to add Indian literature until such time as the people cease to use it as a synonym for the narrow, self-serving parochialism of Europe, until their horizon extends to include all over the world. Hence submission to one hegemonic culture, is unacceptable possibility.

However, John Dewey mentions about a 'Great Community' very much in the spirit of the benevolent spirit of *Vasudhaiva Kutumbakam.* But by this he did not mean an undifferentiated homogeneous community where individuality is submerged and the concept of human unity is established. His vision was of a community of communities—a large community where smaller communities negotiate, interact, expand and recast themselves. He, however, was perceptive enough to record in many of his speeches and writings that the larger community would not make sense unless we concentrate on and appreciate the local community and its life world. In other words he is rejecting the concept of binary opposites, which is so dear to the Western world and hence they talk of great and little tradition; Huntington speaks of clash of civilisations as the battle lines of the future. In India, things are quite different for us. *Loka and Shastra* are two poles of the same continuum. We have inherited a culture based on a universal vision which views man not in terms of his variable and alienable characteristics, such as caste, creed, colour, race, language and social status, but in terms of the inalienable and invariable divine spark inherent in every being.

Unity in Diversity

Vivekananda speaks about the vision of the One in and behind the many.

God is described by Sri Krisna in the *Gita* (7.7) as the Central Thread of Being like the thread that unites all pearls into a garland.

मयि सर्वमिदं प्रोतं सूत्रे मणिगणा इव।

India built up a universal humanistic tradition on the basis of this vision from the time of the Vedas, over five thousand years ago. In the

Veda when it is said, *amritasya putrah* (everybody is son of God), actually the notion of human unity is acknowledged with the Supreme Power as the binding factor. From this notion have come into existence two other notions:

1. The importance of man—
   नहि मानुषाद् श्रेष्ठतरं किंचित् (There is nobody bigger than man as acknowledged in the *Mahabharata*). One can hear the echo of the same in the medieval poet Chandidas, सबार ऊपर मानुष सत्य ताहार ऊपर नाइ (Man is the supreme truth and there is nothing beyond it).
2. Tagore is induced to move a step further and speak about the Ocean of Universal Humanity: हे मोर चित्त, पुण्य तीर्थ जागोरेधीरएइ महामानवेर सागारतीरे (Oh my mind, awake heroically on the shores of the Ocean of Universal Humanity). *Vedanta* has initiated this idea of universal humanity. There is no difference between man and the supreme soul. In other words Man is an universal entity. अहं ब्रह्मास्मि।

Herein is proclaimed the unity of the human beings in the midst of all their diversities. This is based on the concept of unity in diversity, instead of uniformity. India has never tried to suppress any group in society, but allowed all groups to grow and flourish, and at the same time, all this rich diversity is held together by a central thread of unity given by that spiritual vision of the sages. In Indian context, man's constant effort is to move from living to better living or to reach a level of excellence in his life by working through *annamaya* to *anandamaya kosha*—the five dimensions of human life:

Annamaya—physical body sustained by food and shelter.
Pranamaya—the life force sustaining the existence of an individual.
Manomaya—mental identity of an individual who thinks, acts, resolves, loves and hates.
Vijnanamaya—intellectual awareness that is capable of discriminating, of judgements.
Anandamaya—a state of being in bliss.

This indicates that some kind of moral or spiritual ideal is a precondition of all social life. Moral ideal or in other words values are important factors for human unity. There are five principal values—*satya, dharma, shanti, prem, ahimsa* (truth, morality,

The biggest threat to multiculturalism is globalisation which is averse to economic and cultural pluralism.

peace, love and non-violence), which can tie up together human beings of different cultures and different dispositions into one humanity. Plurality is the basic ethos of Indian culture but it never proved to be a hindrance in realising the unity of man. Pandit Nehru has said:

> "Though outwardly there was diversity and infinite variety among our people everywhere, there was that tremendous impress of oneness, which has held all of us together for ages past, whatever political fate or misfortune had befallen us.
> "The unity of India was no longer merely an intellectual conception for me. It was an emotional experience which overpowered me."

However, this unity is not a melting pot like America is, a synthesis or amalgamation of diverse identities but it is like an Indian meal that is a plate full of selection of sumptuous dishes in different bowls. Each tastes different and does not necessarily mix with the next, but they belong together to the same plate and they complement each other in making the meal a satisfying repast. The important thing is that a Victor Banerjee, or an Abu Basar or a Sunil Gangopadhyaya or a village boy Kanu or a village girl Jabunnisa still sings the same songs and dream the same dreams together which they inherited from their culture, the composite culture of thousand of years. This is what Pandit Nehru hinted at that tremendous impress of oneness which can be termed as pluralistic universalism which justifies pluralistic differences and at the same time seeks for some universal oneness.

Now about the second part of the paper regarding the growth of multiculturalism. The multiculturalism of India is ancient; the multiculturalism of European nation is recent. We are multilingual, multireligious, multiracial and multicultural since last five thousand years. In multi-ethnic societies, multiculturalism is not a choice but a standard and etiquette—a mindset for coexistence if not integration. India, whose multicultural concerns have long informed India's history and traditions, constitutions and political arrangement, has always found unity in its diversity. This unity is either the spiritual vision of the one behind the many, of the one in the many. Or it is seeking some kind of a sense of commonality in these differences.

The *Atharva-Veda* says (12.1.45) : "That this earth is one home which holds together, according to their respective attitudes and interests, people speaking different languages and people following different religions; like an immovable steady cow (while milking) makes us prosperous through thousand streams of wealth and welfare." Multiculturalism in the post-industrial society in America, Canada, Europe and England is used as a political weapon, a method of ruling a country of people of different cultures and ethnicity. A journalist Yasmin Alibhai has argued that multiculturalism is backward looking and divisive. Multiculturalism fosters the notion of celebration of cultures. The totality of cultures cannot be damned because of some of its strands. Each culture has some value and so one has to think before making a stereotypical judgement about the people who belong to such cultures. Each culture also emphasises that no individual culture should carry the burden of all the communities' misdemeanours (wife-beating or clitoridectomy of women and dowry abuse and Isalimist terrorism).

Pluralism and Multiculturalism

The notion that pluralism should be welcomed and tolerated is something that necessitates the birth of the idea of multiculturalism. But as said earlier it is now used in the West more as a political weapon.

In multiethnic societies, multiculturalism is not a choice but a standard and etiquette—a mindset for coexistence if not integration.

The principle is that we rule and they, the lesser breeds, may get on with their lives and breedings. Master would not dream of intervening unless something is done that might undermine his place at the top in which case all this cultural relativism goes quickly through the window. This is what exactly happened after 9/11 disaster or 5th July bomb explosions in the London underground. Two years ago, Briton's Chancellor of Exchequer and now Prime Minister, Gordon Brown, supporting his colleague Jack Straw, admonished Muslim women for wearing the *hijab*, as it impedes communication between people and set them apart from the rest of Britons. He asked British Moslem women to familiarise themselves with the Magna Carta—in other words—take on English thought, English dress and manners—was the message. France some years ago also banned *hijab*, head scarf of the Muslim women and turban of Sikh community and even cross skullcap in public schools. Holland which was more liberal and followed a highly relaxed form of multiculturalism, changed its policy, after a Dutch Moroccan slashed the throat of a Dutch filmmaker, Theovan Gogh, for desecrating Islam in one of his films. In a revealing survey by the Pew Global Attitudes Project, 16 per cent Muslims in Europe, 81 per cent in Britain, 66 per cent in Germany, 46 per cent in France think of themselves as Moslem first and then as citizens of the country in which they reside.

But at the same time there is no denial of the fact that because of multiculturalism Asians particularly in US and UK are making their presence felt in the mainstream living and at times calling the shot. Minority identities should not forget that they have to be a part of the national identity or they have a national identity based on the participative democracy of India and other countries. Upholding and supporting what is practiced in one's culture and entertaining a biased approach towards what is valued in other areas can be very harmful for the proper development of multiculturalism.

It is said that multiculturalism gives people hyphenated identities and Ayn Rand Institute of US calls it the racism of diversity and maintains it clearly that multiculturalism is racism in a politically correct guise. It holds that an individual's identity and personal worth are determined by :

(i) Ethnic-racial membership.
(ii) Equality of cultures regardless of their moral views or how they treat people.
(iii) Multiculturalism which holds that ethnic identity should be a central factor in educational and social policy decision.

It is a threat to education because it does not encourage a student to question assumptions and the assumptions of his parents and society. The demand for approvals of faith has sparked a debate about the state utilising its funds to fund new faith (Hindu, Sikh and Muslim) schools, a development lamented by people like Prof. Gundara. He argues that state sponsored segregation is not justified on the grounds of race or religion as separate is not equal. Multiculturalism demands that students accept blindly what they are given. Instead of encouraging reason and independent judgement, multiculturalism demands obedience to authority—the authority of the ethnic. By allowing different communities to lead their own separate lives, it fosters ghettoisation rather than points of common contact.

The celebration of plurality leads us to human unity. The unity is based on our realisation of the divine spark which is inherent in every human being.

India always had a tradition not only of multiculturalism but pluralism in which linguistic, cultural, ethnic and linguistic identities irrespective of numerous situations of inter-community conflicts found local space for survival. Thus, the identities that India nurtured were not hyphenated but integral to our history of civilisational survival. In spite of the fact that social anthropologists like Furnivall, Jenkins, Vincent endorsed the notion of pluralism, and respect and celebration of cultural differences, there is a strong group which shows its apprehension that it will promote ethno-nationalism and may disintegrate the existing world order. The vocal protagonist of this idea is Huntington and his theory of clash of civilisations and Fukuyama's assertion that American Liberal democracy may constitute the endpoint of mankind's ideological evolution and the final form of human government and as such constitutes the end of history. In the West, liberal democracy as perceived and practiced by them is the only political order acceptable.

Adding referenda to a political system could help prevent the evolution of a liberal democracy into an oligarchy. In this frame of thought the celebration of differences either in the political domain or in the cultural or economic domain smacks of clash of civilisations. As a reaction people create enclosures to prevent their annihilation. They want economic prosperity and at the same time do not think that in the bargain they have to forgo their cultural individuality and their ethnic identity. In a multicultural situation, the demand for separate identity is symptomatic of the desire for self-realisation rather than an ultimate objective in itself. Each group is just saying give us our space, in which we can live with others and with honour. Problems arise when the identity that is sought to be asserted is rigid and non-negotiable rather than one which can be accommodated into the national stream. Exclusive concerns for either the dominant or the minority interest is bound to hurt both and destroy society. However, the process of globalisation rooted in Western Science and Liberal Capitalism had no place for pluralism. India's unity is based on our diversity, on our multilingualism, multi-religious and multi-racial existence, on our plurality. Pandit Nehru says that our unity is the unity of heart and mind, which makes us feel like a large family which has to be defended, which has to be worked for and which will lead us to cooperate with one another. This sense of commonality is as old as the Indian civilisation and is the force unifying the Indian people and their activities, social, religious, political and intellectual. It is also said very correctly by Anantha Murthy, the noted Kannada writer that if we take the popular slogan, unity in diversity, one will understand that by overstressing diversity, one begins to see the unity and if one insists on looking for unity in India, then what one sees is diversity. In other words plurality is the basis for keeping the unity intact of the country or, in other words, human unity.

Multiculturalism can be best understood, as says Bhikhu Parekh, neither as apolitical doctrine with a programmatic content nor as a philosophical school with a distinct theory of man's place in the world but as a perspective on or a way of viewing human life. It has three central insights :

(i) The cultural embeddedness of human beings. We oragnise our lives and social relations in terms of a culturally derived system of meaning and significance.

(ii) The inescapability and desirability of cultural plurality. Culturally self-contained life is virtually impossible for most human beings in the modern, mobile and inter-dependent world. Moreover, it helps to understand one's culture better if it expands intellectual and moral horizon and stretches its imagination and guards it against the obvious temptation to absolutise itself.

(iii) Plural and multicultural constitution of each culture. Every culture is internally plural because it reflects a continuing conversation between its different traditions and strands of thought. This does not mean that it is devoid of coherence and identity, but that its identity is plural, fluid and open.

The biggest threat to multiculturalism is globalisation which is averse to economic and cultural pluralism. Many theatre forms are disappearing because of small screen. Proscenium theatre is already responsible for many folk forms to disappear. Its agenda all along is homogenisation. Its theory is profit over people (Chomsky, 1999). Poverty is blamed for all the ills of the society and with our saying so, it implies that if poor are not able to keep with the demands of the market system, they have no right to survive. Economic success stories have completely stifled the voice of the marginalised and the impoverished both of right and left politicians. The hegemony of the West, in particular that of US, in deciding the future of the world has taken ominous proportions.

In the name of multiculturalism, it is creating a global order, a global village. In the meditative Upanishadic time we felt that the world is a human family and the divine spark is the guiding principle and we are the divine spark. But as world citizen of the new village, we realise that this is a creation of Western Civilisation, a point in the relentless process of westernisation of the globe. The terms and conditions for living and participating in the life of this village are laid down by the West. We, who live in India in homes and forests, sometimes even on the pavements of the roads of metropolitan cities, are being asked to live in this village as world citizens primarily for two reasons:

1. We matter as a potential market. The global players of the West would like to buy and market India, also in India and, therefore, the allurement of the global citizenship. The global market ideology is now telling us that your plurality does not count except that it adds to the variety of taste and what matters is our potential consumer capacity for the market. GATT, WTO, IMF are all used as tools to conscript us as world citizens for the benefit of the West and its market and maintain the inequality in the age of globalisation which according to James K. Galbraith is a perfect crime. Its hegemony has blatantly eroded human rights of the poorest of the poor. The Kalinga Nagar violence, Singur crisis, Nandigram debacle, growing Naxal red left in the country are only minor pointers in that direction.

2. After 9/11 attack on the twin towers by the terrorists we are asked to be partners in the war with terror started by USA. In other words our world citizenship is, in fact, an invitation from the most powerful country of the world, who initially started an unholy war long back in establishing their supremacy by throttling democracy in different parts of the world. Those who remember history will recall another 9/11, September 11, 1973 when US actively suppressed democracy in Chile. The current pattern of events in Afghanistan and Iraq is quite ominous. Democracy is still a distant mirage in these countries and the Bush administration had failed in establishing it and the US army is no more a liberating army but has become an occupying force.

In this kind of a situation I shall like to move a step ahead of just argumentative tradition of India as explained by Amartya Sen to register my protest and also show my inclination to subvert the hegemonic world order which appropriates, homogenises and coopts all plurality unless cross-cultural exchanges become reciprocal and language of liberalism, multi-lingual pluralism continues to struggle to define its own domain.

The Goal of Human Unity

My conclusions are:

1. The celebration of plurality leads us to human unity.
2. The unity is based on our realisation of the divine spark which is inherent in every human being.
3. We accept certain civilisational values (*satya, dharma, shanti, prema and ahimsa*) which can tie up human beings into one humanity.
4. Multiculturalism should avoid solely the dominant and the minority interests and create a feeling of commonality unifying the people of a nation and also nations together. This can be termed as pluralistic universalism.
5. Lastly, we must have the wisdom to perceive the inter-connectedness of all life and living; the courage not to fear or deny difference, but to respect and strive to understand people of different cultures and the compassion to maintain an imaginative empathy that reaches beyond one's immediate surroundings and extends to those suffering in distant places.

CHAPTER 5

Human Rights Debate Need for Fresh Approaches

DR. SUBHASH C. KASHYAP

Democratic polity is based on the respect for human rights and dignity of the individual. It cannot survive in a situation where human rights are violated and dignity of the individual is infringed with impunity. Human rights are very much the **inthing** these days both nationally and internationally for intellectual discussions in the academia as also for discourses by politicians around the world. Yet, there is a case for stressing the desirability of new approaches to the ongoing debate on human rights.

Human memory being proverbially short, the tendency has always been for every society to regard its own perceived body of values as some kind of an immutable legacy and universal yardstick valid for all times. However, there are, in fact, no constants in human history; all social political concepts, norms and values are in a state of perpetual flux. Woven into the warp and woof of human history, the concept of basic or fundamental human rights or of the natural or inalienable rights of man also has been a variable one. There is no single, simple conception of human rights. It has varied from generation to generation and evolved with the changing times and under constantly shifting conditions.

There are, in fact, no constants in human history; all our social political concepts, norms and values are in a state of perpetual flux.

Defining Human Rights

The foundational norm governing the concept of human rights is the respect for human personality and its worth, regardless of colour, race, sex, religion or other considerations. These rights are essential for the adequate development of the human personality and for human happiness. Without getting involved in definitional controversies, therefore, human rights may be said to be those fundamental rights to which every man or woman inhabiting any part of the world should be deemed equally entitled merely by virtue of having been born a human being.

The concept of human rights today essentially has political, social and economic connotations. It is founded on the ideal of the realisation of equality of all men, freedom and liberty for all men and, basic to them, all, social, economic and political justice for all men. Guarantees of political and civil rights without social and economic rights are incomplete just as the latter alone are insufficient to satisfy the spirit of man. The social and economic rights are primary while the civil and political rights are higher. If the former constitute the foundation of the building, the latter provide the elevation.

Basic to human rights is the concept of nondiscrimination. But, if we look into the pages of the history of mankind, this basic principle of nondiscrimination between human beings or of the universality of human rights has not always been so self-evident or accepted as being axiomatic. There has been a perennial conflict between the elite's perception of their individual liberties and the fundamental human rights of the common people. Also, there has always existed and continues to exist a wide gap between precept and practice, and between abstract principles and their application or implementation.

Without taking sides in the old controversies between the school of Natural Law and the school of Legal Positivism, it can be safely asserted that in a modern democratic State all rights flow from, are authorised and protected, and, where necessary, restricted, by the organised will of the community. In other words, all rights are given by the people to themselves and the sanction behind them is the Constitution and the law of the land and not any natural, divine or immutable commandment or endowment.

Also, all rights, in the final analysis, are essentially social, involving as they do relationships between individuals in a society. It is for each society to determine in its discretion what disciplines from time to time it must accept to ensure that the rights of the people at large are safeguarded. It follows as a corollary that while conceptually human rights must be the same for all societies, their implementation would necessarily remain culturally bound and variable. In the actual realisation of the rights for its members, each society has to evolve its own model of implementation and protection which may be best suited to its own circumstances and needs. Foreign models can hardly be apposite or be of much direct avail. The performance of a country in this sphere has to be adjudged solely by the test of how far it has succeeded in actually securing the rights for the widest possible number of its people and how well it has managed to accomplish a harmonious adjustment of the rights of all by establishing a well secured and legally well engineered society, with the rights of the weaker sections properly protected.

In this situation, the importance of positive law as against natural law and the role of the legislature become all too evident. In its efforts to secure social justice to the people, every state is consciously committed to economic growth and, therefore, to planning, direction and control of social change. In the present day world of rapid scientific and technological advances, as society gets more structured and complicated, human rights get more substantive and more dependent on legislative action. "Society itself comes to have rights." Legislation comes to play a more significant role in the creation of new norms and standards. For, in order to be relevant, it has to become an instrument of development and social change by helping to remove or alter existing socio-economic stratifications and inequities that are found to hamper the smooth realisation of economic, social and cultural rights for the community as a whole.

Today, the ramifications and facets of human rights debate are multifarious. Fresh approaches to human rights would be unfolded when we understand them not only in terms of international law and national constitutions, but also in terms of politics, economics and diplomacy of human rights, on the one hand, and in terms of international commerce and trade in human rights, on the other.

Human Rights in the International Perspective

Western writers would like us to believe that it was the British charter known as the *Magna Carta* which for the first time formulated and put down in writing the human rights and liberties of the individual against the authority of the state. The truth is that the *Magna Carta* was actually a charter of concessions which the 'nobles' or the 'feudal potentates' wrested from King John in 1215. It was far from being a charter of the rights of the people or of the common man. The rights for which the barons and nobles petitioned the King, were intended to be no more than their own liberties or special privileges which distinguished them from the mass of the British people. The *Magna Carta* was followed by the Petition of Rights (1627) and the Bill of Rights (1688). While these three provided most of the terminology and the spiritual impulses of the English Revolution and much of the metaphysical inspiration of the modern declarations of human rights, it must not be forgotten that it was throughout a struggle between the barons and landed aristocracy, on one side, and the King, on the other, while the people as such were nowhere in the picture.

The term 'Human Rights' was introduced in the United States under the Declaration of Independence in 1776. The Bill of Rights in the form of the first ten Amendments to the Constitution of the United States, and the Declaration of the Rights of Man adopted in 1789 by the French National Assembly and prefixed to the Constitution of 1791, marked the radical innovation of the acknowledgement of the inherent rights of human beings in the constitutional law of modern states.

The Western ideas of rights and liberties were conceived in a particular socio-political framework, in situations of oligarchy, feudalism and highly restricted franchise. Natural rights and natural law in the context of doctrines of *laissez-faire* meant basically the right to freedom of trade and enterprise, equality of opportunity in trade and business, freedom of contract and free competition. Liberty was conceived as absence of interference by the state. Right to property was put on a higher pedestal than right to life itself. Even slavery was justified under rights to property and to freedom of trade, contract and competition. Slaves were herded as animals in dark cages in the holds of ships and sold to the elite of society in Europe and America. Trade was financed by leading merchants of England, Spain, France and other countries. If 50 per cent of the "merchandise" reached the destination intact, the average was considered 'not bad'.

It seems never to have troubled the conscience of those vexing eloquent on the theories of human rights of freedom and equality that they traded in human beings or held them as slaves, working in their homes and on their farms. That there was anything reprehensible in their hunting the native American Indians and depriving them of their land or in their owning slaves and perpetrating the practice of slavery did not occur even to those who were assembled together to sign the noble Declaration of Independence and proclaim the self-evident truths that 'all men are created equal' and endowed with certain inalienable rights to 'Life, Liberty and pursuit of Happiness'. All these people presumably thought that in putting to use their human chattel as they liked, they were merely exercising their individual liberty to enjoy their 'property' without interference.

That there was anything wrong in the practice of serfdom did not bother the framers of the *Magna Carta* and the Bill of Rights. Also, those who were propounding the doctrines of freedom and democracy at home and priding themselves in their parliamentary institutions did not find anything incompatible in their subjugating whole nations and races of men and following policies of blatant colonial repression abroad. The human rights of their conception were thus meant to be applicable only to the select nobility of the white race and not to all mankind without discrimination of race, sex, colour or creed.

After the First World War, a declaration of human rights became almost a normal feature of Constitution making and a general principle of the constitutional law of all the so-called civilized states. The Russian Revolution widened the concept of human rights and added a new vital dimension of socio-economic justice or of the social and economic rights of the people. International Charters and national constitutions framed after the Second World War have shown an increasing realisation of the truth that peace within and among the nations can be lasting only if it is based on human rights and socio-economic justice. They assign, therefore, a visibly important place to human rights which again are conceived as covering both the traditional political and civil rights and the relatively new socio-economic rights.

Those who were propounding the doctrines of freedom and democracy at home and priding themselves in their parliamentary institutions did not find anything incompatible in their subjugating whole nations and races.

What may be regarded in our times as the inalienable rights of all members of the human family were crystallised in the Charter of the United Nations and for the first time became the concern of international law. The Charter recognised that international peace and a stable world order could be established only on the foundation of social justice and human rights. It reaffirmed "faith in fundamental human rights, in the dignity and worth of the human person, in the equality of men and women and of nations large and small". Setting out a common standard of achievement for all peoples and nations, the Charter expressed the resolve of the United Nations 'to promote social progress and better standard of life'. It laid stress on the promotion of "the economic and social advancement of all peoples" and pledged the endeavours of the United Nations to "encouraging respect for human rights and for fundamental freedoms for all without distinction to race, sex, language or religion".

On December 10, 1948, the United Nations General Assembly adopted, characteristically without a dissenting note, the now famous Universal Declaration of Human Rights which may be said to be almost the first ever international effort to codify the fundamental human rights. The Declaration was followed by a series of covenants and conventions.

The civil and political rights listed in the Declaration were, among others, equality before law; protection against arbitrary arrest; the right to a free trial; freedom of opinion and expression; freedom of peaceful assembly and association; freedom of thought, conscience and religion; and the right to own property. To these were added economic, social and cultural rights, such as the right to work and to choose one's work freely; the right to equal pay for equal work; the right of everyone to 'a standard of living...adequate for the health and well-being of himself and his family'; and the right to education. The general principles, set out in the Universal Declaration, have since been spelt out in more precise and legal terms. Thus, the close interdependence of civil and political rights, on the one hand, and of economic, social and cultural rights, on the other, finds recognition and is reflected in the International Covenant on Civil and Political Rights, 1966, the International Covenant on Economic, Social and Cultural Rights, 1966 and the International Convention on the Elimination of All Forms of Racial Discrimination, 1966. The International Covenant on Economic, Social and Cultural Rights opens with the following preambular words:

> "Recognising that, in accordance with the Universal Declaration of Human Rights, the ideal of free human beings enjoying freedom from fear and want can only be achieved if conditions are created whereby everyone may enjoy his economic, social and cultural rights, as well as his civil and political rights".

As of now there are over 100 international covenants, declarations, treaties or other such instruments of the UN in the human rights area. These include those against apartheid, on elimination of racial discrimination and on the Rights of the Child. The views expressed at successive UN seminars and in many UN reports, also reveal a consensus on the point that without a minimum of social justice or without ensuring the satisfaction of basic human needs of the people at large, the enjoyment of traditional civil and political rights and freedoms of life and liberty could not have any meaning, relevance or legitimacy. Freedom from want and hunger and freedom from fear, oppression and discrimination are both equally necessary.

Developing World and New Approaches to Human Rights

There has been great divergence between the resources and rights available to people in the developed and the developing world. As one looks at the genesis of the human rights movement after the Second World War, it may need to be examined whether it was in its conception and motivation as altruistic or as devoted to the professed noble cause of human rights as it is made out to be and to what extent was it only a by-product of the cold war or intended to be a counterweight

There has been great divergence between the resources and rights available to people in the developed and the developing world.

to the Soviet initiative of starting a worldwide Peace Movement, again with ulterior motives of its own.

In more recent history, we have been withnessing Hiroshima, Nagasaki, Vietnam, Iraq, Afghanistan, Bosnia, Kosovo. One is tempted to ask the deity of human rights: "Oh God! what crimes are not committed in thy name?"

History apart, the fundamental questions in connection with the concept of human rights today are: whose rights do we mean—of the individual or of society? Who authorises, who takes away and who protects these rights? Who determines when and what constitutes violation of Human Rights? Can the powers who themselves have been the greatest offenders against humanity and exploiters of mankind and who built their own national mansions of affluence and development with the sweat of slaves, indentured labour and colonies be now allowed to assume the role of policing the globe in the garb of protecting human rights?

There was a time in recent past when international law was supposed to apply to the conduct of what was called the comity of "civilized" nations of the world. The colonies were inhabited by the uncivilised "natives". It was the white man's burden to civilise them. In somewhat similar vein, now in the neocolonial age of multinationals, market economy and globalisation, the developing countries are being subjected to preachings, admonitions and pressures in the name of human rights.

Obviously, Western discourses on human rights promotion cannot be expected to be acceptable in the context of national and international societal conditions and objectives. The contents and contours of the 'natural' and 'inalienable' human rights need continual reappraisal and redefinition against the shifting backdrop of contemporary realities. As with development, so with human rights, the struggle is a continuing one. In the matter of human rights all countries of the world are at best at the developing stage. Even among the so-called developed countries, there is perhaps none where the human rights may be said to have been fully secured for all men or women or where they are not violated or subjected to various limitations. In fact, if we look around the world we find instances of blatant discrimination between human beings and violation of basic human rights. To quote from the *Times of India editorial* of September 30, 1999:

> "It is rare for human rights violations to occur on a massive scale without being preceded by the interference and involvement of the big powers. The Indonesian occupation of East Timor had the blessings of the US and its allies during the Cold War era. The Rwanda Burundi massacres of 1994 were preceded by the flow of arms from Belgium and France. The atrocities in Sierra Leone were

> linked to the interests of multinational diamond companies operating there. Religious fundamentalism, terrorism, the interests of narcotics traders, multinational companies and weapons manufacturers, the expansionist designs of some states and the geostrategic designs of the big powers are all factors which can lead to humanitarian catastrophes. Often, the very nations responsible for instigating trouble subsequently use the intra-state violence which follows as an excuse for urging international intervention. Slowly but surely the world is sought to be taken back to the period of the 'White man's burden'.

Racial discrimination, women's inequality, growing rate of crime, unemployment and infringement of civil liberties of individuals are still affecting millions of people in some of the otherwise most advanced, affluent and developed countries of the world. The hard fact to be remembered is that the Western countries started preaching lessons of human rights, rule of law, constitutionalism, and civil society to others after they had themselves become highly affluent and developed by flouting all the norms and concerns.

Again as with development, so with human rights, the problem is very largely one of distribution and equality, nationally and internationally. Sometimes, even modest plans to secure basic human rights for the people of developing countries are thwarted by international monetary and economic pressures. National and international *dadas*, gangsters or terrorists use human rights as a weapon against lawfully constituted democratic governments in the Third World countries. Leaders of the armaments lobby who specialise in weapons of mass destruction and causing maximum pain, misery and devastation, are in the forefront of the human rights movements.

While the most blatant violations of human rights in 'friendly' countries with totalitarian regimes are glossed over with impunity, verbal rebuffs, propaganda and sanctions are not the only weapons against those who try to assert themselves. Big corporations acting as go-betweens and tempters attempt to "corrupt ruling groups and to destabilise from the top and subvert from below". The neocolonialism under the garb of economic liberalisation and globalisation and similar standards takes "the shape of mercenaries, multinationals, money and manoeuvres". It may be legitimately asked: "Is it fair to expect us to acquiesce in its perpetrating relations of inequality and conditions of discrimination?"

Some of the non-democratic countries which have refused to be signatories to the Universal Declaration of Human Rights remain close allies and friends of the United States. The US does not have the courage to criticise even China who hardly had a creditable record of respecting human rights. No questions are asked about the use of child labour in China, South Korea, Latin American countries and similar other countries.

That there are a good number of child prostitutes or sex workers, both male and female, in some of the advanced countries of the world does not seem to agitate the conscience of the international human rights activists. The Western powers are dictated by their own narrow strategic, economic and purely commercial interests and not by human rights record of the countries concerned. For example, faced with a tough competition in the area of textiles, leather goods, carpets, handicrafts, readymade garments and not being able to beat Indian goods on grounds of quality or prices, the bogey of the use of child labour was raised under the banner of human rights. It was well known that India was the second biggest exporter of carpets in the world and 34 per cent of these exports went to America alone. Some traditional arts and handicrafts like carpet weaving in countries like India were hereditary engagements and required long training right from childhood. In fact, it was part of their vocational education and the father's workplace was their school.

While the most blatant violations of human rights in 'friendly' countries with totalitarian regimes are glossed over with impunity, verbal rebuffs, propaganda and sanctions are not the only weapons against those who try to assert themselves.

According to a study published in *The Observer*, the number of children working in North America, Europe and Latin American countries was also large and their working conditions were simply not in consonance with the ILO Guidelines. A report of the American General Accounting Office held that economic hardships and state's neglect forced 25 to 30 per cent children in the age group of 11 to 18 years in the USA to work. Of these, children belonging to ethnic groups and immigrant stocks worked in very unfavourable conditions.

In what had somehow come to be called the "Third World" countries, the human rights situation was rendered more complicated by massive problems of poverty, economic and social underdevelopment, backwardness, illiteracy, economic disparities and social inequalities often attributable to long colonial domination or continued economic domination or political interference by outside powers. There was grossly unfair and unequal sharing of earth's resources among the peoples of the world. Human rights should recognise no borders and there must be equal sharing of prosperity coming from natural resources which were the common heritage of all mankind.

The familiar spectacle in the developing countries is one of scarce resources as against a host of competing claims and of a vast population living on the margin of subsistence restively looking for immediate amelioration. This situation imposes a need for choice, for laying down priorities and effecting a series of balances. In these countries, if economic, social and cultural rights are to have any meaning, it is essential to establish some just and equitable means of production and distribution. The achievement of a minimum level of economic development and of raising the living standards of the masses, so necessary for effective realisation of human rights, become the primary concern of the state and the struggle for liberty itself takes an economic turn. It cannot be left to the economists and theorists of liberalisation policies who would like to see the rich to grow richer before the poor can grow less poor through the trickledown and leftover effects.

In all discussions on the subject of human rights, a climate is often sought to be created either by design or through prejudice or ignorance whereunder the developing countries may appear to be in the dock and on the defensive while the affluent ones can lecture them about human rights. Such rights all over the world are, in fact, threatened by:

(a) excessive concentration of wealth and means of production and distribution and the most extravagant *per capita* consumption patterns in the so-called advanced and developed countries of the world;
(b) racial discrimination, new economic imperialism and restrictive trade practices;
(c) overt or covert interference by some powers to dictate and determine the national policies and programmes of other countries, using nations as pawns in their global aims and for that purpose to prefer more pliable, docile, subservient and unstable military or other junta governments without popular base;
(d) the growing and ever increasing gap between the developed countries and the poor developing countries of the world; and
(e) the most affluent and powerful countries using the stick of human rights in their trade war to bar the entry into their country of more competitive goods from developing countries.

It needs to be particularly stressed that there is no conflict at all between the protection of human rights and promotion of development plans for building a 'no poverty society' or going for 'economic liberalisation with a human face'. It is wrong to suggest that in developing countries civil and political rights should take a back seat 'to economic and social growth'.

The real issue in the developing as in other countries is not of making a choice between the two sets of rights, but of finding an acceptable compromise. The situation calls for a harmonisation in which all the basic human rights are accorded their rightful place for the general well-being of the community and of the individuals themselves as members of the community. It would be wrong to assume that the poor need only bread and the satisfaction of their economic want or that the demands of human personality and the rights of individual freedom are of no value to them. The poor need both food and freedom. Freedom is their birth right and food is the obligation of the state towards its citizens.

Rigid insistence on abstract civil and political liberties of the individual alone could amount to ignoring the social realities and lead to perpetuation of injustices to the detriment of the common good. In the words of Ole Algard, once permanent representative of Norway, an affluent country, to the United Nations :

> "You cannot talk about human rights in the abstract. Freedom of speech does not mean very much to a person about to starve to death. Therefore, economic development is a precondition for proper safeguards of human rights; and human rights are dependent on development."

It is hardly relevant to discuss the different theories of natural rights or utilitarianism, or the theory of justice or of synthesis or the generational theory. American social scientists specialise in presenting various conceptual constructs, models and paradigms in the area of human rights as in all other areas of writings in social sciences. But, it is important to emphasise that in the developing or underdeveloped countries of the Third World, many of whom have suffered for long exploitation under centuries of colonial rule, vast numbers live at below human subsistence levels and their priorities are those of fighting hunger, disease, poverty, illiteracy, paucity of drinking water. In this background, we need to examine the new approaches of the basic Human Rights to development.

The General Assembly of the United Nations, as early as in 1979, had resolved that the right to development was a human right and that both nations and individuals were entitled to claim equality of opportunity for development. Also, under the new fundamental human development objectives, development was no more to be conceived in terms of industrialisation, consumerism, size of the market, growth of GNP, among others, but from the angle of improvements in living conditions and in the quality of life leading to all-round development—social, economic and political—for individual human beings.

The 1986 Declaration on the Right to Development by the UN General Assembly recognised the right to development as an emerging human right for the protection of the interests of large communities in developing countries inasmuch as necessary development and improvement in the conditions of the nations of the Third World was an essential prerequisite for safeguarding any civil, political, economic or cultural human rights of individuals. The Declaration spoke of inalienable human right by virtue of which every human person and all peoples are entitled to participate in, and contribute to, and enjoy economic, social, cultural and political development, in which all human rights and fundamental freedoms can be fully realised."

The United Nations as early as in 1979 had resolved that the right to development was a human right and that both nations and individuals were entitled to claim equality of opportunity for development.

The 1993 Vienna Conference on Human Rights again stressed the importance of right to development being an integral part of the concept of human rights and the economic development of the Third World nations as the collective responsibility of the world community.

While the developing countries were thus engaged in trying to bring issues of right to development as a human right on the centre stage of international deliberations, the Western powers were perfecting their strategy of using human rights as a political, strategic, economic and diplomatic weapon in international relations. *What we witness today is not so much a concern for the rights of human beings as such under national or international law but a struggle in the pursuit of politics, economics, commerce and diplomacy behind the mask of protecting human rights.*

Human Rights in Indian Ethos and History

The concept of human rights is neither entirely western in origin nor so modern. It is a crystallisation of values that are the common heritage of mankind. In India, references occur as early as in the *Rig Veda* to the three civil liberties of *Tana* (body), *Skridhi* (dwelling house) and *jibasi* (life). Long before Hobbes, the Indian epic *Mahabharata* described the civil liberty of the individual in a political State. Ancient Indian society was a highly structured and well organised affair with the fundamental rights and duties not only of individuals but of classes, communities and castes clearly laid down. The concept of *Dharma* was precisely that of rule of law—the supreme law which governed the sovereign and the subject alike and covered the basic principles involved in the theory of rights, duties and freedoms. Before the second century BC, we find mention of elective kingship and the law of nature which even kings had to obey on pain of deposition. Also, kings were required to take a pledge never to be arbitrary and always to act according to "whatever law there is and whatever is dictated by ethics and not opposed to politics". Kautilya, the author of the celebrated political treatise *Arthashastra*, not only affirmed and elaborated the civil and legal rights first formulated by Manu but also added a number of economic rights. While categorically asserting that an Arya can never be subjected to slavery, he ordains that "the king shall provide the orphan, the aged, the infirm, the afflicted and the helpless with maintenance, provide subsistence to the helpless expectant mothers and also to the children they give birth to." Private ownership in land was not recognised. Land could not be made a private property even by a decree of the King. Recognising the institution of private property and the individual's proprietary rights over various forms of wealth, the *Arthashastra* says that "lands could be confiscated from those who did not cultivate them and given to others".

The ancient ideal that has survived in the consciousness of the millions of ordinary Indians has been that of the welfare and happiness of all *Sarvesham Mangalam Bhavatu, Sarve Bhavantu Sukhina* and of the whole world being one family—*Vasudhaiva Kutumbakam.* We are supposed to pray everyday not only for our own well-being but for the well-being of all mankind. The ancient Indian perspective of a global society is that of a family giving and sharing and not of a market place where everything is bought and sold and where the spirit of essential human unity becomes subservient to the supremacy of crude market forces.

Fundamental human rights in India in the sense of civil liberties with their modern attributes and overtones are, however, a development more or less parallel to the growth of constitutional government and parliamentary institutions from the time of British rule. The impetus for their development obviously came out of resistance to foreign rule when the British resorted to arbitrary acts such as brutal assaults on unarmed *Satyagrahis*, internments, deportations etc. There was no fundamental law guaranteeing the subjects, rights and liberties and they were humiliated and discriminated against in many ways, in their own country. From its earliest stages, the national struggle for freedom in its practical manifestation was largely directed against racial discrimination and to securing basic human rights for all the people. The freedom movement and the harsh repressive measures of the British rulers encouraged the fight for civil liberties and the demand for constitutional guarantees of some fundamental rights. The avowed objective of several national organisations—including that of the Indian National Congress—in the beginning was only to secure some civil liberties and human rights of non-discrimination on grounds such as of race and colour in the matter of access to public places, offices and services. As far back as 1895, within a decade of the establishment of the Indian National Congress, the Constitution of India Bill (described as the Home Rule Bill) envisaged for India a constitution guaranteeing to everyone of her citizens certain basic human rights like freedom of expression, inviolability of one's house, right to property, equality before law etc. Following the Montagu-Chelmsford Report in 1918, the Indian National Congress at its special session held in Bombay in August that year made a demand for writing into the Government of India Bill then on the anvil "a declaration of the rights of the people of India as British citizens" including therein, among other things, guarantees in regard to equality before law, protection in respect of liberty, life and property, freedom of speech and press, and rights of association. In the same year, at its Delhi session in December, the Congress passed another resolution claiming the recognition of India as a nation "to whom the principle of self-determination should be applied" and as a first step demanding the immediate repeal of laws, regulations and ordinances which denied basic civil liberties to the people, restricted free discussion of political questions or empowered the executive to arrest, detain, intern, extern or imprison outside the processes of ordinary criminal law.

Under the inspiration of the Constitution of the Irish Free State of 1921, which included a list of fundamental rights, the Commonwealth of India Bill, finalised by the National Convention in 1925 embodied a specific 'declaration of rights' visualising for every person certain fundamental rights in terms practically identical with the relevant provisions of the Irish Constitution.

A resolution passed at the Madras session of the Indian National Congress in 1927 reiterated that the basis of any future Constitution for the country must be a declaration of fundamental rights.

The Motilal Nehru Committee appointed in 1928 by the All Parties Conference pursuant to the 1927 Madras Congress resolution, in its Report declared that the first concern of Indian people, as of the Irish people, was to secure fundamental human rights that had been denied to them. The rights recommended by the Committee were, incidentally, a close precursor of the fundamental rights in the 1950 Constitution of independent India, with ten of the nineteen rights enumerated in the Nehru report appearing in the Constitution substantially unchanged.

The famous Karachi Resolution of 1931 on "Fundamental Rights and Social Change" further clarified the goal and added another dimension to the demand for constitutional rights. The resolution was in three parts: (1) Fundamental Rights and Duties, (2) Labour, and (3) Economic and Social Programme. It was significant that as early as in 1931, the Congress thought of an enumeration of fundamental duties along with fundamental rights.

Also, along with the right to form unions, the Resolution demanded several social and economic rights like those to free primary education, a living wage and healthy conditions of work for labour, protection against old age, sickness and unemployment, protection of women workers, protection against employment of children, relief to the peasantry etc. The Resolution also enjoined the state to control key industries and own mineral resources. It declared that "in order to end the exploitation of the masses, political freedom must include the real economic freedom of the starving millions"—an evidence of the awareness on the part of the leaders of India's freedom struggle that political freedom by itself was of little value unless it led to socio-economic revolution, "to the eradication of poverty and disparity, and the breaking down of the outmoded apparatus of superstition, privilege and hierarchy." Civil and political rights of the individual, therefore, were neither appreciated nor demanded in isolation but always in conjunction with positive social and economic rights of the masses.

It would thus be seen that human rights were not a matter of a new found love for India. They had been part of the Indian ethos and history.

Constitution of India and After

Representing the crystallisation of the values and concepts held dear in India's varied and rich cultural heritage and having its roots deep in the motivational forces of the national struggle for Independence and coming closely on the heels of the Universal Declaration of Human Rights, inclusion of a Bill of Rights in the Constitution of India accorded with the contemporary democratic and humanitarian temper and constitutional practice in other nations of the world. Also, it reflected in no small measure the anxiety of the founding fathers to incorporate and implement the basic principles enunciated in the Universal Declaration. In fact, within a year of the adoption of the Universal Declaration of Human Rights, the Assembly incorporated in the Constitution of India the substance of most of these rights. The two parts—the Fundamental Rights and the Directive Principles—of the Constitution of India between them covered almost the entire field of the Universal Declaration of Human Rights.

The Indian constitutional format in respect of human rights was remarkable as a significant and unique attempt at conflict resolution for the delicate balance it sought to achieve between political and civil rights, on the one hand, and social and economic rights, on the other, or between the individual rights and social needs. The whole scheme was based on a philosophy postulating a dialogue between individualism and social control. The Constitution makers believed in the equal importance of the two sets of rights as a cardinal tenet of their philosophy. Human Rights for them were indivisible and civil and political as well as social and economic rights had got to coexist to make for true human happiness and lead to the fullest flowering of each human personality not only in individual but in wider community interest.

To begin with, the ideals, objectives and the basic philosophy of the Constitution are contained in a nutshell in its Preamble. The words of the Preamble, largely a reproduction of the Objectives Resolution earlier adopted by the Constituent Assembly, set the tone and represent the spirit of the Constitution of India.

The Indian constitutional format in respect of human rights was remarkable as a significant and unique attempt at conflict resolution.

The Fundamental Rights incorporated in Part III, the Directive Principles in Part IV and the subsequently added Fundamental Duties in Part IVA actually constitute one organic unit which itself flows or follows from the Preamble. It is, thus the preambular assurance of the dignity of the individual—and this happens to be the basic principle underlying the Universal Declaration of Human Rights as well—which is sought to be implemented through Parts III, IV and IVA of the Constitution.

For every right, there is a corresponding duty. Duty is an inalienable part of right; the two represent the two sides of the same coin. What is duty for one is another's right and *vice versa.* If all men have a right to life, a duty is also cast upon all men to respect human life and not to injure another person. When Gandhiji was requested to give his thoughts on the Universal Declaration of Human Rights, he said:

> "I learnt from my illiterate but wise mother that all rights to be deserved and preserved come from duty well done. Thus the very right to live accrues to us only when we do the duty of citizenship of the world. From this one fundamental statement, perhaps, it is easy enough to define duties of men and women and correlate every right to some corresponding duty to be first performed. Every other right can be shown to be a usurpation hardly worth fighting for."

Gandhiji sought to emphasise the economic and social responsibilities of all citizens. It was in keeping with his ideas that the Constitution (Amendment) Act, 1976, added to the Constitution the new Part IVA titled 'Fundamental Duties' after the original Parts III and IV of Fundamental Rights and Directive Principles, respectively.

The institutions specifically devoted to protection and promotion of human rights norms under the Constitution of India and fulfilment of commitments under the international human rights law include:

- The National Human Rights Commission
- The National Commission for Women
- The National Commission for Scheduled Castes
- The National Commission for Scheduled Tribes
- The National Commission for Backward Classes
- The National Commission for Minorities
- National Commission for Religions and Linguistic Minorities

In discharging its responsibilities in the area of operationalisation of human rights, the Parliament of India has made full use of the parliamentary processes and of the various substantive and procedural devices available for questioning, criticising and influencing the Government and even for correcting or modifying polities.

Human rights issues having been highly emotive in India, Members of Parliament have been quick to take note of any instances of arbitrary or high-handed executive interference with individual rights or violations of the liberties of citizens or oppression of weaker sections and have raised these issues in the Houses of Parliament. The devices like 'Calling Attention Notices', 'Adjournment Motions', 'Questions' and 'Short Notice Questions' etc. have come handy for the purpose.

Discussions on human rights' issues have contributed a great deal in keeping the administration on its toes and ensuring that any case of blatant violation of fundamental human rights particularly of the less privileged sections of society, did not go unnoticed. Parliamentary committees on Petitions, Empowerment of Women and on the Welfare of Scheduled Castes and Scheduled Tribes also have been seized of issues of human rights.

Besides, the Parliament has enacted a large number of laws in the category of social or human rights legislation, that is legislation for giving effect to positive human rights like the Protection of Civil Rights Act, 1955, National Commission for Women Act, 1990, National Commission for Minorities Act, 1992, Protection of Human Rights Act, 1993.

Lot of vicious and motivated propaganda was unleashed against India in the matter of human rights violations. Quite often eyebrows were raised in the name of child labour in handicraft industries like carpet weaving, handloom textiles. Armed forces were accused of atrocities on civilians while dealing with infiltrators, terrorists and secessionist insurgents. The police were blamed for employing primitive and barbaric methods of crime investigation. While not all the accusations were entirely unfounded, everything had to be seen in perspective. First and foremost, a country had to defend itself, its freedom and territorial integrity and then it had to give the highest priority to providing security and protection to the dignity of its citizens.

Police Atrocities

The police are often accused of using third degree methods to draw information and confessions from the suspects, of causing custodial deaths and of engineering fake encounters. All these are cited as violations of human rights. It is true that the conduct and functioning of the police leave much to be desired but the crime situation and the milieu in which they have to work cannot be ignored. It is almost impossible to find witnesses or other evidence acceptable to courts of law against hardboiled criminals and gentlemen gangsters well known to the police and the people.

A police officer who is not able to extract a confession is considered incompetent and unfortunately there are serious limitations to the more humane methods of interrogation yielding results and scientific methods of investigation are hardly available to the Indian policeman. Also, where the criminal is a person with plenty of money or political influence, it is almost impossible to get him convicted and punished. We read in the papers everyday stories of how one after another prosecution witnesses in important criminal cases turn hostile or get eliminated. As it is, when everybody knows that a serious crime has been committed and also who the criminal is, he often goes scot-free. The rate of conviction is very low which is demoralising for the affected citizens and the police.

Naxalite groups, militants and terrorists are engaged in committing egregious abuses including murdering of policemen, security personnel and citizens and their family members. There are caste based or other private armies. Mafia gangs rule. In large parts of the country there are no signs of administration. The main job of the police is to look after the security and interests of the VIPs. They have hardly any time to think of ordinary human beings, much less of their rights.

Human Rights Violations by Armed Forces

Indian armed forces have been operating under the most difficult circumstances and in the most hostile terrain in the North East, in Jammu and Kashmir and most recently in other parts of the country in warlike situations. Their record in respecting human rights norms has been exemplary particularly when viewed in the face of the character of terrorists and insurgents who have no moral compunctions and who could not care less for any codes of conduct or for anybody's human rights. Investigations have revealed that in overwhelmingly majority of cases, the stories and accusations of human rights violations and atrocities committed by the paramilitary or regular armed forces have been utterly unfounded, and that internal machinery for detecting any violations exist and that severe action has been taken in a few cases where violations had taken place.

Speaking at the 50th Session of the Human Rights Commission at Geneva on February 17, 1994 as the leader of Indian Delegation, Atal Bihari Vajpayee had put the record straight by pointing out that the very aim of terrorists is to destroy the rule of law through calculated violence against both the individual and the state. In Punjab, terrorist violence had taken a toll of about 12,000 lives. In Jammu and Kashmir, more lives were destroyed. This included a large number also of Muslims for whom they confess to be working. Innocent citizens are abducted, tortured, raped, killed and brutalised. Political leaders, workers and the relatives are eliminated to prevent all democratic political activity. Government officials are killed to silence the administration. Members of the judiciary and the press are intimidated to create a breakdown of the legal system and of independent journalism. Intellectuals, educationists, journalists and community leaders are abducted and killed to silence dissenting opinion against terrorism. The systematic religion based extremism by terrorist elements has resulted in the exodus of 250,000 members of other religious communities including Hindus, Sikhs, Buddhists and Christians from the Kashmir Valley to other parts of India. Indeed, as many as 50,000 Muslims also felt compelled to flee the Valley to seek safety and succour in other parts of India. The spectre of cross border terrorism threatens the survival of democratic civil society. It was imperative to bring massive pressure of world public opinion against terrorists and subversives and for not protecting them in the name of human rights. A situation cannot be allowed in which human rights are seen to be the preserve of the practitioners of terrorism while those dealing with the menace courageously, under extremely difficult circumstances, are falsely condemned for violation of human rights. Human rights must not be used for sectarian ends and their genuine promotion can only be achieved if we all work together to create an environment of trust, understanding and friendship.

We may write books in defence of human rights. But, in the context of the way our population keeps growing, the way the poor children in some parts get literally sold for a few hundred rupees, thousands of people get killed everyday in natural and manmade calamities, accidents, orgies of violence and hundreds and thousands meet premature death due to reasons of undernourishment, disease and poverty. The value attached to human life in India (unless it is one's own) is very small. In any case it is

The intelligentsia must be able to unmask the marauders masquerading as protectors of human rights nationally and internationally.

nowhere like what it is for, say, an American. The yardsticks for measuring human rights violations have necessarily to be culture and country specific. Poverty has a culture of its own. When the real struggle for millions is for sheer survival, when there are no worthwhile schools for miles together, where families live in abject poverty, somebody has to discard hypocrisy and call a spade a spade and say whether it is better for the children to die of hunger, get sold, join the force of street beggars or to do some honest work for a living, presuming that some such work opportunity is available.

As a Chairman of the Human Rights Commission, Justice Venkatachaliah, once said, "over 88 per cent of pregnant mothers in India are anaemic. The IQ of the children born to them gets frozen at 50 per cent of the normal level; millions of such children are born every year in India in what is the most serious crime, not just against humanity but against our very future as a country."

We are living in conditions where, as a country, we the people, after more than sixty years of independence, have amongst us the largest number of illiterates, the poor and the unemployed, where hunger is rampant, where more than a lakh villages do not have drinking water and where mothers are constrained to kill their children. While crores of public money is spent and armed security forces are engaged in safeguarding the politicians—their sons and daughters and in-laws—many of whom should be behind bars, even the most basic security of life for the ordinary citizen is nonexistent. Where political processes and polity are so polluted that criminals become law makers and rulers, what human rights are we writing about and whose human rights? How will heavily funded human rights institutes and journals be able to help?

The intelligentsia must be able to unmask the marauders masquerading as protectors of human rights nationally and internationally. When free thinking intellectuals with no axe to grind get thinking, they are expected to handle the theme without any preconceived notions in all its facets, with an open mind, freely, frankly, critically and fearlessly.

CHAPTER 6

The Human Society Yesterday-Today-Tomorrow

SHARU S. RANGNEKAR

The Backdrop

The anthropologists define man as a primate that habitually makes and uses tools. The tools he uses are not only material tools, but also social tools, that is, organizations. There is evidence of use of stone tools by man 95,000 years ago. However, the concept of organization started when the human beings started group hunting and then developed agricultural cultivation and animal husbandry about 10,000 years ago.

In physics, flame is defined as a region where two or more gases meet to provide heat and/or light. Similarly, organization can be defined as a region where two or more persons meet to provide survival and/or growth.

The development of organizations involved treating human being as resource for survival and growth. This brought in the concept of "role" and "discipline". The organization must allocate specific roles to the human beings in the organization and inculcate discipline whereby the roles will be adhered to with minimal conflict.

Confucius opined 2500 years ago that the Human Society is based on six relationships. The first three relationships create the concept of family and the other three create the concept of community.

The most important role is the role of the "chief". In the herding animals, the role of the chief has to be earned by individual combat giving the phrase *balabhogya vasundhara* (world is ruled by power). However, this concept meant continual destructive conflicts in the organization.

So myths were created about "divine right of kings" and authority becoming hereditary. Pharaohs of Egypt and many ruling princes of India considered themselves descendants of God and their authority could not be questioned by human beings.

The problem became complex when there were several claimants to succeed the ruler. The concept of the eldest to succeed was not always accepted and there were bloody battles for succession. In India, such battles amongst the Rajput kings and Mughal emperors are well known. Perhaps the most severe case was that of the Ottoman Empire in Turkey. To avoid family rivalries, Muhammad II the Conqueror (1451-1481) decreed that all male relatives of the reigning Sultan should be executed at his accession. This was literally carried out and Muhammad III put his nineteen brothers to death and sewed several of his father's concubines who were pregnant, into sacks and had them thrown into the sea—just to be on the safe side in case a possible claimant to the throne was born.

Even at that time, these measures were considered too drastic and it was decided not to kill the princes but to keep them safely locked up in cages in the *harem* without any knowledge of the outside world and without any education. This was called the *Kafas* (cage) System. By coincidence, some of these princes became rulers after having been in such cages for a long time (39 years in the case of Suleman II and 50 years in case of Osman III). These men were expected to take up the reigns of government at a moment's notice and rule over one of the most extensive empires. Obviously, it did not work out and led to the decline and fall of the Ottoman Empire.

Over a period, a "non-destructive" succession system had to be evolved—by election in the case of political power and by selection in the case of administrative power.

For this selection, the Chinese started the system of competitive examinations to select the best talents and the idea was picked up by many colonial powers that created a civil service. An interesting alternative was used by the Ottoman Empire in Turkey. The system known as *Kapi Kullari* comprised a group who were legal slaves of the Sultan. All were born Christians and converted to Islam. All of them were trained by the state for their official functions. The slave status carried no social stigma, but divested the member of any personal claim outside the service of the Sultan. They were forbidden to have legal marriage to have acknowledged children or to own private property. They were paid, promoted, demoted and even executed at the Sultan's will and their possessions reverted to the Sultan at their death. The best regiments which formed the backbone of the

Ottoman army, all officials from the cooks and gardeners to provincial governors and ministers, were drawn from this institution. By this method, the Ottoman Empire obtained a superlative group of administrators, entirely devoted to their duties, undistracted by personal allegiance and preoccupations and dependent for their careers (and their very lives) on their demonstration of efficiency and loyalty. Simultaneously, the non-heredity status precluded the formation of powerful elite which could threaten the authority of the Sultan.

Today, managements of large organizations are using methods which are similar to either of these two strategies. The multinationals, by and large, create cadres of management trainees who are recruited every year and trained to go up the management hierarchy. The chairman is often a management trainee recruited about 25 years ago, trained and promoted within the organization.

In the so-called Marwari concerns, basically the second strategy is followed by recruiting people from the ethnic clan and making them fully dependent on the *babu* for their career. The personal loyalty does not always last—particularly when the industrial empire is divided amongst the family members. However, many of these executives—though excellent in their contribution value—have a low transfer value (ability to get another comparable or higher level job elsewhere) due to lack of formal qualifications, systematic training and even command on the English language. They continue to stick to the organization—even when they find that the organisation is recruiting so-called professional managers, that is, executives with formal qualifications, who are given higher emoluments and perquisites. This creates a running feud between the "loyalists" (that is, who have worked for a long time but have no formal qualifications and consequently unable to get change) and the "professionals" (who have commanded better employment terms but are suspected regarding their loyalty by the loyalists. The "professionals", in turn, feel that the "loyalists" are Hottentots who are overvalued and would not be able to get half their emoluments in the open market.

The multinationals, by and large, create cadres of management trainees who are recruited every year and trained to go up the management hierarchy. The chairman is often a management trainee recruited about 25 years ago, trained and promoted within the organization.

The ogranisations entered the twentieth century in three distinct structures:

- Family enterprises managed by traditional traders,
- Multinational branches or subsidiaries managed by expatriates,
- Government organizations managed by bureaucratic administrators.

The organizations were characterized by:

- Rigid structures controlled from the top with hierarchy and rules,
- Desire for stability, predictability, large size integrating vertically,
- Operations characterized by closely guarded information, quantitative analysis, reactivity, risk minimisation and sustainable competitive advantage.

Relationships underlying the Human Society

Confucius opined 2500 years ago that the Human Society is based on six relationships. The first three relationships create the concept of family and the other three create the concept of community.

The three concepts on which the family is based are:

- Father-Son
- Husband-Wife
- Elder Brother-Younger Brother

The situation changed with the education of females and now they are able to pick up every technology and compete with males. Consequently the Husband-Wife inequality has vanished.

As in all other species of animal, the only two natural relationships for the human beings are: Male-Female and Mother-Child. However, to build a family the above three "unnatural" relationships have been given more importance. Furthermore, in these relationships there is a built-in inequality. Father is superior to Son, Husband superior to Wife, Elder brother superior to Younger brother.

Decline and Fall of Unequal Relationships

Confucius himself felt that this superior-inferior relationship may not last for ever. The first relationship typified by Ram-Lakshman came apart long ago. The younger brothers refused to accept the superiority of elder brother, particularly where property and power were involved. This led to fraternal fights typified by the succession in Mogul empire. This happened right up to the village level and fraternal fights leading to break up of families became all prevalent.

The relationship, Father-Son, continued till the twentieth century. Twentieth century created catastrophic changes. Earlier, typically a son received his technology from his father and continued practicing the vocation of the father. Consequently, even at older age the father was important—

partly for the gratitude for providing the livelihood and partly as a consultant to refer to for a complicated problem. This was valid when the *Vaidya's* son became *Vaidya*, Carpenter's son became Carpenter, Goldsmith's son became Goldsmith and Dacoits's son became Dacoit. However, in the twentieth century several new technologies became available suddenly and there were sources other than the father to learn the technologies.

As Akbar Allahbadi puts it:

Tifl me kya bu aayegi ma baap ke aitbar ki
Dudh to dibbe ka hai, talim hai sarkar ki

What culture can be imbibed in the child by the parents—after all, the milk is coming from the tin and the training from the government. Consequently, the father became increasingly redundant in today's society and fastest growing industry is *Vriddhashram* (Old Peoples' Home).

Similarly, the husband's superiority received a shock when the female education got prevalent. In America, the key to keep women subjugated was: "Keep them pregnant and keep them barefooted". This made them incapable of absorbing any technologies from outside the home. So they were confined to cooking and bringing up children. The situation changed with the education of females and now they are able to pick up every technology and compete with males. Consequently, the Husband-Wife inequality has vanished.

Confucius predicated that when these three inequalities would not be accepted, the human society will give more importance to the relationship of equality, that is, friend-friend relationship. Thus a family can exist today only where the father treats son like a friend; the husband treats wife like a friend and the elder brother treats younger brother like a friend. This was advocated in our scriptures regarding father-son relationship:

Panchavarshe Rajavat
Dashvarshe Dasavat
Prapte tu Shodshevarshe
Putre Mitravat Acharet

First five years pamper him like a king. Next ten years discipline him like a slave. But on his reaching the 16th year, treat him like a friend.

This advice to promote friendship was advocated several centuries ago—but is being implemented only in this generation. However, looking at tomorrow, friend-friend relationship rather than blood relationship will be the key to human social groups. The professional relationship between the people of some profession, social relationship for example, relationship like that between the members of Rotary Club, will take precedence over blood relationships.

Community Relationships

For the formation of the communities, Confucius described three relationships:

- Ruler-Ruled
- Master-Servant
- Guru-Disciple

These were also relationships of inequality and ruled for several thousand years. However, they were disrupted in the last few centuries. The divine right of kings was questioned and was overthrown in the battle of Bastille with the slogan of liberty, fraternity, equality.

Now most of the countries have democracy which means that the *rulers* have to beseech the *ruled* periodically for "sanction of authority". Thus, the power is not automatic or hereditary, but has to be renewed periodically.

Similarly, in Master-Servant relationship, the master's superiority was through his providing capital and technology. Particularly, provision of capital was important. However, with the advent of IT industry, the technology became more important than capital. The servant could have a greater technological knowledge than the master and the master could build an effective team with the servant through relationship involving identity, mutual importance and development.

Similarly, in Guru-Disciple relationship, the guru was supreme when typically the disciple went to his *Ashram* for 12 years and got all knowledge to carry him through the rest of his life. Now an educated person is likely to have had more than 100 *gurus* and will continue his learning almost to the end of his life. In such a situation the permanent primacy of the *guru* is not possible and the person can have only a fleeting loyalty to a *guru.*

The Society of Tomorrow

Thus the six basic relationships to create a human society have undergone a sea change. The society of tomorrow has to be based on equality and relatively short duration relationship. To prepare a human being to accept this equality superseding his ego as well as making capable of building intense but short term relationship is a problem of the human society of tomorrow.

CHAPTER 7

Dilemmas of Contemporary Human Society in Turbulent Times

DR. S.R. MOHNOT

Historic Advances

The history of human society has taken many twists and turns in the last five decades cutting across the twentieth century and the early years of the new millennium. Most of these have been historic milestones. Living in the midst of the drama, the recent generations are not fully cognisant—*albeit* not wholly oblivious—of the portentous developments.

That the world has been able to absorb the shocks in its own stride is a great tribute to the contemporary generations. That the shocks have posed challenges as they emerged is a matter of history. The more exciting are the formidable challenges which these offer in human behaviour and its absorptive capacity. It is difficult to visualise what is in store in years and decades to come while the demands on human ability to face these are, unmistakably unfathomable.

Today's human society lives in an era of civilisation which is characterised by speed, volatility, turbulence, division and harmony. The first-three phenomena are the elements of the same set. Volatility is a concomitant of accelerated speed; and it leads to turbulence. Beyond volatility, division is a pervasive phenomenon, which is a product partially of turbulence. An interesting facet of the processes of rapid change is

Today's human society lives in an era of civilisation which is characterised by speed, volatility, turbulence, division and harmony.

harmonisation and integration. While division is a negative element, it is countered by harmony and integration. Technological advances engineer human progress which enables consolidation and integration. In these mingled and conflicting processes, what wins and what loses eventually, is only a matter of crystalgazing (or speculation).

The contemporary civilisation is thus an amazing configuration. In the midst of plenty, thrives poverty. The world produces enough to give a decent human life to all but distortions are many and glaring such that it baffles imagination. Motivated by self interests, the fragmented society generates and witnesses disastrous conflicts. Despite unprecedented scientific advances, the world is infested with islands of primitive life shorn of basic humane and human instincts and emotions.

The Milestones

A brief inventory of the milestones through which the human society has passed through in the recent eventful years is simply baffling:

1. *Exploration of the space* through technological breakthroughs (opening up new vistas for all).
2. *The electronics revolution* with all its multifarious manifestations, culminating in landing on the moon and finding water on that erstwhile mysterious planet.
3. *The emergence of Information Technology and Internet*, nearly magical in their operating processes.
4. *The new world of telecommunication and cellular telephony* transforming the world into a global village.
5. *Robotics*, venturing to replicate God's most complex creation, the human being.
6. *Advances in medical sciences and technology*, such as those related to cardiac surgery, oncology, laparoscopy, organ transplants and new thrusts in diagnostics and stem cell technology, seemingly conquering nature.
7. *Exploring genetics, biogenetics and biotechnology*, opening up doors to a new technological world.
8. *Demographic controls* attempting to find a preventive solution to the Malthusian Law, while religious faiths continue to raise constraints born out of self-assumed supremacy.
9. *Assertion of human rights*, a reassuring breakthrough in the midst of primitive disparities and inequity.
10. *Death of apartheid and racial discrimination*, a slap on the face of imposed human arrogance.

11. *Globalisation in trade, investment and intellectual property* enhancing the concept of borderless world generated by technology.
12. *Discovery of television and digital photography* enabling the trillion miracles which the human race is continuously witnessing.
13. *Petrochemicals*—transformation of hydrocarbons into synthetic polymers, fibres, elastomers, resins and agri-nutrients, changing the global resource profile.
14. *Air travel* faster than speed of sound.
15. *Nuclear power* and deadly nuclear weapons which pose to be the most powerful deterrence and menacing destruction at the same time.
16. *Emergence and spread of religious fundamentalism*, leading concomitantly to terrorism, the unabashed saga of killings and crimes, rationalised in the name of God, the Almighty, religion, language or segmental ill treatment.
17. *The fast march towards the global village* overcoming deterrent constraints and roadblocks of political and localised economic interests.
18. *The rising urge for global fellowship* disregarding fragmentation of the society, ardent chauvinism and archaic nationalism.

Each one of these concepts, technologies or developments represents a distinct idea—some highly positive, some devastatingly negative—but one which has produced or possesses the potential to impact the course of human history, civilisation and nobility of humans.

The well-known *Time* magazine carried a cover story in its issue of June 29, 2009 with the caption "20 Years Ago the World Changed". The identified events may be juxtaposed with the foregoing historic events in the nature of world revolutions:

The contemporary civilisation is thus an amazing configuration. In the midst of plenty, thrives poverty. The world produces enough to give a decent human life to all but distortions are many and glaring such that it baffles imagination.

1. *Moscow's Revolution*—the collapse of the soviet system with the initiatives taken by Gorbachev. (It gave a new direction to economic history. Dictatorship once more received condemnation like Hitlerism and democracy gained ascendancy. It has also reemphasised the supremacy of free markets and free—not necessarily—fair competition).
2. *The Net's-Big Bang*—creation of web by Trim Berners.
3. *The Chinese Reality*—reflected in 'the rebellion in Tiananmen Square'.

4. *Setting a Tone for History*—the meeting between F. de Klerk and Nelson Mandela which made a miracle in South Africa.
5. *About Turn*—when Vietnamese troops left Cambodia in 1989.
6. *Dethroning of Tibet's Nobel Man*—Dalai Lama flees from the country and lives in exile. (While the world recognises him by honouring him with the Nobel Prize, he is treated as a delinquent by the Chinese Government forbidding world leaders to meet or any country to receive him).
7. *Rushdie's Mumbai. The Satanic Verses* was not a meditation on Islam, it was about the author's faith in his hometown but a *Fatwa* was issued by the Iranian religious chief to kill him.
8. *A Triumph for Love*—Denmark becomes the first country to legalise gay lovers. (*Time* says, "it provided a mode of tolerance for the rest of the world to follow". Rightly or wrongly, only future twists and turns in civilizations will show).
9. *After the Bubble.* Japan's economy had been in the doldrums for so long because it revelled in excesses. (It appeared that it would soon recover. It did not for quite some time but soon after, it was again caught by the financial crisis and economic meltdown of 2008. One wondered if the US economy in the wake of 2008 might meet eventually a similar fate with huge external debt, unprecedented fiscal deficits and printing of unlimited quantity of greenbacks.)
10. *Publishing Big River Amazon* was out to shape the future of books and reading. (It was doing it, but Internet was to supersede with digitized reproduction and accessibility of knowledge—destined to change the civilisation's greatest gift—writing and reading).

These are no doubt momentous events but not as fundamental in their impacts as the identified milestones.

Role of Intelligence in creating Artificial Life

Anticipating that a robot can spread viruses that no one can stop, a press report on the conference of leading scientists, artificial intelligence (AI) researchers and robotics at California, USA, gives an alarm that because of the advances in AI, one wonders if there should be limits on research that might lead to loss of human controls over computer-based systems that carry a growing share of society's workload from waging war to chatting with customers on the phone. A neuroscientist has claimed that within a decade, the scientists will be able to create a model which replicates the functions of human brain. It shall have the understanding of electrical-mechanical-chemical patterns of the brain. The only constraint will be financial resources, according to Professor Markran of the Brain Mind Institute of Switzerland. He also says, "The brain is of course extremely complex because it has trillions of synapses, billions of neurons, millions of proteins, and thousands of genes. But they are still finite in number. Today's technology is already highly sophisticated and it allows us to reverse engineer the brain rapidly." The concern is that further advances could create profound social disruption and even lead to dangerous consequences. The long-term possibilities are enormous: machines empathising with patients and prescribing medicines.

Craig Venter, an independent researcher to Rockville, Maryland, USA, has claimed that his team has crossed a critical hurdle to creating man-made organisms in a laboratory which will lead to the creation of artificial life within four months. He has been working on the project for a decade. He claims to have developed a method of transplanting DNA into bacteria.

That is not the end of it: it is reported that Chinese researchers have managed to create powerful stem cells from the skin of a mouse and have these to generate fertile live mouse pups. They include skill cells (IPS cells) that are programmed to look and act like embryonic stem cells. These cells taken from day's old embryos are claimed to have cell type and, in mice, can be implanted into a mother's womb to create living mouse pups. This means mice can be grown in labs without fertilisation. This is another step in the advancement of life sciences, which seems to know no limits, as from mice to humans might be another jump.

Another story from France says that a child-sized figure styled as iCub with big eyes and a white face might turn fiction into reality. It will learn how to react to different actions, offering new insights into the development of human beings. Six versions of the robot are operating in Europe and scientists are working to make it learn like a child.

With the introduction of digitisation, written books are going out of fashion steadily, not slowly. Digitisation is penetrating all walks of life. Not only books and referential material, even accounting records and fiscal systems are getting digitised fast. The colossal polling system in India with over 500 million voters spread out in half a million villages have been digitised making it immensely easier for the giant-size operation and making it almost fool-proof, practically eliminating all pollrigging.

It is apprehended that although the computer systems did not displace work opportunities, but robots of the future can create sooner than later societal turbulence, which will not be manageable easily because of loss of employment and privacy. As in the past, this apprehension could prove wrong as the human ingenuity could discover alternative options. The fact still remains that the direction in which the human society is marching will create severe jolts—not merely vibrations—and sooner the world discovers the preventives, better it is for the much needed balance before it creates serious disruptions and imbalances.

In short, in whatever way one views the changing scenario, it is a revolutionary world exposed to turbulences as never before. Present indicators are ominous: it will be a more turbulent world in the years to come. Whether it will usher in a new era of people's supremacy, freedom, happiness and peace or autocracy and human catastrophy, nobody can foresee and predict despite all human ingenuity and intellectual prowess. All that is certain is that several new more far reaching milestones, are likely to emerge.

The Imponderables

The epoch-making milestones have also generated diverse dilemmas of contemporary human society, some of which are created by the explosive developments.

Space explorations and landing on the moon, for example, have several technological, cultural and emotional ramifications. It has once and for all changed some basic assumptions of human life. To both, the Islamic and Hindu world, Moon was an object of some sublime values. Moon was also a symbol of celestial life leading to a very meaningful symbol in Indian literature. It stands for beauty and something unattainable and unreachable. All these beliefs are devalued, if not wholly discarded. Although historical association of the planet persists, it will, in due course, diminish further and human ingenuity will have to discover a new model or a new set.

The technological breakthroughs are not limited to rocketry, these extend to newer domains like satellite-moored communication systems, mapping and knowledge penetration into unknown spaces, usage of solid fuels. Their implications to the day-to-day life have yet to be unfolded and explored. It will have even more far-reaching impacts on warfare.

The epoch-making milestones have also generated diverse dilemmas of contemporary human society, some of which are created by the explosive developments.

Robotics has attained a new revival. Until recently, robotics remained limited in its applications. It performed some functions in work places, such as in machines and factories or gaming. The Japanese ASIMO broke a new ground. Robots are now showing signs which indicate that it could understand and talk. It has great potential in surgery. Drone, unmanned fighter produced by the Americans and used to fight Talibanese in North West Pakistan throws up new possibilities (and dangers). It may alter the very basics and strategies of warfare and generate new global alignments and realignments.

Instead of armoured tanks and human armies, unmanned aircraft may fight wars. It will then become a war moored in technology, involving no human lives and thus changing the political relationships worldwide. The supremacy of the army and physical strength will be overtaken completely by technological supremacy. This would, no doubt, call for the induction of colossal resources in men, material and money. Such technological advances will tend to shift the application of world's attention and resources from human welfare to political and technology moored warfare.

In that context, geographical boundaries denoted by political entities, that is nations, will fade, if not disappear. If that happens, nation states will turn into powerful technological groupings. The future scenario is, indeed, difficult to visualise but it has unfathomable fallouts.

Imagine illustratively, a future robot will autonomously be able to kill thousands of people. Since it will be computer-operated through remote control, the consequences are infinite.

On the other hand, robots will open up new opportunities. Robots, it is pointed out, will be able to interact with patients and even carry out intricate surgeries. At the same time, robots will soon perform tasks which will reduce human drudgery by undertaking difficult, hazardous or repetitive tasks.

In short, it will be a New World—a strange new world—of a global village technologically driven and armed with knowledge, always churning, and always explosive and yet seeking human peace and happiness for the humankind.

An Explosive World

U Thant, the then United Nations Secretary General observed a long time ago:

> "I do not wish to be seen overdramatic, but I can only conclude from the information that is available to me as Secretary General, that the Members of the United Nations have perhaps ten years left in which to subordinate their ancient quarrels and launch a global partnership. If such a global partnership is not forged within the next decade, then I very much fear that the problems I have mentioned will have reached such staggering proportions that they will be beyond our capacity to control."

The dangers on which he desired immediate action (within a decade) were arms race, human environment, demographic explosion and underdevelopment. While the world has been struggling to move in the charted directions, the progress has been very limited and tardy. It is an explosive world we live in and anything turbulent can happen at any time. If worse is not happening, it is only because of the innate quality of the human race and its desire to survive the turbulent times. U Thant has referred basically to animosities among nations and the political and military leadership, which have deepened in several areas.

It will be a New World—a strange new world—of a global village technologically driven and armed with knowledge, always churning, and always explosive and yet seeking human peace and happiness for the humankind.

The Secretary General was, perhaps, an ardent optimist. Despite the warning, there was no chance of something substantially occurring within the short time span he envisaged. The political leadership around the world is too hard-headed and self-centred to permit the changes to occur in a short-time of a decade. Even if it were to happen in four decades, it would have been a great achievement. Look at the huge stockpile of problems—of Palestine, Talibanism in Afghanistan, Somalian anarchy, chaos and piracy, Indo-Pakistan enmity, religious fundamentalism expressed through terrorism, gross underdevelopment infested with poverty, hunger, disease and extreme disparities, arms race, preservation and proliferation of stockpiles of nuclear weapons, and the damage to environmental balance and stability endangering the existence of the planet. All these human concerns have witnessed only expansion, and not any mitigation or perceptible relief. Serious human risks persist and have multiplied, costing precious lives of innocent people and imposing misery on a large part of the human race, but with little mitigating correction.

Dilemmas born out of Turbulence

Turbulences from the developing dynamics have taken on at least nine distinct manifestations:

- *Terrorism:* The worst face of human society.
- *Religious fundamentalism*: Denial of human equality and freedom of belief and expression.
- *Hunger and poverty*: Hungry millions and abject poverty.
- *Militarism*: Supported by deadliest weapons—nuclear, chemical and biological—in turn, supported by advancing logistics of delivery systems.
- *Decadent political islands*: Autocratic regimes in large and small countries ignoring basic human rights despite a new awareness worldwide to the contrary.

- *Erosion of basic human values*: Unethical human behaviour at family, group, national and international levels.
- *Social degeneration*: Ascendancy of social conflicts contrary to basic human values and rights.
- *Economic oscillations and abject disparities*: Disparities and economic cycles perpetuating disparities, unemployment and human misery.
- *Growing incidence of killer diseases*: Impairing human life and happiness.

These turbulences have resulted in a number of global dilemmas or contradictions and grave problems to resolve. The visible faces of a few selected dilemmas may be highlighted for clearer understanding of the enormity of the human concerns:

- Terrorism when powerful powers (despite states with unlimited security power) are apposed to it.
- Misuse of noble name of sublime God and ennobling religions for committing criminal acts in defence of make-beliefs and concocted false positions.
- Poverty in midst of plenty.
- Hungry millions against the world's capacity to produce surplus food.
- Fragmented world against the declared aspiration of One World.
- Delayed and fractured justice with an army of well-meaning judges and judicial systems.
- Grossly undemocratic acts by declared votaries of democracy and self-styled champions of people's good.
- Unemployment in midst of unprecedented rise in investments.
- Pursuit of restrictive trade practices and protectionism—direct or indirect—while recognising that free trade is in the interest of all.
- Growth of high incidence of diseases despite the monumental advances in medical technology and processes.
- Use of child labour amidst the realisation that child's education is a must for a healthy human society.
- Intensification of urbanisation in the face of the realisation that it raises unlimited social (and economic) costs.
- Excessive use of essential non-renewable resources despite the recognition that they will soon get exhausted.
- Increasing animal cruelty amidst intense love for acquired pets and fanciful animal antics, natural, induced or forced.
- People's repressions by self-proclaimed democracies.

- Increasing perversity and promiscuity contrary to historical social repugnancy and respect for women.
- Continuing environmental degradation by an environmentally conscious world.
- Aggravating climate change and global warming despite the realisation that it will endanger the planet and all billions living on it now and later.
- Stockpiling nuclear weapons and spending huge resources knowing that even a fraction of these if used will destroy the whole world, including the perpetrators.

The negative dimensions of the dilemmas have generated and aggravated the global miseries. Ironically, these are pursued with ever new vigour, rationalised through vigorous justification, make-believes or convoluted logic intended to mislead others and, in the process, misleading the propounder.

These dilemmas have led to some glaring global problems a few of which may be recalled and highlighted in the wider human and cultural context.

The World's Serious Problems

Before the world today, aggravated by the foregoing dilemmas, there are numerous basic issues which continue to plague the human society and which demand urgent attention:

1. Terrorism and violence.
2. Religious fundamentalism and aggression.
3. Flagrant violations of human rights.
4. Hunger and poverty among millions.
5. High incidence of diseases like HIV, cancer and cardiac disorders.
6. Extensive use of child labour and denial of education.
7. Denial of or delayed justice.
8. Unfair or unequal treatment of women.
9. Carbon emission and climate change.
10. Depletion of non-renewable and essential resources.
11. Extreme economic and social disparities which breed unemployment, economic misery, hatred and violence.
12. Nuclear conventional militarism and consequential waste of resources.
13. Rampant corruption and misuse of acquired political, regulatory or market power.

14. Extremely low ethical standards in individual, group, social and national conduct and behaviour.
15. Cruelty to animals.
16. Absence of democracy and prevalence of autocratic power, concealed, camouflaged or open.
17. Widespread adulteration of food articles and medicines causing diseases and preventing cure and even causing fatalities.

Some articulation of a few of the major global problems which have far-reaching ramifications will broadly indicate what goes wrong with the present day world.

Climate Change and Carbon Emissions

Environmental pollution is posing to be the worst crisis the world is getting exposed to threatening the very existence of the planet earth as the future of all humanity is at stake. An Oxfam Australia report says that in the next four decades, global warming may render 75 million in Asia Pacific region alone as refugees. There will be rising water and food shortages and loss of lives.

According to a recent Global Carbon Project Study produced by scientists from several countries, the world is on course for a catastrophic 6°C rise in temperatures by the end of this century. This is because carbon dioxide (CO_2) emissions have increased dramatically since 2002 and the Earth's natural ability to absorb the gas has declined. They found that there has been a 29 per cent increase in CO_2 emissions from fossil fuels between 2000 and 2008, the latest year for which figures were available.

In the matter of arresting the depletion of ozone layer, several initiatives taken by India have succeeded well. The Ministry of Environment has made it public that India has been successful in phasing out ozone depleting substances like chlorofluorocarbons (CFCs) 17 months ahead of the target date (2010). It was accomplished by various initiatives backed under the Montréal Protocol which has explicit financial arrangements for transfer of technologies. Developing countries are expecting similar arrangements for mitigation technologies under the Copenhagen Summit.

There are several institutions world over which are attempting to address this problem but a great deal more needs to be done. Ira Magazines' Chairperson of the Clinton Climate Initiative of William J. Clinton Foundation, has disclosed that the Foundation was setting up four solar parks around the world with a total capacity of 20,000 MW. The largest one is to be set up in Gujarat (India) with a capacity of 3000 to 5000 MW.

It will require some 5000 ha of land and an investment of Rs. 8 to 15 billion. It is expected to be operative in 2012.

While, in the past, and presently, the industrial nations have primarily been responsible for the global damage in both absolute and relative terms through huge quantities of carbon emissions, the incremental damage in future is expected to be generated increasingly by the developing countries because of their much needed developmental needs. The estimates show that the USA has been emitting per capita 19.9 tonnes of CO_2 and Japan and European countries like Russia, the UK and Germany about 10.0 tonnes of gases against the world average of about 4.0 tonnes only. The emissions from the developing countries have been much lower. The corresponding level for China is 3.2 tonnes and for India as low as 1.2 tonnes. Even by total country emissions, the USA tops the list with 5900 million tonnes against India's only 1330 million tonnes. And yet the affluent countries insist on equal effort and are unwilling to share the mitigation cost.

The major differences arise from mitigation responsibility which involves financial commitments. The United Nations' World Economic and Social Survey Report, 2009, has estimated that the increase in energy investment shall have to be doubled from the existing US$ 500 billion to US$ 1000 billion per year and it will require some US$ 20 trillion in the next 20 years to move on a low carbon growth path. The European Union has estimated that the developing countries will need some 100 billion Euros per year by 2020 to address the issue of climate change. (They promised Euro 5 to 7 billion per year by 2012).

The US supported by the EU argues that Kyoto Protocol be abandoned as the context since 1990 has changed. In advancing this argument, it is overlooked that the US had not agreed even when the Kyoto Protocol was concluded and the context had not changed then. In other words, the US was not ready to shoulder the global responsibility while it was the major polluter. Realising the adverse implications of the US aversion to the Kyoto Protocol, new ways are being explored on the pattern of WTO (World Trade Organisation) regimen and it was hoped that a new way would be found at Copenhagen meet of the United Nations in December 2009. While a new effort, howsoever small, has been made, the only consolation is that Copenhagen was not a washout although Kyoto Protocol seems to have been an unfortunate casualty.

Four recent studies on greenhouse gas (GHG) emissions have indicated that India's per capita emission will continue to be below the global average even after 20 years from now. Two of these studies were prepared by McKinsey, the global consultants. It is estimated that India's per capita GHG emission in 2000-01 was only between 2.77 tonnes, equivalent of five tonnes of CO_2. In 2031, it will be lower at about 4.00 tonnes against the corrected global average of 4.22 tonnes.

Climate Change is a universal problem. It concerns the future of the entire planet and, therefore, all mankind. It is interesting that of the 192 countries participating at the Copenhagen Summit, the USA has been the only one which had not signed the Kyoto Protocol, while it has been historically the largest contributor of GHG emissions. The principle to follow by all is simple, which everyone must accept: the polluter must own the responsibility and pay for the damage affecting others. Apart from this, the world has also to recognise that the developing world has to make the leeway to give a minimum of human life standards to the millions of the poor.

Free Trade

Like the climate change, as indicated earlier, free trade has become a knotty problem because of the differences between the rich and the developing countries. India took the initiative in organising the New Delhi mini-ministerial conference of 30 WTO member countries in the second half of 2009 to iron out differences. It seemed to breaking the ice, if not achieving a breakthrough. But as usual, the talks stumbled once again. Special Safeguard Measures (SSM) were an important issue for the Doha Round's collapse.

The basic problem relates to the agricultural subsidies—over US$ 200 billion in the US alone—being granted, while the richer countries want free trade in other products. The earlier attitude of the affluent countries was to help the developing countries to attain a minimum standard of living for their teeming millions, but that approach is severely diluted. The richer countries have ceased to be cognisant of the realisation that "poverty anywhere constitutes a danger everywhere" and that free trade is good for all countries.

Hunger, Malnutrition and Food Security

One in every six people in the world goes hungry or undernourished according to a report by United Nations Food and Agricultural Organization (FAO). In statistical terms, 16 per cent of the world's population gets less than 1800 calories a day, a norm considered as the minimal requirement for living a healthy life. The FAO estimates that some one million were added to this tally because of the 2008 recession. Most, if not all, of these people inhabit the developing world of the twenty-first century.

The reports of FAO show that the world will need some 70 per cent more food output to feed 2.3 billion more mouths that will be added by 2050. This will call for raising cereal production from 2 billion to 3 billion tonnes and meat output by over 200 million tonnes. The capacity of most of the food producing countries has reached saturation levels. It would thus pose a herculean challenge to the world community.

The Asia-Pacific region, the world's most populous area alone, has over 64 per cent of the hungry. The Sub-Saharan Africa has the highest hunger rate with 265 million people remaining undernourished, representing about one-third of the total population. The hungry millions are a disgrace for the technologically advanced world of the twenty-first century.

The Government of India has announced that it plans to introduce genetically modified (GM) veggy foods, such as tomato, brinjal and cauliflower in the country within the next three years. It is one way in which increase in food availability is intended to be expanded. With biotechnology making significant advances, the nature of food and pharmaceuticals will undergo a major change. However, the global opinion is divided: while the US is all for it, the EU by and large is wary—if not apprehensive—of development.

India's National Sample Survey Organisation (NSSO) has been maintaining that people below the poverty line (BPL) in India had gone down to 28 per cent (61st round). A Committee of the Ministry of Rural Development has put the figure at 50 per cent of the population. The Planning Commission of India had also been working on that estimate for 2004-05. It is based on monthly income of Rs. 560 (some US$ 12 at the present exchange rate), which enables an intake of 2100 calories of food per day. In 2007, Dr. Arjun Sengupta Committee came to the figure of 77 per cent of the population based on the per capita income of Rs. 20 per day or Rs. 600 per month.

The persistence of a large number of beggars and people under BPL with less than US$ 2 a day, many of whom commit suicide because they cannot maintain their family, is a problem of great social magnitude. They are a challenge to the society which claims to be humane and democratic. While billions of dollars are spent or frittered away in luxury goods, wastes, and in odd projects and armaments, it is highly disappointing that the society is not able to give them a basic human life.

India has been implementing development plans since 1950s and has spent hundreds of billions of rupees on diverse types of development programmes. The objective of Indian economic planning has always been

The Asia-Pacific region, the world's most populous area alone, has over 64 per cent of the hungry. The Sub-Saharan Africa has the highest hunger rate with 265 million people remaining undernourished. The hungry millions are a disgrace for the technologically advanced world of the twenty-first century.

inclusive and integrated development, but it has failed to address this basic human and social problem.

That it is a threat to peace can be easily seen if a proper indepth analysis is made of the contemporary violence in the world. The hungry poor become an easy prey to the lords of violent movements. Suicide bombers—not their masters—commit the heinous acts only for one reason, which is economic misery of the self and the family and consequent frustration and desperation.

What is more interesting is the fact that the world can easily produce and supply enough food for all only if there is the wherewithal for the hungry to access food. Hunger is thus a concomitant of poverty. The triumvirate of hunger, poverty and unemployment constitute the most depressing manifestation of economic misery and degradation of the society. The three phenomena are interlinked and mutually cascading, each thriving on others.

The Scourge of Terrorism

Above all aberrations of human society in the world of today, terrorism has become a matter of grave concern to the civilised society. Scattered worldwide, terrorism is inspired, planned and perpetrated by self-serving causes. While a precise definition may be difficult to design, it is consciously planned and repeated violent acts by one group against the state, a target group or innocent people who come within the range of the criminal acts of the terror groups. Ostensibly, it is taken recourse to or inspired in the form of revenge by some assumed cause, it takes the form of hateful revenge. Irrational and wholly unjustifiable excuses are as divergent as could be conceived, none has any rational or justifiable reason. The assumed-repeat assumed-causes could be religious or class enmity, imposed supremacy of religious faiths, retaliation against some occurrences which are not liked by the attacking groups, caste or social arrogance (or subjugation), hunger, unemployment, poverty or economic or social disparities.

When the history and operating systems are probed, it could easily be established that the two motivations of terrorism are none other than POWER and MONEY (often transformed in the form of SELF-GLORY), the vicious goals of all greedy people. All other excuses are attempts to rationalise or justify their actions or to mislead their own followers (poor and ignorant) and the people at large. The political grievance or class hatred is given the guise of people's liberation struggle or holy *jehad* or any similar description.

Terrorism takes many forms: direct killing, maiming and torturing people, burning homes and hearths, hijacking, exploding or burning buses, trains and aircrafts, exploding time bombs, raping women and killing children, destroying villages or other habitats, or waging outsight civil war. The victims do not necessarily belong to any specific caste, community, race, religion, region or nation. Nobody is spared, even the most honourable and the respected people of all ages, and even those who are not directly or remotely related to the targeted victims.

There are institutions engaged in programmes to indoctrinate *fidayeens* for *jehad's* from their childhood. In a recent operation in Swat, Pakistani army is reported to have discovered that 200 children as young as 6 years old were being prepared for *jehadi* operations. Once one enters a group or gang, he has no choice; he must follow what he is asked to do. All escape routes are sealed. If later a better sense dawns, it is of no avail. One must follow or else meet the same fate as the intended victims are exposed to.

It is hard to imagine that the Palestinian problem defies resolution despite the desire of the whole world except the involved communities or nations. The same applies to the conflict between India and Pakistan over Jammu and Kashmir. It defies all reasonable understanding that one nation carries on an undeclared war through cross-border infiltration and violence for years, for decades. It inflicts unmeasurable losses in money and men. Those killed, maimed, orphaned or widowed are not the target people—even if that could be ever be justified—but innocent people of the same segment of society in whose name the proxy war is waged. What is worse, despite the open and insurmountable evidence, basic facts are outrightly and publicly denied.

The former President of Pakistan and a military ruler for eight long years eventually admitted that his country or its state agencies promoted terrorist groups. However, to the astonishment of many, the present Pakistani President, democratically elected, also confessed that the state agencies supported cross-border terrorism, which was denied for at least two decades despite the open secret that they did. It was no different when the national identity of the only living terrorist caught in 26/11 Mumbai attack was denied until it was found indefensible. In doing all this, the policy designers in Pakistan do not realise that they have been nurturing a venomous animal which recoils on its own masters. In the recent period, it has become crystal clear that it has recoiled upon them. The army has to fight almost a civil war within its own borders. The Talibanese have attacked Pakistan's military establishments at will at different locations. When the Islamic University killing took place, the government was forced to close schools and colleges for a week to avert similar adventures. What could be more glaring evidence than that terrorism has no set targets and it could recoil upon its own sponsors and its own followers. One can only hope that better counsels will prevail burying in self-interest, the animosities to prevent consequences the like of which Pakistan is now facing at colossal and unbearable national (especially human) costs.

When the history and operating systems are probed, it could easily be established that the two motivations of terrorism are none other than POWER, and MONEY (often transformed in the form of SELF GLORY), the vicious goals of all greedy people.

In most cases, states have been fighting terrorism, in some on their own; in others in conjunction with others. But there are not many cases where the state itself promotes or supports terrorism. The states, when they support terrorism are not compelled by anybody, it is the powers of the time that propel it.

It is also widely known that terrorism is supported by internal and external financial assistance or by supply of arms and equipments by diverse agencies and sources, some voluntary, some out of compulsion or threats. Devoid of such support, terrorism will collapse and meet its own natural death. Common citizens in any country do not support such activities, they are only compelled to do so.

Khalil Gibrain explains: "The love of one's country is a splendid thing. But why should love stop at the border". To be faithful to one's faith is a great quality, but why stop at one faith, all faiths have the same sublime source, God, called by whatever name. If that one simple lesson can be learnt, much of violence around the world could be reduced, substantially, if not totally.

All religious teachers ask their followers to serve and help the downtrodden and the poors. Charity and philanthropy is part of all religious cultures. While all religiously-oriented terrorists swear by the Almighty and the religions assumed to be followed by them, what they intend to do is to hurt or kill innocent human beings, which no religion permits. They do not serve their respective religions, they follow their own common religion of which the Gods are power and money—not the Almighty in whose name they swear and justify their acts. (As these lines are being written, a news items is being flashed on the television that two suicide *jehadis* killed 40 people in a mosque in Rawalpindi and then bombed themselves. Is it not ironical that two *jehadis* sacrificed their own lives to kill 40 of their fellow beings following the same faith and faithfully praying to God in a sacrosanct place like a holy mosque?)

Terrorism has played a deleterious role in several phases of the development of the human society. But the enormity the world has witnessed in the last few decades is staggering and would far exceed the losses for centuries taken together including the losses of the First and Second World Wars.

If the costs of terrorism are computed for the world community, it would certainly exceed a trillion dollars in sheer monetary terms. Social and non-monetary intangible costs could easily exceed equivalent of 10 trillion dollars. If the losses could be saved and used for the weak, poor and the downtrodden, great human misery could be prevented or minimised.

The UN System and Veto Power

The aberrations of the contemporary world are not limited to these glaring inhuman developments. These extend to seemingly normal constitutional systems and practices.

Let alone the autocratic regimes of some nation-states, a look at the international organisations presents glaring distortions. Those who champion democracy and democratic systems become, willing or unwilling, protectors of undemocratic systems.

The United Nations system which has existed for over half a century and has played a commendable role in sorting out several — certainly not all — international conflicts and in promoting economic and varied aspects of social development, is itself beset with veto power in the most important of its organs, the Security Council, the protector of security in the world. In principle, all nation-states are equal members. What then is the need for a veto power of a selected few? There was, perhaps, some object in providing for it in the wake of Second World War because of the fragile global strategic situation and the need to act quickly and effectively in response to violent international conflicts. It was, perhaps, also necessary, because the world was bipolar and divided into two powerful blocs. The third group of nations did not matter militarily. But after half a century of operations when the exigencies of the aftermath of the World War have disappeared and politically the world is not divided between the two power blocs in confrontation with each other, there is no valid justification for the veto power in the hands of five nations. These nations got this privileged power because they were powerful combatants in the World War. How can that status be perpetuated indefinitely? If the permanent member status and/or

While all religiously-oriented terrorists swear by the Almighty and the religions assumed to be followed by them, what they intend to do is to hurt or kill innocent human beings, which no religion permits.

veto power has to be continued, how can anybody justify that the second most populous and the first largest democratic country be denied that status while much smaller countries are invested with that power. India possesses much more than 10 times the population of the two of the five member nations. If, unfortunately, military power is the criterion, India has the second largest army in the world and is also a nuclear power. If regional distribution be the criterion, how is it that Europe should have three permanent members? In other words, no logic or rationale justifies the present status.

India has had to lobby hard for a seat on the UN Security Council with all kinds of member countries but some countries have deliberately blocked the move, directly and some indirectly. What is worse, India has not been elected even to a non-permanent, non-veto seat for the last 18 years. A permanent seat on the Security Council after all does not matter. The powerful (and politically obstinate) states do what they like without caring for the constitutional logic. But it does reflect how the global political and power-ridden system operates irrationally.

Armaments and Peace Dividend

Another associated problem is the issue of armaments, especially, nuclear armament. Arms and ammunitions worth trillions of dollars are produced, amassed, discarded or intended for mass destruction in the nature of genocide. A civilised world with a pervasive United Nations Organization and an International Court of Justice could settle issues by mutual parleys, arbitration or at worst adjudication, why do they have to go to war unless the objective is to impose one's point or position by force. If the civilised mode is observed, the peace dividend to the world community could be huge, capable of banishing poverty and hunger from the world. The only reason for not being able to ensure the more civilised options is the unwillingness of some countries or groups to permit a reasonable course of action. When a few countries insist on amassing armaments, others have to develop for defence or as deterrence. It is interesting that a recently held convention on international trade on arms in Vienna, a proposal to limit small arms business by engraving a unique number was opposed by four countries—United States, China, Pakistan and Iran. It is understood that 80 per cent of the arms supplies are sourced from these countries.

While non-proliferation is the right and civilised goal, deals are surreptitiously made and development of nuclear weapons is secretly carried out for both good and bad reasons. If a hostile state has developed and amassed nuclear weapons, others need a deterrent and the only deterrent could be the ownership of nuclear weapons. The irony of the continuing position is that recognised nuclear powers, whatever their size and importance in world affairs, could hold on the explosive arsenal but all others must keep away. The logical outcome is proliferation, open or surreptitious. In some cases, hue and cry is raised and the imbroglio continues with charges and counter-charges. A nation which has demonstrably indulged in proliferation is otherwise helped militarily by those who champion the cause of non-proliferation under some different objectives. As a result, for one or other reasons, proliferation continues and the objective of anti-proliferation is frustrated.

Indian case is, perhaps, a unique one. It had to develop its own nuclear weapons capability because of the hostile environment in the neighbourhood. The US, the global leader and champion of non-proliferation, made a very outstanding deal to transfer civilian nuclear technology with a thoroughly negotiated mandate from the world organisation, the International Atomic Energy Agency (IAEA). That implies that India was indirectly admitted as a nuclear power state. But if one examines the case deeply, it would not have happened but for the commercial interests of the decision-leader despite other overwhelming considerations. Enlightened self-interest is an admitted principle of international diplomacy, relations and policy, but this goes much beyond that.

At any rate, the critical issue is that India is asked to sign the non-proliferation treaty (i) without being clear what the status of its nuclear weapons is; (ii) the existence of two belligerent neighbours, one possessing and multiplying nuclear weapons programme without any international sanction and the other sitting with a pile and delivery systems which can destroy the whole world, let alone India; and (iii) the continued possession of stockpiles of nuclear weapons by some countries which continue to call upon others not to do so. A simple question which cries for a legitimate answer is: while two largest nations of the world are poised against each other with thousands of kilometres of common border, one must continue to sit on the stockpile of nuclear weapons and the other be prohibited to have any. This position certainly defies any logical answer and needs to be attended to without coaxing one to accept the unequal position.

A simple question which cries for a legitimate answer is: while two largest nations of the world are poised against each other with thousands of kilometres of common border, one must continue to sit on the stockpile of nuclear weapons and the other be prohibited to have any.

Nonetheless, this should not be construed to be an argument for a fillip to nuclear or even conventional armament. On the contrary, it is the opposite. It only carries the message that nuclear disarmament must be assigned equal priority if not precedence, over non-proliferation.

Honour Killings : A Matter of Shame

India and similarly configured countries in other geographies (the Middle East, South and South East Asia, Africa and Latin America) still remain, in isolated parts, like a primitive society in some ways. The impact of modern civilisation has yet to dawn on some segments of the society. The way the people live (or are forced to live because of illiteracy and poverty) in slums in urban centres and dirty habitats in rural areas, speaks of a culture which ought to have been consigned to the dustbins of history a long time ago. Lack of education and economic destitution have prevented the change. There are other similar but even more shameful things which occur. While millions of children are denied access to education, some are offered as sacrifice to self-discovered 'deities'? Dishonour—styled as honour-killings are resorted to by the families because siblings of different castes, clans or following different religious or dogmatic faiths want to be united in wedlock. The Home Minister of India, P. Chidambaram had to say as late as August 2009. "The violent crimes are committed in the name of defending the honour of the family or women; we should hang our heads in shame when such incidents take place in the twenty-first century."

The 'dishonour killings' are only one form of inhuman behaviour of human beings in a society which claims to be an advanced and modern knowledge society. The violations of almost universally acknowledged norms of fundamental human rights are infinite and are pursued with self-righteousness. And what happens is known to all the activists and other public leaders who overlook these under one guise or the other.

Organ Replacement and Swaps

A social issue of great significance related to the prevention of human suffering is the one of organ swaps and donations. The problem is worldwide but experiences differ from country to country. It is estimated that in India some 250,000 of cornea are required for replacement but only 25,000 are donated every year. Out of those donated, 30 per cent are not usable. Similarly, some 30,000 liver transplants are required but only 400 are available; some 150,000 need kidney transplants, only 3,800 get the organ for replacement. The cadaver donors in the US are estimated at around 9000; in India it is a miniscule 50. In several countries such donations are prohibited.

While organ donations save lives, the system in some areas has degenerated into scandalous proportions. Several cases have come to light where organs are traded for money. Many poor people whose organs are extracted are cheated by some medicare centres. In some cases the latter have taken out organs under the guise of needed surgeries. A human act, which could be a boon to the suffering people, has turned into a social evil. What ails the society is the criminal practice in the guise of a benevolent act, which is creating these distortions.

The unavailability of the organs is partially due to the fact that the present statutes are inadequate or misguided. In India, the statute of 1994 permits only blood relatives to donate, while the blood-relatives' organ may not be compatible with the needy. An amendment is being proposed to permit swaps by the relatives with others willing to donate.

Trafficking in organs (especially kidneys) is not limited to the poor countries. A recent report says that a self-styled matchmaker was found to be involved in the US getting people from Israel to give away their kidneys at an estimated price of US$ 10,000 and sold these to patients in US at US$ 160,000. While all such despicable acts use a serious social aberration, these occur basically because of poverty emerging from disparities, exploitation and ignorance.

Mercy Killings and Death Penalty

Associated, albeit remotely, with this issue is the debate about mercy killings, that is, allowing a person to die in case of brain death or extreme terminal suffering. Opinions are divided because of the intrinsic risk that, if permitted, it could be misused. There have been many cases where family members wanting to get rid of ailing parents or other members resorted to the option and placated it as mercy killing.

A similar debate rages about death penalty. Many humanists oppose the imposition of death penalty irrespective of the intentions, deliberate or not, of the perpetrators of heinous crimes such as murders, genocide and blatant gang rape. The basic arguments are two: first, that the society has no right to take the life of anybody; and second, that by hanging a person, one more similar crime is being unwittingly committed. Moreover, when a person is hanged, he dies instantaneously and does not suffer the penalty of pain for the harm done to the victims. For many diehard criminals or those who commit crimes only out of deep frustrations or compulsions in life, death is a blessing in disguise and not a punishment. Since many heinous crimes are committed in the society and those who are given death penalty are only a few, it is quite reasonable to take the position taken by the humanists that death penalty be abrogated from the statutes all over the world. Several countries have abolished death penalty while many others are contemplating to do so. It is hoped that this will be followed by all countries. Nevertheless, many other punishments which are cruel and not human in nature continue and the civilised world will have to deliberate on these very seriously. Several countries adopt extreme torture for different types of crimes even to those who have not been convicted by constitutionally constituted or competent courts or against whom no undisputable evidence has been established. Many continue to suffer for years because of dilatory processes of legal administration, sometimes engineered. These are all inhuman acts and are a blot on human civilisation. For any advanced society, these are disgraceful.

The Problem of Child Labour

Another dilemma facing millions is the engagement of child labour. It is rightly condemned as a social menace, as millions of innocent children are denied education and normal human life. In principle, all conscientious societies are agreed on the abolition of child labour. But some have gone as far as to take undue advantage of the menace and have used this in matters of trade by disallowing imports of goods produced with the use of child labour.

There is, however, also another side to the issue. What does one do if the family cannot earn enough to feed itself including 'the working' child? It is a hard truth that millions of parents ask their children to work and earn because they do not have adequate means to feed the family. If they do not ask the children to work and earn whatever paltry income they get, not only is the family starved, it is denied basic medicines, let alone education, decent and protective clothing or safe housing. This is a big dilemma for the society. Abolition of child labour is a very laudable objective but a really positive answer is needed to resolve it recognising the basic economic conditions. Of the hungry in the world, there are 200 million poor children who do not receive needed nutritious food, according to a UNICEF report released before a three-day summit conference on the problem of world hunger. If children are forbidden to work, more children will go hungry.

The society must first provide basic minimum for human life to all before banning child labour. This is not a precondition which defies solution. If nations can be given billions to undertake projects and development programmes of diverse types and sizes, some certainly not as essential as providing a future to the new generation, why could not a similar programme be undertaken to ensure that the people in poverty are guaranteed a minimum decent human life. If social security can be organised for those engaged in 'organised activities' in a country, why not economic security be extended to the destitute, downtrodden and disadvantaged helpless people? Except for the chauvinistic emotions around nationality, people in other countries are as fellow humans as those living in one's own country. The real problem is that those who write development plans and those who carry them out are not fully aware—or do not want to be aware—of the stark ground realities and the consequent priorities. Problems and solutions to problems are considered in isolation, not in a holistic and practical way. Inclusive economic growth is a prerequisite of the abolition of child labour. The abolition of child labour will remain a dream until a basic human life is assured to those who live in abject poverty.

Economic Meltdown and its Fallouts

The foregoing delineation establishes one dimension clearly—social, political and economic problems, globally or domestically, are inextricably interwoven with each other, and, therefore, call for a composite configuration of responses for all involved.

The 2008 economic meltdown triggered by the sub-prime debacle and collapse of giant investment bankers like Lehman Brothers and others like the world's largest insurance company, AIG, was no less than an economic tsunami with hard social fallouts. It carried in its trail grave social and economic impacts. It shook the entire world's economic system. Its strong waves travelled to the European continent, to Asia Pacific engulfing Japan and to other small and big nations, developing and developed, affluent and poor. Hundreds of thousands of businesses had to be closed down and millions of poor people were thrown out of employment. The turbulence was not limited to selected organisations in the financial world. Almost concomitantly, corporate icons of the dimensions of General Motors and Ford Motor Company faced bankruptcy. The governments had then to come to the rescue of the most powerful organisations with an estimated 4 to 5 trillion dollars of bailouts. The bailouts came from the taxpayers' money, which was resented vehemently even in affluent America. Apart from the losses and setbacks, millions lost billions in their businesses on the stock markets. Lifetime's hard earned money disappeared in no time. Colossal unemployment was created.

The critical question is: why did this happen and can this be prevented to recur again? The hard fact of life is that it is inevitable in the given economic model. The free market system which promotes individual enterprise and innovation, has the seeds of turbulence in-built in itself unless regulated. Adam Smith's invisible hand does correct it but after a great deal of irreparable damage done to all.

Symptomatically, the meltdown was a failure of the system. If analysed deeply, at the bottom of it is nothing but human greed to acquire material resources generated or owned by others by hook or by crook, grabbing whenever an opportunity comes by. This kind of turbulence shall continue to haunt the human society unless it develops the capacity to restrain wants through *sanyam* or self-restraint and be ethical in the conduct with each other. Given the prevailing ambience, it is difficult to achieve that goal. But in the interest of human welfare, happiness and peace, it is an indispensable need.

Several distortions are imbedded in the very system as it operates. Low production costs lead to low prices, which in turn result in extravagant use of scarce resources, an extreme example of which is that of petroleum, a pervasive but exhaustible source of energy. In 1973, the first oil crisis emerged because crude oil price was raised from US$ 1.3 per barrel to US$ 2.5 per barrel (except for the low sulphur Libyan oil). And there was a hue and cry worldwide. Nobody realised that the low price was playing havoc to world's energy resources. Had the low price persisted, experts agreed that there would be a catastrophe: the world would exhaust its vital fossil energy resource very soon.

Thankfully, the price of crude rose and was stabilised at around US$ 20 a barrel. But then the crisis took the opposite direction. While for some time the price rose to a manageable and perhaps optimal level of US$ 35 to 50, later it catapulted to US$ 145 a barrel. It was a shock to all countries, rich and poor, which depended on imports of crude. It badly affected even the richest, the United States of America. But the apex price was fortunately only a matter of speculation—not of an imbalance in supply and demand. Soon after, the price went low to one-third of the peak and was hovering around half of the peak. While it has been a product of global demand and supply, the case speaks how free markets operate—added and abetted by concerted effort of powerful cartel of oil producing and exporting countries (OPEC). Even with the prevailing crude price at US$ 70 to 80 a barrel, it is predicted by knowledgeable world experts that the fossil fuel would get exhausted in about 25 to 30 years. What then, is anybody's guess.

The critical question is: why did the global economic downturn happen and can this be prevented to recur again? The hard fact of life is that it is inevitable in the given economic model.

Free markets are free only in name. These are regulated by powerful operators through huge resources of dominant market shares or by the creation of monopolistic markets through brand-building with or without differential USPs (unique selling proposition). It has become crystal clear that free competition will not remain free and fair unless *socially regulated.* Lessons after lessons have been learnt that social—not state regulation—is a must. Its coverage, intensity and modalities will need to be carefully designed, but devoid of an independent and professionally organised system, the distortions and manipulations will persist. At the bottom of all this is ethics in economic affairs and behaviour. Unethical behaviour leads to extravagance of individuals and the extravagance of the populace extends to the profligacy of the state.

Profligacy at all Layers

In 2009, the fiscal deficit in the US was estimated to quadruple from a staggering US$ 489 billion to an astronomical US$ 1300 billion—from 3.2 per cent of GDP to over 13 per cent of GDP. It is a far cry from the accepted norms of fiscal prudence. And where does this money come from? Not taxes mercifully, but from public debt, and a public debt is only a tax on future generations. The total debt of the Government of the United States of America, home of the most affluent in the world, is over US$ 2 trillion. The paradigm is: the more you have the more you desire, a basic human behavioural trait. Unlike in conventional economics, more does not give more satisfaction, it generates more hunger. It is estimated that it will make each US family indebted more than by US$ 60,000. As a result, the US economy triggered the worst financial crisis—leading to equally severe economic meltdown—there should be no wonder.

By societal economic norms of the yesteryears, it is so amazing that the materially and economically the most affluent nation in the world is most indebted. What does it imply? It basically means that the urge for possessing and enjoying wealth knows no bounds.

By societal economic norms of the yesteryears, it is so amazing that the materially and economically the most affluent nation in the world is most indebted. What does it imply? It basically means that the urge for possessing and enjoying wealth knows no bounds. If in this kind of lifestyle the world is faced with environmental degradation, there should not be any surprise. Now that the growth (or deceleration) indicators were threatening extinction of the planet, there is at least the realisation that something ought to be done. But that is a short-lived wish as international bickerings continue to haunt the world. The richer communities do not want to permit a dent on their wasteful life and the poor world cannot afford to do what is necessary to provide a minimal standard of civilized life to its people, millions of whom live in abject poverty, a living which is devoid of adequate nutritious food, shelter, essential medicines and educational facilities for the children.

The Coloured Mindsets

Among other reasons for the malaise is the distorted mindset around the world. Guided by some not-so-positive media and vested interests, the affluent world still see emerging societies with their coloured glasses. For many decades they repetitively qualified India as *Hindu India* not realising that India, by its adopted Constitution, declared itself unequivocally to be a secular country. Countries with ardently self-styled theocratic associations, however, were called by their internationally recognised denominations. In the recent years, the media was forced to acknowledge some of the achievements of countries like India and China but it is always with a handful—not a pinch—of salt. The widely circulated American newsmagazine *Newsweek* carried a story under the title "*Unqualified for the Overrated*" in regard to Nobel Peace Prize in 2009: "You might have thought that 1946 would have been a good year for Mohandas K. Gandhi known to Hindus as 'the Mahatma', I might not agree." Mark the words: "known to Hindus as the Mahatma"—Who would believe that the author did not know that Gandhi is called the Mahatma world over. The Oxford English Dictionary like others carries the word 'mahatma', derived from Sanskrit mainly because Gandhiji has been addressed as Mahatma and not by his full name, Mohandas Karamchand Gandhi. The mindset is demonstrated by many more similar sarcasms.

The supposed to be an independent and objective newsmagazine, *The Economist* of London, in giving a story on the 2009 general elections in India, in which the ruling party unexpectedly won a resounding victory, starts a long piece with the caption: "India is a land of bright promise". And then immediately, it reverts to its make-belief with the concealed mindset:

> "It is extremely poor. About 27m Indians will be born this year. Unless things improve, almost 2m of them will die before the next general election. Of the children who survive, more than 40 per cent will be physically stunted by malnutrition. Most will enrol in a school, but they cannot count on their teachers show up. After five years of classes, less than 60 per cent will be able to read a short story and more than 60 per cent will be stumped by simple arithmetic."

The story of successful massive elections in the largest democracy had to be discounted! And how better could it be done by the brilliant editors? The commentators from the Western world continue to be obsessed by the old ingrained legacy—the so-called imperial mindset. They fail to realise that the world has transformed itself.

Howsoever out of context, the facts mentioned are no doubt broadly true, but needed to be discounted by the facts that despite such conditions, India dons the second largest technical manpower and the Indian students in schools, universities and business schools and institutes of technology come out at the top not only in India but against those from the advanced countries. Today these very Indians head some of the world's largest corporates like Indira Nooyi, CEO of PepsiCo or Vikram Pandit of Citigroup, let alone likes of Rajat Gupta once heading the global consulting firm of McKinsey. L.N. Mittal, an Indian, became the largest steel producer in the world. At least two Indians figure in the richest ten persons on the planet. Indians are also honoured with Nobel Prizes in diverse fields—from Rabindra Nath Tagore in Literature, as far back as 1919, and C.V. Raman in Physics, to Hargovind Khurana and Amartya Sen in Economics. The latest addition is Professor Venkata Ramakrishana in Chemistry in 2009. India also boasts to send *Chandrayan* to moon, discovering for the first time water on that mystical planet.

The basic question is about the lingering negative mindset of the affluent world which strikes at the emerging nations at the fall of a hat. Such mindsets cloud international relationships and matters of vital interest in the comity of nations and global developments of critical importance. An extended version of such mindset is the racial prejudices. Apartheid might have been given up in South Africa after a long struggle, but it perpetuates itself. In Australia, Indian students are brutally beaten up on several occasions. Under diplomatic pressures, the government spokesperson and ministers have assured that it was not due to racial prejudices and that they were stray events. However, when Indian inhabitants were protesting against it, the Australian Prime Minister issued a stern warning to the Indian students not to take law in their own hands. It did not matter to him that the perpetrators of the crimes were taking law in their own hands without provocation and it was his duty to restrain them. The implication, perhaps unintended, was that the Indian students must meekly suffer.

In a newly emerging global village and global cultural configuration, a broad globally-oriented mindset is the need of the hour.

The Ethical Standards

A basic reason why these problems persist is the unprecedented erosion of ethical standards. The ethical standards in different walks of society have witnessed perceptible decline, be it the family, the local habitat, business, religious rituals, public governance, political life or international relations. These have been eroded even in education and medicare and other social services. In some areas, the phenomenon is more pronounced; in some less. The dent, however, has crossed acceptable bounds in all areas.

It is now being increasingly recognised that the trend must be reversed if the human society has to live in peace. Some initiatives have been taken. In the realm of education, for example, lessons on ethics are being introduced at primary and higher levels. Corporate social responsibility (popularly styled as CSR) is being promoted as an essential parameter of performance in the business world. And an essential component of CSR is ethics, ethical conduct in business, although the emphasis continues to be on philanthropy, which touches only the fringe of the problem.

There has to be a committed realisation that upholding the interest of the society is not only an obligation of each enterprise, it is also in its own interest to foster it, says R.K. Pachauri, Chairman of the Nobel Prize winning United Nations Inter-governmental Panel on Climate Change (IPCC). It is an age when unethical corporate behaviour is highlighted instantly and information about it is disseminated through the internet and other instant communication channels. While the corporates or other business entities earn profit—which is their legitimate right—it is their obligation to protect and promote societal interests if for no other reason than that the corporates receive several unidentified benefits, tangible and intangible, and inflict several direct and indirect negative fallouts on the societal interests. In fact, their very existence depends on the social fabric.

In a newly emerging global village and global cultural configuration, a broad globally-oriented mindset is the need of the hour.

In political and public life, ethics is as urgently needed as in the business world. Even the noble medical profession has witnessed erosion of ethics and needs a surgery. Business ethics may be considered an empty slogan in the prevailing environment of business practices and behaviour, vitiated by corruption, but it is a basic prerequisite of good social life.

Explosive Risks of Falling Standards and Values

The pervasive multiple turbulences call for deeper factor analysis about why they occur. At the bottom of these is the growing human greed and arrogance. The more the man has, the more he craves to get. Satisfaction of specific wants generates more wants as aspirations and expectations get multifold. Given the urge to compete and excel, man becomes acquisitive and aggressive. In the advancing contemporary world, the process is both aggravated and accelerated. The process must be reversed if peace and happiness has to prevail.

The humans have three primary possessions: brain, heart and sensual organs. Brain is the producer of intellect—to discern, to design, to plan, to command and be commanded. The heart emits emotions for self-satisfaction and actualisation and for satisfying others—the spouse, the family, the society. Sensual organs enable a person to feel, to taste, to smell, to enjoy. The three—brain, heart and sensual organs—establish their own interrelationships. They function together and together they make the human a total being, a personality. To taste good food, one needs all the three, more of brain and sensual organs. To feel the pleasures of affluence or pains of poverty, one needs all the three, more of heart and sensual organs. To be socially harmonious, the three elements operate together with the dominance of the first two. These give rise to love and hate, pleasure and pain, good and evil, greed and philanthropy, lust and abstinence, intelligence and stupidity, emotional burst and mental calm and meditation. They function together also to make the humans human, humane and spiritual.

In political and public life, ethics is as urgently needed as in the business world. Even the noble medical profession has witnessed erosion of ethics and needs a surgery.

For a physical, mental, social and spiritually healthy life, a happy equilibrium and a meaningful equation and sustainability in the relationship of the three are a *sine qua non.* When such balance is missing, humans encounter turbulence which generates social upheavals (within or between defined groups, such as social or economic classes and nations), and impacts divergent human and social equations. This basic nature of turbulence in the context of the three basic human possessions has to be understood to prevent and withstand wider turbulences.

In more than two decades of studying and writing about world religions, historian Karen Armstrong, author of *A History of God, Faith After September 11,* and more recently, *The Case for God* was repeatedly struck by the emphasis that all the great traditions place on compassion. It would be only appropriate to recall the words of the greatest scientist of our times, Albert Einstein:

> Take care not to make intellect your God.
> Intellect has powerful muscles,
> But no personality.
> Intellect cannot lead, it can only follow.
> It is not particular about the choice of its leader.
> Intellect has a sharp eye for tools and methods,
> But it is blind to ends and values.

Gautam Buddha has said: "Health is the greatest gift, contentment the greatest wealth, faithfulness the best relationship." The three elements are grossly devalued. Health is impaired by pollution and stress; contentment has been replaced by greed to get more and more of material means and sensual diversions, while trust is a rare commodity to find in the contemporary life. Distrust is pervasive in individual, family, societal, professional and political relationships.

And it is the ends and values which determine the quality of civilisation, not the devastating power of nuclear weapons or the billions of dollars of wealth.

Admittedly, right thinking people around the world—and there is no dearth of such people—are doing their best in the spaces they occupy, but a quick glance at the dilemmas and the problems will bring into bold relief the stark fact that the human society is exposed to explosive dangers. Some of the dangers are persisting from the past and some are newly emerging out of the current social and economic standards, values and milieu. The dangers arise only out of greed of some. The greed is born out of loss of fellowship at all levels—the family, the small homogeneous groups, the small and large habitats, nations and the world. The social standards and values have fallen precipitately in the present age. The daunting challenge before the world is to raise the social standards and values, apparently a simple, but in real life, a most challenging task.

The Need for Positive Thinking

The genesis of a powerful idea is the power to think. Whatever be the walk of life—be it production of goods and services, writing or speaking, planning strategies of wars or forging relationships—thinking plays a vital role. Thinking leads to innovation and innovation is key to success and advancement. Action is also born out of thinking. Since thinking is so vital, it must be positive, ethical and humane. The ills of the world today are moored in thinking which is negative. Positive thinking can change the world and the fabric of human life in the world.

Victor Hugo has rightly said that "there is nothing more powerful than the idea for which the time has arrived". But then here is a juncture in which a whole pack of powerful ideas have dawned. There is, no wonder then that the contemporary world is a lot bewildered and finds it difficult to cope up with the multidimensional impacts. The multiplicity and complexity of ideas have also led to divergent

And it is the ends and values which determine the quality of civilisation, not the devastating power of nuclear weapons or the billions of dollars of wealth.

conflicts, conflicts of behaviour and interrelationships and conflicts between rights and obligations.

World Charter of a Civilised Social Order

In the context of the stocktaking of the currents and cross-currents of the present day world, with immense negative baggage carried by an extremely positive, forward-looking and intelligent world, let us recount what could be done to ensure a happy, peaceful and prosperous planet (See Annexure).

It is both easy and difficult to follow the principles of the proposed Charter. Dreams are not always easily achieved. It may easy because, it is born out of natural human conduct and sensitivities. It refers to the basic human goals which a just and happy society must try to achieve. While admittedly, the world is far from the target but good human feelings and behaviour have the intrinsic capability to imbibe and to operationalise these in practice. If these human standards are internalised, established and ensured, the human society will find itself in a painless and civilised world.

Needless to say at the end that this essay is a symbolic tribute to the memory of Dr. L.M. Singhvi. It is amazing that he had actively propounded, professed and promoted all the contents of the Charter through his innovative thinking, convincing and articulate writings, powerful and persuasive speeches and supporting institutions and programmes in pursuit of the causes. It is amazing because it is a great feat that one individual can espouse and promote all that is good in the human society. While we are debating the alternative options for the human society at the crossroads, he had chosen the route which leads one to all that is good in the human mind and the human society.

ANNEXURE

World Charter of a Civilised Social Order

THE VISION

The world looks forward to a just, peaceful and happy global order, a goal to which every world citizen, individually and collectively, is committed and dedicated.

To achieve this goal, the word community will strive to ensure that:

1. Every person is guaranteed basic human rights recognized by the world community.
2. No discrimination is made on account of gender, race, religion, nationality, language or any other discriminatory denomination, spatial or otherwise.
3. Every person is guaranteed the freedom to follow his/her faith (religion) chosen by him/her on own volition without any compulsion or constraint.
4. Women enjoy equal social status and rights and privileges as do men.
5. No person is denied the opportunity of living a sustainable life and of employment to pursue any avocation because of his place of birth, gender, race, nationality or religion.
6. Every person willingly and honestly shares equitably the social costs and benefits.
7. No religious, social or economic practice, or obligation is forced on any individual, which is in violation of the accepted fundamental human rights.
8. Every individual is assured fair justice within a reasonable time and which does not penalise him for acts not committed and without due processes of law.

9. No individual is punished by another or by the state or society except for deliberate unlawful act.
10. Every person is treated equally in the eyes of law without discrimination of any kind.
11. Every person is assured of employment or means of income which is enough to sustain a respectable human life for self and the family unless he/she declines to work.
12. No individual remains without food, shelter or medicare, because of no access to means.
13. Every child is provided, irrespective of social or economic denomination, gender or any other attribute, a decent level of education.
14. Every person is allowed the privacy in life which does not impinge on the rights of others.
15. Every individual is assured of equal rights under the country's laws and by those who are assigned the task to administer the laws and regulations.
16. Every individual is committed to honour law enforced by the state.
17. Every person willingly and honestly repays due debts and obligations willingly undertaken by him/her in any form—relational, economic or social.
18. Every individual considers it his/her duty to be 'FAIR' and 'NICE' to others in any behaviour or transaction—not in one or some cases, but ALWAYS.
19. Every individual follows ethical practices in her/his behaviour, transactions or acts.
20. All nations or groups of nations refrain from taking any action that leads to wars.
21. Death penalty is abolished from the statutes of all countries.
22. No person or groups of persons inflicts cruelty on animals in any form.
23. Every individual, individually or collectively in association with others, prevents waste of essential and scarce resources to the best of his/her ability.
24. Everybody exercises legitimate care to protect the environment and refrains from doing anything which endangers the environment.

Module II

Focused Themes
On Culture, Governance & Judiciary

CHAPTER 8

Friendship in Classical Indian Thought*

LORD BHIKU PAREKH

My theme[1] is the idea of friendship in classical Indian thought[2]. Our current ideas of friendship are shaped by many traditions of thought, such as the modern western, the Islamic especially the Persian, and beyond that the classical Indian reflections on the subject. This is seen in the variety of words we use to describe friends, such as mate, friend, alter ego, soul mate, *dost*, *jigari dost*, and *mitra*[3]. I wish to concentrate on the classical India. This is a large area covering the *Vedas*, the epics, the *Puranas*, the Buddhist and Jaina literature, and the rich poetic and dramatic writings of Kalidasa, Bhavabhuti, Bana and others. Since I cannot discuss them all, I shall largely confine to the two epics with occasional references to other writings.

Most examples of friendship in the two epics and other religious and literary texts relate to men. Friendships between men and women are discussed, but they are either between two lovers, or between God and his devotees as in the case of Krishna and the Gopis, or more often between husband and wife as in the case of Kalidas's *Meghdut* and *Aiavilap*. Female friendships receive some attention and are generally presented as more intimate, more reliable, more durable, more easily made, and less self-conscious than those between men. However in most other respects they are like male friendships.

Friendship is a unique and complex form of human relationship. First, it is non-biological in the sense that unlike parents and children or siblings, it is not based on the ties of blood or heredity. This is not to deny that parents and children or brothers and sisters may become friends, but their

---

* Revised version of Dr. L.M. Singhvi Memorial Lecture delivered on August 8, 2008 at New Delhi.

their natural relationship sets limits to the quality and depth of their friendship, and that the latter is irreducible and autonomous in nature.

Second, friendship is a voluntary relationship. Although it is not based on conscious, let alone rational, choices, and often grows unconsciously and involves an elusive mental chemistry, it contains elements of deliberation, choice, and decision. The parties involved are aware of the development of their relationship, and freely decide whether or not to sustain and intensify it by required acts of reciprocity. Since it is entirely voluntary and not embedded in a network of other relations, friendship paradoxically may end at any time or last forever.

Third, friendship is relation between two individuals. One might have many friends, but one is a friend of each of them individually. Friendship is not and never can be a mass or collective relationship.

Fourth, since friendship has no basis outside of itself and is a free creation of two individuals, it is entirely dependent on what they care to make of it. It takes whatever form they choose to give it, has such content and depth as they succeed in putting into it, is a unique expression of the kind of persons they are, and reveals their individuality to a much greater degree than most other human relationships.

Fifth, friendship is open-ended and admits of degrees. One person is 'just' a friend; another is a 'good' friend; yet another is a 'close' or an 'intimate' friend, a 'fast' friend, as Indians call it. Friendship covers a large spectrum ranging from a perceptible degree of warmth to a near total merger of two selves, and often occupies a place somewhere between the two extremes.

Sixth, friendship is reciprocal and involves mutual acknowledgement and shared understanding. I cannot be your friend unless you are my friend. Friendship cannot come into being and last unless the parties involved acknowledge its existence, are broadly agreed on what it means and entails, and behave towards each other accordingly.

Finally, unlike the relations between spouses and parents and children, friendship has no legal or even social sanctions and must rely on its own energy and vitality to sustain itself.

The Concept

Friendship then is a non-biological, voluntary, open-ended, informal, uninstitutionalised, and mutually acknowledged relationship between two individuals based on their goodwill and fondness for each other. Given these and other constitutive features, it is only possible under certain conditions. Friendship can be a socially threatening even subversive relationship because it creates pockets of intense loyalty and can cut across social hierarchies and transgress social conventions. Friendship presupposes a society or a culture in which human relations are not totally structured and formalised, and leave adequate space for informal and self-generated relationships. It also presupposes that individuals are able to rise above their socially defined roles, are willing and able to undertake the adventure of creating new and unpredictable relationships, and have the courage and the disposition to share their intimate thoughts, feelings, and vulnerabilities with other and mortgage their happiness to other's precarious feelings. It also implies that individuals have the patience, constancy of contact, and the emotional energy required for a slowly maturing relationship; share enough experiences in common to have something to talk about; have the capacity to rise above their narrow self-interest and establish non-calculative rapport with others; have the emotional and moral maturity to understand and to adjust to each other's moods and eccentricities; and that they do not take so narrow a view of morality that it leaves no room for partiality and preference.

These and related conditions do not obtain in all societies, and hence friendship is not a universal phenomenon. Some societies, such as the tribal, have only a limited space for friendship; some others, such as the modern individualistic and largely privatised societies, encourage it up to a point but not beyond; some others such as the communist societies frown on it and prefer the collectivist ethos of comradeship based on dedication to a common cause. Many religious communities discourage friendship because it detracts from the love of God and breeds pockets of deep personal attachments. For the stoics, the wise man has no friends, and Kant has difficulty reconciling friendship with the principle of universal impartiality.

I intend to inquire if Indian thinkers identified a form of relationship analogous to that of friendship as described above, how they analysed its nature and structure, and what value they placed on it. If the orientalist writings on Indian society were correct, and if this society were as rigid and collectivist as they imagined it to be, it would have left no room for friendship. In fact the opposite is the case, which only goes to show that the classical Indian society and, indeed, the Indian society in general bore only a limited resemblance to the orientalist view of it. The classical India has one of the oldest and richest traditions of discourse on friendship that is second to none in its subtle analysis of the nature, levels, forms and obligations of friendship. Indeed it is unique in the world literature in regarding friendship as a deeply moral and even spiritual relationship, condemning *mitradroha* or betrayal of friends as a *paap* (sin) and seeing friendship as one important *bhava* (instinct) or mode in which to relate to God.

Friendship in Indian Literature

Indian thinking on the subject goes as far back as the *Rigveda* composed around 1000 BCE. The *Rigveda* uses three terms to describe the relationship of friendship, namely *sakha*, *mitra*, and *suhrd*. None of these is the exact equivalent of the modern conception of friendship, but none is wholly dissimilar either. Although sometimes the *Rigveda* uses the three terms to characterise different forms of friendship, on other occasions it uses them interchangeably. Indian thinking on friendship was further developed in such subsequent texts as the *Atharvaveda*, the epics, the *Puranas* and the classical literary works of Kalidasa, Bana, Bhavabhuti, and other eminent scholars.

Some societies, such as the tribal, have only a limited space for friendship; some others, such as the modern individualistic and largely privatised societies, encourage it up to a point but not beyond; some others such as the communist societies frown on it and prefer the collectivist ethos of comradeship based on dedication to a common cause.

Almost from the very beginning, the Indian discussion of friendship took place at two levels, which for convenience I shall call metaphysical and social. At the metaphysical level, Indian thinkers asked what should be the proper human orientation, disposition, or attitude (*bhava*) towards the rest of the universe. In contrast to the anthropocentric and theocentric views of the universe dominant in the West, most Indian thinkers took a cosmocentric view of it. For them the universe was an internally articulated and ordered whole whose constituents were all its equally legitimate 'co-tenants' enjoying the right to exist and to avail themselves of its resources. Human beings, therefore, had a duty of universal friendliness and goodwill (*maitre*) towards the other orders of being. Rather than grudge their existence and destroy them in pursuit of their narrowly defined species-interests, they are enjoined to cherish them and take delight in the infinite beauty and diversity of the universe.

A remarkable prayer to God in *Sukla Yaiurveda* reads: *'Mitrasyaham caksusa sarvani bhutani samikse'* ('I look upon all living beings with the eyes of a friend'). In *Taitiriya Samhita*, the author wishes 'peace' to earth, trees, plants, waters, and indeed to all sentient beings and prays that he may not unwittingly injure even the root of a plant. As the *Mahabharata* puts it, "he verily knows the substance of *dharma* who is always the friend of all". Friendship to all living beings leads to non-violence (*ahimsa*), meaning not only abstention from harming them but also the absence of a wish to harm them.

As Vyasa puts it in one of his *Bhasyas*, it is *sarvatha sarvada sarvabhutanam anabhidroha* (absence of hostility to all living beings in every way at all times).

While being oriented to all other human beings and the rest of the universe in a spirit of friendliness, the individual also stands in a relationship of friendship with particular individuals. Indian thinkers distinguished several forms or kinds of friendship, of which three are regarded as the most common and important. Each has its own logic and morality. The three forms are often given different names. One is *maitri* the second is *sauhardya*, and the third *sakhya*. In other words, a friend is either a *mitra*, a *suhrd* or a *sakha* or *sakhi*.

Although the term *maitri* is sometimes used in a generic sense, it is often used in the philosophised literature to refer to the most elementary level of friendship, or what we might call friendliness. As Shankaracharya in his *Gitabhashya* points out, it is based on mutual interest and expectation of reciprocity, and has an instrumental rather than an intrinsic value. This is more a case of an alliance than that of friendship. It lasts as long as the interests last, and is only as strong as the interest involved. It is a shifting relationship and lacks mutual trust and goodwill. As Bhishma on his deathbed tells Yudhishthira, this is generally the case in political life, and this is how a king should view his 'friends'. Many relations of friendship begin like this, and either stay there or over time become the basis of genuine friendship. In the *Ramayana*, when Rama first meets Sugriva in his search for Sita, the two view each other warily, and ask what each can do for the other. As Rama says, "our friendship will develop and last because we need each other". Their relation was initially fraught and marked by mutual suspicion and misunderstanding. But as each fulfilled his part of the bargain and as they worked together, they began to like each other and developed genuine friendship that transcended considerations of self-interest and reciprocity. When Bharat welcomes Rama and his associates at the end of the war, he calls Sugriva a friend and a brother. *Tvam asmakam chaturnam tu bharata Sugriva panchamah.*[4]

Friendship to all living beings leads to non-violence (ahimsa), meaning not only abstention from harming them but also the absence of a wish to harm them.

The second level of friendship represents friendship proper. It is based on the 'bonding of hearts'. Friends are *suhrd* or good-hearted towards each other. As Bharat puts it in the *Ramayana*, '*sauhardai iavate mitram apakarorilaksanam*' (from good-heartedness is born friendship; harm is the sign of enmity'). My friend is someone who instinctively feels for and with me, and participates in my joys and sorrows. Our hearts are bonded; we are related 'at the level of heart.' And our hearts converge and communicate with each other (*hridaya samvad*). In the classical Indian literature heart is often the seat of instinctive understanding. A charioteer who knows the moods and understands the movements of his horses is said to have the heart of the horse (*ashvahriday*). Friends understand each other without speaking and anticipate each other's moods and thoughts.

Individuals can become *suhrds* in various ways. Growing up together in childhood is one of the most common. The relation between Krishna and Sudama is an excellent example of this. The two had grown up together, gone to the same school, and were close to each other. Having lost contact with each other for years, the two met together and resumed their friendship as if their separation had made no difference. The two had little in common save shared childhood memories. Their abilities, wealth, social status and power were vastly unequal. Not surprisingly they had little to say to each other, yet they delighted in each other's presence.

One of the best examples of *sauhrd* is the relation between Karna and Duryodhan. Karna, an illegitimate child abandoned at birth by Kunti, was found and raised by a lower caste couple. All his life he suffered the stigma and humiliation of a *sutaputra*. Duryodhan recognised his talents, accepted him as an ally, and made him the king of Anga, and thus a nominal Kshatriya. Over time the two became great friends. When during the great war Krishna and then Kunti revealed to him his real identity and tried to persuade him to abandon Duryodhan in favour of Pandavas, he was uncompromising in his rejection. Duryodhan, he argued, had done him great favour (*upkar*), given him his pride and self-respect, and placed him under a 'deep debt of gratitude'. Additionally he had shown him affection and asked for nothing but affection in return. As he says, Duryodhan had asked for nothing but 'just my heart' which 'has been in his keeping ever since'. As a result 'my heart is not mine to give you, it belongs to my friend Duryodhan'. To betray him was unthinkable, sinful, and Karna could not possibly entertain such a thought.

Sakhya represents the third and highest form of friendship. It implies greater intimacy and transparency bordering on substantive mutual identification, deep love and total mutual commitment. Although the term *sakha* is sometimes used loosely, its most common usage is to convey the highest form of intimacy. *Sarnanashilvvasneshu sakhvarn.* Sakhya is possible between those who have the same basic orientation to the world and similar habits or tastes, and is generally forged through facing common difficulties. When Garuda announces his friendship with Rama in the *Ramayana*, he says: *aham sakha te kakutstha privah pranobahiskarah* (I am your dear friend, Rama, your external self)[6]. The complex and fascinating concept of *pranobahiscarah* or what is sometimes called *bahisprana* or external self implies that closest friends reflect each other's life-breath, spirit or self (*prana*), and discover themselves in each other. Friends draw their sustenance from each other, and cannot live a full life without the other. The *prana* or self of each partly lies outside him, and needs the other to complement and complete it.

The paradigmatic example of *sakhya* of course is the friendship between Krishna and Arjuna in the *Mahabharata*. As Krishna says, 'Let it be understood that Arjuna is one half of my body', and that they are really 'one self that has been made twofolds.' For his part, Arjuna tells Krishna, *sakheti matva prasabham yaduktam, he Krishna he yadav he sakheti* (I have addressed you in the past as a sakha, thought of you as a *sakha* and taken many liberties)[7].

In the *Mahabharata*, Krishna and Arjuna are inseparable. They have much fun together; they fight, plot, and conspire together; they adore, love, and care for each other; and they instinctively understand each other's feelings. moods, and thoughts. Krishna helps Arjuna elope with his sister Subhadra against the opposition of his family. He reluctantly tells occasional lies and even breaks his vows to protect Arjuna in difficult situations. When he fears that Arjuna might not be able to keep his pledge to kill Jayadratha before sunset the following day, he observes that he does not wish to live in a world in which Arjuna is absent, and decides to break his pledge not to engage in active combat himself. He acts as Arjuna's charioteer during the great war, a job involving not only high risk and a low status but also total and instinctive understanding of the plans, strategies, and thoughts between the warrior and his charioteer. Later on when he realises that the moment of his death has arrived, his last thought is for Arjuna, and his final wish is to see him and relieve his likely distress. Krishna summons him in a telepathic encounter, bids him a most affectionate farewell, and consoles him with the thought that once a man's purpose in life is realised, he must not only accept but welcome and even invite death. In the *Mahabharata* the friendship between the two men is said to be so close that they are described as 'aspects (*amsa*) of one another,' as 'really one self.' The Karnaparvan refers to them repeatedly with an air of mystery as 'the two Krishnas,' and Karna speaks of 'having seen the two Krishnas together on one chariot'.[8]

At one level the relation between Krishna and Arjuna is simply a relation between two close friends. At another level it exemplifies the relation between the devotee and God. God can be conceptualised in several different ways, *sakha* being one of them. Indeed *sakhvabhakti* is generally viewed as the second best form of *bhakti*. The devotee sees God as his *sakha* and the latter in turn does the same. Each is devoted to the other, reaches out to other, and loves and misses him. Their relation is not based on fear but love, playfulness and commitment, and involves mutual submission and *ekrupata* or total identification. In *Srimad Bhagavatam,* when Durvasa gets angry with Ambarisha, Narayan saves Ambarisha, saying 'I belong to my *bhaktas.* They have renounced everything and have chosen me as their sole companion. In return I have sworn that I will never abandon them. Their sorrow is my sorrow, and their happiness mine. This is why I am called *bhaktaparadhin*'.

I have briefly sketched several forms of friendship. Whatever its form, friendship is associated with the three related ideas of *ananda, sahava,* and *abhaya.* Friends are dear to each other and give each other *ananda.* In the *Mahabharata* Yudhisthira refers to Karna as *suhrdanandavardhana* (one who enhances the joy of his friends)[9]. In the Indian classical literature friendship is often associated with fun, merry making, playfulness, agreeable and amusing conversation, escapades, and disregard of social conventions. Indeed friendship is the only relationship in which these things are permitted, and those involved are released from the stern demands of duty characteristic of other relationships. In the *Mahabharata,* Krishna and Arjuna often banter about their military and romantic adventures (*vikrantani ratani cha*), get drunk and behave unconventionally.

Since friends care for each other, they render useful services to each other and make uncalculating sacrifices of time, energy, money, and even life. The classical Indian view of friendship has a strong practical orientation and makes mutual help its touchstone. True friends are tested in adversity, and both the classical and popular literature are full of false friends being exposed in times of need. Krishna helps Sudama when he goes to him for financial help. Sugriva helps Rama when the latter is desperate. Karna stands by Duryodhana during the *Mahabharata* war. And Krishna is always by Arjuna's side when the latter gets into trouble. By contrast Drupad, a boyhood friend of Drona who had promised him help when needed, spurns the latter when he goes to him for financial assistance. 'Friendship is only possible between equals' he argues, and Drona's hope for one was a 'fantasy'. Although Drona later forgave him, their deep enmity remained that ended with Drona's death at the hands of Drupad's son-in-law. If a friend does not help me when I need it, he is not a true friend. And if a stranger helps me, he shows goodwill towards me and lays the foundation of friendship. It is not the act of help *per se* but the feeling of goodwill which it reflects that betokens friendliness, and forms the basis of their friendship. In Indian thought a good deed (*upkar*) is seen as a sign of goodwill or favourable disposition just as harm is a sign of hostility (*apakarorilaksanam*), and generates a debt (*ma*) of gratitude and goodwill.

Friendship also involves fearlessness. In the *Mahabharata,* Krishna describes Kama as *mitranam abhavamkarah,* one in whose presence his friends know no fear or anxiety[10]. The concept of fearlessness (*abhaya*) is subtle and complex. It implies not only that friends have nothing to fear from each other but also, and more importantly, that when friendship comes under severe strain or those involved cease to be friends, they must never betray each other, divulge information obtained during their friendship, nor behave as if they had never been friends. This is a recurrent theme in the various stories of *Panchatantra*. The *Hitopadesha* puts it well: 'If a friendship breaks, a true friend's feelings towards that former friend undergo no change, as a lotus stalk, though cut, holds its shape.' Friendship is supposed to entail lifelong commitments, and while it may be loosened, suspended, or even ended, it can never be 'broken' and its obligations violated.

Loyalty to friends does not imply that one may not criticise them or point out and protest against their wrong doings. Indeed, in the Indian discussion of friendship, friends are almost invariably described as sources of sincere advice and acting as each other's conscience, and those acquiescing in their friends' mistakes and misdeeds out of blind loyalty, self-interest, or cowardice are generally condemned. Friendship is one of the few relationships in which honest and fearless criticism is both permitted and required. While friends should be open and honest with each other, they are required to refrain from gossiping or saying unpleasant things behind each other's back, revealing their limitations to outsiders, and doing things likely to harm or demean them in others' eyes. Critical in private, friends are expected to present a loyal and united front to the world. The two are complementary. It is precisely because friends can count on each other's good feelings and loyalty that they enjoy the privilege of fearless criticism, and *vice versa*.

Since friendship involves bonding of hearts, which is also what characterised familial and kinship relations, the Indian thinkers have as a rule conceptualised friendship in familial terms. A close friend is a 'brother' (*bhratr*) or 'kinsman' *(bandhu)*, and friendship is often called 'brotherliness' or 'brotherly disposition' (*bhratrabhava* or *bandhutva*). A close friend is a brother; one not so close is like a brother. In either case friendship is familialised and assimilated to kinship. At its best friendship, a purely voluntary and inherently fragile relationship, acquires the thickness of blood and the solidity of natural ties. A friend is an adopted member of the family. He shares food with the family, an important privilege in a caste society with its rigid taboos, helps in the household chores, stays with the family, enjoys more or less unrestricted access to it, and is generally given more or less equal love. Even the caste restrictions on marriages are slackened and occasionally waived in relation to friends. Since friendship is familialised, it is subject to a dual logic. The family determines whether an individual should be admitted to its inner realm, and hence limits who one can have as one's friend. However, friendship also has its own dynamics, and can redefine the family's social conventions and subvert its taboos.

Since friendship is recognised as an important social relation, several authors of moral treatises (*dharmasastras*) took cognizance of it and gave it a ritual status. In the *Ramayana* there is a reference to *maitrividhi*, a ceremony in which when Rama offers his friendship to Sugriva, they shake hands and with fire as witness go around it to confirm and sacralise their new relationship. In the marriage ceremony, one of the steps in the *saptapadi* involves the newly wedded couples often promising to be friends to each other. Some *dharmasastras* invoke the remarkable concept of *mitradroha* and call it a sin (*paap*). When Rama wonders if Sugriva really intends to help him as promised after Bali's death, he says that when those who betray their friends die, even the crows do not eat their flesh' (*tan mritan api krivvada kritaghnan na upabhuniate*)'[11]. According to Manu, a person guilty of betraying a friend is barred from participating in a *shraddha* ceremony involving offering oblations to dead ancestors; killing a friend is as much a sin as giving false evidence in a court of law or reviling the *Vedas*; having sex with a friend's wife is as much a sin as having sex with one's own sister; and when one's intimate friend dies, the impurity is supposed to last for a whole day[12]. According to *Vishnu Purana*, those guilty of betraying friends invariably go to hell.

Friendship also earns spiritual merit. He who has been true to his friends acquires spiritual power that can be as great as that acquired through an austere penance. In the *Mahabharata*, when Arjuna is about to kill the indomitable Karna with an arrow suggestively entitled *anialika* (a respectful tribute), he puts all his spiritual merit behind it and invokes, among other things, the power of his friendship. Uttering *satvakriva*, he says, 'If I have sincerely practised all the austerities, pleased the gurus, and if I have heard only good things about my friends and never wished them ill, may that truth give this arrow the power to behead *Kama*'[13] (Taposti *taptam guruvasca tosita mava vadistam suhrdam tatha srutam*). It is striking that friendship is given equal value with loyalty to the *guru* and intense penance. I know no other tradition in which friendship is given such a high value and assigned a quasi-religious and sacred status[14].

Since friendship involves loyalty and helping each other out in times of need, it creates a moral dilemma. Friendship is a most valuable human relationship, both intensely moral and deeply spiritual in nature. Yet friends have a duty to help each other, and may, therefore, need to bend moral rules, cut moral corners, and engage in *adharma*. How is one to deal with this? For the classical writers there are two ways of coping with it. First, friendship should be limited to those with *samanashila*, that is, those with similar disposition and character, so that neither will make unacceptable demands on the other. Second, one might avoid forming friendship altogether, so that one is never morally compromised. This is what

Yudhishthira does. He is *dharmavatar* or *dharmaraj*, and it is striking that he has no close friends. He has brothers who are all equally dear to him. He has a wife to whom he is not particularly attached or partial. This form of friendless life; however, has its limits. It deprives life of fun, merry making or *ananda*. It also renders it intensely lonely and insecure. Human life is, therefore, unimaginable without friends, and friendship naturally brings with it its inevitable attachments, partiality, some degree of favouritism. For the Indian writers wisdom consists in choosing one's friends most carefully, building one's relations with them on a moral basis, encouraging them to be good human beings, and reducing to the minimum such moral compromises as friendship entails.

The dilemma, however, is not that easily resolved. If a friend asks for minor moral violations, the epics argue that these are permissible. Human life in general is impossible without some immorality, and this is particularly permissible in such a deep and valuable relationship as friendship. But what if a friend is guilty of gross *adharma* and asks for a most *adharmic* deed? The epics' answer seems to be that in such situations one's response depends on the enormity of the evil involved. Vibhishana was right to leave his brother Ravana, though wrong to refuse to perform his funeral rites, for which Rama criticised him and urged him to perform them on the ground that enmity ends with death (*maranantani vairani*). As for Kama, the situation was more complex. Duryodhana behaved badly but was not as evil as Ravana. This is why Bhishma and Drona chided him but ultimately stood by him and fought for him. Kama's reasons were similar. Betraying and breaking his promise to Duryodhan was gross *adharma*. Staying loyal to him also involved *adharma*, though not of the same magnitude. As Kama says, this was his fate, meaning both something predetermined and a tragic situation, and he had to make his choice and live with it. Whatever he did was both right and wrong, though in his view staying loyal to the demands of friendship was on balance far more right. The fact that the outcome of the war was more or less certain and the Kauravas were fated to lose was also a factor in his decision. Here as elsewhere in the *Mahabharata* the idea of fate plays a complex and sometimes discussion-stopping role.

Friendship also poses another problem for Indian thinkers. *Anasakti* or total detachment is often held up as the highest ideal. It implies that one is *samadarshi*, above likes and dislikes, and treats all human beings impartially. Friendship militates against this, raising the question whether it has any place in the life of a person aspiring for perfection. The question does not receive systematic treatment in Indian thought, but the general view seems to be that such a person can have friends and families, be fond of them and even love them, provided that he is not attached to them and does not morally prefer them over others in cases of conflict of interests. This fascinating and highly suggestive idea of detached love, love that cares and agrieves and has depth and energy but is not dependent on and possessive about or possessed by its object, love that is calm and non-emotional and in full control of itself, is a recurrent theme in Indian moral and philosophical thought. This is how God is supposed to love his creation, especially human beings, and it represents the ideal which a long line of Indian saints and spiritual aspirants including Mahatma Gandhi sought to approximate.

As far as I can see, there seems to be a striking gap in the otherwise extremely rich Indian discussion of friendship, namely, celebration of intellectual friendship viewed by Plato, Aristotle and some European writers as the highest and even the only true and lasting form of friendship. Such friendship is based on intellectual partnership, a shared pursuit of truth and knowledge, mutual exploration of common problems, delight in the exchange of ideas and arguments. This kind of friendship does not receive much if any attention in Indian thought. The Indian tradition is of course full of fascinating philosophical discussions, but these are either between the *guru* and his disciples or between the protagonists of different schools of thought. If I am right, those more familiar with the Indian view of friendship than a layman like me would need to explain why it does not give as much importance to the bonding of heads as to that of hearts.

Summing Up

I would like to conclude this discourse with a general plea. I hope to have shown in this lecture that in the classical Indian thought, friendship occupies an unusually high place in the hierarchy of human relations. It is a sacred human relationship, like that between parents and children. It represents an expansion of the individual self to take in another without losing one's individuality, such that what is mine becomes his. As Bhavabhuti puts it in *Uttarramcharita*, you are my *sakha* because whatever is mine is also yours (*Tasmat sakha tvamasi vanmama tattavaiva*). What I have said in my lecture scratches only the surface of the vast and subtle literature on the subject, and ignores many fascinating discussions of different forms, limits and moral dilemmas of friendship. Sadly there has so far been no systematic study of the classical Indian discourse on friendship, indeed, I cannot easily think of a single significant book on the subject. As a result, we have lost access to a great treasure, a rich and inspiring tradition, that has sustained our civilisation for several

Such friendship is based on intellectual partnership, a shared pursuit of truth and knowledge, mutual exploration of common problems, delight in the exchange of ideas and arguments.

millennia. I very much hope that this treasure will be explored, and the tradition retrieved and critically appraised, by scholars with the sensitivity and care it deserves. That would be a worthy tribute to a remarkable man whom this lecture commemorates.

NOTES

1. I am grateful to Professors Mukund Wadekar, Rajendra Nanavati and Gunvant Shah for their most helpful comments on the text of this lecture. For parts of it, I rely on my 'An Indian view of Friendship' in Leroy Rouner, ed., Friendship (Notre Dame; University of Notre Dame Press, 1995).
2. For the Greeks and Romans, friendship was primarily a political relationship and was largely an alliance based on mutual interest and support. The idea of disinterested friendship (philia) as opposed to Plato's eros was first fully articulated by Aristotle, but it was limited to those 'who are good and alike in virtue' and united by their common or shared love of good. See Nichomachean Ethics 8, 3, 1156a, 1419. For a good discussion see A.W. Price, *Love and Friendship in Plato and Aristotle* (Oxford: Clarendon Press, 1989). The Epicureans saw friendship as an escape from social and political relations, and based it largely on a shared intellectual life. For Saint Augustine friendship was only possible among those sharing a common faith, and even then its intensity was always suspect. In China friendship was traditionally seen not as a private relationship as in the modern West, but as a public relation subject to social constraints.
3. The term *dost* or *dosti*, which is largely of Persian origin and implies informality, deep emotional bonds and loyalty, introduces a new conception of friendship in Indian thought from around the 17th century onwards. The Western idea of friendship arrived towards the end of the 19th century, and did not get assimilated into Indian thought and regional literature until the mid-19th century.
4. *Ramayana* 6.130. 44-46.
5. *Ramayana* 6. 130. 44-46
6. *Ramayana* 6.50. 46.
7. *Gita*, 11: 41. See also 11: 44.
8. *Karnaparvan* 8.57.48 talks of *drstva krsnavekarathe sametau* (having seen the two Krisnas together on one chariot).
9. *Karnaparvan*, 8.46.9.
10. *Karnaparvan*, 51.61.
11. *Ramayana*, 4: 30: 73. See also 4: 30: 81/2.
12. G. Buihler, ed., *The Laws of Manu* (Delhi; Motilal Banarsidass, 1948), 3,160; 5,82; 11.59. See also *Vishnu Purana* 2.6.11.
13. *Mahabharata*, 8.67.20. Far a further discussion, see Norman Brown, 'Duty as Truth in Ancient India.' *Proceedings of the American Philosophical Society* (1972), pp. 252-68; and Myles Dillon. The Hindus' Act of Truth in Celtic Tradition, Modern Philosophy (1947), pp. 137-38.

14. Karna accuses Salya of being a *mitradrohi* (one who betrays or injures friends). He could kill him but does not, 'Because you are a *sakhi*, a suhrd and also a *mitra* (*sakhibhavena sauhardanmitrabhavena caiva hi*), for these three reasons, O Salya, you now live. Karna has clearly in mind three different relations in which he and Salya stand, for which he needs three different terms. It would appear that he regarded Salya as a *mitra* because he was an ally of and supported Duryodhana, as a *suhrd* because tree was generally, though not during the great war, well disposed to Karna, and as a *sakhi* because he was his charioteer. It is striking that the *Karnaparvan* represents one of the major occasions for a careful articulation of the vocabulary of friendship in the classical Indian literature.

CHAPTER 9

State of Governance in Rising India

DR. BIMAL JALAN

The Perceptible Change

For nearly three decades after 1980, India has registered one of the highest rates of growth among developing countries, and is now regarded as an emerging global power. Poverty ratio has also improved during this period. Nevertheless, more than half of India's population—as many as 600 million to 700 million persons—are still dependent on government for providing basic needs and services like nutrition, education, health, sanitation and housing. In all these areas, the record of public agencies in delivering services to the poors, despite high growth, has been abysmal. India has been one of the worst performers and enjoys a low ranking in human development indices compiled by international agencies, including the United Nations and the World Bank.

This chapter is an attempt to examine briefly the causes and reasons for this state of affairs in a rising India, which now has one of the highest rates of growth, savings and investment in the world. Compared with the past, another striking change has been in respect of India's balance of payments, which provides considerable freedom to India in the management of its economy.

Earlier, we were supposed to be a 'hand-to-mouth economy', dependent on food aid as well as financial aid from abroad. After 1956, only 10 years after independence, for nearly three decades, there was hardly a year when India did not go through a severe balance of payment crisis. The primary task of government planners and policy advisers during that period was to make both ends meet and keep India going. This position has fundamentally changed.

I believe that for the first time in its post-Independence history, India is now in a position to do and accomplish whatever it wishes to do in the economic field. There is no constraint of resources, foreign exchange or entrepreneurship.

Causes of Dysfunctionality

Let me now deal with the reasons for deterioration in the state of governance despite substantial gains in the country's overall resource position and economic strength. The deterioration in governance is most visible in respect of public delivery of services to the less disadvantaged persons, maintenance of law and order, and provision of basic municipal services.

A fundamental reason for this state of affairs is the proliferation of ministries and offices of government. There is no item of government business for which a single ministry can be held responsible, except perhaps taxation or the budget making. The number of ministries has shot up from 18 in 1947 to 65 or more now, and there has been a sharp increase in the number of Cabinet Ministers, independent Ministers of State in-charge of separate Ministries, and large number of Ministers of State who report to Cabinet Ministers. Many of these Ministries have very little to do. All Ministries also have more than one department and several subordinate agencies. The rigid hierarchy in the delivery and decision-making process further ensures that horizontally, as well as vertically, a dozen or more offices are likely to be involved from different ministries including Planning Commission even when there is no policy to be decided, such as, say, provision of drinking water or electricity to rural areas.

In addition to the centre, there is similar proliferation of governmental organizations at the State and district level. It has become a routine matter for policy to be announced by the central government, but implementation remains in the hands of State government and their subsidiary organizations. Central government blames State governments, and the latter blame the Central Government for rigidity in the provisions of the scheme or inadequate allocation of funds. Within the Central Government, it is now common for one department or Ministry to blame another department for any drawback in either policy formulation or policy implementation.

India, at the time of Independence, inherited a civil service structure which was generally referred to as the "steel frame" and was supposed to be the envy of the post-colonial world. What made India's civil service an extremely effective instrument of governance was the independence that civil servants enjoyed in effectively implementing policy decisions, which were taken by political leadership. There was a clear separation of executive powers between ministers and civil servants within the executive. Gradually, but surely, all this seems to have undergone a change, particularly after the emergence of coalition governments at the Centre and States with short life expectancy.

The rigid hierarchy in the delivery and decision making process ensures that horizontally, as well as vertically, a dozen or more offices are likely to be involved from different Ministries including Planning Commission even when there is no policy to be decided.

As emphasised by several former cabinet secretaries and other high level officials in their memoirs, most of the administrative powers which were earlier in the hands of the civil servants have now been taken over by political masters at the ministerial level who have no direct or indirect experience of administration. As politics has become more combative and personalised, and coalition governments have become less secure about their tenure in office, transfers of civil servants have also become very frequent. Some years ago in UP, for example, where two parties resolved to have a 6-monthly tenure in government, there were as many as 1000 transfers ordered within a year amongst members of the IAS and the IPS. First head of government ordered transfers of senior officers at an average rate of 7 per day. The second head of government who took office after the expiry of 6-month period, decided to beat this record and transferred officials at the rate of 16 per day!

As a result of frequent transfers, administration has naturally become weak. What is even worse is that civil servants, instead of being independent of political leaders or parties in power, have now become subservient to them. As a result, corruption has also become rampant, both to avoid transfers as well as secure remunerative postings.

I must make it clear that I am referring here to the system as a whole and not to individuals. We are fortunate to have many outstanding civil servants at different levels who perform efficiently without fear or favour.

Recent developments in politics are too well known to require any elaboration. While we can take justifiable pride in our vibrant democracy and system of free and fair elections, there is also very little doubt that the shape of India's politics has changed fundamentally with the emergence of multiparty coalition governments without a shared programme or agenda. We simply have to reflect on political events in States of Goa, Jharkhand, Bihar and Chhattisgarh, and more recently at the Centre. What is happening in our several States, and to some extent at the Centre, are not accidental. Some recent developments are reflective of a deeper malaise that is beginning to affect our political system. Let me just highlight three political developments which are likely to have substantial long-term significance:

- The first is the power of small parties in recent coalitions, particularly since 1989. As we have seen, a party with less than 5 per cent of the seats can enjoy immense clout—and many of these parties have no national agenda, but only local agenda.
- The second is the shrinking role of the Parliament. Even the Union Budget of the government is often passed without a discussion and with a "voice vote". A couple of years ago, the second part of the Budget session was first cancelled after approving the budget and then reconvened. Leaders of major parties decide what will happen. Members of Parliament themselves have very little say.
- The third political development is the erosion of collective responsibility. There has been an erosion in the constitutional concept of collective responsibility of the Cabinet and Government power in regard to all matters of public importance. On several issues of public importance, there are many disparate voices emanating from different sources from the same government (on Special Economic Zones or internal security issues, for example).

Thus, the three essential pillars of parliamentary democracy are now weaker than ever before—majority party rule, role of parliament, and collective responsibility. The expectations of a short-term in power in several states with unstable coalitions has further eroded the respect for political propriety.

The Overview of the System

Let me now summarise and give an overview of where we are in relation to politics, civil service and governance in emerging India. On the economic front, there is no doubt that India's fundamentals are strong with high growth, high domestic savings and investment, and a very strong external situation. However, we face substantial problems in the areas of governance and administration. In Indian politics, we are now going through a new phase in which coalition governments with a large number of small regional parties with differing

There has been an erosion in the constitutional concept of collective responsibility of the Cabinet and Government power in regard to all matters of public importance.

agenda are likely to become the norm rather than an exception. Several of the constitutional provisions about the working of our rightly applauded parliamentary democracy are also facing question marks.

On the whole, we seem to be going through a period of transition with a growing connect between economics, on the one hand, and governance and politics, on the other. As we look to the future, the overarching issue that India faces is whether in the years to come we will be able to resolve what can perhaps be described as "public-private" dichotomy in the functioning of our country. It is a striking fact that economic renewal and positive growth impulses are now occurring largely outside the public delivery system at the levels of private corporations, autonomous institutions and individuals at the top of their professions in India and abroad. In the functioning of the government and politics, once elections are over, we see a marked deterioration at all levels.

Three essential pillars of parliamentary democracy are now weaker than ever before—majority party rule, role of parliament, and collective responsibility.

Agenda for Public Reforms

Can something be done to resolve this dichotomy and improve the functioning of politics and governmental system in the future? Elsewhere, I have suggested an agenda for political reforms with a view to improving a system of accountability and functioning of political parties once they form a coalition (see *India's Politics : A View from the Backbench*, Penguin, 2007 and 2008). Let me briefly mention a few areas where I believe reforms are absolutely essential if we have to realise our full potential as an emerging economic power. Incidentally, I do not think that we need to move from a Parliamentary System of Government to a Presidential System, as suggested by some. In my view, it is much better to stick to a system that we have tried out over the years, rather than to introduce a new system, which has its own perils as we see in several of our neighbouring countries. Some suggestions for political reform which require urgent consideration are :

- Within the framework of parliamentary form of government, an important priority is to further reduce the political role of the government in the economy, particularly the power of multiple ministries and short-lived governments over public sector enterprises. Privatisation is not the only answer. The real question is whether we can create an "arm's length" relationship between the government and these enterprises (i.e. Union Public Service

Commission-type arrangement), where the board is appointed through an autonomous agency, such as Public Sector Enterprises Board (PSEB), and has the power of supervision over the management of public enterprises.

- In the era of coalition politics, it is important to try and provide for greater political stability after the formation of government. This can be done if the anti-defection law is also applied to small parties and independent members who choose to join the government. In other words, those who join the government cannot defect (as happened in Chhattisgarh) without having to seek re-election. At present, the anti-defection law applies only to members of a political party which has had the unintended consequences of providing an incentive for formation of small parties, and reducing the personal autonomy of legislators belonging to a large party.
- There is also need to change the distribution of powers between the Union and States under articles 245 to 255 of the Constitution. For example, it will be desirable to give states much greater economic powers, but transfer inter-regional or inter-State laws and other issues to the Centre.

> ***In the era of coalition politics, it is important to try and provide for greater political stability after the formation of government.***

- The issue of state funding of elections has also been considered from time to time, but has not been found acceptable. Not that state funding would eliminate corruption, but with high cost of elections, the lack of it has become an important defence of corruption in the exercise of political and administrative powers. In a budget of more than 600,000 crore at the Centre and Rs. 1100,000 crore at the State level, even an allocation of 0.5 per cent for State funding of elections would generate sufficient resources for State funding. It is also possible to allocate MPLAD funds amounting to Rs. 1700 crore per year for this purpose.
- Finally, a separation of powers between civil services and ministers for carrying out administrative functions is essential. Greater empowerment of the civil services must, of course, go hand in hand with greater accountability of civil services for their performance and ethical conduct.

There is much more that can be done to make our political and administrative system work better. The above set of reforms will constitute an important step forward, and further measures may be considered after sometime in the light of experience.

CHAPTER 10

Making Democracy Relevant for the Common Man*

SOMNATH CHATTERJEE

Foundation of Democracy

What is the relevance of democracy if it does not make any difference to the lives of the common man, that is a basic question. The effectiveness of any government is judged on the basis of the impact it makes on the lives of those who need the government the most.

The greatest challenge on the Founding Fathers, in the wake of Freedom, was to come up with a viable system of government that would reflect and represent the diversities of India and at the same time constructively govern it for the years to come. We finally adopted a parliamentary democratic system, after a great deal of debate, with the conviction that it best suited us. Our people and their leadership had great expectations from it, in spite of the fact that the world around us was quite sceptical about our ability to successfully operate a democratic system. We can take legitimate pride in the fact that in laying the institutional foundations of our Republic we have made remarkable progress.

Our most significant achievement of the first half century of freedom is that we have sustained a parliamentary democratic system, with all its imperfections, all these years. Having successfully come through fourteen General Elections and experienced a good degree of political stability for over five and half decades, no one today would dispute that Indian

---

* Based on the Author's V.K. Krishna Menon Memorial Lecture, delivered at Kochi, Kerala, on 6th August, 2005.

Democracy has come of age and that democracy is here to stay, which clearly establishes the maturity of Indian electorate.

The institution that has contributed the most to the consolidation and strengthening of democracy in the country is our Parliament. Over the years, our Parliament has come to be identified, both in theory and in practice, to be the pivot of our political system. The responsibility for providing direction, momentum and the institutions for social engineering in India has been on our Parliament.

Our most significant achievement of the first half century of freedom is that we have sustained a parliamentary democratic system, with some imperfections.

The Social Dimension

On the social front, Independent India had to undertake the delicate task of having to blend tradition with modernity, customs with the laws, to bring reason to prevail over superstitions and reconcile issues of faith with the demands of modern administration and governance. Perhaps, the biggest and the most complex issue that India had to address on the social front was the issue of the political, social and economic exclusion of a significant segment of our population and the ways and means for their empowerment by bringing them into our national mainstream. These seemingly impossible tasks, precipitated by historical forces, were sought to be achieved by taking recourse to progressive legislations and by adopting a policy of protective discrimination. Today, we are distinctly recognised in the world community for our democratic and secular values and for establishing the foundations for an inclusive and modern social order.

The responsibility for providing direction, momentum and the institutions for social engineering in India has been on our Parliament.

On the economic front, we have made noticeable gains, in spite of many gaps in achievements, by taking a substantial segment of our people from below the poverty line to a better living. Our planned efforts of the last five decades have helped us, to some extent, in mitigating the extent of privations of the colonial era and in building India into a nation of considerable economic strength within the framework of democracy, federalism and a policy of self-reliance.

I have not presented this positive picture overlooking the other India that lives under conditions of poverty, deprivations, squalor, illiteracy, ignorance, intolerance and prejudices. The social revolution our Founding Fathers had conceived does not seem to have touched upon the lives of a substantial section of our society. It is only when we succeed in making a positive impact upon the lives of those sections that still remain largely untouched by the lofty objectives of democratic governance that we can say that the system of governance we adopted nearly six decades back has become relevant for all our people.

Democracy is not all about periodic elections and political rights. It is fundamentally about providing for the basic needs of the people. "Health for all, education for all, home for all, jobs for all and security for all", should be the end results of democracy, which can be achieved only when the power structure is adequately representative of all sections of the society. Democracy is also about good governance. Only when the government is transparent, accountable, responsive and responsible can we claim to be moving in the direction of good governance.

Nobel laureate, Prof. Amartya Sen, very perceptively analysed that democracy's claim to be valuable 'does not rest on just one particular merit'. He has stressed that "there is a plurality of virtues here, including, first, the *intrinsic* importance of political participation and freedom in human life; second, the *instrumental* importance of political incentives in keeping governments responsible and accountable; and third, the *constructive* role of democracy in the formation of values and in the understanding of needs, rights and duties."

The greatest challenge before our democracy today is about how we make it work for the betterment of the common man. This would involve the creation of enabling social, political, economic and legal conditions that would help every section of the society to participate fully in the process of governance and empowering them to ask questions to hold the State accountable always.

Democracy is not all about periodic elections and political rights. It is fundamentally about providing for the basic needs of the people. "Health for all, education for all, home for all, jobs for all and security for all", should be the end results of democracy.

The dream of our Founding Fathers was to evolve a structure which would be most suited and relevant for the achievement of socio-economic and political justice for the common man, the eradication of poverty and ending the exploitation of the disadvantaged sections of society and providing for the basic needs of the people by ensuring universal education, an effective health care system and job opportunities for all. One of the guiding principles in this regard was Mahatma Gandhi's notion of democracy which was one where the weakest should have the same opportunity as the strongest.

Dr. B.R. Ambedkar put it in perspective when he stressed that we must not content ourselves with mere political democracy; we should rather strive to make our political democracy a social democracy as well. Democracy is incompatible and inconsistent with isolation and exclusiveness resulting in the distinction between the privileged and the unprivileged. With a framework of political democracy already in place, we should embark upon the task of bringing economic and social democracy to the centre stage of all our developmental programmes so that the fruits of development are enjoyed by one and all equally and human dignity remains inviolable under all circumstances.

Millions of our people have still not been emancipated from the vicious cycle of poverty, illiteracy, unemployment, poor health care, gender-based prejudices and other economic and social infirmities and specially so in the case of the disadvantaged and the marginalised sections. The conditions of the working class are no better. Food, shelter and clothing for a majority of our people continue to remain a distant goal.

Inclusive Process of Decision Making

The most crucial factor, therefore, to my mind, is to make decision-making a more inclusive process in which the common man has a say in shaping his life and everyone is given an equal chance to share in the resultant economic and social gains. Promoting democratic politics will not be possible without expanding capabilities such as education, improved health, knowledge and skill to enable people to play a more effective role in decision-making.

For this, it is important to identify the sections that have so far been discriminated against and kept out of the purview of development. Women have to be made equal partners with men in private and public spheres of life and decision-making. People have to be freed from discriminations based on race, ethnicity, class or gender. To achieve all these, our economic and social policies have to be responsive to people's needs and aspirations. We need to have a strong national urge to eradicate poverty and achieve an acceptable level of equity in society, besides broadening people's choices on all fronts. All these are key parameters, which need to be addressed to achieve human development goals so as to make democracy relevant for the common man.

The democracy that we are talking about and all its achievements so far have no relevance to more than 400 million of our citizens who still live unsure of their next square meal. The growing gap between the rich and the poor, between the haves and the have-nots do not make our democracy stronger, rather it only undermines our socio-economic and political systems. As Swami Vivekananda said, "A few thousand graduates do not make a nation, a few rich men do not make a nation." We cannot hold distributive justice as a distant dream any more.

There has to be a firm commitment on the part of all of us to achieve the goals laid down in the Constitution to mete out justice equally to all. As I have said elsewhere too, if the basic issues affecting the everyday life of the common man have to be effectively addressed, the Directive Principles, which have been appropriately described as *the Manifesto of a Welfare State* should be made enforceable to ensure accountability of the administration. Article 38 of the Constitution, which forms the core of those Directives, had made it incumbent upon the state to constantly "strive to promote the welfare of the people by securing and protecting as effectively as it may a social order in which justice, social, economic and political shall inform all the institutions of the national life." This would involve, as Gandhiji said, " … a levelling down of the few rich in whose hands is concentrated the bulk of the nation's wealth, on the one hand, and the levelling up of the semi-starved, naked millions on the other."

Another important aspect of making democracy relevant to the common man, to my mind, is the effectiveness of our judicial delivery system. An independent Judiciary has been accorded an important role in our constitutional set-up to protect the rights and interest of the citizens. No doubt, our Judiciary has played its role towards preserving, protecting and promoting Fundamental Rights of the citizens, in many cases checking administrative lapses and curbing Executive excesses and in strengthening the democratic culture of the country, yet the mounting arrears of cases and slow moving judicial process make the scenario quite distressing as this, in many instances, almost amounts to denial of justice itself to the common man.

Rule of law has to be enforced not by expanding any organ's extent of powers, by encroaching into the areas specifically assigned to any other, but by diligently and effectively discharging each one's assigned responsibilities. In my view, therefore, the Judiciary, one of the three main pillars of our democratic governance, to make itself relevant for the common people, has to demonstrate a greater degree of activism in discharging its primary responsibility of providing speedy and cheap justice and operate in a manner clearly recognising the space provided to the other institutions of democratic governance.

An important aspect of making democracy relevant to the common man, to my mind, is the effectiveness of our judicial delivery system.

Transparency in Public Administration

There is a general perception that the public administration system, which is also an important component of our governance structure, has not been able to deliver the goods to the extent that is expected of it. Red tapism and corrupt practices have been a bane of our public administration. We have to drive in a new sense of urgency into our bureaucracy at all levels about issues of development. A competent, educated and dedicated bureaucracy, well trained in the art and science of administration and functioning transparently, and with probity is a necessary prerequisite for a people-oriented democracy.

Transparency in the public administration and its accountability to the people are important factors in ensuring that democracy delivers good in its concern for the common man. It has a two fold advantage—transparency and accountability tone down the chances of corruption in the system and secondly, they strengthen democratic institutions by creating awareness, involvement and participation of an informed citizenry. Democratic societies are expected to be open and transparent. We had recognised long back that the right to information was implicit in the right to freedom of speech as enshrined in the Fundamental Rights in our Constitution. We have procedural devices provided in our Parliament and the State Legislatures to strengthen Executive accountability but that is not enough to ensure the transparency required of the administration and to satisfy the people's right to know. The Right to Information, now statutorily recognised, should become a tool of grass root empowerment, which would also work against corruption and exploitation. As it is said, it is in secret places that corruption thrives.

It is with this realisation that we have decided to telecast live the entire proceedings of our Parliament. The people have a right to know what transpires in Parliament and how their representatives articulate their concerns and grievances before the highest popular forum of our democracy. It has also been our endeavour to ensure that the institutions of democracy always remained accountable to the highest people's forum. With this objective in mind the functioning of Parliamentary Committees *vis-à-vis* the Executive is being made more effective. A Parliamentary Committee, in its functioning, is treated like a mini-parliament itself. Once their functioning is streamlined and their suggestions and recommendations find adequate reflection in the policy formulation, we will be adding an important dimension to the concept of representative democracy in the country.

The Right to Information, now statutorily recognised, should become a tool of grass roots empowerment, which would also work against corruption and exploitation.

Our Parliament itself has to be ever vigilant about the growing cynicism among our people about the way the institutions of our democracy function. It is on Parliament, more than on any other organ, that the responsibility for sustaining people's faith in democracy as the most sensitive system to the people's problems, rests. Therefore, the institution collectively and the individual members, who constitute it, will have to function as role models for the society at large. As the Presiding Officer of the House of the People, I am acutely aware of this great responsibility.

The civil society and the media also have important roles to play in this. Where the state takes it as a duty to safeguard the freedom of media, it expects of the media to bolster democracy through its varied roles in a responsible and responsive manner and contribute in partnership to secure political, economic and social development in ways consistent with democratic principles.

Empowering People

Once we recognise the common man as an equal stakeholder in the policies and programmes of the country, as a means of capacity building, we must accept that education adequate in quantity and quality with contemporary relevance, is the most powerful instrument for empowering people and for facilitating development. In fact, education is the best tool for empowerment and the key to human development. It is basic to our progress and to the achievement of important goals like democracy, secularism, equity, liberty, fraternity, justice and national integration. To quote Swami Vivekananda again: "The only service to be done to our lower classes is to give them education, to develop their lost individuality.... They are to be given ideas, their eyes are to be opened to what is going on in the world around them; and then they will work out their own salvation ...."

Populist platitudes will not help in addressing the common man's problems. The Eighty-sixth Amendment to the Constitution provides for free and compulsory education to all children in the age group of six to fourteen years. Such initiatives can impact upon the lives of the people only when the injunctions emanating from them are matched by the conviction among the leaders of society of the need for such measures. Otherwise they will only remain paper provisions for the people. A successful education policy would form not only the bedrock of national development in all its dimensions but would also form the foundation for a vibrant democracy, growth of productivity, income and employment opportunities, thus offering quality life to the common man. This is important for bringing about a stable social order also. As Prof. Amartya Sen observed, "If we continue to leave vast sections of the people of the world outside the orbit of education, we make the world not only less just, but also less secure...Not to be able to read or write or count or communicate is a tremendous deprivation...."

For our priorities to be actualised, we have to carry the people with us and make them active partners in our planning and developmental processes. We have taken some measures in the right direction by enacting the Constitution 73rd and 74th Amendment Acts to facilitate decentralised governance and participatory planning. Participatory planning increases transparency, besides facilitating better integration of the developmental process and making the programmes more responsive to the local needs by addressing the problems of the common man.

We still have a lot to do to enable greater participation and involvement of women in our representative bodies. No system of government or polity can afford to sustain itself by ignoring this vital productive human resource which makes for almost half of the world population. This process of democratisation by including women in its fold is sure to make the common man feel the change for a better and secure future for generations to come.

The thrust of our democracy and development has to be, therefore, among other things, on empowering people in the fullest sense. We have to expand the capabilities of the common man to realise his full potential by extending improved health, value-based modern scientific education and increased employment opportunities. With the rising levels of education, employment and income, the common man will be able to secure a better future for himself. This will strengthen his belief in the efficacy of the democratic set-up and he will not take long to understand that democracy is the only political regime which, when fine-tuned with sound governance practices, is capable of ensuring political and civil freedoms, besides promoting more equitable outcomes for the people. The effectiveness of a government in a developing society like ours is not to be judged on the basis of its popularity with the rich but with the poor who need it the most. Those in governance should not gloss over the sadness in the eyes of the poor when they see the broadening smile on the faces of the rich.

As Prof. Amartya Sen observed, "If we continue to leave vast sections of the people of the world outside the orbit of education, we make the world not only less just, but also less secure.

If the man on the street is left at the mercy of forces of exploitation and orthodoxy, if he cannot freely exercise his constitutionally guaranteed rights, if he does not feel part of the political and developmental processes, if he cannot take informed decisions on the issues that affect his worth as a citizen, if he cannot partake of the fruits of development, if he cannot live in dignity and if his social, economic and political future is decided by his standing in an obscurantist, hierarchical social structure, then, democracy makes no meaning to him, it does not hold any relevance for him. Such paradoxes of democracy that he encounters daily, will shake his confidence in the system as a whole. That cynicism, that skepticism, could yet be the gravest threat to democracy as a system of governance. We cannot afford to take even minor threats to democracy lightly. As the distinguished British journalist, Bernard Levin, cautioned, "... remember that every nation that has fallen from democracy into tyranny was at one time only remotely in danger, and we would do well to think of ways that can strengthen our defences." The most important thing to do, to my mind, is to make it relevant for the weakest of our citizens.

Enlightened Citizenry

There should be only one class of people in a just democracy and that is the enlightened citizenry, whose happiness, dignity and self-respect are expected to be guided by laws and institutions in the making and unmaking of which they have a decisive say. As the eminent Justice Frankfurter said, "the highest office in a democracy is not that of the President, but that of being a citizen." This is about the essence of democracy. We should not forget that the most fundamental *raison d'etre* for a democracy is an authentically just social order, as against a 'counterfeit' one. Only so long as the interest of the common man remains at the centre of democratic discourse will democracy continue to be relevant for him. It was such a democracy that our Founding Fathers had visualised and strove all through their lives to accomplish.

It is said that in the early years of a Republic, it is the leaders who create institutions, but later it is expected of these institutions to be capable of producing leaders. Only when our democracy acquires the resilience to churn out leaders of great calibre, from among the common people, in all walks of life, can we say with confidence that it has become really relevant for the real commoners of our country. This can be achieved when leaders, who place the country before them and use the institutions of democracy to safeguard the interests of the country and its people, lead the country.

CHAPTER 11

An Ayurvedic View of Life A Facet of Indian Cultural Heritage*

PROF. M.S. VALIATHAN

Ayurveda, according to Caraka (or Charaka), is knowledge which seeks to weigh life in the scales of wholesomeness and happiness against their opposites. Its main themes of health and disease, and recovery of health from disease take the stage against an inspiring background of intuitive philosophy, lofty idealism, and vivid compassion, which are the hallmarks of India's cultural inheritance. After centuries of neglect and stagnation, Ayurveda has witnessed an unprecedented resurgence from the twentieth century in India and abroad. Ayurveda viewed health as a state of many-sided equilibrium, and disease as its reversal. Ayurvedic practice of medicine aimed at the restoration of equilibrium and, in that process, represented more than the sum of dietary regimen, procedures and medications.

From Thrombosis to Ayurveda

It is an eloquent commentary of our times that this discourse is sponsored by the Thrombosis Research Institute, which does advanced research on thrombotic disorders in its centres at London and Bangalore. Thrombosis is a reversal of the natural state of the blood which remains liquid in the heart and blood vessels, thanks to a state of equilibrium between blood and its conduits—what is technically called 'vascular homeostasis'. It occurs

---

* Based on the Dr. L.M. Singhvi Memorial Lecture delivered in Delhi under the auspices of the Thrombosis Research Institute of Bangalore, on 24th January, 2009.

when the equilibrium breaks down and blood solidifies in blood vessels during life to the detriment of organs or life itself. Triggered by many causes, thrombosis progresses through a biochemical cascade of great complexity. This intricate event evolved over millions of years when organisms with a closed vascular system had to seal any breaches in the vascular compartment to prevent exsanguination by forming a plug or coagulum without causing generalised thrombosis. When the vascular system was open in primitive organisms earlier (e.g. Crustacea), coagulation provided a defence against invading microbes. In recent years, studies on the molecular evolution of coagulation factors and complement system have shown that both processes arose from a single ancestral mechanism which provided defence against microorganisms and against the loss of body fluids. Determination of the coding sequence of coagulation proteins from many species has even allowed an estimation of the order of appearance of coagulation proteins in the evolution of species. The ongoing work to prevent deep vein thrombosis and thrombo-embolic complications of prosthetic heart valves is beneficial and life-saving, but it can have few claims to impinge on the biology of coagulation which will possibly continue to evolve as man finds new habitats with vastly different living conditions. Above all, the breakdown of equilibrium as the trigger for thrombosis has a strong resonance in Ayurveda which postulated a different kind of equilibrium—*sāmya*—as the basis of health and its disturbance as the equivalent of disease.

Its main themes of health and disease, and recovery of health from disease take the stage against an inspiring background of intuitive philosophy, lofty idealism, and vivid compassion, which are the hallmarks of India's cultural inheritance.

Early History

Caraka said that the science of life always existed, and a beginning can be said to have occurred only with reference to the first attempt to put down concepts and practice in writing. The earliest record of the roots of Ayurveda is found in the *Atharvaveda* (*circa* 1500 BC), which has numerous hymns relating to health, diseases, fertility, herbal drugs and anatomy. No wonder Caraka insisted that students of Ayurveda should be loyal to the *Atharvaveda*, which regarded diseases as the punishment of gods for human transgressions. The Atharvan practice of medicine was driven by faith—*daivavyapāúraya*. The Buddhist phase which followed marked a sharp decline in the use of hymns, but Ayurvedic concepts and practice flourished as shown by numerous textual references in the Buddhist period, such as *Milindapanho*, *Dīkhanikāya* of Suttapitaka, *Mahāvagga* of Vinayapitaka and

Visuddhimagga. The universities of Taksasila and Nalanda became famous for medical studies and attracted students from many other countries in Asia. The practice of medicine was driven by empiricism, not faith, in Buddhist India. The next phase was heralded by Caraka's redaction of *Agnivsa Tantra* (first century) when intellectual life in India was in ferment. The six systems of Indian philosophy were differentiating at this time from pre-existing but undifferentiated strands of the *Upanisads*, and they were often in conflict with Buddhist doctrines. The vigorous intellectual climate influenced Caraka, whose *Samhita* stood out for its philosophical bias. It became the foundational text of Ayurveda, used even today by the students and practitioners of Ayurveda, and marked a shift of Ayurveda from faith-based to reason-based (*yuktivyapāúśraya*) practice. The redaction of *Suśruta Samhita*, which was done by Nāgārjuna a few centuries after Caraka, became another classical text widely admired for its surgical orientation and descriptions of operations and instruments. The last of the 'Great Three' of Ayurveda was Vāgbhata, who probably lived in the sixth century and composed *Astānga samgraha* and *Astānga hṛdaya.* The *Samhitā* phase of the 'Great Three' was the golden age of Ayurveda, which was systematised and taught and practised all over India. As the *Samhitās* were translated into Arabic and Tibetan, and texts such as the *Bower Manuscript* were discovered in Central Asia, it is clear that the reach of Ayurveda extended far beyond the Indian subcontinent.

The breakdown of equilibrium as the trigger for thrombosis has a strong resonance in Ayurveda which postulated a different kind of equilibrium—sāmya—as the basis of health and its disturbance as the equivalent of disease.

Stagnation and Resurgence of Ayurveda

The golden age of Ayurveda was over after Vāgbhata. The period of stagnation which followed lasted a thousand years when advances became a trickle, such as the advent of counting pulse, use of mercury and opium in treatment and the description of syphilis. But there were no more Carakas or Suśrutas and no more Taksaśilas or Nalandas. The surgical procedures of Suśruta disappeared from the mainstream of Ayurveda and survived precariously among the 'lower castes' here and there. Surgical operations such as the plastic repair of the nose, couching for cataract, complicated deliveries, setting of fractures and many other procedures were not done by traditional *Vaidyas*, but by illiterate practitioners who passed on their manual skill from one generation to the next. According to P.C. Ray, India's soil at this time was made "morally unfit for the birth of a Boyle, Descartes, or a Newton, and her very name was all but expunged from the scientific world for a time". India's East-West encounter in the nineteenth century spurred the growth of modern science and medicine and brought about a revolution in India's cultural history. Unfortunately the encounter spared Ayurveda, which suffered from neglect if not denigration. Ramnath Chopra's brilliant contributions on the pharmacology of natural products of Ayurvedic origin, commercial production of Ayurvedic drugs by P.S. Varrier at Kottakkal, Gananatha Sen's work in Calcutta and Lakshmipathy's in Madras were a few lamps which shined in a sea of darkness. A dramatic resurgence came after Independence and Ayurveda has never had it so good as in the twenty-first century. In the growth of patient care, education, research, commercial production of drugs, and patronage by the government, the position enjoyed by Ayurveda is enviable today.

The Ayurvedic Canvas

Ayurveda, in the literal sense, is the knowledge of life. P.C. Ray characterised the long phase of India's cultural history from 600 B.C. to 800 A.D. as the 'Ayurvedic period' because he credited Ayurveda with the origins of not only medical sciences but also chemistry and, if one may add, plant and animal sciences. The philosophical climate in the *Samhitā* phase was so vibrant that Ayurveda, especially Caraka, was influenced by, and contributed to, the ongoing philosophical currents in India. An Ayurvedic view of life must, therefore, consider the rich background against which medical themes appeared to complete the big picture. In a great painting, an artist achieves harmony by composing different parts into a unified whole by design. In the *Last Supper*, Leonardo achieved this harmony by emphasizing the figure of Christ, who was silhouetted against a window behind him. All the lines in the background which receded into the distance seemed to converge on him. One could hardly imagine the *Last Supper* if the scene were shifted to a shallow room with different background! Divested of its background, Ayurveda would be reduced to no more than a system for medical practice. It is, therefore, appropriate to outline the background which enlivens the Ayurvedic canvas.

Man and the Cosmos : Common Constituents

The constituent elements of the universe and those of the smaller universe within the human body are identical and their response to varied stimuli is also identical. The universe as macrocosm and the human body as microcosm was always a dominant theme in Ayurveda, which regarded man as a part of all that exists and the human body as a cosmic resonator. The universe is known through our five senses which have specific objects

An Ayurvedic view of life must, therefore, consider the rich background against which medical themes appeared to complete the big picture. In a great painting, an artist achieves harmony by composing different parts into a unified whole by design.

of perception, such as what the eye sees, ear hears, tongue tastes and so on. The elements perceived by the five senses and their derivatives (pancha-bhūtas) constitute the universe for Ayurveda, which has little to say on a supra-sensory universe. The tissues of the body, no less than food and medications, are composed of the five elements and their derivatives. It is this identity of composition which underlies the central principle of Ayurvedic therapeutics that mandates the choice of food and drugs from without for producing effects within the body. It was believed that this principle could hardly operate in the absence of identity between the substances in the external world and the smaller world within.

Evolution of the Universe (*parināma*)

How did the universe with its immense diversity begin? How did it evolve? These questions belonged to a field which had been ploughed earlier by Sānkya philosophers, and which was of great interest to Caraka, whose medicine was deeply rooted in the philosophical soil. According to him, all that exists evolved from *avyakta*—an unmanifest, undifferentiated, incoherent and primordial state of existence. A perturbation in Avyakta led to a cascade represented by Mahat (*buddhi*/consciousness) — *Ahankāra* (individuation) — *Tanmātras* (subtle forerunners of five elements) — *Indriyas* (five sense organs and five motor organs) — *Manas* (mind) — five *Indriyārthas* (objects accessible to the five senses), which totalled 24 categories[1,2].

Evolution of the universe began when a perturbation occurred in *avyakta* by the interaction of the forces of *rajas* and *tamas*, which were latent in it. This event belonged to the realm of chance, a random occurrence which could neither be predicted nor controlled. But once the perturbation occurred, the subsequent course of evolution through a cascade which ended in sense objects and the universe was pre-set, progressive and unalterable. To borrow a Monod's phrase from a different context, the initial perturbation in *avyakta* was a chance event, but subsequent

The constituent elements of the universe and those of the smaller universe within the human body are identical and their response to varied stimuli is also identical. The universe as macrocosm and the human body as microcosm was always a dominant theme in Ayurveda, which regarded man as a part of all that exists and the human body as a cosmic resonator.

steps represented unalterable necessity. However, unlike Darwinian evolution which is irreversible and open-ended, the process of *parināma* in Ayurveda consists of endless alternating phases of differentiation and expansion followed by another when the stupendous variety dissolved into the original, undifferentiated *avyakta*. This process had no external control and was blind to the sufferings of man. Caraka's view of evolution was 'harsh' and admitted no role for God in the process. According to him, the universe in some undifferentiated or differentiated form was always there and would always be there.

Equilibrium (sāmya)

Ayurveda regarded equilibrium as the essential condition of good health and well-being. But equilibrium was a collective term which included several individual components that were not interchangeable. The seven tissues (*dhātus*) of the body (muscle, fat, bone, blood, etc.) had to maintain *dhātusāmya*; the fires (*agni*) which constantly burn in the tissues and make things happen had to preserve *agnisāmya* and *dosas*, the all important products of digestion, without whose perturbation no disease could occur, had to keep dosasāmya. Sāmya involved the interaction between the body and the environment as the six seasons ranged from the very hot to the very cold (*ṛtusāmya*). This called for adjustments on the part of the body, some of which occurred naturally such as sweating during summer and shivering in winter. But Ayurveda prescribed food, drinks, physical activity, medical procedures and general conduct to supplement natural adaptation and maintain equilibrium through the change of seasons[3].

Ayurveda regarded equilibrium as the essential condition of good health and well-being. But equilibrium was a collective term which included several individual components that were not interchangeable.

Sāmya also included *hetu* (cause), which gives an insight into the role of causes in the genesis of disease as understood in far off days. Causes were countless and were classified under four large groups (due to the perturbed *dosas,* to external events such as floods; to the wrath of the gods; to imprudent conduct). They exist all the time, everywhere and can never be eliminated. Nevertheless, people generally remain healthy, suggesting that something more than a cause is necessary to produce disease. Ayurveda held that a breakdown in the equilibrium between the body and the coexisting cause (*hetusāmya*) was the principal factor in the genesis of disease, cause playing a supportive role. Instead of taking arms against innumerable causes in a fruitless and unending chase, Ayurveda argued, it would be wiser to restore *hetusāmya* by appropriate measures, when causes would take care of themselves.

A Full Life

Ayurveda offered a model for living, which stands in sharp contrast to the traditional view that Indians prized asceticism and renunciation, and disparaged affluence and a life of comfort. Caraka stated explicitly: "A person with a normal share of strength and combativeness, who is of sound mind and concern for things here and hereafter, is moved by three desires. These are the desire for life, for wealth and for life hereafter. The desire for life comes first, because the loss of life amounts to the loss of everything. To ensure good life and health, the observance of a code of conduct is necessary, just as careful attention needs to be paid for the proper care of illness. The pursuit of wealth comes next, because wealth takes second place only to life. There is scarcely anything more miserable than a long life without the means to live. One should, therefore, work hard to make a living by engaging in farming, animal care, trade, service and similar occupations. The third desire concerns life in another world after death, which does indeed raise many doubts."

The desire for long life in good health found expression in the prescribed code for living, which is a far cry from asceticism[5]. The code laid great stress on personal hygiene; guidelines on nutrition and tasty food, appropriate clothes and jewellery, sexual intercourse, social relations and enjoyments, which are the elements of a full life. While virtues such as truthfulness, rectitude, fearlessness, modesty, courage, forgiveness and kinship to all forms of life were extolled, there was no bar on the celebration of life and the use of *rasāyanas* to enable one to live for a hundred years. A whole section in *Caraka Samhitā* was, in fact, devoted to rejuvenant therapy[6], which was claimed "to ensure prolonged lifespan, youthfulness, good health, fine voice and complexion, suppleness, intellect, power of retention and strength". Caraka devoted another section to vājīkarana, which consisted of numerous formulations to enhance sexual vigour to the level of a horse's[7].

The elaborate description of various items of food and drinks, the protocol for dining, the enjoyment of many types of wines and a wine party, which are elaborately described in Ayurvedic texts should leave one in no doubt that, barring a minority who were ascetically inclined, the vast majority of people sought to lead a full and enjoyable life.

Training of a Physician

Side by side with the ancient *Gurukulas*, universities such as Taksaśila imparted medical training as recorded in Buddhist literature. The pupils were chosen with great care and were required to possess a liberal education which included sacred and secular literature, grammar, logic, philosophy, astronomy, astrology, mathematics, botany and mechanical arts. The selection was made on the basis of physical, mental, intellectual and moral attributes, besides the aptitude for arduous training for several years[8]. Initiation was done during a sacred ritual, which involved the pupil taking an elaborate oath on the conduct of a physician in training[9]. The academic training consisted of learning by rote and more importantly, by discussions. *Caraka Saṃhitā* is indeed based on such discussions which were vigorous, free and highly educative. Practical training was given at the bedside, during domiciliary visits, and by participation in the identification of herbs during field trips, preparation of drugs and performance of medical and surgical procedures. At the conclusion of training, which was determined by the preceptor, the student had to obtain Royal permission to start practice. The *Arthaśāstra* of Kautilya had laid down severe punishment for those doing medical procedures without Royal permission.

Extraordinary importance was attached to training in debates, and Caraka went to great lengths to discuss hostile and friendly debates, definition of many logical terms, techniques to worst the opponents and so on[10]. This was important for a physician who wished to challenge an opponent for a debate on his doctrine or method and defeat him to win fame and adherents. This tradition of disputation was not confined to Ayurveda. Strict guidelines applied to the debators such as "not a word should be spoken which is not well thought out or which is out of place or which is confusing or lacking in scriptural authority". Triumph in a major debate or disputation strengthened one's claim to become a royal physician.

Side by side with the ancient Gurukulas, universities such as Taksasila imparted medical training as recorded in Buddhist literature.

Destiny (*daiva*)

The human condition is smitten by suffering which is the constant companion of a physician's vocation. *Traditional systems of Indian philosophy regarded false knowledge as the ultimate cause of human bondage and suffering and sought, in different ways, the liberation from bondage by ridding oneself of false knowledge.* Caraka held, on the other hand, that suffering resulted, in the final analysis, from errors of judgement and imprudent conduct *(prajnā-parādha)*. Unlike false knowledge which is a metaphysical concept, erroneous judgement is mundane and offered better possibilities for mankind for avoidance or correction. But how free is man to avoid flawed judgements and imprudent

Traditional systems of Indian philosophy regarded false knowledge as the ultimate cause of human bondage and suffering and sought, in different ways, the liberation from bondage by ridding oneself of false knowledge.

conduct? This question brought Caraka into an illuminating discussion on human destiny, which had been debated in India for centuries. One view held that fate was supreme, and no human effort could make the slightest difference to its inexorable operation; another view known as *pauruseya* and championed by *Yogavāsista*, claimed that the heroic endeavour of man could indeed alter the course of destiny. If predestination is carried to its logical conclusion, Caraka pointed out, much of human effort, including the practice of medicine would become futile. Granted that no human effort could ward off the consequences of evil acts of great sinfulness, he noted that the bulk of what one does in a workaday world lacked a moral content in so far as it related to the business of daily living. Caraka argued that if a person chose to remain well by paying attention to hygiene, nutrition and proper conduct, one could not claim that his consequent well-being had been preordained. While the effect of *Karma* was unalterable for crimes and sins of great magnitude, errors which were the lot of the human condition could be prevented or corrected by adherence to proper conduct. This essentially involved the avoidance of the overuse, underuse and misuse of the senses and the mind. Caraka did not advise the renunciation of desire or non-attachment, but commended a full and righteous life which could be enjoyed in harmony with one's environment. A healthy life, according to Caraka, had to be a righteous life.

Habitat

Ayurveda inherited the *Atharvan* adoration of nature, which was amply reflected in the background of the discussions held in Atreya's hermitage, and in the surroundings of a house for healing described by Caraka. It recognised, however, that beneficent nature and the habitat for living beings were ever susceptible to devastation by epidemics and other calamities, which was termed *janapadodhvamsana*. Polluted air, water, land and disorderly seasons had the power to wipe out populations and destroy the habitat[11]. Ayurveda took the view that the root cause for calamities which devastated human habitat was unrighteous and sinful living. Rulers lacking in probity would treat officers, traders and people so unjustly that righteousness would disappear altogether and even "gods would take leave of the country". Unrighteousness would also invite ruin by war and violence, which were triggered by greed, anger and conceit. Epidemics and devastation were a warning to statesmen of the perilous state of governance. The surest remedy and best prophylaxis for this catastrophe was wise living, ethical conduct and harmony between man and his surroundings[12].

Ayurvedic Approach to the Practice of Medicine

While keeping out of trouble by observing a code of conduct (*svasthavṛtta*) occupied centre stage, Ayurveda recognised man's vulnerability to disease and attached the highest importance to the practice of medicine to get one out of trouble *(āturavṛtta)*. The role of medicine was akin to giving a helping hand to men who had fallen in a pit they had dug themselves and from which they might escape on their own only with difficulty[13]. Medical practice demanded a quartet—physician, medications, helper and the patient—each possessed of special qualities[14]. Among the quartet, the physician was the most important because of his knowledge and his role as a leader and coordinator. When the quartet was complete and each member had the prescribed qualities, treatment would succeed and restore the equilibrium of tissues and *dosas* and make the patient well. However, it was incumbent on a good physician to recognise before treatment whether the disease was curable, palliable or incurable[15]. His guiding principles were friendship and compassion towards the ill, joy in treating those amenable to therapy, and masterly inactivity towards patients with incurable diseases[16]. When a major or risky treatment was contemplated for a grave or incurable illness, the physician was obliged to share the information with the family of the patient. The three great texts (*bṛhatrayee*) made no reference to *yogāsanas* or meditation as ancillaries to the practice of medicine. The use of mantras was infrequent, and astrology played a minimal, if not, no role. Though compassion was recognized as the motive power of medicine, physicians were not forbidden from accepting a fee for service, except from sages and teachers and so on. The texts suggested a line of treatment slanted in favour of the affluent, but Caraka was sensitive to the problems of the poor and prescribed treatment 'without frills' for them[17].

Coverage of Diseases

The *Samhitās* are encyclopaedic in the coverage of diseases, which were always seen and managed through a framework of perturbed *doṣas.* As a bird in flight does not go beyond its shadow, diseases, according to Vāgbhata, do not transcend

Though compassion was recognised as the motive power of medicine, physicians were not forbidden from accepting a fee for service, except from sages and teachers.

perturbed *doṣas*[18]. Every disease would have distinctive clinical features and would require a different treatment depending on whether it was precipitated by perturbed *vāta, pitta* or *kapha*, or their combination. As *dosas* involve the whole body, every disease was systemic in Ayurveda which did, however, recognise, for practical purposes, regional and specialized disorders. Examples are diseases of the head and neck, eye diseases, poisoning, and disorders in children. Surgical conditions were dealt with by specialists who had received training in the discipline (*śalya*) as taught by Suśruta.

On the basis of counting the number of references to diseases in the *Caraka Samhitā* (using a digitised text made by Yamashita of Kyoto University), a probable picture of the prevalence of diseases in Caraka's time (1st century A.D.) could be constructed. This analysis showed that the references to infectious diseases such as tuberculosis, leprosy and cholera were twice that of non-infectious diseases, including heart disease, anaemia, diabetes, epilepsy, etc. in Caraka's India. This finding from archeoepidemiology would sit well with the disease pattern in the 'pre-transition' stage of an ancient society, as postulated by modern epidemiology[19].

The natural history of diseases and their prognosis were always discussed at length in Ayurveda. The elaborate signs of approaching death (*rista*) were required to be learnt by physicians, and they were put together from medical experience and colourful popular beliefs. The exhaustive discussion on the signs of death would suggest that a class of specialists probably existed, who were experts in the care of the dying.

Treatment of Diseases

Diagnosis was given great importance. It was based on interrogation, inspection, palpation and listening to bowel sounds, etc. In fact all senses, excluding taste, were employed in the diagnostic process. Counting of pulse entered Ayurveda long after *Vāgbhata's* keen observation was supplemented by astute inference and the teachings of great predecessors. According to Caraka, physicians who are unable to explore the 'dark interior of the body with a lamp of knowledge and discrimination' could never treat patients with success. An ancient text (*Mādhavanidāna*) was, in fact, exclusively devoted to the diagnosis of diseases.

Once the diagnosis was made in terms of the perturbation of *doṣas*, therapeutic measures were put in place promptly, as delay was condemned. For mild perturbation, simple measures (*śamana*) such as fasting, rest, etc. were sufficient; but copious perturbation which manifested in serious diseases would call for the elimination of accumulated and vitiated *doṣas* (*śodhana*) and the restoration of *doṣasāmya.* This involved rest, dietary regimen, evacuative measures (*pancakarma*) and the administration of various drugs of plant, animal or mineral origin. Lifestyle, dietary regimen, cheerful atmosphere and faith in the physician and his method were as important as herbal drugs and procedures for successful treatment. The drugs and procedures were always chosen on the basis of their properties being opposed to those of the perturbed *doṣas.* If the perturbed *doṣas* were acidic, for example, the medicinal formulation would be alkaline. If the patient's condition was surgical or became surgical, he was referred to the surgeon. Many of the procedures adopted for treatment were based on a 'mechanism of action' as conceptualised by ancient physicians. *Pancakarma* is a good example of their talent to see images of events in the mind's eye when they were absent before the senses, and move them about inside 'one's head' to work out new arrangements for a possible mechanism. This was not done by deduction, but by a blend of speculation and insight, which would qualify as induction. In the treatment of patients, yoga, meditation and astrology played a minor role in the *Bṛhatrayee.* Auspicious configuration of stars was chosen, not always, for conducting major elective procedures, and chanting of hymns reserved for special occasions only.

When evacuative therapy or other major procedures were prescribed, the patient was admitted to a 'house for treatment'[20]. Caraka gave detailed guidelines on its ideal location; building plan with rooms for the patient, attendants, physician, cook, kitchen, store for medicines and equipment, bath, etc. The house had to have in attendance musicians, singers of ballads and associates who could relate to the patient easily. Its locale had to be home for birds, animals like hare and antelope, and gifted with plenty of greenery and supply of pellucid water. Caraka even gave directions on the furniture, upholstery, and vases for flowers in the patient's room! Obviously, the house for treatment was designed to heal the mind as well as the body.

Surgical Procedures

Ayurveda excelled in surgery, which was synonymous with the Dhanvantari School of Suśruta in Varanasi. He probably lived before Panini, who made three references to him in the *Astādhyāyi. Suśruta Samhitā* dealt with cadaveric dissection to learn anatomy; use of fruits, leather bags, and various other models to practice basic surgical techniques such

When evacuative therapy or other major procedures were prescribed, the patient was admitted to a 'house for treatment'. Caraka gave detailed guidelines on its ideal location; building plan with rooms for the patient, attendants, physician, cook, kitchen, store for medicines and equipment.

as incision, excision, extraction, suturing and tapping; pre- and post-operative care; a large number of procedures such as the setting of fractures, couching for cataract, removal of bladder stone, plastic repair of the nose, drainage of abscesses, and surgical methods including ksāra sūtra for treating anal fistula. Among the many surgical procedures Suśruta described, trephining of the skull was not mentioned. It was performed by Jivaka—Buddha's physician—a few centuries later. Suśruta described 20 sharp and 100 blunt instruments, and gave directions on their proper use.

In Suśruta's period, surgeons were respected as Ācaryas, but the position had already begun to change by the 5th-6th century, when surgeons and all others who used their hands to make a living—masons, carpenters, weavers, farmers, blacksmiths—found themselves downgraded by a travesty of social engineering. This was the beginning of a long phase of intellectual stagnation and decline, when brain was disengaged from the hand and the springs of originality ran dry in India.

Epilogue

Echoing the *Mahābhārata*, *Caraka Samhitā* proclaimed 'whatever is found here, may be found elsewhere; whatever is not found here, will be found nowhere'[21]. The vast stage and the immense range of things and events which characterise the phenomenon of Ayurveda would undoubtedly bear out the claim of Caraka. Ayurveda recognised the identity of man and the cosmos as a central reality and upheld the dynamic equilibrium among the constituents of the universe—living and non-living—as the necessary condition of existence. The equilibrium was credited with in-built mechanisms to withstand shocks and restore itself, which could be glimpsed in the spontaneous recovery of function from dysfunction in many a diseased state (*svabhāvoparama*). The role of Ayurveda was no more than to assist the process of recovery and maintain good health by safeguarding the state of equilibrium.

While Ayurveda had ample tools and remedies in its vast storehouse, it enjoined virtuous conduct as the sovereign prophylactic against maladies and the unfailing guarantor of well-being. This was brought out in full measure by Vāgbhata through numerous verses in the *Astāngahṛdaya*.

Consider the following: "All creatures seek happiness in whatever they do: but happiness cannot be had without righteous conduct. Therefore, righteous conduct is obligatory for all."[22]

On the attitude to fellow beings: "One should always regard even mites and ants as no different from oneself."[23]

Towards a foe: "One should be of service to him who may be intent on doing harm."[24]

In adopting the middle path[25]: "Neither torment nor pamper sense organs."[26] In the quest for knowledge: "The whole world is a teacher for the wise in all he does; therefore, a man of action in the world's theatre should emulate its example."[27]

On virtuous conduct in general: "Compassion for living creatures; charity; tamed body, speech and mind; regarding others as one's own."[28] "Nights and days roll on; one who ever reflects—how have I spent my nights and days—would never grieve."[29] "Giving up imprudent conduct; restraining the activities of senses; remembering one's role in his noble calling; and cherishing the knowledge of habitat, time and soul, a physician should follow the path trodden by men of virtue."[30]

"One who enjoys wholesome food and activity everyday; who introspects on his actions; who is unattached; who is generous; who looks on all with an equal eye; who is truthful and forgiving; who delights in the service of virtuous men; he remains free from illness."[31]

How to live a virtuous life was a golden thread which ran through, and bound together, the varied themes of Ayurveda.

Ayurveda prized knowledge and skill highly, but rated compassion and virtuous conduct even higher in a physician's scale of priorities. Therein lies the key to its unbroken practice for 25 centuries and its resurgence in our times.

NOTES

1. *CS Śarīra*, 1: 16, 67.
2. *CS Sūtra*, 1: 53.
3. *CS Sūtra*, 6: 48.
4. *CS Sūtra*, 11: 3-8.
5. *CS Sūtra*, 5: 71-75.
6. *CS Cikitsā*, 1: 1-3.
7. *CS Cikitsā*, 2: 1-4.
8. *CS Vimāna*, 8: 3-4.
9. *CS Vimāna*, 8: 13-14.
10. *CS Vimāna*, 8: 15-26.
11. *CS Vimāna*, 3: 6-7.
12. *CS Vimāna*, 3: 12-18.
13. *CS Sūtra*, 9: 3-12.
14. *CS Sūtra*, 10: 5.
15. *CS Sūtra*, 10: 9-22.
16. *CS Sūtra*, 9: 26.
17. *CS Sūtra*, 15: 19-21.
18. *AH Sūtra*, 12: 32-33.

19. Valiathan, M.S., *The Legacy of Caraka,* Orient Longman Pvt. Ltd., Hyderabad, 2003, pp. xlvi-lvii.
20. *CS Sūtra,* 15: 5-7.
21. *CS Siddhī,* 12: 54.
22. *AH Sūtra,* 2: 20.
23. *AH Sūtra,* 2: 23.
24. *AH Sūtra,* 2: 24.
25. *AH Sūtra,* 2: 30.
26. *AH Sūtra,* 2: 29.
27. *AH Sūtra,* 2: 45.
28. *AH Sūtra,* 2: 46.
29. *AH Sūtra,* 2: 47.
30. *AH Sūtra,* 4: 32.
31. *AH Sūtra,* 4: 36.

Note : CS = *Caraka Samhitā; AH = Astāngahṛdaya.*

CHAPTER 12

Secularism and Rule of Law*

JUSTICE P. SATHASIVAM

Secularism : A Concept

The word 'secular' comes from the Latin word *saeculum*, meaning 'age' or 'generation'. In Christian Latin, it referred to 'the temporal world.' Secular is the word used in Protestant countries. In Catholic countries, specifically France, the term used is 'laicism' from the Greek word *laos*, meaning people, and *laikos*, meaning the lay. Although both terms refer to the separation of church and state, "while the underlying emphasis in the word 'secularism' is on the idea of worldliness, the term 'laicism' emphasises the distinction of the laity from the clergy." On the other hand, Collins English Dictionary defines secularism in a somewhat different manner:

> *Secularism (1851): the attitude that religion should have no place in civil affairs.*

Rule of Law

'Rule of Law' is the supreme manifestation of human civilization and culture. It is an eternal value of constitutionalism and inherent attribute of democracy and good governance.

---

* Revised version of the Dr. L.M. Singhvi Memorial Lecture to the Supreme Court Advocates-on-Record Association of India on February 26, 2011.

The term 'Rule of Law' is derived from the French phrase *la principe de legalite* (the principle of legality) which refers to a government based on principles of law and not of men. In this sense the concept of 'Rule of Law' is of old origin and is opposed to arbitrary powers. It is an ancient ideal and was discussed by ancient Greek philosophers such as Plato and Aristotle. Plato wrote, "where the law is subject to some other authority and has none of its own, the collapse of the State, in my view, is not far off; but if law is the master of the government and the government is its slave, then the situation is full of promise and men enjoy all the blessings that the gods shower on a State." Aristotle also endorsed the concept of Rule of Law by writing that "law should govern and those in powers should be servants of the law." Sir Edward Coke is said to be the originator of this concept, when he said that the king must be under the God and Law and thus vindicated the supremacy of law over the pretensions of the executives. In India, the concept of Rule of Law can be traced to *Upanishads* where it provides 'Law is the King of Kings'.

'Rule of Law' is the supreme manifestation of human civilization and culture. It is an eternal value of constitutionalism and inherent attribute of democracy and good governance.

A.V. Dicey later developed on this concept but his concept of the Rule of Law contemplated the absence of wide powers in the hands of government officials. According to Prof. Dicey, Rule of Law contains three principles or it has three meanings:

1. *Supremacy of Law*: No man is punishable or can lawfully be made to suffer in body or goods except for a distinct breach of law established in the ordinary legal manner before the ordinary courts of the land.
2. *Equality before Law*: No man is above law. Every man whatever be his rank or condition is subject to the ordinary law of the realm and amenable to the jurisdiction of the ordinary tribunals.
3. *Predominance of Legal Spirit*: The general principles of the constitution are the result of juridical decisions determining rights of private persons in particular cases brought before the Court.

British Rule vis-a-vis Secularism

In India, secularism was not a new idea peculiar to the nation building elite. The British introduced the idea that some laws could come from non-religious sources. The first such British law came in 1772, with the Warren Hastings' Regulating Plan, which established a judicial system that codified civil, criminal and commercial laws. Family law and certain property laws were still governed by Hindu and Muslim religious laws. By 1882, all areas of law, with the exception of personal laws, were governed by Codes. Thus, secularisation of the law began with the judicial system which the British gradually put into place. This concept even reached certain religious practices with acts dealing with the caste system and marriage laws.

At the same time, the colonial government also used religious difference as a source of restructuring the legal system. For instance, it made use of a policy known as 'the Islamisation of Muslim law and the Sanskritization of Hindu law.' This policy resulted in limiting the scope of personal laws to rigid textual law since the British followed only their conception of what the religions of the colonised were, rather than what the actual experiences demanded from the law. Not only was the construction of these textual personal laws influenced by British legal concepts, but this policy also "resulted in establishing religion and personal laws as important signifiers of community identity, as the colonial legal structure administered a unified Muslim law hitherto unknown in India."[1]

The Republic of India

Among the seven nations of South Asia forming the South Asian Association for Regional Cooperation (SAARC), India and Nepal stand out as the only countries that have declared themselves as secular States. In each of the remaining five nations, one or another spiritual faith has the status of the officially adopted or legally promoted religion—Buddhism in Bhutan and Sri Lanka; and Islam in Bangladesh, Maldives and Pakistan.

In the past six decades, India has been through partition along religious lines, experienced communal riots and assassinations, and yet managed to emerge as one of the more stable nations of the developing world.

In the 28 States and 7 Union territories of today's India, the level of diversity is unparalleled. There are examples of virtually all known types of societal divisions: six major religions, Hinduism, Islam, Sikhism, Christianity, Buddhism and Zoroastrianism; two major language families, Aryan and Dravidian with eighteen official languages and innumerable dialects and tribal tongues; three racial strains, Aryan, Dravidian, and proto-Australoid; and over two thousand castes, hierarchically ranked, endogamous and occupational.[2]

Although nationalism might be a strong current, amidst this diversity, religion emerges as a unifying factor. According to the Office of the Registrar General & Census Commissioner, India, 80.5 per cent of India's population is Hindu, with the largest religious minority, Muslims, following at 13.4 per cent.[3] This reality of religious identity is well reflected in the Constitution of India.

Constitutionally, India is a secular country and therefore has no State religion. However, it has developed over the years its own unique concept of secularism that is fundamentally different from the other concepts requiring complete separation of state and religion in all matters.

India has developed over the years its own unique concept of secularism that is fundamentally different from the other concepts requiring complete separation of state and religion in all matters.

Secularism: A later addition

Despite the clear incorporation of all the basic principles of secularism into various provisions of the Constitution when originally enacted, its preamble did not then include the word secular in the short description of the country, which it called a 'Sovereign Democratic Republic.' This was, of course, not an inadvertent omission but a well-calculated decision meant to avoid any misgiving that India was to adopt any of the western notions of a secular state. Twenty-five years later, by which time India's peculiar concept of secularism had been well established through its own judicial decisions and state practices, the preamble to the Constitution was amended to include the word 'secular' (along with "socialist") to declare India to be a 'Sovereign Socialist Secular Democratic Republic.'[4]

Development of the Secular Idea in Christian Europe

Secularism as an ideology and a political system was born in Christian Europe. Since its beginning, state and religion existed in separate spheres in Christianity. The Church had its independent institutions. The kings were not seen as representatives of the divine on earth. The Church spoke for the divine, whereas the kings ran the earthly affairs. Thus, there already existed a foundational thinking among the masses that the functions of the state and religion were distinct. After the Reformation, Christian Europe also realised that in order to survive, their communities had to recognise the validity of differing religious beliefs. "In old conditions the state must be intolerant to survive; now it must tolerate or be destroyed." Moreover, Europe had a tradition of thinkers, like John Locke, who emphasised individual freedom, especially freedom of faith.

The Constitution of India

India is neither the force-fed child nor the naturally evolved secular. On

August 15, 1947, when India gained independence, the people of the subcontinent emerged out of colonial rule of about five centuries, first under the Central Asian Mughal rulers and then under the British Empire. Although the Mughal and British rulers differed in many significant ways, they both left their legacy in the Indian socio-economic structure and the Indian psyche.

The Constitution of India was adopted on November 19, 1949 and came into force on January 26, 1950. It was the brainchild of the Constituent Assembly, indirectly elected in 1946 by the provincial assemblies. The Constitution reflected the ethnically, religiously and linguistically diverse make-up of the country. It was, therefore, a compromise between the diverse groups that made up India. After the bloodshed in the aftermath of Partition, the Constituent Assembly sought to write a Constitution that could bring order without compromising the rights of any group. It is this characteristic of our Constitution that has enabled it to endure more than half a century of economic, political and social upheavals that the Indian nation has experienced. The first Constitution to be adapted after the Universal Declaration of Human Rights, the Constitution of India remains the oldest constitution in the developing world.

The Preamble to the Constitution declares that India is a SOVEREIGN SOCIALIST SECULAR DEMOCRATIC REPUBLIC. The words 'socialist' and 'secular' were added in the year 1976 by the 42nd Amendment. This amendment was adopted during 1975-1977 Emergency, as a response to growing unrest. The Constitutional framework for achieving secularism, however, has been a part of the Constitution since its inception, as set forth in Articles 25 to 30 thereof. Indeed, in *Kesavananda Bharati* v. *State of Kerala*, the Supreme Court of India held that secularism is a basic structure of the Constitution.[5]

Articles 25 to 28 describe the right to freedom of religion. Article 25 grants all persons the "freedom of conscience and the right freely to profess, practice and propagate religion." This right, however, is not without limitation and is "subject to public order, morality and health and to the other provisions."[6] Sub-clause 2 of Article 25 gives the State the right to regulate or restrict "any economic, financial, political or other secular activity which may be associated with religious practice." Article 26 deals with the rights of religious groups to form institutions and acquire and administer property. As in Article 25, these rights are subject to public order, morality and health. Under Article 27, no person can be compelled to pay special taxes on the basis of religion. Article 28 prohibits religious instruction in wholly State-funded educational institutions. Articles 29 and 30 set forth certain cultural and educational rights for minorities and are aimed at prohibiting discrimination against minorities in cultural and educational areas of life.

In addition to the specific rights set forth in Articles 25-30, a very significant mandate is provided in the Directive Principles of State Policy of the Constitution of India. Under Article 44 of the Directive Principles, "the State shall endeavour to secure for the citizens a uniform civil code throughout the territory of India." This provision is not enforceable in a court of law because the Directive Principles are not mandates, but are points of guidance to future governments.

While the Constitution advises the State to secure a uniform civil code, it also places an important fundamental duty on its citizens. Article 51A(e) places a duty on every citizen of India "to promote harmony and the spirit of common brotherhood amongst all the people of India transcending religious, linguistic and regional or sectional diversities."

The foregoing provisions of the Constitution have been interpreted and applied by the Supreme Court to prescribe the scope of Indian secularism.

Apex Court's Views on Secularism

The Supreme Court expressed its views on the Secular nature of the Constitution for the first time in *Sardar Syedna Taher Saifuddin Saheb* v. *State of Bombay*[7] where it was held that:

> "Articles 25 and 26 embody the principle of religious tolerance that has been the characteristic feature of Indian civilisation from the start of history. The instances and periods when this feature was absent are merely temporary aberrations. Besides, they serve to emphasise the secular nature of the Indian democracy which the founding fathers considered to be the very basis of the Constitution."

In *Keshavananda Bharti* v. *State of Kerala*[8], three different judges in different ways laid down 'secular nature of the Constitution', 'secular and federal character of the Constitution', 'liberty of thought, expression, belief, faith and worship' as part of the basic structure of the Constitution. Nowhere the word 'secularism' was specifically emphasised as part of the basic structure.

In the case of *Ziyauddin Burhanuddin Bukhari* v. *Brijmohan Ram Das Mehra'* the Supreme Court set the role of State to be neutral and impartial in extending its benefits to citizens of all castes and creeds.

This philosophical logic was also followed in the case of *Indra Sawhney*[9] where it was held that caste poses a serious threat to secularism and as a consequence to the integrity of the country.

In the landmark judgment of *S.R. Bommai* v. *Union of India*[10] the Apex Court without any hesitation held that secularism is the part of the basic structure of the Constitution. The term 'secular' has advisedly not been defined presumably because it is a very elastic term not capable of a precise definition and perhaps best left undefined. Secularism represents faith born out of the exercise of national priorities. It enables people to see the imperative requirements for human progress in all aspects and cultural and social advancement and indeed for human survival itself. It also not only improves the material condition of human life but also liberates the human spirit from bondage of ignorance, suppression, irrationality, injustice, fraud, hypocrisy and oppressive exploitation. In other words, though the whole course of human history discloses an increasing liberation of mankind, all is covered by the term secularism. This attitude is described by some as one of neutrality towards religion or as one of benevolent neutrality. It is absolutely erroneous to say that 'secularism' is a vacuous word or a phantom concept.

'Secularism' in the Constitution is not anti-God and it is sometimes believed to be a stay in a free society.

Later in the case of *M. Ismail Faruqui* v. *Union of India*[11], also known as Ayodhya Acquisition Case, the Supreme Court delineates the role of the State vis-à-vis religion and held it is in the nature of injunctions against the State in this respect. *Inter alia*, it prevents the State with either identifying itself with any religion or engaging in any religious activity. It was held that the Preamble of the Constitution read in particular with Articles 25 to 30, emphasises the guarantee of equality in the matter of religion to all individuals and groups irrespective of their faith emphasising that there is no religion of State itself. It is in this manner that the concept of secularism embodied in the constitutional scheme, as a creed adopted by the Indian people, has to be understood while examining the validity of any legislation on the touchstone of the Constitution. The concept of secularism is one facet of the right to equality woven as the central golden thread in the fabric depicting the pattern of the scheme of the Constitution. It was held in this case that *"Secularism is absolute; the State may not treat religions differently on the ground that public order requires it. The principle of secularism illumines in the provision of Articles 15 and 16."*

'Secularism' is more than a passive attitude of religious tolerance. It is a positive concept of equal treatment of all religions.

The latest trend that the Court has followed in the Ram Janmbhoomi case, *A.S. Narayana Deekshitulu* v. *State of Andhra Pradesh*[12] is by equating the concept of the secularism with the *'Sarva Dharma Sambhav'*, that is, tolerance for all religions which springs from due deliberation for one's own happiness and also for welfare of all beings.

Secularism demands that the State shall not have any religion of its own and no one could proclaim to make the State or endeavour to create a theocratic state. Persons belonging to different religions live throughout the length and breadth of the country. Each person, whatever be his religion, must get assurance from the State that he has the protection of law to freely profess, practice and propagate his religion and freedom of conscience.[13] It was held in that case that secularism is part of the fundamental law and an inalienable element of the basic structure of the Constitution.

The Court's commitment to constitutional secularism was put to the test shortly after the mosque demolition, in May of 1993, when it was approached by a group of Muslim imams—individuals in charge of religious activities of respective mosques. The imams brought a petition challenging ancient Islamic religious practice that denied any form of monetary compensation to Imams because Islamic law imposed by local government officials, required them to offer voluntary service. In *All India Imam Organisation* v. *Union of India & Others*, the Supreme Court demonstrated its ability to uphold its constitutional obligations by disregarding Islamic personal law and protecting the constitutional rights of the imams. According to the Court, the rights of the imams must be interpreted in the context of modern constitutional protections, and not ancient deep-seeded beliefs. The Court explained, "In series of decisions rendered by this Court it has been held that right to life in Article 21 means right to live with human dignity. It is too late in the day, therefore, to claim or urge that since Imams perform religious duties they are not entitled to any emoluments. Whatever may have been the ancient concept but it has undergone change."[14]

The Court's approach in this case seems to reflect a major breakthrough towards constitutional secularism. As one author explains, "Making the prospects for such creative jurisprudence more promising is the fact that the majority emphasised the supremacy of Indian courts, rather than Muslim law as interpreted by Muslim legal authorities, in determining the essentials of Islamic practice."[15]

A strict separatist approach towards secularism is not supportable in a nation like India, where religious beliefs saturate the social ethos of the culture.

Notwithstanding the Court's progress in giving real meaning to secularist constitutional provisions in cases like All India Imam Organisation, a strict separatist approach towards secularism is not supportable in a nation like India, where religious beliefs saturate the social ethos of the culture.

This again illustrates the challenges facing the Indian Supreme Court: how does it strike a balance between allowing citizens to exercise their freedom of religion without infringing on others' rights to be free from the imposition of religion?

The Supreme Court encountered this precise issue in a 2002 case invoking Article 28's prohibition on religious instruction in public educational institutions.[16] In *Roy v. Union of India*, the Court held that teaching religion in State-funded schools was not a violation of Article 28 because an effort "to educate children to understand the common factors in all the religions is not a non-secular step."[17] In fact, the Court asserted that imparting accurate knowledge of all religions to the nation's youth will be a solution to the problems of religious strife, and will ultimately eradicate non-secular sentiments throughout the country.[18] The Court attempted to achieve its balancing act by relying on traditional notions of secularism and religious equality.

The challenges facing the Indian Supreme Court: how does it strike a balance between allowing citizens to exercise their freedom of religion without infringing on others' rights to be free from the imposition of religion?

The real meaning of secularism in the language of Gandhi is equal treatment and respect for all religions, but we have misunderstood the meaning of secularism to mean negation of all religions. Democracy cannot survive and the Constitution cannot work unless Indian citizens are not only learned and intelligent, but they are also of moral character and imbibe the inherent virtues of human-being such as truth, love and compassion.[19]

The real meaning of secularism in the language of Gandhi is equal treatment and respect for all religions, it does not mean negation of all religions.

Freedom to Profess, of Conscience and of Religion

The freedom of conscience gives a person the right to believe in the tenets of any religion that are conducive to its spiritual well-being.[20] The right to profess one's religion granted in Article 25(1) is essentially the right to proclaim one's faith.[21]

Although the Constitution does not define what is meant by the word 'religion,' the Supreme Court of India has expressed divergent views on the meaning of religion. In cases such as *Commissioner of Hindu Religious*

Endowments v. *Sri Lakshimdra Thirtha Swamiar*, the Supreme Court took an inclusive approach to religion:

> "Religion is certainly a matter of faith with individuals or communities and it is not necessarily theistic. A religion may not only lay down a code of ethical rules for its followers to accept, it might prescribe rituals and observances, ceremonies and modes of worship which are regarded as integral parts of religion, and these forms and observances might extend even to matters of food and dress".[22]

On the other hand, some Supreme Court cases have taken a narrower view of religion. For instance in *S.P. Mittal* v. *Union of India*, the Supreme Court took a restricted view of religion and held that Sir Aurobindo's teachings were a philosophy, not a religion, despite his followers' belief that it was a religion.[23] In other cases, the Court has given effect to the egalitarian vision of the Constitution. For instance, in the Temple Entry case, *Sri Venkataramana Devaru* v. *State of Mysore*,[24] the Court found that the state legislation allowing all Hindus, including low caste Hindus, the right to enter temples did not violate the rights of religious institutions under Article 26(b) of the Constitution.

In addition to the general inclusive approach to religion, the Supreme Court has stated that religious practices or performances of acts that are essential to the pursuance of religious beliefs are as much a part of religion as faith or belief in particular doctrines.[25] The question of what practices can be considered to be an essential part of the religion is ascertained by examining the doctrines of that religion.[26]

The Quareshi cow-slaughter case put to test what practices are essential to a religion.[27] The Quareshi case involved a legal challenge by Muslim butchers to state legislation prohibiting the slaughter of cows. The state legislation was partly motivated by the strong religious sentiment of Hindus against the slaughter of cows because cow is a sacred animal in Hinduism. The Muslim butchers, on the other hand, argued that their inability to continue their practice of sacrificing a cow on Bakr Id Day interfered with their religious beliefs. The Supreme Court held that the state law banning cow slaughter did not violate the religious rights of Muslims. The Court reasoned that the Quran did not mandate the sacrificing of cows and that there were economic (and therefore, secular) reasons for the legislation. In a subsequent case, the Supreme Court emphasised that the religious practices included in the freedom of religion are those which are "essential."[28]

Right to Propagate Religion

The right to propagate one's religion, also granted by Article 25(1), is not unrestricted. In *Stainislaus* v. *State of Madhya Pradesh & Orissa*,[29] the Supreme Court delineated the boundaries of the right to propagate in the context of state legislation prohibiting forcible conversions. The Supreme Court held that the right to propagate means the right to "transmit and spread one's religion by an exposition of its tenets." But, the Court was clear that there is no constitutional right to convert a person from one religion to another, because this would impinge on the 'freedom of conscience' guaranteed to all the citizens of the country alike.

As to whether the State has the right to pass legislation restricting conversions, the Court held that the 'public order' provision of Article 25(1) has a 'wide connotation' and that the State could legislate conversions if they "created public disorder."[30] Thus, the Court evolved a standard where the right to freedom to propagate religion is subordinate to the State's power to maintain 'public order.' Because the definition of "public order" is very broad, the State's power to legislate in this area is effectively broad.

Anti-Conversion Laws

Anti-conversion laws have arisen from a long history of religious activities in India.[31] These laws were first seen during the British colonial period, although the government did not promulgate any anti-conversion laws.[32] However, Hindu princely states enacted them during the British colonial period in an attempt to preserve Hindu religious identity in the face of British missionaries.[33] In particular, princely states, now part of Chhattisgarh, passed anti-conversion laws as early as the 1930s.[34]

The first of the post-colonial anti-conversion laws were passed in the states of Orissa and Madhya Pradesh in 1960s.[35] The Orissa Freedom of Religion Act of 1967 and the Madhya Pradesh Dharma Swatantraya Adhiniyam of 1968 are examples of anti-conversion laws still in existence.[36] Similarly, the anti-conversion laws have been adopted by other States such as Arunachal Pradesh, Tamil Nadu, Himachal Pradesh, Rajasthan, Chhattisgarh and Uttarakhand.

The power of these laws is that they have "made forced conversion a cognizable offence under Sections 295A and 298 of the Indian Penal Code that stipulate that malice and deliberate intention to hurt the sentiments of others is a penal offence punishable by varying durations of imprisonment and fines."[37] The state legislatures and the state Governors have played a large role in whether these bills will be enforced, amended, or repealed. Although the Supreme Court of India has created a precedent for these laws, one can see from the diversity of action on them that anti-conversion laws are very controversial, and that religious conversion has inflamed passions.

Personal Laws

The rights guaranteed under Articles 25 and 26 of the Constitution form the basis for religion-based personal laws in India. The personal laws cover areas of marriage, divorce, inheritance and adoptions. In the immediate aftermath of the partition of India along religious lines, the framers of the Constitution could not simply abolish family laws. Religious identity formed the basis of community in post-colonial India. The framers had to indicate to the masses that the new independent nation would respect and protect this identity. Thus, while they included Article 44 in the Directive Principles encouraging the development of a uniform civil code, the framers left intact the system of separate religious family laws.[38] Although India maintains this legal pluralism in the area of family law, only a unitary judicial system interprets and enforces these multiple religious codes.

Soon after the Constitution established the family law structure, the Indian Parliament revised Hindu family laws by introducing Bills passed between 1955 and 1956. Polygamy was abolished, and divorce was permitted. The Hindu personal laws were also uniformly applied to all 'Hindus.' The definition of Hindus includes Jains, Buddhists, and Sikhs. The uniformisation of the Hindu code started the debate as to whether a uniform civil code should be enacted and religious personal codes abolished.

The crux of this constitutional (and political) debate has centred on Muslim personal laws. In *Md. Ahmed Khan* v. *Shah Bano Begum*[39] case the Supreme Court held that under Section 125 of the Criminal Procedure Code a divorced Muslim wife is entitled to maintenance beyond the *iddat* period. It further stated that there was no conflict between this provision and the Muslim Personal Laws.

The Court also called for a creation of a Uniform Civil Code. The Indian Government responded to the civil unrest and protests by enacting the Muslim Women's (Protection of Rights on Divorce) Act in 1986 exempting Muslim men from Article 125 of the Criminal Procedure Code. The Government also amended Section 125 to specifically exclude the Muslim wife's right to maintenance beyond the *iddat* period from the Criminal Code.

The Supreme Court, however, was not discouraged by the amended Section 125 or the Muslim Women's Act, and again interpreted it in a manner that appears to conflict with Muslim personal laws. In *Noor Saba*

Khatoon v. *Mohd. Quasim*,[40] the Court held that the minor children of Muslim parents have an absolute right to maintenance. In a subsequent decision upholding the validity of the Muslim Women's Act, the Supreme Court ruled that a Muslim husband's liability to provide maintenance extends beyond the *iddat* period under the terms of this Act.[41]

Conclusion

The crux of secularism is autonomy, that is, the independence of human reason and secular life from determination by religious authority. Communalism and religious fundamentalism deny this very autonomy. While communalism denies the basic secularist distinction between religious and secular concerns of man by making religious identity the sole criterion or basis of the secular interests of a group, religious fundamentalism denies the autonomy of the entire life and culture of a society by declaring religion to be the sole determinant thereof. If the claims of communalism and fundamentalism were accepted, a disastrous result would follow, that is, there would be several autonomous religious communities with distinct cultures within a pluralistic society like India, and no common culture or shared values or ways would prevail and it would be difficult to call such a society, India, a nation.

The crux of secularism is autonomy, that is, the independence of human reason and secular life from determination by religious authority.

The problems of a multi-religious society are very different from those of a uni-religious one. If religion intrudes into the secular life and culture of a uni-religious society, its intrusion goes almost unnoticed. But in a multi-religious society, the intrusion by any one religion in social life is resented by other religious groups and leads to friction. Hence, there is need to differentiate secular life and culture from religion.

In fact, a pluralistic society is the greatest test for secularism. While the ideal of religious toleration is theoretically accepted in the West, it has to be really practiced and lived in day-to-day life in a pluralistic society. It not only becomes the basis of peaceful existence of different religious groups, but also paves the way for mutual sharing of each other's beliefs. It is only in such a society that its secular commitments can be tested, as the leaders of such a society are faced with the complex problem of harmonizing the claims of various religions with each other, as well as demands of a secular polity. Such a society is forced to evolve a secular culture in order to preserve both its pluralistic character and its integrity.

A pluralistic society is the greatest test for secularism.

No one ever denies the diversity of India; what is unfortunate is that this diversity is being labelled as diversity of nationalities. Religion is, for us, basically a personal affair, which is shared with other co-religionists and may lead to a community fellow feeling, but it cannot be, and must not be the basis of an all encompassing communal identity. At the same time, a total rejection of the category of community may also falsify the reality, just as excessive emphasis on it does. We cannot do away with the category of religious community altogether, as we cannot do away with religion. As it is not religion but its tyranny in all secular matters that is antithetical to secularism, so it is not the religious community but its political or anti-social mobilisation that contradicts all secular values.

It is not religion but its tyranny in all secular matters that is antithetical to secularism.

Secularism in India at times is vitiated by an excessive reliance on the category of religious community. Thus, it is clear that secularism must bodily dissociate itself from any compromise with communalism. It means a total, unconditional rejection of the category of religious community for socio-political dialogue or action.

The task before us is the development of an integrated national identity. This national identity would not deny the pluralism of Indian culture but express it. That is, Indian identity is understood in the form of a complex mosaic whose constituent religions, languages and regional cultures have their own individualities but are at the same time permeated and determined by one common factor of Indianness. This Indianness is characterized by pluralism and tolerance. Significantly, this Indian trait of tolerance has encouraged the thriving of a large number of religious cultures and sects side by side, but at the same time, it has also provided a basis for their partial synthesis. Because Indians tolerate each other's faith, values and customs, they tend to share them, especially at the mass level.

Indian identity is understood in the form of a complex mosaic whose constituent religions, languages and regional cultures have their own individualities but are at the same time permeated and determined by one common factor of Indianness.

India has been a multi-religious country for a very long time, with Jews, Christians, Parsis and Muslim traders arriving and settling in India over the first millennium. Sikhism was born in India, in the same way that Buddhism and Jainism originated in the country. Even pre-Muslim India was not, as is sometimes claimed, mainly a Hindu country, since Buddhism was the dominant religion in India for many hundreds of years and Jainism has had an equally long history and in fact a large continuing presence today. Even in terms of Vedic and Upanisadic contributions, Buddhism and Jainism are as much the inheritors of that tradition as are later forms of Hinduism. The one university for which India was outstandingly famous, namely Nalanda, which attracted scholars from China and elsewhere after many hundred years of existence just around the time when the universities of Oxford and Cambridge were being founded (in the thirteenth century), happened to be a Buddhist university.

Secularism as a concept is very vital to our country and contributes immensely in the realisation of our socio-economic-political objectives. We as a nation have good reasons to resist any anti-secular enticement.

I urge you all to maintain the sanctity of our country by respecting the pillar of Secularism which makes a significant part of the underlying structure supporting our nation.

NOTES

1. Rajeev Dhavan, *The Road to Xanadu: India's Quest for Secularism, in Religion and Personal Law in Secular India: A Call to Judgment*; 301-329, at 308 (Gerald James Larson ed., 2001).
2. Robert L. Hardgrave, Jr. & Stanley *A. Kochanek, India: Government & Politics in a Developing Nation*; 26 (1993).
3. See, http://www.censusindia.gov.in.
4. India Const. preamble: amended by the Constitution (Forty-second Amendment) Act, 1976 (enforced since January 3, 1977).
5. AIR 1973 SC 1461.
6. The "other provisions" refers to the other fundamental rights given to all persons, including the right to equality.
7. AIR 1962 SC 853
8. (1973) 4 SCC 225
9. AIR 1993 SC 447
10. (1994) 3 SCC 1
11. (1994) 6 SCC 360
12. `AIR 1996 SC 1765
13. *State of Karnataka* v. *Dr. Praveen Bhai Thogadia* AIR 2004 SC 2081.
14. *All India Imam Organisation* v. *Union of India & Ors.*, 1993 SOL Case No. 098, para. 5, available at http://www.supremecourtonline.com/cases/ 2939.html.
15. Gary Jeffrey Jacobsohn, *The Wheel of Law: India's Secularism in Comparative Constitutional Context*, 13 (Princeton University Press 2003).
16. *Roy* v. *Union of India*, 2002 SOL Case No. 502.
17. Id. para. 85.
18. Id.

19. Id. para. 84, 86.
20. *Ratilal Panachand Gandhi* v. *State of Bombay*, AIR 1954 SC 388.
21. *Punjab Rao* v. *D.P. Meshram*, AIR 1965 SC 1179.
22. AIR 1954 SCR 1005, 1023-24, *Bijoe Emmanuel* v. *State of Kerala*, AIR 1987 SC 748. (upholding the religious beliefs of Jehovah's Witnesses to not sing the National Anthem).
23. AIR 1983 SC 1
24. AIR 1958 SC 895.
25. *Ratilal Panachand Gandhi*, AIR 1954 SC 388, 392; *Venkatamana Devaru* v. *State of Mysore*, AIR 1958 SCR 895, 909.
26. *Lakshimdra* AIR 1954 SCR at 1025.
27. *M.H. Quareshi* v. *State of Bihar*, AIR 1958 SC 731.
28. *Sarup Singh* v. *State of Punjab*, AIR 1959 SC 860. *Cf. Jagdishwaranand* v. *Police Commr.*, Calcutta, AIR 1984 SC 51, 57 (holding that tandava dance in public is not an essential part of Ananda Marga after examining the practices of that religion).
29. 2 S.C.R. 616 (1977).
30. *Ramji Lal Moti* v. *State of U.P.*, AIR 1957 SC 620 (upholding constitutionality of criminal law punishing deliberate and malicious outraging of religious feelings based on the "public order" restrictions in Articles 25 and 26).
31. Jonathan K. Stubbs, Persuading Thy Neighbor to be as Thyself: Constitutional Limits on Evangelism in the United States and India, 12 UCLA PAC. *BASIN L.J.* 360, 363-68 (1994).
32. Arpita Anant, Anti-conversion Laws, *The Hindu*, Dec. 17, 2002.
33. Id.
34. Faisal Mohammad Ali, Christian Anger at Conversion Law, *BBC News (Central India)*, August, 2006.
35. Stubbs, *supra note* 32, at 378-80.
36. Id.
37. Anant, *supra note* 33.
38. Indian Const. Art. 44.
39. AIR 1985 S.C. 945
40. AIR 1997 SC 3280.
41. Ruling on Muslim Divorce Act, *The Hindu*, September 29, 2001, at 9.

CHAPTER 13

Increasing Relevance of Vivekananda and Aurobindo

L.N. JHUNJHUNWALA

The Inspiration

A great Bengali author, Sankari Prasad Basu, had written in Bengali nine volumes under the title *Vivekananda and Contemporary India* comprising more than three thousand five hundred pages of fine print in Bengali. It took me two years to complete these volumes. This was around 1999. Singhviji did not know Bengali, so I translated some portions and narrated the following:

> "Maharashtra was ravaged by plague around 1898. British army had a contempt for the native language, culture and religious feelings. They created a terror in Poona. People fled from Poona. They entered the kitchens and destroyed the food, entered the shrines of homes and spat on the idols and threw them on the streets. Whatever remained of these people after the famine was taken away by the soldiers and the rest was burnt. Soldiers enjoyed the fun of burning goods. Many ladies committed suicide. The streets were blockaded, shops were broken open in Rand's presence and the whole scene was like the sacking of a conquered town.
> The men were completely stripped in the presence of others. Women were asked to expose their bodies and to hold up their wearing apparel. When complaints were made, Rand thundered,

"the inmates of the native houses must be inspected in broad day light as there was not sufficient light in the houses for efficient inspection."

Two brothers Damodar Chapekar and Balkrishna Chapekar could not tolerate this insult of the ladies. Their blood boiled. They went to Lokmanya Tilak and wanted his blessings to retaliate. Lokmanya Tilak was highly moved and told them that they are hardly eighteen years old and they should not risk their lives. Chapekar brothers stole revolver and two rifles from a shop at Bid in Nizam's territory. They also stole bayonets from sepoys, who used to sleep at Blanti temple in Pune. They assassinated plague officer Rand and Lt. Aiyerst. Damodar Chapekar was arrested on the 18th October, 1897 on the charge of blackening the statue of Queen Victoria and putting a garland of shoes around her neck and burning University pandal where a memorial for Queen Victoria was to be held. Ganesh Shah Dravid gave information about Chapekars. He got a reward of Rs. 10,000 and the Chapekar brothers were arrested. But Dravid and his brother were murdered in 1899 by revolutionaries. Vasudev Hari and Ranade were convicted for this murder. Vinayak Ranade was hardly 15 years old when Damodar Chapekar was executed. Vinayak Ranade took a vow to throw out the Britishers and organised *Mitra Mela* to unite Indians against the Britishers. *Mitra Mela* was able to attract members like Bal Gangadhar Tilak, who later became a premier of Bombay. Vinayak Ranade took part in *Mitra Mela.* The Bengal and Maharashtra revolutions were fully coordinated. Maratha revolutionary Bapat met Bengali worker Hemchandra Das in Paris and both of them learnt bomb manufacturing. Damodar Chapekar was hanged on the 18th April, 1898. He requested Lokmanya Tilak to send him a copy of *Gita* which he wanted to hold at the time of execution. Lokmanya Tilak did hand him over the *Gita.* His brother Balkrishna Chapekar was caught in 1899 and was also hanged.

Vivekananda was overwhelmed with emotion at the heroic act of Chapekars and said "Ah, then the Indian manhood is not totally dead ...why were not the statues of the Chapekar Brothers installed and worshipped." Kumud Bannerjee has said that he saw Tilak standing before Swamiji with folded hands and narrating the story of Chapekars.

It was in this background that I felt highly inspired when Singhviji told me that Shree Somnath Chatterjee, the Speaker, has agreed to allow him to install two life size statues of Swami Vivekananda and Aurobindo

Ghosh in the Lok Sabha. It was the 23rd August, 2006. The Parliament was overcrowded with all the devotees of Ramakrishna Mission and Aurobindo Ashram. Everybody got interested to read and listen more about these two great sons of India. The Prime Minister, the entire Cabinet the entire Opposition were present and praising Singhviji for inspiring the nation with the spirit of Swami Vivekananda and Shree Aurobindo Ghosh.

Singhviji in heavens will feel happy if we purify our minds by recollecting the life story of these two great sons of India, which I am giving very briefly.

Swami Vivekananda's Teachings

Swami Vivekananda was born in a rich family on the 12th January, 1863. His father Vishwanath Dutt was a famous legal practitioner. Swamiji was a voracious reader. He studied Socrates, Plato, Aristotle, Leibnitz and Hume. The vastness of the galaxies in the sky and the smallness of electrons and neutrons aroused his interest in God, who created all this. He developed a strong conviction that if there was a God, he can also be seen and must be seen by him. He met the greatest religious leaders and philosophers of his times in Calcutta. But nobody could tell him that they have seen God. Finally, he met Shree Ramakrishna at Dakshineshwar in 1882, who told him that he sees God more clearly than he is seeing Vivekanand and could also make him see God.

The vastness of the galaxies in the sky and the smallness of electrons and neutrons aroused his (Swami Vivekanad's) interest in God, who created all this. He developed a strong conviction that if there was a God, he can also be seen and must be seen by him.

Shree Ramakrishna made Vivekananda go through long *sadhana* and gave him the experience of *Nirvikalpa Samadhi*. Before leaving his mortal body in 1886, Shree Ramakrishna entrusted all his other disciples to continue their *sadhana* under Vivekananda's leadership. Swami Vivekananda toured the whole country from 1888 to 1893; sometimes staying in the palatial houses of the maharajas and sometimes in the poor huts of cobblers.

Around the 24th December, 1892 he reached the far end of India at Kanyakumari. He was overwhelmed at the sight of the tri-junction of Indian Ocean, Bay of Bengal and the Arabian Sea. There was a rock a few furlongs away from the sea shore. The Swami swam to the rock and sat there and remained in meditation for three days and nights. He saw the vision of the ancient India with its pristine glory and prosperity. He then saw the decline of India, invasion by outsiders and defeat. He was greatly moved at the poverty of the country and was inspired to go to Chicago for

World Parliament of Religions. He came down to Madras. Raja of Ramnads and various princess were highly influenced by his knowledge and oratorial skills. They all encouraged him to go to the World Parliament, but none made any offer to make any financial contributions for this trip. Ultimately the Maharaja of Khetri gave him the necessary funds and he went to Chicago. His seven minutes address to the parliament made him the leader of the parliament. He spent four years in America and Europe. He and the other disciples of Shree Ramakrishna along with household devotees formed the Ramakrishna Mission in 1898. While Swamiji was travelling from Japan to US in 1893, Jamshedji Tata also happened to be in the same ship. They both talked about the use of Indian resources and putting up large industries and scientific research institutes in India.

Jamshedji wrote to Swami on the 23rd November, 1898 the following letter:

> Dear Swami Vivekananda,
>
> I trust you remember me as a fellow traveller on your voyage from Japan to Vancouver. I very much recall at this moment your views on the growth of ascetic spirit in India and the duty not of destroying, but of diverting it into useful channels.
>
> I recall these ideas in connection with my scheme of Research Institute of Science for India, of which you have doubtlessly heard or read. It seems to me that no better use can be made of the ascetic spirit than the establishment of monasteries or residential halls for men dominated by this spirit where they should live with ordinary decency and devote their lives to the cultivation of sciences—natural and humanistic. I am of the opinion that if such a crusade in favour of an asceticism of this kind were undertaken by a competent leader, it would greatly help asceticism, science, and the good name of our common country; and I know not who would make a more fitting general of such a campaign than Vivekananda. Do you think you would care to apply yourself to the mission of galvanising into life our ancient traditions in this respect! Perhaps, you had better begin with a fiery pamphlet rousing our people in this matter. I shall cheerfully defray all the expenses of the publication.
>
> With kind regards, I am, dear Swami,
>
> Yours faithfully,
> Jamsedji N. Tata."

Thereafter, he spent more than a year in India organising RK Mission, went again to US for a little more than a year. He left his mortal body in 1902 even before he reached the age of 40.

Lessons from the Life of Shree Aurobindo

Now let me recall for you the story of Mahayogi Shree Aurobindo. Nine years younger than Vivekananda, he was born on the 15th August (our Independence Day now) 1872. His father Krishnadhon was absolutely Anglicised. He hated everything Indian. Aurobindo was kept away from Indians. At the age of five, he was sent to a special school in Darjeeling for English children with instructions that he should not come in touch with any Indian language or Indian students, and grow up with English children, imbibing only English ways. He did not know his mother tongue Bengali.

At the age of 7, his father took Aurobindo and his two brothers to England. They were left with the family of a clergy man with instructions that he should be kept away from Indians. Aurobindo spent fourteen years in England. The first five years passed easily and money came from India regularly. Then came hardships, no money came.

Thousands of miles away children suffered from poverty and want. His eldest brother, Benoy Bhusan, took a job and maintained brothers on a semi-starvation diet. Aurobindo continued to study English poetry and fiction, French literature, history of Europe, a little of Italian, German and Spanish. He was brilliant and carried away all the prizes. Aurobindo then took up ICS and started getting stipend. But he was filled with fiery love for the motherland and became the Secretary of a secret society with the romantic name "Lotus and Dagger". Every member had to take a vow to dedicate his entire life to the liberation of India. Aurobindo delivered many fiery speeches. He qualified for the ICS, but did not want to be a slave of a foreign Government. Shree Sayaji Rao, the Maharajah of Baroda happened to meet him in London. He was impressed with Aurobindo and employed him for Rs. 200 a month. He landed in February 1893 at Bombay harbour. With his first step on Apollo Bunder, he had his first spiritual experience. Gaekwad appointed him in Baroda College first as Professor of French and English and then as Vice Principal.

Aurobindo had a very strong conviction that pranayam could make him strong enough and this will help him to get Indian Independence.

Hardly had six months passed, he started writing fiery articles for a paper *Indu Prakash* bitterly criticising the soft policy of the Indian National Congress. Aurobindo went to Bengal in 1902, organised revolutionary activities in Calcutta, practised rifle shooting and organised revolutionaries there. Under the cover of sports groups for lathi play, fencing, riding, he prepared them for a violent revolution. Aurobindo formed a Committee of revolutionaries. Swami Vivekananda's disciple, Bhagini Nivedita, was a member of this committee. Aurobindo wanted one of his dedicated followers to join the military and learn making bombs. Bengalis were not admitted in military. Therefore, he had to have a different name common in UP and entered the army. He went to England to learn to make bombs. Aurobindo had a very strong conviction that *pranayam* could make him strong enough and this will help him to get Indian independence. By 1904, Aurobindo started *pranayam* for six hours a day under his Guru "Lele". This electrified his brain. He could now write 200 lines in half an hour what normally took a month. He realised that yoga gives power and he wanted power to liberate India. He speaks in one of his letters "you stand before a temple of Kali beside a sacred river and see what?—a sculpture; a gracious piece of architecture; but in a moment mysteriously, unexpectedly, there is instead a Presence, a Power, a Face that looks into yours; an inner sight in you has regarded the World Mother." Ramakrishna also was a worshipper of Kali.

In 1905, British Government passed the black act of partition. Aurobindo wrote a small revolutionary booklet, *Bhawani Mandir* which was circulated throughout the country. He joined Bepin Chandra Paul and started editing *Bande Matram*, which became very popular. Aurobindo entered Congress and tried to convert it into an instrument of revolutionary action. He wanted Congress to discard the wrong ideas of British justice advocated by Gokhale, whom, however, Gandhiji regarded as his Guru later. Aurobindo made a revolutionary group in Congress with a plan of increasing non-cooperation with the foreign Government and an open revolt all over the country. Aurobindo gave *diksha* of revolution to a number of young people.

It seems to me that no better use can be made of the ascetic spirit than the establishment of monasteries or residential halls for men dominated by this spirit where they should live with ordinary decency and devote their lives to the cultivation of sciences—natural and humanistic.

Aurobindo left Congress and joined the underground movement. On April 30, 1908 a bomb was thrown on District Magistrate at Muzzafarpur. Early in the morning of May 2, while Shree Aurobindo was still sleeping, the British Police charged up the stairs of his house, revolvers in hand and arrested him. Aurobindo was implicated in the case. Trial began on the 19th May, 1908. It was a huge trial and 142 people were accused, 4000 exhibits were produced and 222 witnesses were examined. The whole country was waiting for this trial. C.R. Das left his legal practice to defend Aurobindo. Aurobindo was lodged in a solitary cell—nine feet by six feet, which served as bedroom, dining room and toilet. He was not allowed to meet anybody. This small cell had two jars, one for his toilet and another one for drinking water. He was not allowed to go even for a walk.

But very soon, a miracle happened. Aurobindo saw Krishna all round. Various supernatural experiences followed. For a fortnight, Vivekananda spoke to him constantly. Aurobindo himself writes, "I looked at the jail … and it was no longer the high walls that I was imprisoned; no, it was Vasudeva who surrounded me. I walked under the branches of the tree in front of my cell but it was not the tree, I knew it was Vasudeva, it was Krishna whom I saw standing there and holding over me the shade. I looked at the bars of my cell, the very grating that did duty for a door and again I saw Vasudeva. It was Narayana, who was guarding and standing sentry over me … "I lay on the coarse blankets that were given me for a couch and felt the arms of Sri Krishna around me, the arms of my Friend and Lover… I looked at the prisoners in the jail, the thieves, the murderers, the swindlers, and as I looked at them I saw Vasudeva, it was Narayana whom I found in these darkened souls and misused bodies." The jail turned into a pilgrimage.

Shree Ramakrishna told him that he sees God more clearly than he is seeing Vivekanand and could also make him see God.

C.R. Das was able eventually to get Aurobindo released.

Motilal Ray took care of Shree Aurobindo and Aurobindo reached Pondicherry in 1910. He was busy with his intense *sadhana* and writing great works. The Second World War erupted. Stafford Cripps came to India to negotiate with Congress and Muslim League for cooperation in British war efforts. Aurobindo sent a special message to Gandhiji to accept Cripps proposal. In retrospect now we find that if Gandhiji had accepted Aurobindo's advice, the partition of the country would not have taken place and lives of millions of people lost during partition would have been saved. Crores of people migrating from one place to another place would have been avoided.

Singhviji wanted this country to be filled up with the great spiritual as well as dynamic ideas of these two great sons of India whose statues were to inspire the law makers of the country. It was an inspiring function with all the devotees of R.K. Mission and Aurobindo Ashram attending the Parliament. The Parliament was elevated to a high level of spiritual ambience. Singhviji was the hero of the event. Vivekananda wanted the statues of Chapekars. Singhviji got the same inspiration and got Swami Vivekananda and Mahayogi Aurobindo's statues installed in the Parliament.

I only pray to God to give strength of Swami Vivekananda and Mahayogi Aurobindo to my country.

CHAPTER 14

School Education in Relation to Freedom of Religion and Belief, Tolerance and Non-Discrimination*

PROF. ABID HUSSAIN

Dubious Role of Schools

The anti-freedom, illiberal and intolerant attitudes which vitiate life and suppress human rights and human freedoms reflect a state of mind, which is generally shaped by anti-liberal schools to which we send our children. None of us is born intolerant. Intolerance is an acquired behaviour. It is in the schools that young minds are indoctrinated to hate and despise others who are different from them in terms of race, religion, castes, culture and beliefs. Seeds of hatred are thus sown early in their minds in the schools to which they go and which soon transform them into uncritical morons. Partisan learning in impressionable formative age causes incalculable damage to the psyche and the pupils accept the conscious distortions as the global truth. It is, therefore, important to treat schools as the key to the development of national ethos.

To elaborate the point, schools that propagate that there is only ONE TRUTH are not being loyal to their noble calling. In these schools fanaticism is manufactured and students are taught to hate 'others'. Being so brought up, these children are unable to imagine 'someone else's world'. They do not learn to understand that there could be different forms of life

---

* Revised text of a discourse at the Human Rights Commission Conference on 'Education and Religious Tolerance', Madrid (Spain), 2002.

styles and schools of thought. Thus these schools become perfect breeding grounds for extremism. It is in this context that schools assume a critical role in the future development of a just society based on universal Human Rights. Since school going comes at a formative stage in a child's life, what is imparted to him at this early stage of life stays with him for ever and gains high ground. Prejudices, once acquired, stay and condition his mind, fostering a miasma of ignorance and intolerance which vitiates his whole life. Thus, this everwidening area of ignorance causes incalculable harm to society by destroying its unity and sullying its mystique. Later, as they grow up they fail to recognise that by taking away certain rights from others, they diminish the very essence of the human condition—treating people as equals. Insensitivity turns them into irresponsible and petty tyrants and, if unchecked in their behaviour, dehumanises them further.

Partisan learning in impressionable formative age causes incalculable damage to the psyche and the pupils accept the conscious distortions as the global truth.

Testimony of History

History is full of instances, where young minds once made intolerant at the school stage later become willing agents such as the HOLOCAUST in Germany; ruthless creators of GULAGS in the Soviet Union and savage barbarians in theocratic states. In Afghanistan we have seen how intolerance has led to distortion of a great religion by fanatics and how religious men have joined the forces of political terrorism. It is ironic that education which should have enlightened minds, once distorted by intolerance, has thrown people into dungeons of darkness and savagery. Indeed, the moment you submit yourself to a rigid unidimensional message you become a fanatic.

Ubiquitous Urge for Religion

It is a fact that people of different faiths have engaged in violent religious conflicts through the ages. Though socialist states of the twentieth century argued in favour of atheism and banned religious practices and rituals among their citizens, the enforced age of reason lasted as long as the people were arbitrarily ordered to conform. In former Communist countries, religious fervour returned as worship, hitherto neglected, became visibly functional. This occurrence reminds us of Voltaire's witticism, 'If God didn't exist, man

It is ironic that education which should have enlightened minds, once distorted by intolerance, has thrown people into dungeons of darkness and savagery.

would have to invent him'. Since the beginning of human history, religion has in various manifestations dominated man's conscious. Effort to make some kind of sense out of one's sudden adventure into what he has always considered the 'unknown'. Indeed, religious faith is unique in human beings and lives on. When guided by positive motivation, it imparts a healing touch to society. Conversely, a confrontationist approach creates social upheavals engendering more prejudices and animosities.

Advocates of Inter-Religious Understanding

Despite a welter of conflicting fanaticisms in all societies, there are men and women who emphasise and preach inter-religious understanding. The great Indian emperor Ashoka in his twelfth edict proclaimed:

> He who does reverence to his own sect, while disparaging the sects of others, wholly from attachment to his own, with intent to enhance the glory of his own sect, in reality by such conduct, inflicts the severest injury on his own sect. Concord, therefore, is meritorious, to wit, hearkening and hearkening willingly to the law of piety as accepted by other people.

This is a noble thought (as far as it goes). However, in nine cases out of ten, the followers of one religion hold that their faith does good, but other faiths do irreparable harm. Hence the not-so-infrequent eyeball-to-eyeball confrontations among religions. When the aim of all religions professes to be the betterment of humanity, each striving to seek in its own way to help the individual become a better human being and society and a better place to live in, then what prevents the religions from coexisting without friction and feuding? A few comments, though seemingly digressive, will be in order to provide to comprehend this baffling question.

Spiritual and Ritual Realms of Religion

Any religion broadly comprises two realms—the spiritual and the ritual. The spiritual realm is the essence, the core, the very substance of a religion. Its influence on the individual through the content of worship and meditation (mark the words, content and not mode of worship) serves a dual purpose. First, its metaphysical and philosophical content serves as a guiding light to the individual, drifting rudderless as a lonely being in this vast universe, to seek self-knowledge and approximation to some higher reality. But the individual is also a social being. Hence the second purpose of the spiritual realm is to sublimate his natural instincts and raw emotions and passions through a structured value system to enable him to fulfil his societal obligations—ranging from his family, class and tribe to yet wider and wider social configurations.

Even after making due allowance for the necessary exclusivisms which demarcate one religion from another owing to the exigencies of age and clime and cultural milieu, the spiritual realms of blatantly 'poles apart' religions display a remarkably high degree of *transcendent unity.* That is why some savants preferred the expression 'religion' in the singular, to the one 'religions' in the plural, to describe the multiplicity of religion(s). For describing the multifarious religious beliefs, they chose the phrase 'forms of religion'.

The second purpose of the spiritual realm is to sublimate his natural instincts and raw emotions and passions through a structured value system to enable him to fulfill his societal obligations.

The other realm, viz. ritualism, which is the outward shell of a religion, is mainly concerned with religious modalities and externalities, some exoteric and some esoteric, such as modes of worship (mark the words, modes and not content of worship), codes spelling out the do's and don'ts about dress, personal appearance (like tonsured head or wearing one's hair, moustaches, beard, in a very specific manner), food, ablutions self-flagellation of several kinds, sexual behaviour and other. Not only transgressing but even the slightest deviation from these so-called sacrosanct and inviolate ritual injunctions is most likely to invite the wrath of the presiding pontiffs of religions and theocratic powers-that-be; resulting in the severest punishment like excommunication or even worse imposed on the hapless 'dissenter' or 'blasphemer'.

Undeniably, it is the over-emphasis on the ritualism of most religions that tends to breed exclusivisms and fissures in the social fabric. The differences between religious beliefs keep surfacing in minor sporadic incidents of confrontation and even violence, fraught like a ticking time-bomb, with the danger of turning into a major catastrophic upheaval in society.

Such being the nature of the bonding element of religion, *vis-à-vis* their dividing element, there is no reason why the *transcendent unity* emanating from the spirituality of religions should not override and nullify the divisive influence at times cast by their ritual practices.

Constructive Role of Schools

Remedy, now lies in undertaking well thought out measures to restore schooling and education to its rightful place in society by transforming education into an art of respecting others and endowing youth with a passion to go against orthodoxy, exposing the postures of ritualistic exclusivity to celebrate transcendent unity in the midst of diversities. Such an education can remake men into good human beings, reconstructing them to embody something beyond their individual selves, some inscrutable deeper spirit of friendship, love and humanism. Guided by ethical, normal and just values, life would become for them a performance before divinity, putting them several steps ahead of the so-called *gurus* pretenders to holiness.

Many practical steps could be taken to create harmony and mutual respect among the various religious traditions. School children could be taken on visits to holy places of different religions and asked to spend some time praying together. They should also be given a chance to listen to discourses of different religions by religious practitioners. They should also be encouraged to join the celebrations of different religions and participate in their festivals. These would make a deep impact on children's mind and open their hearts to value the traditions of other religions thus learning to approach each other with respect. This will be a fitting fulfilment of Khalil Gibran's exhortation, "Say not, I have found the truth, but rather, I have found a truth."

Need for Reformed Syllabi

Reformed education syllabi giving due emphasis to the spiritual elements of religions, can go a long way in creating and promoting tolerance, harmony and mutual respect for various religious teachings. It is, therefore, extremely necessary especially for multi-religious democratic states, to promote a general study of all religions so that the citizens can understand each other better and live together amicably. Syllabi giving well chosen information about each of the major religions should be included as part of the course in citizenship or as part of general education to be introduced in schools and colleges. Careful analysis is required to ensure that biases do not creep into revised texts. Different perspectives must be present lest students grow up with a truncated or doctored version of religious histories. Racial and ethnic stereotypes should be thoroughly purged. Reordering of text books is a sensitive issue and should not be left to the discretion of those who are not academics in the real sense of the word but pseudo-scholars and more-loyal-than-the-king type bureaucrats only too willing to toe the political line. Even the best of the scientific findings ultimately reach dead ends and without critical appraisal and revision, science cannot progress further. As Dr. S. Radhakrishnan said, it is "the homage that the finite mind pays to the inexhaustibility of the infinite".

Unity, not Uniformity

Through good inter-culture based scientific education, we can achieve unity in diversity in a world which is becoming global and interdependent. But we certainly do not advocate attempting to merge our various traditions and diversities into one uniform practice. We need different traditions even in the realm of religion, because a single tradition cannot satisfy the needs and mental dispositions of the great variety of human beings. Moreover, it is diversity that enhances the seductive attraction of a mosaic; the beauty of a bouquet lies in the fact that it is made of flowers of different colours. The symphonies of Beethoven and Mozart, though rendered through different musical instruments, each with its distinct characteristic, when synchronised create an enchanting melody. Education should aim to develop similarly, sharing and respecting each other's religion and beliefs through well-thought-out syllabi, to know each other's differences and enjoy a harmonious blending of differences, which in turn can lead to the much coveted *transcendent unit.*

To achieve a synthesis and coexistence of different beliefs and cultures with respect for human resources is the aim of good education. It is through imbibing the values of respecting all religions in their multiplicity and duality that the essential unity of mankind is achieved. It is through good education based on tolerance taught and practised in school rooms and in play grounds that we lay the foundations of a just and moral society, where life is not divided by parochial considerations and 'the world has not been broken up into fragments by narrow domestic walls but where common humanity is fostered and led forward into ever widening thought and action'. This is how our schools can pay homage to the inexhaustible possibilities of a life of freedom, innovation, happiness and human rights for all.

Through good inter-culture based scientific education, we can achieve unity in diversity in a world which is becoming global and interdependent.

Conclusion

Borrowing from Bertrand Russel, we might repeat that the world we should wish to see would be one freed from the virulence of group hostilities engendered either by differing religious doctrines or clashing political ideologies. Then and then only shall we be able to realise that happiness for all that is to be desired from co-operation rather than from strife. We should, therefore, wish to see a world in which education is aimed at mental freedom rather than at imprisoning the minds of the young in a rigid armour of this or that dogma or ideology. The world needs open hearts and open minds, and it is not through rigid systems, whether old or new, religions or political, that these can be attained. The human goal must be to break the cycle of hatred, intolerance and violence, and instead to invigorate vision out of which spontaneous impulse springs to bring about unity and progress.

Module III

Economic and Business Dimensions

CHAPTER 15

Emerging Role of Business in Society

RAHUL BAJAJ

India's Long Tradition of Business

Business exists to fulfil the needs of the customer. In the process it creates wealth and employment, pays taxes, rewards its shareholders. If business is to continue to exist it has to continually reinvent itself and grow.

India has a very long tradition of business. We were trading over 2,000 years ago. We were manufacturing cloth and many other things and trading with East Asia, Eurasia and Africa. The *hundi* was invented by us long ago to settle long distance accounts. In our society, governments were advised to tax lightly, generally around 25 per cent. In our country, the strong are expected to protect the weak; the fortunate to aid the unfortunate. Schools and places of higher learning and dharmashalas and even healthcare centres were built by the rich. In our temple at my home town, Wardha, which celebrated its centenary this year, at the gateway sat an Ayurveda practitioner hired by the temple to provide free medical care. The same temple was also the first temple to be opened to *Dalits* as far back as 1927.

Even under the Mughal rule, trade and industry prospered. With the advent of the British and of British trade and industry, things started to change. The pride of place went to British interests. In 1947, much of the total capital in the stock exchanges was in British hands. There was some Indian business, including sizeable ones like the Tatas, but it was just about tolerated, but certainly not encouraged.

Unfortunately, after Independence, with the emphasis on the public sector and the establishment of a licence-permit *raj*, the Indian private

I am taking this historical walk to outline how we came to be where we are today. Why are we like this only? We have 200 years of baggage, some of which we continue to carry, advertently or inadvertently.

sector again shifted to the periphery. The mood of the establishment was anti-business. Also, because of distortions crept in due to policy decisions of the government, a large section of Indian business became unsavoury in its dealings and did not endear itself to the public at large. Shortages bred low quality, black markets, and the like.

I am taking this historical walk to outline how we came to be where we are today. Why are we like this only? We have 200 years of baggage, some of which we continue to carry, advertently or inadvertently.

The Sea Change

There has been a sea change in public perceptions in the last two decades. Making money has become a global obsession. When even Deng Tsiao Peng says that to be rich is glorious, then it cannot be that bad! If one is rich one must be good. That may be debatable. If one is good one should be rich, that is also debatable. Although this appears to have become the world view, I am not in full agreement with it. It has an upside and a downside. How one makes or uses money is important. Money should not confer legitimacy to crooks. Also, there are values much more important than money. To me, the soldier, the teacher, the doctor, for example, have a higher calling than businessmen. At the same time, the political class and, perhaps, the bureaucracy have lost their sheen. Therefore, businessmen are becoming the new role models.

Despite this new role assigned to them, the credibility of businessmen world over is not too high. Enron and WorldCom, for instance, shook public confidence. The recent subprime crisis in the US too has reflected both incompetence and irresponsibility of very reputed companies. CEOs of banks have been bailed out in golden parachutes. The uproar against CEO pay continues to rise. We have enough cases of investors being duped in IPOs.

Business has to understand that it can operate only if it has public legitimacy. The economy is embedded in a society. We realise this clearly when things we take for granted do not exist. Some States in our country do not attract major investments because of business perception of their law and order. Illustratively, what business can be done in Zimbabwe today? I believe that it is our responsibility to make the process of reform and liberalisation a large and growing constituency in the country. It is neither the job of the government alone nor does it have the capacity to do so.

With rising inequalities in our country and rising cost of housing, education and health, there is a real danger of liberalisation getting a bad name and our sliding back into tokenism. Corporate India has a huge stake in this process. We have to proactively create situations wherein more and more people have a stake in the system and in the economic system being fair, sensible and sustainable. For achieving this I believe four things are necessary:

1. Provision of good quality products and services at reasonable prices,
2. Good Corporate Governance,
3. Corporate Social Responsibility, and
4. Philanthropy.

The first three are necessary. The last element is optional, though much of the positive public perception is quite often based on philanthropy. The Tatas have been institution builders and philanthropists par excellence. I am mentioning the first because all others are futile if this basic contract between business and the customer is not kept.

Corporate India has a huge stake in this process. We have to proactively create situations wherein more and more people have a stake in the system, a system which is fair, sensible and sustainable.

Good Corporate Governance

Good Corporate Governance is a matter of observing, in letter and spirit, a regime of disclosure, transparency and accountability. It is a mandatory responsibility one accepts when one manages a publicly-held company.

Corporate Social Responsibility (CSR) is what one does upstream and downstream to be socially responsible and also to enhance one's business. For us to manufacture environment-friendly vehicles in an environmentally responsible manner would be CSR. To train people to drive safely would be CSR. To assist educational institutions in our area would be CSR. CSR in my view is done in enlightened self-interest.

Philanthropy is simply giving back to the society in which we function and from which we get so much.

There can be a discussion of this categorisation, and its refinement, but I believe it is important to keep things simple, even at the risk of over-simplification.

Recently the ICAI (Institute of Chartered Accountants of India) has initiated an effort to suggest a framework for Sustainability Reporting in our country. At times one finds them using Sustainability Reporting and CSR inter-changeably. To me Sustainability is an important dimension and issue, but a subset of CSR. I believe companies should be encouraged to report their carbon footprint and the key aspect of their operations that could pose a serious risk. But I believe that principle-based rules deliver more than overly detailed micro management.

I continue to believe that the Maslowian hierarchy of needs works. Beyond a minimum, people prefer meaning to meaninglessness, prefer contributing to build something, prefer camaraderie to hostility.

In any system there is a structure and a process. Mandating certain things, say in Corporate Governance, provides a structure. But the process of governance determines outcomes. One can have a majority of Independent Directors on a board, but this does not guarantee its independence. What does it guarantee is the quality of management of that company. In our country, we have a tendency to make structural changes, unmindful whether processes support or undermine that structure. We have democracy and poor governance, a bureaucracy and rampant corruption. In such a system scoundrels can get away scot free and the straightforward can find themselves tied up in red tape or worse.

Therefore, I believe we should minimise regulation and have it largely for laying out the broad principles of the rules of the game and for cases when gross travesty of justice occurs. For the rest, the market is more likely to achieve the desired objectives than regulation.

Now, I come to the question of how do we run organizations such that the four things we outlined earlier, good product, corporate governance, CSR and philanthropy happen to them, in this greed-centred world? I believe that it is the culture of the organization that can ensure it.

Again and again, it comes back to what is one's conception of people: what drives them, what motivates them, what gives them satisfaction. And I continue to believe that the Maslowian hierarchy of needs works. Beyond a minimum, people prefer meaning to meaninglessness, prefer contributing to build something, prefer camaraderie to hostility. I believe that the lovely Greek word "*oikodomein*" or to "build up a house", is a basic human urge. People leading organisations have to create an environment conducive for their colleagues to have this sense of contribution. This comes from having an ethical organisation and by being governed by good values, where integrity, quality, dignity and a sense of fair play exists. This does not mean a saintly organisation. Business has its exigencies. However, from such an environment comes pride in one's work and in one's organisation.

The Right Order of Priorities

I have found that if one has the nation, the organization and the individual hierarchy in this order in decision making in a company, then things become relatively simple. This means that a national priority should take precedence over a company priority which should take precedence over an individual priority. If this is done consistently, it moulds behaviour the right way. I should add that the top management of a company has to be specifically disciplined, because it is there where individual priority has the latitude to override organizational priorities.

Pangs are intrinsic to the process of birth. Diversity facilitates sustainable development. So, neither pain, nor the lack of a single path, should deter us from finding our way.

Business was always knowledge-based. This aspect was hidden for a while in our country due to controls on entry. Now we have to develop our own knowledge and integrate knowledge from elsewhere. This requires much greater engagement and involvement of our employees. In this race to attract and retain talent, at the margin, the reputation of an organization matters. Its results: better culture and CSR image. This is another factor driving us to be good corporate citizens.

Corporate India has driven change in our country and would continue to do so. At what pace, in which direction and with what values it drives this change, is the point in question. Mere lip sympathy won't do. We in India have a historic responsibility. I am confident that with our mix of underlying age old societal norms together with the requirements of the new economy, a new Indian model of CSR would emerge.

Pangs are intrinsic to the process of birth. Diversity facilitates sustainable development. So, neither pain, nor the lack of a single path, should deter us from finding our way.

CHAPTER 16

Corporate Social Responsibility The New Direction for Indian Business

K.N. MEMANI

The Historical Background

One common sight any traveller in our country would never fail to spot in even remote corner is a well or a *choubutry* or a temple built in memory of some leading member of a business house or a trader. In *mandis* across the country traders set apart a small part of their earnings of the day in a special fund to build these little monuments as part of their Corporate Social Responsibility (CSR).

Over the decades, business has taken a big stride in raising its commitment to society. Corporate Social Responsibility has moved from being a peripheral charity to a commitment to improve societal welfare in different directions and further on to a change in business processes leading to a building up of ethical values in products and processes. If we go through ancient literature we have Kautilya emphasising in his *Arthashastra* ethical principles while doing business. Ancient religions also mandated on the rich their duty to the society. Hinduism has the concept of *dharmada*, Islam *zakkat* and Christianity and Judaism exhorted the affluent to set apart 10 per cent of their earnings for charity. Charitable foundations and trusts supporting community welfare in one form or other are a common institution over the ages.

Worldwide, the term CSR itself came into vogue some time in the 1970s lifting mere charity by business to a commitment to social benefit.

In some two decades, a majority of large businesses made CSR as part of their corporate plan. This is seen in the activities of global corporations that have adopted regular CSR initiatives. In 1977, less than half of the Fortune 500 companies had mentioned CSR in their annual statements; by 1990-end, 90 per cent had flaunted CSR initiatives.

Indian business houses have had several examples of corporate involvement in the upliftment of the socio-economic environment outside their firms and factories. The Tatas' pioneering work in Jamshedpur is a shining example. Tata-sponsored foundations had set up a string of institutions across the country from the Indian Institute of Science in Bangalore to Tata Memorial Cancer Hospital and Tata Institute of Fundamental Research, Tata Institute of Social Sciences in Mumbai to sponsoring scholarships for advanced studies abroad. We hear a lot more about Western foundations with their worldwide reach like the Ford Foundation, Rockefeller Foundation and others. As a proportion of the revenues of Indian businesses, the contribution to multiple social initiatives can stand abreast of the best in the world.

In a study of CSR initiatives in 2001, Tata Energy Research Institute (TERI) (now The Energy and Resources Institute), classified four stages in the evolution of business involvement in social welfare. The first stage was between 1930 and 50 when an ethical model with trusteeship as its philosophy was dominant. With the state becoming a major player in industry after 1950, a statist model came to the fore till 1970. In the 1970s Milton Friedman, the evangelist of free enterprise said that generation of wealth found was the main concern of business and that CSR should be circumscribed by the businesses' accountability to the shareholders. In effect, it meant that the bottom line was the limiting factor in corporate social responsibility. But ever since 1990s business has begun to question its own justification and found that it has a stake in society. That has altered the perception on CSR. The stake-holder model has begun to inform CSR initiatives. It is no longer just shareholder alone who has a stake in business; society too has a stake.

The Emerging New Concept

The World Business Council for Sustainable Development has expressed the social concerns of business in a new definition of this initiative. It says: "*CSR is a continuing commitment by business to behave ethically and contribute to economic development while improving quality of life of the workforce and their families as well as local community and society at large.*" Thus defined, CSR has assumed quite a different role from the earlier one represented by charity foundations. Behaving ethically meant that the business processes and products have to be transparent and business has a social accountability to fulfil, apart from just financial rectitude. The stakeholder here is not just the shareholder but the workforce of the business and its families, the community around and society at large. This demands a business imperative, a linkage with sustainable development and value-embedded business management.

This wider definition has led to CSR becoming a part of the Millennium Development Goal set by the UN set in year 2000. Under this voluntary initiative, the UN Global Compact requires business to build a social legitimacy for itself. It asks the companies to have a set of core values in areas of human rights, labour standards, environment and fighting corruption. Several advanced countries have now legislation forbidding corporations from bribing their potential clients abroad and their political bosses especially in some of the Third World countries.

This new understanding of corporate social responsibility also widens the scope of corporate behaviour in achieving the millennium goal. To achieve such a wide range of social responsibility, corporates would have to partner with governments and non-governmental organizations, with the workforce itself, with environment management organizations and keep regular evaluation and reporting system in a transparent manner. From a single bottom line of shareholder value that Milton Friedman set forth in the 1970s, corporate world is now moving into what is termed Triple Bottom Line of accountability and transparency to shareholders, workforce and society in general.

The UN Global Compact requires business to build a social legitimacy for itself to have a set of core values in areas of human rights, labour standards, environment and fighting

We may recall here the pioneering work that my friend and philosopher, the late Dr. L.M. Singhvi, did in integrating his own commitment to human rights, his scholarship in international jurisprudence and business management to evolve such a compact as the head or member of several global institutions including his contribution such as International Human Rights Commission. One of his multifaceted initiatives was to alert mankind to the imperatives of ecology and cultural values and how business should adopt them in their core plans.

CSR Initiatives of Indian Corporates

As mentioned earlier, the Tata group's investment in social capital dates back to the early years of the twentieth century. Some other Indian business houses have also funded or otherwise supported different social activities including construction of temples, low cost rest houses for pilgrims, hospitals and educational institutions. The Birlas set up one of the foremost engineering education institutes in the country at Pilani (BITS) that has reached world standards. In more recent days, many corporates have launched multifaceted initiatives in the communities they live in and some extend these globally.

Infosys Technologies carries out CSR at four different levels : at the group level through Infosys Foundation; at the corporate level by the Internal Board of Directors; by its employees at individual or group level that the management encourages. One significant initiative is the lending of its business talent at Board level for various government and non-government activities in areas as different as corporate governance, global warming, education and training, health-care, rural upliftment. Top level executives are allowed to take sabbatical for involving themselves in non-profit organizations for social welfare. For six consecutive years, Infosys has been named "most admired company" which is a barometer of its CSR effectiveness. Good work in community development by corporates helps them in building a better brand image and thereby enhancing their competitiveness.

Another significant CSR initiative is by JSW Steel in women empowerment. Next to the passout, company's steel mill at Tornagallu, the company runs an all-women non-voice village BPO. These village women, though Tenth passed, are trained in computers, English language and several other aspects before absorption. The company has found that this helps transformation of families in villages creating brighter future for the women engaged as BPO employees. It is planning spread of this initiative to other rural areas.

Multi Commodity Exchange has developed an innovative public-private partnership model leveraging on the strength of one of its partners, Indian Post, by setting up Gramin Suvidha Kendras to disseminate information on commodity prices to farmers to enable them to take decisions regarding their choice of crop. Another benefit is to make the farmers price-sensitive to take advantage of changing demand for their produce.

Reliance Industries produces a corporate sustainability report, the first in the oil sector in this country to come out with the eco-evaluation of their business products and processes. Reliance's collective action programme with other Baroda-based industries binds industry and rural communities together. The giant corporation is totally committed to the green initiatives, such as, recycling treated effluents to create acres of greenery. From cow sheds to education, vocational training of women to community revitalisation, there is a range of action programmes in social welfare that the corporate takes up through its many partnership initiatives.

ACC Ltd. has taken up work to contain the spread of diseases like HIV/AIDs and also provide treatment for victims. The innovative part is the partnership with the famous Christian Medical College at Vellore and a treatment centre at Wadi. These are the two most affected regions with this disease. ACC prides itself at being the first corporate to venture into this type of treatment for HIV/AIDs outside the government sphere.

One can go on like this and fill pages after pages with myriad initiatives by hundreds of Indian corporations involving themselves in social action plans. The wide range of target groups that the corporates have chosen, especially empowering of women, micro credit disbursement, education and healthcare and rural development are spread across India. In many cases, they are in partnership with NGOs and government organizations as well.

In this context, a ground reality has to be reckoned with the conventional system is dwindling rapidly. Urgency has arisen to further accelerate the process to bridge the gap between the Corporate Sector and Social Development. This is because already the phenomenon of social convergence has become the need in day-to-day life. A survey conducted by IMRB suggests positive mood of corporate sector in this regard. The survey covers 150 companies with sales between Rs. 200 crore to Rs. 500 crore. It was found from the survey that about 83 per cent of companies apparently showed interest in contributing to social development. Ten years old estimates reveal that the share of private corporate sector in total investment in the economy was 36 per cent in 1997-98, equivalent of Rs. 131,531 crore. The gross investment by private sector for the same year has been estimated to be about 8.4 per cent of the GDP. If we assume a situation where 83 per cent of companies annually invest a mere 1 per cent (of their total amount of Profit after tax) in social development, the total corporate investment in social development will be about Rs. 100,000 crore. This sum is more than the Government of India's projected expectations from the Indian corporate sector. This sum is enough to change the grim picture of Indian social development. To substantiate this logic, an international example may be taken. South Africa's corporate sector spends 1.3 per cent of profit after tax for social development. This shows that for India it is not a mere assumption.

The wide range of target groups that the corporates have chosen, especially empowering of women, micro-credit disbursement, education and healthcare and rural development are spread across India.

Other CSR Initiatives

In addition to such wide range of CSR initiatives, India Inc has impressed the world with some fundamental changes in their corporate activities that link them with the disadvantaged people creating new developmental perspectives that are broadly inclusive and, above all, that have led to impact their own products, business processes and vision. A look at them shows how these pioneers have helped change the very concept of CSR and business itself. ITC, Hindustan Unilever (HUL), Arvind Eyecare, are among such pioneers who have proved much before its recent theoretical framework was formulated that there is a huge business opportunity for corporates to leverage their talent and resources benefitting the people at the bottom of the economic pyramid (BOP).

There is, in fact, a new face of CSR that leading Indian corporates like ITC and HUL have conceived and created at considerable risk to their bottom line. But exceptional corporate leadership and commitment has seen to it that the bottom line itself has swelled due to such initiatives that have touched lives of lakhs of people, on the one hand and created social capital on a wide range. ITC, for instance, under the innovative and out-of-the-box creative leadership of its chairman, Y.C. Deveshvar, has done wonders. When ITC wanted to get wood pulp for its speciality paper and board, Deveshvar rejected the easy option of importing the pulp and got his R&D to find the right and fast growing soft wood the seedlings of which he got distributed widely to farmers who were willing to grow them on degraded wastelands. To improve the supply chain of soybean that his company procured, ITC Chairman thought out the *e-chaupal* approach where Internet-enabled information kiosks spread information about every aspect of soybean to farmers including prevailing market price. The result, in the Chairman's words, ITC has created "value chains that today provide livelihood opportunities for over five million people, many of whom represent the poorest, particularly in rural India." ITC "is today an acknowledged example of Triple Bottom Line Performance". The pulpwood initiative alone has helped regenerate 80,000 hectares of degraded wasteland and 35 million mandays of employment for forestry farmers who are free to sell their products to the highest bidder while it has also created ecological wealth for the country. Despite considerable investment that ITC made in these areas, the company's profit after tax, net worth as well as market cap have taken a quantum jump over the years from 1998 to 2006. PAT has risen from Rs. 261 crore to Rs. 3,120 core and net worth from Rs. 1,121 crore to Rs. 12,058 crore.

Hindustan Lever, now Unilever (HUL) supported women's self-help groups and organized people at the bottom of the economic pyramid to become sales persons for its products specially designed for the poor. 'Project Shakti', as it is called, empowered women by turning them into earners by making them part of its sales force. It benefited the company as well as the people who were turned into small scale entrepreneurs. For HUL, this was an "exciting opportunity to penetrate the rural BOP". This direct-to-home sales with products designed for the people meant that even families with incomes less than Rs. 1,000 per month could become consumers of HUL products. "We are offering economic opportunity to your community" is how rural sales officer for Project Shakti A. Balasubramanian put it (as quoted in Michigan University Business *guru*, Professor C.K. Prahlad's book *Fortune at the Bottom of the Pyramid*).

Pioneers who have proved much before its recent theoretical framework was formulated that there is a huge business opportunity for corporates to leverage their talent and resources in benefiting the people at the bottom of the economic pyramid (BOP).

Candy marketed to the BOP through Project Shakti has become HUL's fastest growing product, the book says. The project aims both to "change the lives of people in rural India" as well as broaden the company's market. Its success rate in product sales in BOP in rural areas is as high as 90 per cent.

These are the distinguishing marks from earlier CSR activities. The new direction of CSR is a total win-win situation. Both HUL and ITC have themselves benefited from their attempt to build social capital outside their campuses while improving the lives of people even far away from their offices and factories. No wonder Professor Prahlad's path-breaking book draws pretty lot from the experience of these and other Indian initiatives.

The new perception on uplifting of the poors that the Michigan business *guru* has put forward starts from the ingrained belief that governments, agencies like NGOs, large firms and organized business "had believed that market-based solutions cannot lead to poverty reduction". 'That belief', Professor Prahlad says, 'is no longer true.' (*ibid.*, pp. 9-10) Calling this as an "intellectual trap", the professor says: There is now widespread realisation in business circles that the "BOP market is a major engine of growth".

Behind this discovery is the realisation that poverty alleviation cannot be done through charity. "Charity rarely solves the problem" says the business *guru*. The new approach is to make product unit packages small enough to be affordable to the bottom, like the shampoo revolution brought about by sachets costing just Rs. 5 each. When the private sector gets involved in actual poverty alleviation at the ground level, it creates products that the poor can afford and then invents business processes where the poor could be both consumers and marketers of these products (HUL Shakti project or Amul's icecream, for example).

Private sector involvement in creating products and business processes at BOP level brings into existence a new partnership that replaces the traditional CSR by businesses. ITC has made thousands of poor farmers into good income earners through its initiatives in persuading them to become entrepreneurs. The initiatives generate trust between the top tier and bottom tier of the socio-economic classes. The net result is not only in terms of better bottom lines for the corporates and more opportunities for income generation at the bottom tier, but the narrowing of the social divide. Capitalism itself becomes a creator of stake for the poor.

The initiatives generate trust between the top tier and bottom tier of the socio-economic classes. The net result is not only in terms of better bottom lines for the corporates and more opportunities for income generation at the bottom tier, but the narrowing of the social divide.

Catching on this trend, the world's richest man, Microsoft Chairman Emeritus, Bill Gates, has developed a new concept of "creative capitalism", "compassionate capitalism". This is the direction which business must now seek and evolve. Significantly, before Gates delivered the now famous speech on creative capitalism at the World Economic Forum at Devos in 2008, he had a long meeting with Professor Prahlad whose book, *Fortune at the Bottom of the Pyramid* and *The New Age of Innovation* have defined a new paradigm for business in the global context.

The basic thesis of Gates is that "we have to find a way to make the aspects of capitalism that serve wealthier people, serve poorer people as well." To do that "companies should create businesses that focus on building products and services for the poor.... Twin missions—making profits and also improving the lives for those who don't fully benefit from market forces." Gates who created the world's largest foundation from his wealth recently (with Warren Buffet also joining him, it is now said to be over 70 billion dollars) said: "The idea that you encourage companies to take their innovative thinkers and think about the most needy—even beyond market opportunity—this is something that appropriately ought to be done."

Ushering in a New Era

We probably are living in a new age of innovation in all respects. Our political leaders have coined a new word for development: inclusive growth. At the same time, global business leaders like Gates and business *gurus* like Prahlad want shift of capitalism to a compassionate and creative one that would include the poor. This is, to quote Bill Gates, "the sustainable way to reduce poverty in the world."

This was also the dream of Dr. L.M. Singhvi who had the same vision. Indian corporate world is increasingly realising its responsibility towards their role for the deprived Indian people. But, no doubt, much more is required to be done in this vital area.

CHAPTER 17

Ethics is Good Business

DR. ABHISHEK MANU SINGHVI

The Concept of Corporate Governance

If one were to encapsulate the subject into two words, Ethical Business, one may be forgiven for caustically describing it as a classic example of an oxymoron. Certainly, some books and dictionaries trying to illustrate and describe the word "oxymoron" give not only grammatical illustrations like "bitter sweet" but also professional ones like "legal ethics". There can, therefore, be no greater validation for a subject like this than to discuss the decline and/or the absence of ethics and morality in business, in the professions, in public life, in politics, in governance and in the media than the sad fact that we live in an era where ethical governance, ethical business, ethics in law, or in medicine are etymologically defined as "polar opposites" or oxymorons.

If we start with business, good or better corporate governance has been a buzzword for the past decade. If ethical corporate governance had been a musical tone, people believe it would have "been top of the pops" as far as activity over the last few years is concerned. The Turnbull Report and the Cadbury Report in the UK, the Kumar Manglam Birla Report, the Government of India Committee recommendations, and the amendments to the Companies Act in India, all sought to address the central dilemma of morality in corporate governance of ethics in business, a dilemma summed up by Lord Thurlow when he said: "Did you ever expect a corporation to have a conscience when it has no soul to be damned and nobody to be kicked?" It is a lament which is centuries old even in corporate jurisprudence. The English jurist, Edward Coke, lamented many centuries ago: "Corporations cannot commit treason and they cannot be outlawed or excommunicated for they have no souls."

Good corporate governance (GCG) is what corporate governance does. But if this has to go beyond the realm of mere slogans, shibboleths and verbiage, we have to address some of the nitty-gritty issues and uncomfortable questions involved in good corporate governance. First of these is the creation, and more importantly, the vigorous and honest policing of anti-insider trading (IT) codes. The IT regulations, many of which were revised after the report of the second Kumar Mangalam Birla Committee (of which this author was a member) provide codes of corporate disclosure practices to ensure timely and adequate dissemination of price-sensitive information, trading restrictions on designated employees, creation of limited trading windows which have to be closed during the price-sensitive periods (like declaration of annual six monthly results) and creation of Chinese walls within a corporate entity separating those inside certain sensitive departments from other public departments. There cannot be even the beginning of GCG without reducing the pernicious yet widespread practice of IT.

The central dilemma of corporate governance or ethics in business is one summed up by Lord Thurlow: "Did you ever expect a corporation to have a conscience when it has no soul to be damned and nobody to be kicked?"

Second is the entrustment of more powers to the market policeman—SEBI. Presently, it has no powers to impound documents, to obtain information from banks or PSUs, no powers to award compensation to aggrieved investors, no power to levy punitive penalties of up to three times the amount of benefit received by the concerned corporate and no power to direct the corporate to disgorge its ill-gotten gains. We cannot police the primary and secondary markets with a toothless tiger which seems almost impotent compared to its US counterpart.

Third, we have to bring into our corporate and legal lexicon a word conspicuous by its absence, viz. "punishment". Fifteen hundred years ago, a Japanese prince said in one of the oft-quoted works on GCG, "Do not fail to bestow a reward, nor impose a punishment". India's record of punishment for corporate misgovernance is almost non-existent. From the 1993 securities to the contemporary UTI scam, no accused was finally convicted in endless time capsule of legal proceedings.

In contrast, other countries like USA and Australia are not paragons of virtue with no corporate dishonesty or fraud but instead regimes which accept the human propensity to commit wrong but police such wrongs vigorously and promptly and arrive at a final conclusion one way or the other within a short time frame. Even before the current spate of skeletons tumbling out of corporate cupboards like Xerox, Enron, WorldCom, Tyco *et al.*, Australia had banned several directors for corporate frauds for over 20 years. Milken—a far more powerful Singaporean than the Indian Harshad Mehta was punished and imprisoned and served out his full term. Within a few weeks of the spate of accounting scandals hitting corporate America, President Bush not only formed a corporate task force but both Houses of Parliament passed a law creating a new oversight board for the hitherto self-regulating accounting industry, quadrupling penalties for fraud up to 20 years and creating a new offence of securities fraud with punishment of imprisonment up to 25 years.

Corporate social responsibility is not only about good governance and philanthropy but it is also about something more than both. At its core lies ethics—a sense of shared participation and responsibility towards not only shareholders but also towards stakeholders and to society at large.

Fourthly, reform of and a hard relook at several established accounting malpractices is a must. For example, several accountancy frauds occurred because the auditor—supposed to be an independent policeman—was (as with Arthur Anderson) also a management consultant to the same company. Earning a million dollars as consultancy fees involves a serious conflict of interest when the same person has to audit the accounts and blow the whistle on corporate frauds. Further, the power of the corporate to appoint and sack its auditor has colourfully been described as the most absurd contradiction, viz. allowing a thief to appoint the judge in his own case and giving him the power to sack any judge who gives inconvenient verdicts.

Good corporate governance is an issue as large as the universe and one can do more than perform like a fan dancer-touching upon some aspects without really covering them. The only fitting answer to Lord Thurlow's question at the beginning was provided by the French philosopher Henry Thoreau who said: "It is truly enough said that a corporation has no conscience: but a corporation of conscientious men is a corporation with a conscience."

Ethics in Business

Ethics in business is, therefore, all about injecting the core values of transparency, accountability, integrity, equity and responsibility in corporate governance. It is to ensure that corporate vehicles do not become an impervious device for obtaining individual profit without individual responsibility. But the concept of corporate social responsibility goes even further than good corporate governance. Corporate social responsibility is not only about good governance and philanthropy but it is also about something more than both. At its core lies ethics—a sense of shared participation, a sense of responsibility not only towards shareholders but towards all stakeholders and to society at large. It is all about the adoption, by businesses and by companies of a sense of shared values, more nurtured from within and less imposed from without.

It is a different matter that for every example of ethical corporate functioning, numerous corporate scams and scandals litter the legal and moral landscape. For every corporate innovation like e-choupal which leverages information technology to confer power and expert knowledge on the smallest farmer and aligns and aggregates farm output, there are numerous Enrons and Tycos. For every social forestry success story or economic empowerment of rural women by socially responsible corporate India, there are many Harshad Mehtas—symbolising the wrecks and ruins of corporate rapacity.

There are two dictionaries worth consulting by everyone to restore one's own balanced sense of reality. One is the Devil's dictionary and the other is the Doubter's dictionary. "Ethics" is defined in the Doubter's dictionary "as a matter of daily practical concern, described glowingly in commercial terms by those who intend to ignore it". And the Devil's dictionary defines ethics "as a body of rules and a declaration of intent compiled by those who have no intention of following it". The heart of the matter, regrettably, is that for all the usefulness of voluntary codes, for all the sermonising and preaching on ethics, which we may all do till the cows come home, the bottom line and end result is that without the sanction of punishment, a culture of morality and ethical behaviour is impossible to create, to enforce and to police. The United States legislators took less than 90 days to enact the Sarbannes-Oxley Act after the corporate scams of Enron, Tyco and others, an Act more intrusive, draconian and severe in penal consequences than anything India or most parts of the world have ever seen.

Truth cannot be compromised in a discussion like this, especially not one in the presence of a *Maha Atma* like Acharya Mahapragaya and, therefore, let me touch on two unpopular and unpleasant aspects of ethics in business before moving on to other areas. Few people know that the Enron investigation was triggered by three women—all Enron employees—who blew the whistle on significant wrong doings by that company. They were rightly described as "insiders" but with "outsider ethical values". They were able to do it only because of an established whistle blower statute in the USA, which gave them complete protection and immunity for revealing illegal activity. We are only now struggling to enact such a facilitative framework after the sad and sorry episode of Dubey and the highway construction industry in Bihar. Incidentally, the description of women as the "fair sex" gained greater credence after the Enron episode.

The Role of Professionals

The second issue relates to the role of accountants (and indeed also legal advisers) in the context of ethical business and good corporate governance. In old ancient jurisprudence, such professionals were described as "bloodhounds". Slowly, over the years, case law started using the milder but still appropriate term "watchdogs". More contemporary scams and collusive practices have led them to be referred to as "lapdogs". Enron and Tyco could not have happened unless these professionals cooked the books with a zest and flair which would put the chefs of Taj Hotel to shame.

There is also the much wider issue of conflict of interest, a more direct ethical dilemma. Most accountancy firms, including Arthur Anderson who were auditors to Enron, were not only auditors but also had management consultancy contracts with the company. Fees earned for the latter outstripped many times the fees paid for being an auditor. Pointing out wrong doing as an auditor is unlikely if that risks losing your management consultancy contract. The power of corporations to hire and fire auditors once led an outside objective observer to lament an ethical conundrum. He said it amounted to the accused having the power to fire the Judge trying him if the judge was likely to come to a finding of guilt. In the context of bloodhounds and lapdogs, there is an interesting story of Sherlock Holmes who reached with the police inspector to investigate a robbery which had occurred the previous night. After much investigation and humming and hawing, when the police inspector thought he had the case cracked, Holmes stroked his chin and observed: "Ah, but there is the curious case of the dog at night". The police inspector, in surprise, said, "But Mr. Holmes, what about the dog in the night. The dog did nothing at night." To which Holmes replied "Ah, there is precisely the curious case, namely, why the dog did nothing at night."

Since society no longer has the overarching vision and the spiritual enlightenment of seers like Gandhi, Vivekananda and Aurbindo and since pathfinders like Acharya Mahapragya are few and far between, we lurch from one spiritual crisis to another. Our budgetary deficits can be controlled if we have now passed a Fiscal Management Act, but our moral deficits cannot be wished away by a legislative magic. This is a deficit which encompasses all sections and sectors of our activity—from law to medicine, from media to business. Indeed, this spiritual deficit encompasses all. It has the power to control the political crisis of a fragmented polity and a fractured consensus, be it the economic crisis of transition from a controlled economy to a liberal, globally integrated economy, be it the social crisis of breaking up of the joint family support systems and structures, be it the demographic crisis of galloping population growth.

In my own profession, the words of Yale Law School Dean Mr. Anthony Kronman about American lawyers can be transplanted appositely to the Indian legal scene. He said: "The book is about a crisis in the American legal profession. Its message is that the profession now stands in danger of losing its soul. The crisis, in essence, is a crisis of morale. It is the product of growing doubts about the capacity of a lawyer's life to offer fulfilment to the person who takes it up. Disguised by the material well-being of lawyers is a spiritual crisis that strikes at the heart of their professional pride." The multiple and simultaneous duties of lawyers to his client, to the Court, to society and to his own professional standing, all of which he has to harmonise, are neither understood nor appreciated. Lord Denning, the most famous judicial icon in the Commonwealth of Nations said, "The lawyer has a duty to the Court which is paramount. It is a mistake to suppose that he is a mouthpiece of his client to say what he wants to, his tool to do what he directs. He is none of these things. He owes allegiance to a higher cause. It is the cause of truth and justice. He must not knowingly conceal the truth". Friedman puts it pithily when he said: "A lawyer's technical knowledge will supply the tools, but it is his sense of responsibility to the society in which he lives that must inspire him to be a jurist as well as a lawyer." Our approach can change only when we remember that "We have not inherited this earth from our forefathers, we have borrowed it from our children."

Enron and Tyco could not have happened unless the involved professionals cooked the books with a zest and flair which would put the chefs of Taj Hotel to shame.

Legal education has to introduce mandatory, comprehensive courses, presently too few and too far between on legal ethics. An all India Code of Ethics for the legal profession and for judges alike is the need of the hour, even without legal or penal sanction. Its very existence will deter casual violation. As Cranston put it: "All law teachers have a responsibility to give attention to the ethical underpinnings of legal practice. We have a responsibility to sensitise students to the ethical problems they will face as practitioner, to provide them with some assistance to the task of resolving these problems and to expose them to wider issues such as the unmet need for legal services."

The legal profession deals with high stakes of life, whether it is life itself, liberty, property, reputation or dignity of a person. One has to remember that the legal profession is different from business. An element of service is very much a part of the profession which is more than a mere earning of a livelihood. In fact, the famous jurist Prof. Roscoe Pound has rightly pointed out the distinction between a profession and business. He says that, historically, there are three ideas involved in a profession. These ideas are of organization, learning and a spirit of public service. These are an essential part of a profession. The remaining idea, that of gaining livelihood is incidental. This may sound very unrealistic today. But that is the difference between a business and a profession. In the old days, it used to be said that a doctor and a lawyer are paid only to enable them to earn so that they can practice their chosen profession.

A Scottish lawyer has rightly said that the practice of law is more than a mere trade or business: "Those who engage in it are guardians of ideals and the tradition of what is right, and to which they should from time to time dedicate themselves." The crucial conditions precedent for creating ethics in society is to return to value-based education.

Value-based Education

In our urge to create educational factories which mass-produce robot-like matriculates and graduates, we have ignored the farsighted and fundamental emphasis on value-based education which many eminent educationists have repeatedly advocated. Former President S. Radhakrishnan, who headed the pre-independence General Education Subcommittee of the National Planning Committee established by the Congress in 1937 and Chaired by Nehru and D.S. Kothari, Chairman of the Education Commission (described by the redoubtable Education Minister, M.C. Chagla, as "a brilliant scientist, a great teacher, an educationist of the highest calibre and God's good man") have opined that cultivation of the rational and scientific temper without moral and value-based educational paradigms is akin to creating rudderless ships.

The Indian tradition and culture has shown us the way for centuries. It encapsulates the three jewels which provide the 'framework' of value-oriented education. *Jnan*, *Darshan* and *Charitra* reflect a holistic approach, insisting that knowledge of life, of universe, of mind and of matter must lead to the right perception and the right perspective, which, in turn, must lead to right conduct and character.

The educational process is not only incomplete but misleading unless data, transmuted into a body of coherent knowledge, is then formulated into philosophy which, in turn, is translated into conduct and character. Cynics, defined by Oscar Wilde, as those who knew the price of everything but the value of nothing, have tried to play havoc with value-based education by generating imaginary apprehensions in the name of secularism and modernisation. They forget that Nehru, Chagla and Kothari were giant rationalists who saw no contradiction in these themes. There is a vast distinction between religious education, on the one hand, and education about religions or the ethical principles of the inter-faith, on the other.

We have to revisit and repackage the norms and paradigms of value-based education in the new millennium to reclaim our younger generations. That connectivity has to be established by redesigning our moral science classes to rescue them from the stereotype jokes they have become. These classes as now conducted lost much of their relevance.

We have to redesign the curriculum and make it interesting, multi-disciplinary, anecdotal and biographical—a veritable journey through the best of our history and literature. We have to experiment with new ideas and models, for example the option of yoga classes as a subject taught, which I have found in only one school in Delhi. We do not have inter-faith jurisprudence as a subject taught in most schools whereas it should be a compulsory subject. But a compulsory subject is not to be taught in an insipid or didactic manner, unleashing tons of reading material and deadening the entire imbibing process.

As Acharya Mahapragaya has said in his delightful book: "We give maximum importance to information, less to intellect and least to ethics". We have to change this sequential paradigm.

Ethics and Morality

In conclusion, I must turn to the general holistic issue of good governance, of which ethics and morality in business are only a part. For good governance and democratic governance, we need to have reconstruction of our patriotism, revitalisation of our public morality and reclamation of national character. We need to rebuild the moral fibre and the patriotic texture of our civil society which appear to suffer from all the seven deadly sins named by Mahatma Gandhi. Those sins afflict our democracy, and indeed democracies in many other countries. Those seven deadly sins were described by Mahatma Gandhi as follows:

1. Politics without Principles
2. Wealth without Work
3. Business without Morality
4. Education without Character
5. Pleasure without Conscience
6. Science without Humanity
7. Worship without Sacrifice

The crisis of democratic governance is, indeed, the crisis of character and the crisis of civil society and not merely of institutional structure. I recall an inspiring poetic prayer which reminds us that though we are living under law, the quality of governance depends on the quality of human beings who make the laws and administer and adjudicate upon them. That poetic prayer (translated) is as follows:

> God give us men! A time like this demand;
> Strong mind, great hearts, true faith and ready hands;
> Men whom the lust of office does not kill;
> Men whom the spoils of office cannot buy;
> Men who possess opinions and a will;
> Men who have honour;
> Men who will not lie;
> Men who can stand before a demagogue;
> And damn his treacherous flatteries without winking!
> Tall men, sun-crowned, who live above the fog;
> In public duty and in private thinking.

There is an endearing rustic saying, which describes the joy of the peacock in his splendorous plumage and his tearful sorrow and grief when it looks at its unshapely legs. To an extent it can be equated with the pride we have in our democratic plumage and the shame and concern we feel in our ugly feet and in the cancerous growth of crime and corruption, and in the strife and violence in our democratic life.

The crisis of democratic governance is, indeed, the crisis of character and the crisis of civil society and not merely of institutional structure.

Democratic governance has its flaws, faults and pitfalls, its limitations and failures. But it has also promises to keep, the promises of Justice, Liberty, Equality and Fraternity as well as the promise of people's constructive and creative participation. I do not know if the best or the worst is yet to come.

CHAPTER 18

The Rural-Urban Divide
The Persistent Indian Milieu

DR. P. C. BANSIL

While 'Bharat' has been predominantly rural, agricultural and poor, reminiscent of the colonial era even after the end of the Raj, India is now a notional entity, largely anglicised and relatively better-off, as if a legacy of the British.

Mahatma Gandhi said that real India lived in the villages. Recognising this, one would expect that the focus of the development strategies of the government in post-1947 period should have been on rural India. The ground reality after over 60 years of Independence does not, however, bear any testimony to the cherished goals.

Out of 638,596 villages in the country, a large number, nearly one-third (217,000) do not have access to safe drinking water. Only 55 per cent of the villages are connected by road. Rural teledensity is just 1.6 per cent as compared to 25.90 per cent in urban India (at the time of writing in 2008). The Punjab state shines with 99.87 per cent of its rural homes wired, but it is just 17.82 per cent in Orissa. The gap between the towering skyrises of affluent India and uninhabitable huts of those that go to bed hungry, cannot easily be measured in figures. Much of new India regards the other with less empathy and more scorn, and considers it to be a burden on the country's bright future. This leads to a clear realisation that there is a Rural-Urban Divide and 'Bharat' is still far behind in the race for its equal share in the development paradigm.

Socio-Economic Indicators

Despite a high growth rate of urban population (Exhibit 18.1), rural areas

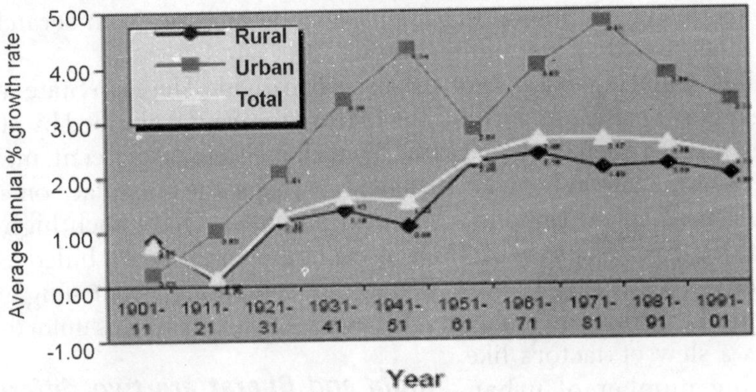

Exhibit 18.1 : Rural-Urban Growth of Indian Population

still continue to claim the habitat of over 70 per cent of the population of India. Because of the poor rural health infrastructure and resultant conditions, rural infant mortality rate (IMR) is much higher than it is in urban India. As compared with urban India, literacy rate is again much lower in rural areas. The differential is all the more pronounced in respect of the female population. A look at the household expenditure pattern shows that nothing better can be expected in near future. In 2004-05, rural households spent roughly about the same amount on education as on consumption of *pan*/tobacco and other intoxicants. Significantly, education featured way down on the family budget in rural India.

We may also consider urban/urban slum dwellers and rural/rural, small/marginal farmers. The Census of India 2001 defines slum as a compact area with at least 300 persons or about 60-70 households of poorly-built congested tenements, in unhygienic environment, usually with inadequate infrastructure and lacking in proper sanitation and drinking water facilities, notified or not under any Act including the Slum Act. More than half of the residents of India's financial capital, Mumbai, live in slums. Almost 15 per cent of all urban Indians live in slums according to the Census of India, 2001, although some recent independent studies put it at a relatively higher figure of 22 per cent.

The top 100 most populated cities in the country alone account for as many as 29 million slum dwellers. One in every two Mumbaikars, one in three Kolkatans and one in every ten Delhiites is a slum-dweller. Thane (near Mumbai), Chennai, Nagpur, urban areas of North 24-Parganas (near Kolkata), Hyderabad, Pune and urban areas of Rangareddi make up the top 10 cities with the highest slum population in the country. With over 640 cities and towns reporting slum population, slums in India are not just a metro or big city phenomenon. Fast urbanising India needs millions of square metres of additional urban space to be built up from scratch, to prevent the growth of yet more slums.

Delhi is a glaring example of urban/urban divide. Here is a State which has the highest per capita income but IMR in the capital climbed by 50 per cent per year between 2005 and 2007 from about 13 to 26 per cent, making Delhi the only State in the country—and, perhaps, the only place on earth outside some hapless regions of central Africa—to have such high and rising IMR. The steep rise of IMR in Delhi in what is being billed as the global city of emerging India, indicates that something is alarming at the core of the health system in the city. What actually explains this unfortunate trend is a slew of factors like the rising number of urban poor, a crumbling public health system and floundering welfare schemes (particularly targeted at the slums) like the Integrated Child Development Services.

India and Bharat are two different habitats living in contradiction. There is urgent need to end disparities and bring them closer.

Let us recall that over 70 per cent of rural people depend on agriculture. There are 115 million families or say 600 million persons who are getting their livelihood from agriculture or allied activities. The share of agriculture in the country's GDP, however, is less than 20 per cent. Per capita income of an average person in the country was estimated at about Rs. 29,600 in 2006-07 at current prices. This would translate to around Rs. 11,000 per capita for those getting their livelihood from agriculture. Some 86 per cent of the average income in this group with the poorest of the poor depending upon agriculture would be about Rs. 4,500—which is just 15 per cent of the average income of an average person in the country.

This highlights the real issue of the agriculture sector in particular and rural India in general. Even these averages do not tell the whole story. In the absence of an alternative employment and ever declining share of agriculture in GDP, the condition of marginal/small holders is getting worse.

The *Forbes* magazine's 2007 rankings of the world's richest people included 53 Indian billionaires out of the global total of 946. Globally, the number of billionaires has grown by 19 per cent and their total net worth rising by 35 per cent to $3.5 trillion (nearly five times India's GDP). India added 14 new billionaires in the preceding year. The combined worth of the 53 Indian billionaires was placed at $335 billion equal to one-third of India's GDP. India replaced Japan as the home for the largest number of billionaires in Asia. India's rich are marching towards the top of the rankings and now have three in the upper echelons, second only to the US. A billion plus population minus these 53 individuals share the balance of the 66 per cent of India's GDP.

Per capita income of small/marginal farmers is further reduced when adjusted for the share of these billionaires in the GDP. If the income of those billionaires and other super rich is taken into consideration, the income of the poorest of the poor will be a mere small fraction. The highest per capita income of a person in Haryana is about Rs. 32,700 and the one in Bihar is only Rs. 5,800. There are again wide variations within Bihar itself—Rs. 6,960 of Patna and Rs. 2,220 of Sheohar. It needs to be understood that even the most optimistic rates of agricultural growth can only support a fraction of the population in rural areas and smaller towns across the country, especially villagers who are semi-literate or illiterate and minimally skilled.

Add to this the issue of nutritional challenge, which is evident from the Food Security Index (2004-06) for Rural India. The index computed by a study is based on several parameters like food availability, access to nutrition and sanitation. This is different from the definition of food insecurity that is equated with food availability. The following facts revealed by the study would highlight the situation:

- 230 million people in rural India are undernourished.
- These account for 27 per cent of the world's undernourished population—the highest for any country.
- Almost 40 per cent of children below three are underweight and 45 per cent are stunted.
- Incidence of anaemia has gone up since 2001—from 74 per cent to 79 per cent in children below five and from 52 per cent to 56 per cent in young women.
- 40 per cent women suffer from chronic energy deficiency.
- 50 per cent of child deaths are due to malnutrition.

Role of Agriculture

In a country like India, where agriculture has been a way of life and continues to be the backbone of rural economy, the memory of pre-green revolution period when India was living from hand to mouth and was declared a basket case by the international community, makes one shudder. However, starting from the late 1960s, for a period of two decades, a chronically food deficit country had achieved food self-sufficiency. For some time it became a net exporter of foodgrains. However, the country was forced to import 6.1 million tonnes of wheat during 2006-07. It is now struggling to maintain the desired growth tempo to achieve food self-sufficiency. This sorry state of affairs is the result of:

(a) stagnating agricultural production;
(b) actual decline in the crop sector growth rate during the Tenth Plan period;

(c) stagnation or small increase in gross irrigated area, despite investment of over Rs. 113,233 crore from 1999-2000 to 2005-06 (Table 18.1).

While the total potential created was of 103 million ha, actual utilisation is just 87 million ha, leaving an unutilized potential of 15 million ha. Actual irrigated area according to *Land Use Statistics* was 79.5 million ha. Limitations include

(d) lack of proper seed replacement rate;
(e) deficiency in distribution and optimum utilisation of credit despite increase in credit. Total institutional credit increased from Rs. 69,560 crore in 2002-03 to nearly Rs. 180,500 crore in 2005-06, disbursement for 2006-07 was Rs. 20,300 crore and Rs. 22,500 crore for 2007-08. Estimated disbursement for 2008-09 is placed at Rs. 264,455 crore. (Table 18.2).
(f) Limitation of technology used. Indian agriculture suffers from technology fatigue. There are wide gaps in the yield potential as demonstrated by the data for 2003-05 provided by the Planning Commission *(Agricultural Survey for the Eleventh Plan, Concerns and Way Ahead, 2007)*

- Wheat: 6 per cent (Punjab) to 84 per cent (MP)
- Rice: over 100 per cent in Assam, Bihar, Chhattisgarh and UP
- Maize: 7 per cent (Gujarat) to 300 per cent (Assam)
- Jowar: 13 per cent (MP) to 200 per cent (Karnataka)
- Mustard: 5 per cent (Haryana) to 150 per cent (Chhattisgarh)
- Soybean: 7 per cent (Rajasthan) to 185 per cent (Karnataka)
- Sugarcane: 16 per cent (AP) to 167 per cent (MP).

Table 18.1: Irrigated Area and Investment

Year	*Gross irrigated area (mn ha)*	*Under Irrigated area foodgrains (mn ha)*	*Exp. on irrigation and flood control (Rs. cr)*
1999-00	78.8	55.3	14,210
2000-01	75.8	52.5	13,529
2001-02	78.1	52.8	14,552
2002-03	72.9	48.7	11,965
2003-04	77.1	52.1	12,900
2004-05	79.5	53.0	19,024
2005-06	82.6	55.5	25,007

Source: Directorate of Economics and Statistics, Ministry of Agriculture, Government of India, *Land Use Statistics and Agriculture At a Glance.*

Table 18.2: Ground Level Credit Flow for Agriculture and Allied Activities

(In Rs. 100 crore)

Agency	*2002-03*	*03-04*	*04-05*	*05-06*	*06-07*	*07-08*	*08-09*
Cooperative Banks	237	270	314	398	425	483	357
Regional Banks	61	76	124	152	204	253	259
Commercial Banks	398	524	814	1255	1665	1811	2029
Total	**696**	**870**	**1253**	**1805**	**2294**	**2547**	**2645**

Source: National Bank for Agriculture and Rural Development in Government of India *Economic Survey, 2007-08.*

The total debt waiver for fiscal 2008-09 stood at Rs. 65,300 crore, benefiting 3.6 crore farmers. Additionally, Rs. 15,000 crore were allocated to the scheme in the interim budget announced in February 2009. The amount was to be disbursed to banks and financial institutions during the following financial year.

Pumping of credit of this magnitude and debt waivers during the last 5 years have not, however, translated into either increasing production or improving the lot of the common farmer. It must be recognised that all these credit facilities in the ultimate analysis have no meaning, if these do not reach the most deserving marginal/small farmers who constitute over 86 per cent of the farming households. Present system of credit disbursement works against the interests of the small/marginal farmers. The data from Punjab (a developed State) shows that the share of institutional credit increased in direct relation to the size of holdings (Exhibit 18.2) and inversely to the outstanding institutional loans. (Exhibit 18.3)

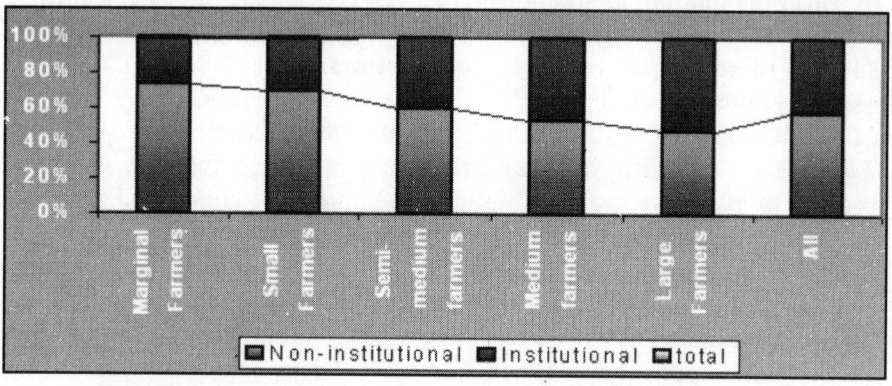

Exhibit 18.2: Share of Different Types of Holders in Total Credit, 2002-03

Source: Sukhpal Singh and M.S. Toor, in *Indian Journal of Agricultural Economics*, Conference Number, Volume 60, No. 3.

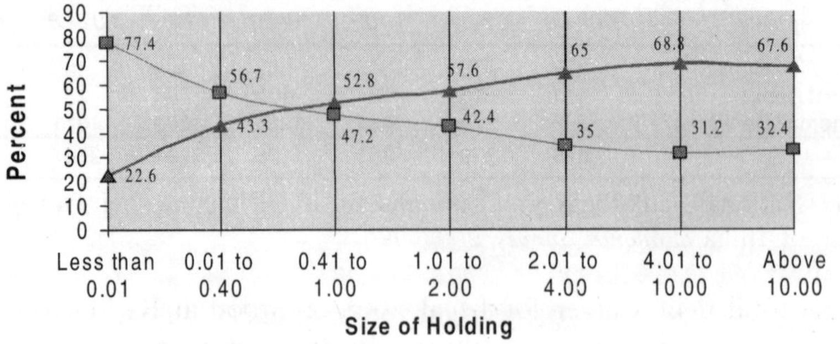

Exhibit 18.3: Outstanding Loan-by Size of Holdings

Source: Ibid.

The Punjab Case

The four-way division of Indian society has shown widening gaps over the years in diverse areas. Against the all-India picture, a peep into the socioeconomic status of Punjab (the leader of the Green Revolution) would be of interest. Inequality within households, across households and in the society as a whole has deepened in the post-Green Revolution era in Punjab. Without ensuring an upward movement of rural population, inequality among various sections of the society in terms of income, assets, education and health cannot be reduced. A study titled *Human Capital, Household Inequality and Public Policy in Punjab*, has found that there is a huge diversity in various regions of the State as far as human development is concerned.

Unless we succeed in providing additional employment (and that of quality) to the huge chunk of the underemployed and marginal/small farmers, the prosperity of agriculture and hence of rural India will remain only a dream.

Not even a single district of Punjab can be ranked high on the human development index, thus establishing that the economic prosperity of Punjab has not translated into increased welfare of people. The State has been frittering away its well earned resources on liquor and drugs. Rural Punjab has a high degree of inequality in terms of income, productive assets and household assets. The richest rural class (20%) has a five times more share in the total income than the bottom (40%) and the rural middle class (40%) likewise has approximately three times higher share in the total income than the lowest class.

Of the total productive assets, the richest 20 per cent rural population had 67.7 per cent share, the middle level (40%) 30.3 per cent share, and the bottom level (40%) possessed only 2 per cent share in such assets. The magnitude of inequality was more pronounced in Mansa and Amritsar Districts compared to Ludhiana, which dons better human development index level.

Punjab is a State where poverty ratio (9.2% rural and 7.1% urban) is about the lowest in the country. However, the data related to the district-wise poverty ratio shows that some districts in the State have as high an incidence of poverty as the all-India average. The proportion of BPL population in rural and urban India stood at 28.3 per cent and 27.5 per cent, respectively, in 2004-05. Muktsar district of Punjab had 28.3 per cent rural and 22.8 per cent urban population living below the poverty line, while Gurdaspur in the north had 2.3 per cent rural population below the poverty line and all districts of Doaba region like Jalandhar have the corresponding level of 0.9 per cent.

Prospects for Bridging the Gap

Indian agriculture today is not only fatigued, it is sick and impoverished. The situation is really worrisome and calls for greater attention. The sad experience of Punjab is a sufficient reminder of the fact that even the best programmes, if not properly handled, can lead to the perpetration of adverse conditions. For its revival, Indian agriculture needs heavy doses of modern technology so as to operate it on sound scientific and economic principles. Allocation of expanded budgetary resources alone towards agriculture administered by a bureaucracy—clearly unequal to the task—has little chance of delivering results to the target beneficiaries. Increased credit at cheap rates has also not done the trick, nor will it do. It has, on the other hand, led to ostentatious spending and unproductive uses. The farmer has invariably suffered because of the use of spurious seeds and fertilizers. What is required is a timely supply of necessary inputs—quality seeds and fertilizers—along with water at reasonable prices. Once this is assured to the farmer, he does not need the subsidies. The role of the government is to promote research and development with a longer-term perspective and to act as a facilitator, a watch dog, a friend and a philosopher. Welcome as it is, the corporate sector has made its entry with the supply of quality inputs and an assured market to the farmer. It has also created a market for agri-business professional services.

Poverty and Agricultural Development

It has to be realised that agricultural development on a priority basis is important not only for the supply of food and fibres to meet the increasing demand, but also to ameliorate rural poverty. Ironically, *agricultural development*, particularly involving small/marginal farmers and landless labourers, and the level of poverty are intensely related. In a country like India where poverty is rampant, agricultural progress and poverty reduction must go hand-in-hand. The whole strategy of creating surplus value in agriculture rests on synergising the three crucial resources—people, land and water. This is to be done through a catalysing combination of research, technology, production inputs, free pricing and marketing options, supplemental non-farming activities and public investment in rural infrastructure. Intensification, diversification and value addition are the key directional goals. Exploiting micro-irrigation potential and liberating the agricultural markets are the two leading thrust areas in this exercise.

The key to reducing inequality is not charity or philanthropy, but innovation and entrepreneurship. Poverty and inequity are worst in rural India. Any attempt to mitigate this would call for another Green Revolution programmed to drive the next wave of agricultural productivity growth on the Gujarat model (described later). Bihar and UP are possibly other States which can accept this challenge.

Exhibits 18.4 and 18.5 present the comparative growth of rural and urban poverty levels in China and India. The sharp decline in poverty in China from 1981 to 1985 was spurred by agricultural reforms that started in 1978.

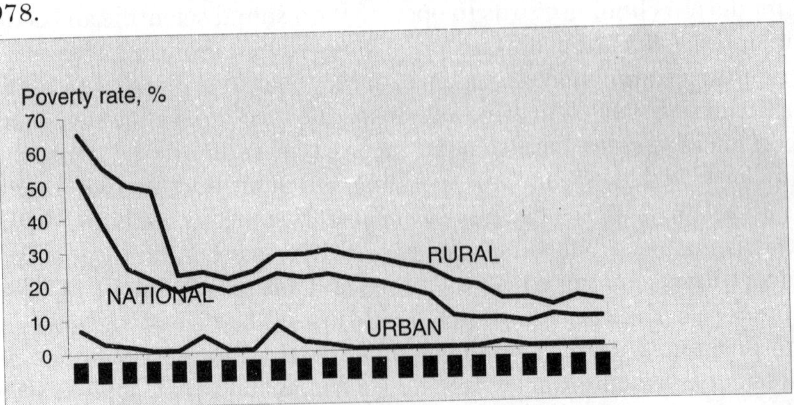

Exhibit 18.4: Urban and Rural Poverty in China

Source: The World Bank, World Development Report, *Agriculture for Development.*

In the 1960s and 1970s, the introduction of semi-dwarf varieties of wheat and rice during the green revolution period in India led to dramatic leaps in agricultural production and raised farmers' incomes, especially in north-west India. Rural poverty fell from 64 per cent in 1967 to 50 per cent in 1977 and further to 34 per cent in 1986.

A great deal of innovation, entrepreneurship and creative public-private partnerships will be required to provide affordable access to essential services to those at the bottom of the pyramid. Fortunately, more and more people are waking up to the idea that social commitment is also good business. As such, saleable business models that help the poor to access markets or essential services represent huge economic opportunities waiting to be tapped.

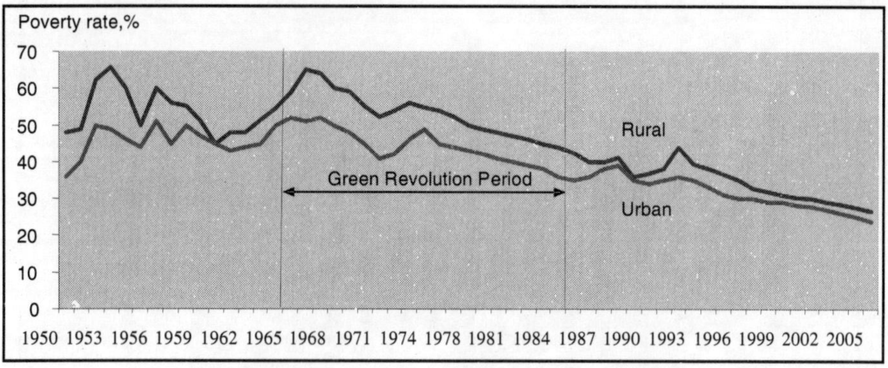

Exhibit 18.5: Urban and Rural Poverty in India

Source: Ibid.

Gujarat Model

During our search for a model, which could address the problem of rural poverty, we found that Gujarat strategy could lead us to the cherished goal of ushering in the Second Green Revolution. Though there is high volatility in agricultural growth rates for almost all States, the growth rate in Gujarat is more than thrice that of all-India, and certainly a way above that of UP and West Bengal, two large agricultural States (Exhibit 18.6).

There are three main sources of growth in Gujarat's agriculture. First, cotton output soared from 3.05 million bales (of 170 kg each) in 2002-03 to 11.2 million bales in 2007-08, primarily driven by BT cotton. Along with BT cotton, more and more maize farmers of two districts of Gujarat, i.e. Panchmahal and Dahod, took to Dekalb hybrid seeds under Project Sunshine. The farmers have registered a three-fold increase in production. Second, the State witnessed rapid growth in the high value segments, livestock, fruits and vegetables. While Gujarat's dairy success is well-known, which is growing at 6-7 per cent per annum on a sustainable basis, the recent phenomenon of high growth comes from fruits and vegetables (dominated by banana, mango, potato and onion) which have grown at almost 12.8 per cent annually during 2000-01 to 2007-08. Third, a superior wheat variety 'Lokvar', developed in Gujarat is giving much higher returns to the farmers. After a low of 0.6 million tonnes in 2000-01, production of wheat jumped to 3.8 million tonne in 2007-08, logging an average annual growth rate of 28 per cent (See Exhibit 18.6).

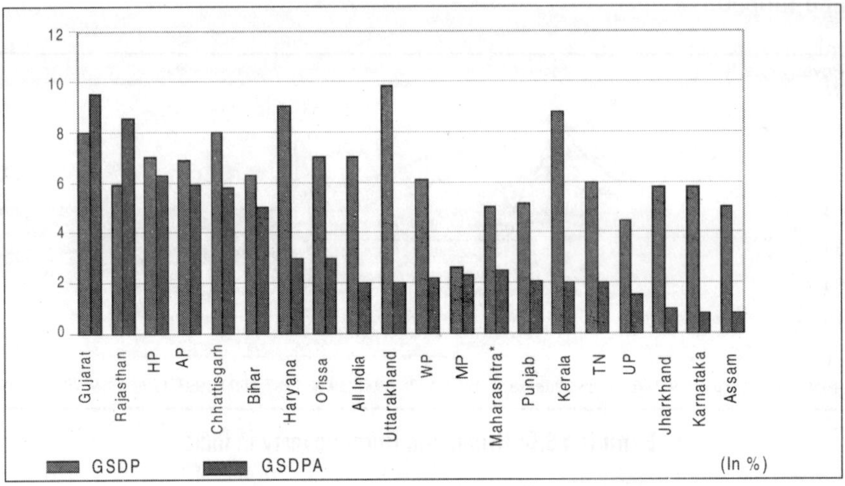

GSDP: Gross State Domestic Product
GSDPA: Gross State Domestic Product from Agriculture

Exhibit 18.6: Growth Rates of Gross State Domestic Product and Agriculture of Major States 2000-01 to 2007-08

Source: Government of India, Central Statistical Organisation.

Technology development and dissemination is a key driver of agricultural growth in fuelling cotton production, raising both the production frontier as well as farmers' incomes substantially. While the public sector has played a role in production and distribution of High Yielding Variety (HYV) seeds like that of wheat, the private seed sector has taken a lead in developing and promoting the use of cotton seeds. In Gujarat, 26 private seed companies have registered 113 varieties of BT cotton. Not only has the yield more than doubled in just five to six years, at present more than 50 per cent of the total cotton area in Gujarat has come under BT cotton.

Again a key driver is increased access to water. Gujarat is a drought-prone state, with an irrigation cover of just 36 per cent of gross cropped area. Increased water supply from Sardar Sarovar project, higher investments in check-dams and watersheds led to higher production. As of June 2007, a total of 297,527 check dams, boribunds and *Khet Talavadi* (farm ponds) had been constructed by the State in cooperation with NGOs and the private sector. Of course, good rainfall for the past few years have also helped propel growth. Concerted efforts to recharge water table, regulated electricity for agricultural use (by separating feeder lines for irrigation and other uses under the Jyotigram scheme) as well as providing high subsidy to farmers with modern water saving technology like drip irrigation, are other factors contributing to the change. Investment in water management and supply for agriculture has led to increased irrigated area under wheat, cotton, fruits, vegetables that have boosted production. Continuing investment in roads since 1990s have paid off, as there are good quality roads even in most rural areas (98.74% of villages are connected by pucca roads).

The key to reducing inequality is not charity or philanthropy, but innovation and entrepreneurship.

Another driver is the rejuvenation of agricultural research. Introduction of agricultural research systems and innovative extension services have enabled research and know-how available to the farmers. The *'Krishi Mahotsav'* programme is the latest initiative in extension services. Under this programme, approximately 100,000 government officials, from the Chief Minister to Taluka level staff from 15 Departments along with about 1582 agricultural scientists and several other stakeholders like civil society organisations, elected representatives, farmers and women spend a month during April/May in rural areas demonstrating the best of technologies, systems and practices to farmers. Such initiatives indicate a strong political will to ensure that development reaches the rural sector. Krushi Mahotsav, 2008, toured all 18,600 villages of the State, providing information and counselling on soil health, organic farming, technology and inputs, irrigation, besides infusing a new spirit of change and mass mobilisation.

Andhra Pradesh : A Case of Local Initiative

In the State of Andhra Pradesh, growth has been promoted with local level initiatives whereby seeds of Green Revolution II have been sown. As the debate on food security rages on, it is worth looking at the success of Deccan Development Society (DDS), a sustainable model with women farmers in Medak District for some 5000 women from 75 villages, 'marginalised' both economically and in terms of gender and caste, DDS in partnership with other NGOs are involved in education, watershed and aforestation projects. The initiative has facilitated the cultivation of more than 5000 acres of fallow land.

In Zaheerabad, where the average employment was less than 200 days in a year, the society brought in 100 additional days of employment. Women *sanghams* have worked on 1,000 acres, creating eco-employment opportunities. Besides, in the last 5-6 years, the DDS farmers have produced 10-15 quintals of bio-fertilisers per year, half of which is consumed in-house. The initiative also involves the production of bio-pesticides, which ensuring that everyone gets 2-3 months of employment besides creating seasonal employment in nearby villages. The society's most impressive achievement lies in pushing food sovereignty. Seed banks are run at the village level and the women earn a dividend on sales. Once achieved, DDS form of parallel agriculture is bound to grow.

Innovative Policy Needed

While highest level of agricultural productivity/production is a national goal, the more pertinent issue at this juncture is whether this alone can provide the required lift in the quality of life in rural areas. To elucidate the point, we may set the gains in the best economies from one ha of irrigated piece of land under optimum conditions in a State like Punjab (Table 18.3).

Table 18.3: Economies of a Small Farmer in Punjab

(in Rs. '000)

	Gross return	*Cost of production*	*Net balance*
Paddy	42.4	31.8	10.6
Wheat	33.6	26.7	6.9
Total	**76.0**	**58.5**	**17.5**

Source: Report of the Commission for Agricultural Costs and Prices, 2007-08.

Cost of production includes the labour cost at Rs. 4,800 for paddy and Rs. 2,900 for wheat. Adding this to the net returns of Rs. 17,500, the farmer earns Rs. 25,200 for the whole year. We are assuming that under the most favourable conditions, the farmer goes for a three-crop rotations and mixed farming whereby he earns from livestock as well. We do not have sufficient data to estimate his additional income from these sources. But under best conditions, this cannot be more than the net income from the two main crops or say Rs. 25,000. If we add another Rs. 10,000 to cover any type of underestimation, net income of the farmer even under ideal conditions cannot exceed Rs. 60,000 annually or Rs. 5,000 per month—less than the salary of a peon in cities. All this assumes that every thing is normal, which is rare in agriculture.

The obvious conclusion then is that whatever we might do to improve agriculture (highly intensive with mixed farming), an average person engaged in agriculture, particularly the subsistent and marginal farmer cannot sustain himself on agriculture alone. Not only that, with the increasing movement of the population where agriculture continues to remain the dumping ground for all the rejects in other sectors and shrinkage of available land as a result of urbanisation and industrialisation, an average person in agriculture even under most favourable conditions will become poorer with time.

This means that we have to frame our policies so that the small and marginal landholders and landless laboures are encouraged to get into occupations other than agriculture. The steps taken in this direction in the past show more or less a complete failure of the country's rural development programmes in which a large number of schemes, often working at cross purposes, are being implemented in rural India. The Community Development Programmes of early fifties through the latest NREGS along with Bharat Nirman, have sunk billions and billions of rupees without any visible impact on the rural economy or country's economy. A Reserve Bank analysis shows that the number of households below the poverty line in rural India, as indicated earlier, is highest among those engaged in agriculture. Even when fully implemented, these programmes will not provide an answer to the real issue—honourable and respectable living conditions for a resident of rural India.

If IT was the driver in professional services for India, then retail could be the engine of rural growth. But for this engine of growth to thrive and prosper, it requires a broad and growing base of consumers with sufficient buying power.

Available skills in rural areas are not capable of adopting modern technologies in any of the rural activities. We need to have a clear policy to introduce an integrated programme to cover:

(a) Micro level assessment of human and natural resource base;
(b) Appropriate training facilities for those living in the villages so as to exploit the full potential of the available resources; and
(c) Introduction of appropriate technologies directed not only to generate farm employment and additional income, but also to empower rural people to enable them to stand with pride as citizens of India of our dreams.

The *India Labour Report 2007* from Team Lease Services India points out that while only about 8 per cent of India's youths are unemployed, more than half face some form of skill deprivation and 57 per cent of them (roughly 82.5 million) suffer some level of unemployability. One of the main reasons for the unemployability is the big disconnect between what the industry needs and what the student learns through the education system. Around 90 per cent of employment opportunities are estimated to require vocational skills. But a majority of students who graduate are equipped with bookish knowledge rather than practical vocational skills. The consequence of this skill deficiency has a debilitating impact on the national economy, in addition to widening inequality between the haves and the have-nots.

For India to prosper, it must integrate its diverse population segments, especially its youth who are the future. But this can only be done if the 4Es are in place—education, employability, employment and excellence. With the 4Es will come the fifth E—economic growth. It is a daunting challenge. And the figures are staggering. A little more than half (around 270 million) of India's workforce is employed in rural areas primarily in agriculture (many of them underemployed). Of the current total workforce, 40 per cent are illiterate and another 40 per cent constitute school dropouts. Of the nearly 455 million jobs available today, almost 90 per cent require some level of skills, while 9 per cent are knowledge-based and 1 per cent a combination of both knowledge and skills.

Clearly, there is an urgent need for both quick, short-term solutions as well as long-term planning. No single stakeholder, whether government or industry, can bridge this massive employability gap. It requires a collective effort, as public-private partnerships (PPP) will be crucial. The concept of public-private partnerships is not new, nor is its application to education. In fact, the Planning Commission has endorsed the use of PPP in education. However, the new initiative calls for a new vision and a strong will for action.

While the country has witnessed increased literacy rate from 18.33 per cent in 1951 to 64.84 per cent in 2001, we still have a long way to go, both in terms of the number of people educated and the quality of education they receive. While short-term solutions, such as courses to bridge skill gaps are necessary, they are not sufficient. For a long-term impact, we need to go to the root cause and address the challenges of overcoming an education system that is entrenched in a pattern of learning by rote rather than equipping students with adequate numerical, verbal and analytical abilities. Again, this deep-rooted system cannot be changed overnight. It requires co-participation, commitment and investment from the private sector right from the primary level.

Employability and inclusive growth does not necessarily have to come from jobs alone. It can come from entrepreneurship. Take the case of Wal-Mart's *Tierra Fertil* (Fertile Land) programme in Central America. It offers technical expertise and business management advice to more than 5,000 small farmers. Producers get annual contracts at a fixed price, enabling farmers to plan ahead. With a contract in hand, farmers who are traditionally excluded by credit providers, can obtain business loans. The benefits are not all one-sided. Wal-Mart is provided with a reliable, more diverse net of suppliers. The *Tierra Fertil* model is successful and replicable. It has been exported from its established base in Costa Rica, Nicaragua and Honduras to new areas in Guatemala and El Salvador.

While there are no two opinions about the urgent need of improving the lot of the rural poor, there is a strong lobby (World Bank) against creating employment facilities in rural areas. Their worry is that more the handouts to the rural people, less incentive will they have to move to urban areas. While it is true that fields can never be as productive as factories, Nobel Economist, Paul Krugman, rightly argued that the miracle economies of South-East Asia were little more than a repeat of the West's farm-to-factory taking place over a very compressed period of time. The same is the China story. It is absolutely necessary to get rural Indians off their handkerchief plots of desperation—and lift the 100 million landless farm labourers and help them to prosper.

Factories to Farms

Urban India, like its rural counterpart, is already loaded with over 25 per cent people below the poverty line with living conditions of slums which are really inhuman. Following the World Bank model, shall we encourage the rural poors to be attracted to the flickering lights of towns and cities and add to their own miseries as well as those of the people in slums? The villager is living in his congenial neighbourhood and reasonably healthy environment. To uproot him from his family does not go well with Indian conditions.

What really is required, on the other hand, is to undertake simultaneously two independent programmes for the development of rural and urban areas. First and foremost is the need to provide social and health infrastructure both to the rural areas and urban slums. This is a must and should be independent of any other programme. Following the experience of cur Asian neighbours, Indian strategy should aim at taking the factories to the farms rather than the reverse of this. This will, of course, call for implementation of programmes for Providing Urban Amenities to Rural Areas (PURA) as recommended by India's former President, Dr. A.P.J.

Abdul Kalam. This is a programme which is germane to Indian conditions and is broadly similar to the one being followed by other Asian countries.

Any programme—public or private—aimed at improving the lot of rural India should be welcome. Lakshmi Mittal of Arcelor Mittal, for example, is finally about to deliver on his promise to invest in his home country. The plans he has unveiled are mind-boggling: Rs. 1,00,000 crore ($24 billion) to be invested in two steel plants and iron ore mines in Jharkhand and Orissa that will produce 24 million tonnes of steel annually when they come on stream. On a conservative estimate, Mittal's investments will generate at least a hundred thousand jobs directly, in the two plants and associated mines, and anything between a million to three million jobs indirectly, which will include rural areas. Add to this the plants being proposed by POSCO of Korea and the Vedanta Group and Steel Authority of India.

All such developmental activities have to be pursued in the basic spirit of the Eleventh Plan which says, 'Our practices regarding rehabilitation of those displaced from their land because of development projects are seriously deficient and are responsible for a growing perception of exclusion and marginalisation. The costs of displacement borne by our tribal population have been unduly high, and compensation has been tardy and inadequate, leading to serious unrest in many tribal regions. This discontent is likely to grow exponentially if the benefits from enforced land acquisition are seen accruing to private interest, or even to the state, at the cost of those displaced. To prevent greater conflicts, it is necessary to frame a transparent set of policies that address compensation, and make the affected persons beneficiaries of the projects.

International Experience

Even smaller countries like Korea, Indonesia and Thailand have implemented such programmes with success. There is no reason why India will not succeed. The future, therefore, lies in an optimum blend of technologies, old and new, which can lead to a new paradigm of rural development based on the principles of ecological sustainability, economic viability and social equity. The corporate sector can take a lead for such technology blending.

The problem of small/marginal land holders is not peculiar to India alone. There are around 240 million subsistent farmers, pastoralists and landless groups that represent about three-quarters of the agricultural households in developing countries. Without adequate opportunities to earn a living, these resource-poor households will be caught in a poverty trap that induces them to over-exploit the limited resources just to survive.

This is not to suggest that all resource-poor, small scale farmers and pastoralists degrade the environment. These rural households have often developed highly efficient agricultural and livelihood systems that make the most rational and conservative use of the scarce resources available to them. Traditional systems are often optimally adapted to the prevailing environmental conditions, even though they function under the constraints of marginal land, scarce capital, and virtually no modern inputs. But the sustainability of many resource-poor farming and pastoral systems can be easily undermined, aggravating the poverty of rural households and the degradation of the environment. There is thus the need to provide them with regular additional sources of income/employment without uprooting them from their homes and hearths. That a strategy based on rural small scale industries can be made to work is evident not only from experience in Punjab but also from developments in several South-East Asian economies, including China, the Republic of Korea, Malaysia and Taiwan. There are a number of countries in South-East Asia where the problem was acute but has been mitigated to a large extent.

South Korea

The experience of South Korea in this context will serve as a good example. The small agriculture holders of South Korea have witnessed a rapid rate of both horizontal and vertical diversification. The share of agriculture in GDP declined from 38 per cent in 1965 to 7 per cent in 1994 and the proportion of agricultural labour force to total labour force declined from 55 per cent to 18 per cent in the same period. Agro-industrial output is rising at an annual rate of about 13 per cent, while the annual growth rates of output of fruits, meat, milk and fish also provide phenomenal support in the form of additional income to small holders.

South Korea is a land of small holdings. However, a sound policy of rural industries fully integrated with farm economy led to substantial rise in household incomes, sharp decline in the number of farm households and farm population with a steady increase in the size of the average holdings since 1970. This was accompanied by a decline of 26.8 per cent in the share of small farmers owning less than 0.5 ha of land during the period 1970 to 1981. This trend has continued even later. As would be expected, the number of small farmers owning less than 0.5 ha of the area under total farm land declined during this period because of parts of agricultural lands having been taken over by the non-agricultural sector, rural/urban households, industries and roads.

One noteworthy feature of the policy introduced in the area of rural development in South Korea was the implementation of *'Saemaul Undoung'* during the early 1970s. Today, this has taken firm roots in the rural areas and has become the base for stable growth of agricultural production by consolidating its foothold as an agrarian, cultural and spiritual movement. The Saemaul movement has brought about sweeping changes among the rural communities. The development of Saemaul factories has reduced the urban-rural income gap through increased non-farm income for farmers and increased employment by utilising idle rural workforce. This development has discouraged the movement of the rural populace towards cities, increased financial revenues for provincial administration and created self-sustaining rural communities. According to UN Food and Agricultural Organisation (FAO), the normal income per farm household increased 14.4 times during 1970-1981, more than one-third of this being contributed by the non-farm sector.

This has brought about such a dramatic change that, while in the second half of the 1960s, an average farm household's income was 60 per cent below that of an urban worker, during the mid-1970s, it outpaced that of urban workers by over 10 to 15 per cent. In addition to the Saemaul rural factories, the policy was also directed towards greater participation of farm women in the productive activity so much so that their share of farm labour increased from 32 per cent in 1970 to 42.6 per cent in 1980.

Japan, Asia and other South-East Asia

It might be of interest in this regard to study another highly simplified concept, Network Alliance Scheme (NAS) of the Japanese model. This is being adopted with some modification to suit the cultural and social environment in Thailand, Indonesia and even China. Thailand has implemented the scheme in a bold and imaginative way.

In Indonesia, the network system called *'Bapak Angkat'* (father unit) and *'Anak Angkat'* (related units), successsfully and effectively covers large sections of industry and agriculture. As a matter of fact, Indonesia's most prestigious Presidential Awards recognise accomplishment in this kind of employment generation and value addition.

In addition to contractual networking, the *Bapak Angkat* provides technical and financial assistance, leases plant equipment and trains people. This eventually leads to higher employment and lowering of the cost of production. Indonesia's experience shows that the output-network alliances achieve a cost advantage which can be as high as 30 per cent. This is, indeed, impressive when considered along with the fact that such networks generate three to fourfold increase in employment compared to fully integrated units.

The average farm size is as low as 0.99 ha and farm families possessing more than 2 ha of land are very rare. The small farms in Java today earn as much as 70 per cent of family income from non-farm activities. During the Fifth Five Year Plan of that country covering the period 1989 to 1994, there was renewed emphasis on diversification of the rural economy, involving activities ranging from introduction of new technologies into existing farming system to development of off-farm employment opportunities.

Taiwan

Ho (1979) has shown that in Taiwan, income from non-farm sources increased from 25 per cent of total rural household income in 1962 to 43 per cent in 1975. Although total rural employment rose at a slower rate than urban employment, employment in many rural industries rose more rapidly (manufacturing employment in rural Taiwan grew at 7.2 per cent between 1956 and 1966) and led to a large shift towards non-agricultural rural jobs. In 1956, agriculture employed 73 per cent of the rural labour force. By 1966, this share had fallen to 54 per cent, with the rest employed in manufacturing, commerce and services. Further, industrialisation has not been accompanied by a concentration of non-agricultural employment in major metropolitan areas.

In rural areas, small scale units with low capital intensity predominate, establishments with fewer than 10 workers employed 41 per cent of the manufacturing workers in rural Taiwan. Fixed assets per person employed in rural areas were half of those in urban areas, the output-capital ratios were higher in some industries, and the ratio of net value added to fixed assets did not differ much from those in urban Taiwan. These facts suggest that rural-based industries used capital as efficiently, if not better than, as urban-based industries.

The impact on rural employment was particularly significant. With the labour force growing by over 2.5 per cent and the size of holdings averaging about one ha (Fei, Ranis and Kuo, 1979), increasing non-farm employment enabled farm households to combine farming with part-time or full-time employment (for some members of the household). This eased the pressure on land and on rural-urban migration. In 1960, 45 per cent of all farm households relied exclusively on farms while 23 per cent earned more income from non-farm activities. By 1970, these ratios stood at 30 per cent and 29 per cent contributing greater equality of total incomes in rural areas. Non-farm activities grew by 12 per cent a year between 1960 and 1970.

China

Rural linkages and non-farm activities are strongly emphasised in China. Although non-crop agricultural activities have always been important (especially pig iron production) they have been accelerated and integrated since the 1970s at both the private and the communal level. Non-agricultural rural employment, for example, rose from about 15 per cent of the labour force in 1957 to over 24 per cent by 1975.

More than 100 million people worked in China's non-farm rural sector in 1975, reflecting a growth rate of over 7 per cent a year between 1957 and 1975. The expansion was most marked in collective commune industries in rural areas. Trade, food processing, personal and financial services, health, education, transport, and communication—all showed above average rates of growth (Rawski, 1979). Social services like health, education, and population control, have been actively encouraged and have grown rapidly.

One unique feature of rural development in China has been the promotion of village centred small-scale industries designed to meet local production (intermediate) and consumption (final) demand locally. A second important feature has been the integration of these activities with agricultural seasons. In the slack period, much of the labour force is employed in non-crop and non-agricultural rural activities. Communes and 'brigades' run small scale enterprises organised on this basis. In the 1980s, these were largely decollectivised through the use of the Personal Responsibility System (PRS). The enterprises almost doubled in number and in the value of their output between 1975 and 1978. The subject activities were expected to contribute about half the total value of the output of the communes by 1985 (Perkins and Yusuf, 1984).

The Chinese have also gone to unusual lengths in promoting indigenous intermediate technologies in support of the official strategy. Locally developed methods, equipment and adaptive innovatives are encouraged (Riskin, 1978). As a direct consequence, in addition to the considerable intensification of agriculture, the vast rural economy not only absorbed nearly 100 million new entrants into the rural workforce between 1957 and 1975, but also raised the average number of days of employment for the entire farm labour force of more than 300 million men and women (Rawski, 1979).

Between 1978 and 1987, while the value of gross agricultural output expanded at 6.8 per cent a year in real terms, gross value of industrial output in rural areas grew at more than 23 per cent a year in real terms, while rural employment in industry, commerce, transport, and construction increased by 124 per cent. The growth of value added in industry during the recent years is around 15 per cent. This impressive growth of rural, industrial and other activities has been accompanied by a large increase in personal incomes and in the demand for rural housing and consumer goods. As a result, millions of new township and village enterprises (TVEs) have emerged to meet this demand. Large increases in rural credit have been provided to the TVEs by the expanding banking system and internal accumulation of funds has been generated in part by concessional tax treatment. Rapid growth in income in the rest of the economy (at rates of more than 10% a year) together with high investment demand (gross investment to GDP) ratios in the 1980s, exceeding 30 per cent a year have helped support this expansion.

The growth in the TVE segment has also brought about massive shifts in the rural labour force. In 1978, about 11 per cent of the total rural labour force of around 306 million was in non-farm activities. By 1986, this share had grown to about 20 per cent in a total rural labour force of 380 million.

Lessons for India

In its Eleventh Five Year Plan, the Planning Commission of India has an entire section dedicated to skill development and training. It is not by accident that the same report bears the title "Inclusive Growth" on the cover. Inclusive growth, of course, does not mean charity. Companies from all key sectors have a stake in furthering education and increasing prosperity. If IT was the driver in professional services for India, then retail could be the engine of rural growth. But for this engine of growth to thrive and prosper, it requires a broad and growing base of consumers with sufficient buying power. If India fails to grow 'inclusively', the consumers' collective buying power will erode, and the Indian growth story will fail. Inclusive growth is more than a clever slogan. It is a call for action not only for government, but also for the private sector, and people to join hands, in identifying problems, developing solutions and growing together.

Based on the position as it exists today and the international experience, one could come across any number of development models in the world, which may or may not have a potential applicability under specific Indian conditions, but could possibly be applied with certain modifications. Unless we succeed in providing additional employment (and that of quality) to the huge chunk of the underemployed and marginal/small farmers, the prosperity of agriculture and hence of rural India will remain only a dream.

The Indian situation stands out as being somewhat unique and it is imperative for us to find solutions relevant and sustainable within our own agro-climatic and socio-economic framework. What we are struggling to achieve ought to be recorded by historians as one of the greatest economic and social experiments to achieve economic growth, fair income distribution and social upliftment, concomitantly with the highest traditions of democratic commitment in which the individual remains supreme.

It needs to be realised by the policy makers that the problem calls for immediate political and economic solutions. Indian agriculture has certainly gained strength, but if farming is to emerge as an honourable and respectable avocation, immediate attention is called for to improve the economic conditions of the farmer. Small and marginal farmers will not change their farming practices and current uses of the resource base unless they have the appropriate economic incentives to do so. It would be necessary to undertake a proper economic analysis of various policy options and their impact on marginal/small farmers. All this will require relevant data, methodology and analytical tools for economic evaluation of the recommended package and its environmental impact at the micro level.

India will have to find solutions—both within and outside the agriculture sector—which are completely indigenous and germane to our heritage. The solutions will vary from region to region and even within the regions according to various agro-climatic, socio-economic and cultural situations. A number of studies have already been conducted all over the country looking into the problems of one or other aspect of this class of cultivators. It would be advisable to compile all this information at one place so as to derive some meaningful results for various policy options in each case. Since there could remain some gaps to complete the story, it will be necessary to undertake specific studies on the following aspects :

1. The present farming practices including livestock as well as non-farm activities of marginal/small farmers.
2. An evaluation of the rationale for different practices being followed by small and marginal farmers in the same area under more or less similar conditions.
3. Resource base of the farmers in terms of human skills and aptitudes and that of the region in terms of the availability of raw materials for processing.
4. An inventory of the schemes to be introduced which are technically and economically feasible and socially desirable as well as acceptable.
5. The possibility of such programme being integrated into the local economy as well as environment.

The government will then be required to develop agriculture to run on business lines, provide urban amenities to rural areas and at the same time provide them with regular employment on a sustainable basis. This will not only reduce pressure on city slums, but also go a long way in achieving our cherished goal of one India—politically, socially and economically—that is Bharat. India and Bharat are two different habitats living in contradictions. There is urgent need to end disparities and bring them closer.

REFERENCES

Bansil, P.C. *Agricultural Statistical Compendium*, Volume I, Techno Economic Research Institute, 1992. Supplement (in Press).

——*Rural Labour and Employment Opportunities*, Paper in *Challenges Facing Agriculture and Rural Development*, edited by T.K. Velayudham, 1994.

——*Second Green Revolution, Role of Corporates, Consulting Ahead*, July 2007.

——*Sustainability and Viability of Small/Marginal Farms*, Paper read at a NIRD Seminar, Hyderabad.

——*Economic Problems of Indian Agriculture*, 6th edition, 2002.

Census Commissioner, Government of India.

Chaudhri Pramit Pal, Bright Lights, Pramit Pal Chaudhri. *Dim* Policy, *Hindustan Times*, 3-6-2009.

Food and Agricultural Organization (FAO), *Poverty Alleviation in Korea*, 1984.

——*Selected Indicators of Food and Agriculture Development in Asia and Pacific Region*, Various Issues.

Fei, John C.H., Gustav Ranis, Shirley, WY Kuo. *Growth with Equity: The Taiwan Case*, Oxford University Press, 1979. New York.

Government of India. India Labour Report, 2007.

Gulati, Ashok, Ganga Shreedhar. 'Emulate Gujarat's Agricultural Success', *Economic Times*, May 5, 2009.

Ho, Samuel PS. 'Decentralised Industrialisation and Rural Development: Evidence from Taiwan', *Economic Development and Cultural Change.* 1979.

Jain, Raj. 'Increase Employability to Fuel Inclusive Growth', *Economic Times*, May 25, 2009.

Perkins Dwight H. and Shahid Yusuf. *Rural Development in China*, John Hopkins University Press, 1984, Baltimore, USA.

Pramila, B. *Problems and Prospects of Agri-business in Selected Developing Asia-Pacific Countries.* Proceedings of the APO Seminar held on August 4-14, 1992, Jakarta.

Rawski Thomas, G. *Economic Growth and Employment in China*, New York, Oxford University Press. 1979.

Report on the State of Food Insecurity in India, 2008, M.S. Swaminathan Research Foundation.

Riskin, C. 1978, *Intermediate Technology in China's Rural Industries.* World Development 6.

Singh, Inderjit, *The Great Ascent, The Rural Poor in South Asia*, World Bank, 1990.

World Bank, *World Development Reports.*

CHAPTER 19

Emerging Indian Society and the Role of the Corporate World

S.A. KHADAR

Development and Indian Society

Advances in Science and Technology and, of late, in the management processes have made a profound impact on the lives of people around the world. The technological revolutions continue to transform the work methods and processes and the quality of life. A survey undertaken in 1994 revealed that more than 70 per cent of rural households in India enjoy the facilities of a portable radio and TV. Several other dramatic developments are being witnessed in the recent years. The number of mobile connections in India has crossed the half billion mark signifying that every second person on an average holds a cellphone in this country of over a billion people. A similar survey undertaken in 2005 shows further mind-boggling developments in India.

The marked progress has been possible due to the visionary leadership which emerged from an array of freedom fighters, constitution builders, jurists, industry and business leaders, academicians, intellectuals and other luminaries and the democratically participative citizenry. India is now in the Eleventh Five Year Plan. Among other achievements, it has developed the second largest reservoir of scientific and technical manpower enabling the country to build a massive institutional and industrial infrastructure. The latest revolution is related to microelectronics and IT, which has totally redefined the working systems. It will help India to become a global economic and political player.

India has a growing middle class of the size of entire Europe's population, whose purchasing power is increasing, and which is able to sustain the growth through internal demand/consumption. India is increasingly recognised as a prospective global economic power due to its impressive economic growth rate (between 6 and about 10%) in the first decade of the century and continuing to sustain it over 7 per cent even during the global meltdown when many leading economies experienced stagnant or negative growth.

However, if one takes the Human Development Index (HDI) produced by the United Nations Development Programme (UNDP) based on diverse social parameters as a direct measure of economic development and rate of progress, India does not rank even in the first 100. The country has three-fifths of its population living without basic sanitation, one-third without safe drinking water, one-fourth with no housing, one-fifth with inadequate medical facilities and an equal number not getting opportunities to go beyond the fifth standard of education. There is a long way to go to achieve inclusive growth. It makes the country to think and introspect on low consumption levels and living standards on human, ethical and even moral grounds.

All in all, India has more than one-fourth of its population below the poverty-line, possibly due to the dismal performance on the social development front and the inability to bring in better distribution of wealth and incomes amongst different sections of the society. There is a growing realisation amongst millions in India that the recent two decades of Liberalisation, Privatisation and Globalisation (LPG) has only resulted in rich becoming richer, while the poor remain poorer despite the Indian economy registering high rates of growth. There are still millions deprived of even basic amenities (let alone the quality of life), despite continued focus on implementing measures on poverty alleviation and improvement in basic needs of life, both in the rural and urban areas.

Poverty breeds instability, disease, waste of resources and damage to the environment. Poverty leads to broken societies that can become a breeding ground for the anti-social elements of all kinds.

Inclusive Growth

The global financial crisis of 2008 hit most of the underprivileged segments of the society, while the organised sector was relatively better protected through government's support packages. Considering all this and also the need for increasing emancipation of the underprivileged segments of the society, it has become imperative on the part of the successive governments in the recent past to focus on issues of *inclusive growth* by implementing a variety of programmes and schemes to reach out to the people below the poverty line by providing minimal wage, employment, healthcare, social security, access to education and skill building facilities to enhance employability. Consequently, all the major initiatives of the Government of India at present—in agricultural and rural development, in industry and urban development, in infrastructure and services, in education and healthcare—seek to promote 'inclusive growth'. The key components of the inclusive growth strategy include a sharp increase in investment in rural areas, especially infrastructure, spurt in credit to farmers; increase in rural employment through an effective social safety net; and a marked improvement in infrastructure.

Socio-Economic Development

On the socio-economic development front, India faces a number of hurdles emerging out of historical factors, such as neglect of holistic development, regionalism, opportunistic policies and parochial approaches aggravated further by the sharp imbalances in regional development. There is an attempt by the political peers to corner the resources for themselves or their constituent interests, in which basic principles of efficiency and overall balanced development is given a go-by. This had led to agitations and demands for the division of States and resources, wherein optimisation and productivity is sacrificed. The root cause for Naxal and Maoist movements could be traced to such factors. Faulty and motivated handling by the decision makers compounds the position. These have been threatening the basic foundations of India's Constitution and democracy, of which every Indian is proud of being a participant in 'world's largest working democracy'.

There had been a marked mismatch between the aspirations of the people in general across the country and the developmental objectives. This continues to widen the gap across the board between the available resources for development and their distribution. There also continues to be a considerable time-lag between the expressed expectations and their actual realisation. The demand for infrastructure services, for example, is much higher as compared to what is accomplished, thus providing a grim picture of perpetual gap—be it in the area of power or energy or roads. Only, in the communication sector the situation is more promising with a technological leap-forward since the early eighties. The rural telephony has come in a big way in the country supported by the timely entry of the private sector.

On the international trade front, exports constitute less than 1.5 per cent of the global exports while historically, India was known for its quality of goods when in early days European, Arab and Chinese traders were trading with India. Handicrafts from India and items like Dhaka muslin were known for their quality globally over the centuries. The reasons for losing such preeminent position in international markets are not very difficult to identify, considering the current level and competencies in product development and quality assurance.

Illustratively, inflation in food items during 2009-10 could not be attributed only to global factors, it is largely due to hoarding of supplies by the trading and distribution sector. In a large country like India, any kind of effective public distribution system could only bring the required respite to the common man. Monopolistic and opportunistic outlook towards trade and exploitation of scarcity (even by creating an artificial scarcity) has been a perennial disease in every facet of trade in the country.

A billion strong India, historically known for its intellectualism and spirituality, has not been able to throw up a commensurate number of Nobel laureates. A few persons of Indian origin who were awarded this distinction have been associated with the US and the UK. One needs to introspect what could be the basic reasons for such an outcome over the last century while this should not undermine the fact that India has a unique distinction of throwing up a number of spiritual *gurus* around the world.

The so-called 'demographic dividend' of India in near future is considered a major advantage for the country backed by largest pool of English speaking and educated population. But despite the largest pool of scientific and technical manpower, skill levels are nowhere near the world standards. The mushrooming growth of engineering and higher technical institutions without proper consideration of standards have resulted in turning out 800,000 engineering graduates, of whom only about 25 per cent are suitable for employment in the current technological and management enterprises. As such, there is a kind of sloppiness in every segment of India's soft and hard infrastructure mainly due to hypocritical approach marred as it is by a lack of systems, the intensity of corruption and absence of ethical and moral standards.

Socio-cultural Developments

On the socio-cultural front as well, some changes in the society are quite disturbing, considering specially that India is a culturally rich country. It is losing its ethnic and cultural roots by imbibing so-called modern or westernised outlook in every aspect. The joint family system has glided into nuclear families with a see change in lifestyle—be it clothing, outlook towards parents and elders and even children. Social relationships have become predominantly commercial in these days of market competition. A typical Rajasthani woman clad in a veil on her face is a rare experience now, except in the interiors of rural areas. The exhibitionism and open-minded approach in every aspect has overtaken the traditional conservatism, which has its own pros and cons in regard to the value system and ethics and morals in life and outlook. This is despite the agitations and other resistance movements organised by some NGOs and political outfits, demonstrating their concerns on fashion shows, beauty pageants, Valentine's Day or Rose Day celebrations. Such things were unheard of in Indian tradition and culture before Independence. It is understood that these cultural changes are not only changing the society towards so-called modernised Western outlook, it is also encouraging attacks on the fair sex like rapes and molestations, which are manifestations of the cultural change.

It is rather alarming that the changing value system at the family level wherein a son or a daughter expects that the parents should provide, as a matter of obligation, best in life, is a shift from the culture and values that instilled gratefulness to and respect for the parents. One wonders where is our *Great Son*, the proverbial Shravan Kumar, of our epics? Possibly this is the result of the contemporary education and Western outlook to life and the set of competitive environment of one-upmanship trying to achieve success by hook or by crook. The philosophy of contentment and gratitude is wholly missing leading to the basic traditional and cultural fabric torn apart.

Despite technological advancements and innovations like the successful launch of *Chandrayan I*, the traditional mindset of the majority of Indians has not changed, be it in terms of gender equality or equality in race and religion, as evidenced by the honour killings that the families perform and female infanticide reflected in female-to-male ratio of 750 to 1000 in some of the so-called progressive States in India. This is absolutely contrary to the modern thinking and inconsistent with massive economic development through large dosage of science and technology.

Ecological Developments

The basic Indian philosophy and outlook to life had been centred on frugality and refraining from becoming a burden to the society and environment by consuming less and conserving the natural resources. Indian sages led a life of austerity and demonstrated how the right lifestyles could lead to sustainability. Today, inspired by global competition, the quality of life has come to mean higher and higher consumerism resulting not only in depletion of the resources and depriving the future generations of their share, but also damaging the ecology and environment leading to global warming and climate change, which is threatening the very survival of the planet. This vital concern was staring in the face of the global leaders who met at Summit 2010 in Copenhagen to resolve the knotty issues. They called for mutual adjustment through changing lifestyles, while developing alternative and sustainable energy sources. The efforts at Copenhagen could not yield the desired results due to rigid positions taken by the global leaders who appeared more concerned about their respective societies rather than the future of the planet.

For India, it is a matter of serious introspection that a country known for its philosophy and practices of 'austerity' should be unduly wasting very valuable and scarce resources. Despite all the teachings on conservation of resources for the betterment of future generations, the common tendency in the current generation is to be extravagant and paying no heed to conserving the scarce resources. A person from the affluent segment of the society does not know that one more person can be fed by the food wasted by him every time he sits on the dining table. An average Indian in the past used to live with a different kind of ideals and value systems. When he faltered either on moral or ethical grounds, he used to resort to self-punishment known as penance, so that he is reminded that he has committed a mistake in the eyes of the Almighty.

Socio-Political Developments

An average Indian is proud of the country's Constitution that provides freedom to practise any kind of faith, with due regard to a solid foundation for pluralism, 'unity in diversity'. That appears to be getting threatened by the rise of fundamentalist forces which are dividing the society on the assumed lines of religion, caste and creed. As such, the values imbibed in terms of universal brotherhood and humanity and tolerance are very rare these days. Such an environment has become very handy to politicians and radical religious leaders and fundamentalist organizations for their divisive politics, their ulterior motives and vested interests. This menacing issue has become all pervasive in every aspect of societal and economic functioning, apart from disturbing the tranquillity of mind of an average citizen, who is basically hard working as well as peace loving. The emergence of a host of fundamentalist organizations, which were non-existent before Independence, has led to the increasing menace of terrorism, spreading like a wildfire. One wonders how a country that believed in non-violence, universal brotherhood and which spearheaded the Non-aligned Movement and laid the foundation to the Principles of Panchshila has become a major target of terrorist attack. There is something amiss somewhere which needs to be addressed, and addressed urgently.

Socio-Legal Issues

No doubt, we must be proud of our judiciary. People have faith in the judiciary for their rational and dispassionate delivery of justice, except for delays (more than 35 million cases pending to be resolved), in which the executive too is deeply involved. Contrary to the adage "justice delayed is justice denied", the situation persists. Of late, judicial activism is in evidence by increasing incidence of *'suo moto'* issues being raised by the judiciary. However, there is an increasing evidence of the powerful and mighty getting away with non-compliance to rule of law, which has been convincingly established by the media in the cases of (i) Jessica Lal murder, (ii) Ruchika Girotra's suicide, (iii) the murder of DPS School student, Arushi, and (iv) Nithari killings of innocent children. These cases clearly establish the nexus between the politicians and bureaucracy and are pointers to the suspicion that all are not equal before law and also that there is a total apathy of the executive, the administration/police and the prosecuting agencies, in performing their tasks. In fact they take pride in that they have been able to take advantage of the flexibility in the systems and that they are privileged to do so because of their positions of power. A society that used to believe in the philosophy of 'penance' demonstrated by its sages (best example being the Father of the Nation) has undergone a paradigm shift in the mindset of the current generation and the society at large. On the other hand, a silver lining is in place in the form of two new tools, Public Interest Litigation (PIL) and Right to Information Act (RTI), which enable the civil society to raise issues of relevance to the society against mis-governance.

Societal Harmony and Tranquillity

A look at the employment scenario, which is central to the societal harmony and tranquillity, is revealing. While unemployment is about 8 to 10 per cent, it is found that underemployment is pervasive. Since a bulk of the working population is engaged in the agricultural and rural sector, there is a great deal of seasonal unemployment. There also exists discernible exploitation of the working class, especially in the unorganized industry and the organized small enterprises. This leads to considerable social discard and disharmony due to major disparities in the compensation scenario. A semi-skilled or unskilled worker does not even get the statutory minimum wages (of Rs. 2700 per month) in a popular and oldest industrial belt close to Delhi (in Haryana), while his counterpart in the State government gets about 4 times, in the Central government 6 times; and about 6 to 7 times in the organized private sector and more than 10 times in a multinational or large-scale private sector companies. Such disparities cannot be congenial to societal harmony.

The Way Forward

Despite all the foregoing problems, the Indian system functions and is progressing. The common spirit and the slogan of the common man in India is *'This is My India'* and that we (people) make it work. Possibly, this is due to the commitment and conviction that an average citizen has in making things work exercising his imagination and ingenuity and above all his tenacity to put up with hardships. This, perhaps, makes the difference between India and other countries. Possibly, the *Karma* Philosophy (put in best of your efforts and leave the rest to God) inspires an average citizen, and gives him the strength to remain calm under adverse conditions and look forward to better days ahead to put in his best. All this helps to build the realisation that the issues facing the society are neither simple nor can they be addressed very easily by the government or the civil society or any other stakeholder. There has to be a collective effort to address these issues in an harmonious and synergetic way.

The Corporate World and Societal Issues

From the delineated multi-faceted macro scenario in India, it would be interesting to examine what role can the corporate and business world play as it has demonstrated immense vitality in the recent years. It could mobilise resources through technology and managerial processes to fulfil the expectations of its ultimate stakeholders, the people of India. In this process, it will impact the environment—both hard (physical) and soft (traditional and cultural)—through its policies, programmes and practices. The anatomy of these linkages between the processes of the enterprise and the environment would reveal greater insights into the implications for the society in general and its key stakeholders in particular.

To begin with, it is essential to identify the different components of the environment surrounding the enterprise and subsequently the linkages and its impacts on the enterprise.

The environment of an enterprise consists of the following major six components:

- *Physical and Natural Environment*: Such as the quality of air, the noise, flora-fauna, the level of Industrialisation.
- *Economic and Commercial Environment*: Characterised by the quality of life of the people, purchasing power, price equation, market

mechanisms (competition), availability/scarcity of resources/goods and services, consumer awareness, the quality focus, opportunities for subcontracting or outsourcing.
- *Technological Environment :* Including the level of technological infrastructure in and around the enterprise to enable it to absorb and develop technology or to outsource it.
- *Societal (Traditional and Cultural) Environment :* Typically denoted by the values, attitudes towards work, enterprise, and involvement of stakeholders, characterised by group behaviour, degree of unionisation, capacity to absorb technology, change and innovation.
- *Political Environment :* Signified by the level of understanding of politics, its interference, influence and involvement in organizational functioning, and multiplicity of unions.
- *Legislative and Legal Environment :* Extent of compliance with 'Rule of Law', especially rules and regulations governing the enterprise concerning resource mobilisation, environment protection, monopoly and competition, labour laws, and judicial system.

It implies that an enterprise operates in a highly charged framework surrounding the environment (Exhibit 19.1). As a result, the enterprise has a host of directions to control itself in terms of guidelines, statutes and regulations such as conservation laws, competition laws, labour laws, product/patent laws, company laws, to make an enterprise a responsible corporate citizen, emerging out of the concerns expressed by the society through resistance movements, public opinions and public interest litigation. In turn, the enterprise influences the societal processes through its

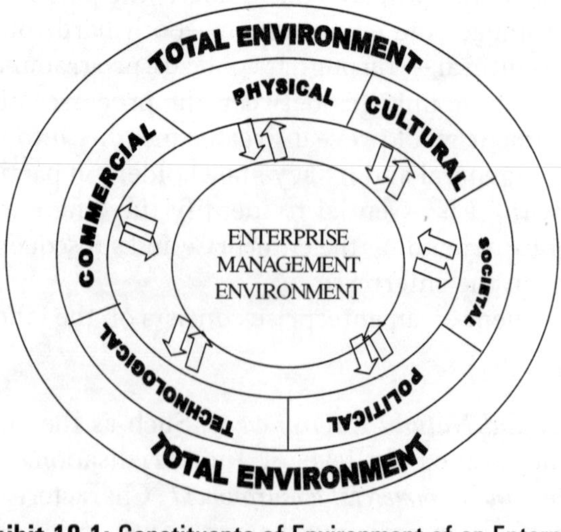

Exhibit 19.1: Constituents of Environment of an Enterprise

behaviour as a corporate entity, which includes the market. From this, a general postulate flows: management processes and their influence (positive and negative) on the societal and holistic environment and the resultant impact on the continuously evolving regulatory framework.

Management Processes and Environment

As indicated, the ethos, values, beliefs, attitudes and style in an enterprise culminate in management policies, systems and processes of decision making. As such, the decisions reflect on the use of internal resources, such as men and materials, impacting customers through quality and pricing policies. These find their way in the market through competitive forces. As a corollary, the pollution at the enterprise caused to the environment affects the society. It means that the corporate behaviour has its impacts on different facets of the total environment inside as well as outside the enterprise. At the same time, like cybernetic (biological) system, these environmental factors also influence, directly and indirectly, the other associated systems of the enterprises. However, by the time the societal components react to the enterprise behaviour resulting in the adjustment of systems, processes and technologies in conformity with social systems. For example, extensive legislation that came up for process control and safety management after the Bhopal gas tragedy (which occurred due to some lapses on the part of the management) is a typical feedback cycle of this nature. The incidence at Bhopal resulted in the MNC (multinational corporate) not only losing its credibility as a responsible corporate citizen but also the erosion of its high market standing.

Similarly, indiscriminate use of scarce resources with no concern for sustainable development would also attract the attention of the society, the government and the consumer. It would lead to legislative control and similar other interventions and may force the consumer shifting to alternate products. The recent Enron episode could be another typical case of this kind. More recently, a similar case of an Indian corporate that of Satyam Computers of Hyderabad was addressed by a number of regulatory authorities. These cases have not only put the corporate managers in the dock, but put accountancy and service firms like Arthur Anderson and PriceWaterhouse in the most unenviable position. Monopolistic approaches, including exploitative disposition of the management, are bound to invoke a sharp response of other stakeholders both from inside and outside the system.

Good corporate governance practices are essentially focused on integrity, accountability, equity, transparency, environmental responsibility and social inclusion.

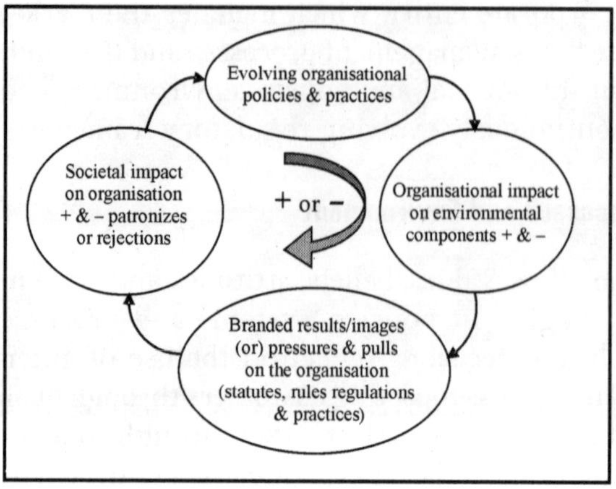

Exhibit 19.2: Enterprise and Environment

On the contrary, let us turn to customer service aspects. The Indian Airlines (currently Air India), hitherto monopolistic enterprise, was forced to compete with a host of competitors ultimately benefiting all the customers by better quality of services. This resulted in a fare-war reducing the cost of travel and the emergence of an era of value added service packages, opening up new vistas of air travel of an average user. The host of alternative private telephone service providers in India in competition with the state-owned BSNL and MTNL have made the telephone system a common man's communication system.

On the technology front, the Indian textile and garment industry, for instance, lost its competitive edge mainly due to inadequate investment in R&D and continuous upgradation of technology. Another typical case in point is the engineering industry of West Bengal, which could not renew itself on a continuous basis and lost its prominent position during the last few decades. Most of such units that have gone sick were taken over by the government to protect employment and have become a great drag on the central exchequer. It is posing to be a Herculean task for the government to rejuvenate and re-build the industry in that State. To understand how an enterprise enhances and enriches the technological environment of its surroundings, take the example of Ranchi in the State of Jharkhand, once a tribal belt of the erstwhile State of Bihar. Now, Ranchi has developed a massive technological infrastructure in terms of a number of SMEs, supply of technical manpower and very good social infrastructure. This has been supported by the huge public sector engineering unit, Heavy Engineering Corporation (HEC).

On the other hand, take yet another case of a sleepy town, Rajahmundry, in the rich agriculture-coastal belt in the State of Andhra Pradesh. It has developed itself into a medium range industrial belt due to the positive impact of the massive expansion and continuous upgradation and modernisation of a large integrated paper plant (earlier owned by the State government). However, industrialisation of that area had an adverse impact on the tradition and cultures as well as the ethnic life of the region. The industrial transformation has greatly influenced the price line of the general products and services, affordable only by the heavy pockets of industrial employees, but not affordable by a common local resident. This ultimately resulted in the alienation of a major part of the society in the region with the enterprise. All this shows that there could be a profound impact of industrial development on the technical and socioeconomic dimensions of the environment around a major industrial undertaking.

The management ethos and style and the human resource perspective determine the behaviour of the supervisory and managerial personnel. Many a time, due to autocratic style, many unpleasant situations may arise. Such behaviour disturbs the peace of mind of the employee but may have reverberations also on the family members of such employees. The ill-effects of such functioning are absenteeism and alcoholism, sometimes disturbing and jeopardising the family life, personal health of the employee. In countries like Japan, Germany and the USA, focused attention is given to the physical and mental health of the employees on a continuous basis to maintain the healthy socio-cultural environment and to ensure sustained and improved performance.

Interesting as it may seem, 'sons of the soil' based employment system adopted as a well meaning social rehabilitation policy by an American MNC has resulted in a workplace culture ridden with fights and feuds, carried directly from the class and caste-based society in a rural area of Haryana where the unit is situated. This MNC has grappled with this kind of work culture for over a decade.

The perceptible entry of MNCs in the 1990s in India had resulted in high salaries and compensation structures. This has influenced the job market and added sufficiently to the inflation-related issues. As a result, Government of India was forced to nearly double the pay of its employees through the Fifth and Sixth Pay Commissions. The effect of such a measure for the government on the fast depleting coffers was felt. This has also been affecting the investment for development both in the States and at the Centre and leading further to deficit financing. It is rather painful to observe the wide disparities in work compensation. With such disparities, societal tensions and turmoil are likely to, and have in fact, developed.

The multiplicity of trade unions and political influences greatly impact the organizational functioning of industrial enterprises in India. The root cause of all this could be traced to the management behaviour and the basic outlook of the enterprise culture towards the working class. It is basically unfair and self-centred management behaviour for enhancing its market leadership or other political gains that result in such strategies. By and large, such approaches lead to corrupt practices of different shades. A wide variety of scams witnessed in India and abroad in recent times stand testimony to this basic premise. As a result, the concepts like Corporate Governance, Corporate Ethics and Corporate Social Responsibility (CSR) have become issues of great relevance to the enterprises now.

The foregoing analysis establishes very clearly the close linkage between internal corporate culture and style and resultant management policies, on the one hand, and the total external societal environment, on the other.

While recognizing that corporate world only cannot be held responsible for the state of affairs (good or bad), there is a lot that a business enterprise can do to address these issues. Possibly, it also has a lot to contribute to ameliorate the hardships of the bottom of the pyramid classes by extending its helping hand in accelerating the processes and initiatives of government in the focused areas of inclusive growth; apart from taking on direct roles of promoting inclusive growth through its policies and programmes.

Inclusive Growth

Inclusive growth seeks to enhance social cohesion (and, therefore, stability), which, in turn, leads to market for goods and services. While Corporate Social Responsibility (CSR) efforts are usually undertaken with a view to increasing company's legitimacy (societal acceptance of a company's right to operate) or building brand equity (public relations), inclusive growth focuses on identifying opportunities—on the demand side, empowering consumers at the bottom of the pyramid by offering goods and services which cater to their context and needs and affordability and on the supply side by building capabilities among the poor to ensure that there is a talent pool from which companies will recruit manpower in the future.

The Indian economy, which has over the last six decades passed through various phases of growth, is now all set to enter an altogether different orbit marked by a high rate of expansion, combined with 'inclusive growth.' The term, inclusive growth, is finding its way increasingly in the lexicon of government leaders, economists, planners, academicians and businessmen, not just in India but all over the world. Inclusive growth is based on the realisation that human welfare and happiness at all levels is a must for a healthy human society. Poverty breeds instability, disease and wasteful use of common resources and damage to environment. Poverty leads to broken societies that can become a breeding ground of the anti-social elements of all kinds. High rates of national income growth alone do not address the challenges of employment, poverty and balanced regional development. Nor does growth in itself lead to human development. Consequently, all the major initiatives of Government of India at present—in agricultural and rural development, in industry and urban development, in infrastructure and services, in education and healthcare—are focused on 'inclusive growth'.

The government's massive efforts since Independence, especially in promoting public sector having a focused mandate for balanced regional development, did have an impact on inclusive growth. However, as the case with usual governmental systems, they are normally bogged down by typical ineffectiveness; the impact did not go far enough. As a former Prime Minister observed that less than 15 paise in a rupee earmarked for inclusive development efforts actually reach the beneficiaries. There is a great scope for enhancing the efficiency as well as effectiveness of a host of meaningful schemes of the government leading to higher convergence and effectiveness in meeting the desired goals and objectives.

Industry too has been giving some attention to this aspect of socio-economic development although only in a small way, in the form of social philanthropy through creation of foundations for serving social causes. In fact, the very existence of business is to serve the society with goods and services, which implies by itself economic and societal development. It can become more inclusive if the policies and programmes take care of the common man and his affordability of goods and services.

In any event there is now a fair amount of consensus on the fact that economic growth has failed to be inclusive, particularly in the post-liberalisation phase. The scenario changed from bad to worse with the widening of gap between the rich and the poor leading to rising figures of people living below the poverty line (BPL), the unemployed and uneducated. This has impelled the forces worldwide to work in the direction of holistic development. Now, both the government and industry are working for the betterment of the bottom of the economic pyramid. Initiatives of the government include investment in rural infrastructure, guaranteed employment and primary education as the principal focuses. Corporates are contributing through CSR, provision of employment for the less privileged ones and investment in skill enhancement of the workforce, particularly in rural areas.

A Development Policy Report in 2006 by the World Bank reveals that inclusive growth is the indisputable way to reform the regional imbalances and to strengthen economic gains. Inclusive growth process implies enhancement of quality of basic services including education, power, healthcare and water supply for every individual across the country. It has also been suggested that the stress should be laid not only on the distribution of economic gains but also on empowering people in enjoying their social life and at creating employment opportunities.

At the macro level, India has been seriously pursuing the way to make its economic growth processes socially and regionally more inclusive. The guiding principle of the government has been to ensure that improved performance of the economy must contribute to employment generation, poverty reduction and human development, while sustaining higher rates of economic growth. The Approach Paper for the Eleventh Five-Year Plan (2007-12) had recommended restructuring of policies that would facilitate greater convergence between objectives of growth and distributive justice under the neo-liberal framework under which high growth remains the core objective to be achieved through broadening the base of effective demand as well as savings. The ambitious programmes of the present government to uplift the rural society include NREGA (National Rural Employment Guarantee Act), PURA (Providing urban amenities in rural areas), Rajiv Gandhi Gramin Vidyutikaran Yojana, Pradhan Mantri Gram Sadak Yojana, Rural Water Supply Programmes, installation of village public telephones, to name a few. The aim of each of Government's leading programmes is to ensure that growth is more equitable and that it empowers the most deprived of the citizens. Employment generation is one important pillar of the strategy of inclusive growth. Towards the same end, India continues to focus on agriculture and at the same time to acelerate growth.

The National Rural Employment Guarantee Scheme

Since August 2005, NREGA provides a statutory guarantee for one hundred days of employment in every financial year to adult members of any rural household willing to do public work at the statutory minimum wage. The Central Government's outlay for the scheme was over Rs. 39,000 crore ($8 billion) in 2009-10. This programme was introduced with the aim of improving the purchasing power of the rural people, primarily semi-skilled or unskilled people, living in rural India, whether or not they are below the poverty line. Roughly, one-third of the stipulated workforce to be engaged should consist of women. The NREGA addresses the objectives of rural development, employment, and social empowerment. It stipulates that works are targeted towards a set of specific rural development activities. The scheme provides irrigation facilities to land owned by people coming under SC/ST categories and beneficiaries of land reforms. NREGA is the first programme having been implemented with IT support. TATA Consultancy Services, India's largest IT sector company had designed the software solution for the State of Andhra Pradesh.

Indira Awas Yojana

The genesis of IAY can be traced to the programmes of rural employment which began in the early 1980s. Construction of houses was one of the major activities under the National Rural Employment Programme (NREP) and the Rural Landless Employment Guarantee Programme (RLEGP). There was, however, no uniform policy for rural housing in the States.

Prime Minister's Rojgar Yojana

This programme has been designed to provide employment to more than a million people by setting up of 700,000 micro enterprises for the educated unemployed youths. It provides for the setting up of self-employment ventures through industry, service and business routes. The scheme also seeks to associate reputed NGOs, especially in the selection and training of entrepreneurs and preparation of project profiles. The implementation agencies at the grass roots level are District Industries Centres (DICs).

Inclusive Growth and Business

As indicated, of late, particularly after the onset of globalisation, industry too started realising the need to enhance its contribution to socio-economic development in the rural areas. It has also started earmarking some funds out of its surpluses and creating foundations to undertake social and community development at the grass roots level, particularly in rural India. The Prime Minister, Dr. Manmohan Singh, in his address to industry leaders on the occasion of annual general meeting of the Confederation of Indian Industry suggested a 10-point charter for industry to focus on inclusive growth as a part of its social responsibility and corporate governance :

- Respect for workers and investment in their welfare
- Corporate Social Responsibility
- Employment of the less privileged
- Resist excessive remuneration and discourage conspicuous consumption
- Invest in people and in their skills
- Desist from non-competitive behaviour
- Invest in environment-friendly technologies

- Promote innovation
- Fight corruption at all levels
- Promote socially responsible media and finance socially responsible advertising

To address the issue of upgrading rural infrastructure alone, the government announced in 2005, the Bharat Nirman programme. Under this programme, the government was to earmark a major investment for rural infrastructure in six areas, irrigation, drinking water and sanitation, roads, electrification, telecommunication, and housing. The lock and key models are aimed to provide finances to the projects undertaken on a priority basis.

The number of alliances between non-profit, non-governmental organizations (NGOs) and commercially-run corporations has dramatically increased. NGOs and corporations, as part of the growing corporate social responsibility (CSR) movement, are forming strategic alliances at an unprecedented level. NGO-business partnerships are truly collaborative, with a jointly defined agenda that focuses on a clearly measurable goal.

Ford Foundation of the US is one outfit of great historical relevance that had been supporting socioeconomic productivity and inclusive growth related issues for over three quarters of a century. Similarly, the Melinda Foundation of Microsoft of late had been earmarking billions of dollars to address the issues of inclusive growth (in particular health and education) in developing countries across the globe. In India, the Tata and Birla Groups continue to have similar foundations right from their inception, extending meaningful service to the society, in general, and weaker sections, in particular.

Business Policies to support Inclusive Growth

It is a happy development that the corporate world has started thinking that operating business on ethical lines imparts credence to corporate governance and sustainable growth and at the same time it adds value to its key stakeholders. An important aspect of corporate governance is to ensure accountability of key persons in an organization through mechanisms that try to reduce or eliminate the principal-agent relationship. It promotes economic efficiency and emphasises on stakeholders' welfare. Corporate governance exists as a complex interjection of law, morality and economic efficiency. Good corporate governance practices are essentially focused on integrity, accountability, equity, transparency environmental responsibility and social inclusion. In the increasingly conscience-focused market-places of the twentyfirst century, the demand for more ethical business processes and practices is increasing. Simultaneously, pressure is applied on industry to improve business ethics through new public initiatives and laws. Business ethics is a form of applied ethics that examines ethical principles and moral or ethical problems that arise in a business environment. It applies to all aspects of business conduct and is relevant to individuals and business organizations as a whole. Technology is central to process efficiency and high productivity. While selecting technologies, enterprises are focusing on factors of efficiency and productivity, cleaner environment, orientation to employment generation, flexibility for further research with extendable capabilities.

All this leads to the basic premise that the journey towards balancing the outcome of economic growth involves many challenges. The dominant challenges include the imperative of maintaining acceleration of economic growth without compromising on human development and sustainability. Indeed, the earlier referred, 10-point charter for the industry leaders is having its influence in the thinking processes of the businessmen, which are increasingly addressing the concerns of inclusive growth and integrating them with their business policies and processes. Examples of these are social pricing for rural products taking into account the affordability for BPL sections.

Talent Development

India, a country of over a billion, with millions of unemployed and underemployed people and harbouring a bustling economy is facing ever increasing need for trained human resources. The most effective way to convert millions of the unemployed and underemployed to trained human resource is vocational and livelihood skills training to take up the managerial and administrative responsibilities of government and corporate-backed programmes that are directed to vocational skills development among the underprivileged. They assist centres through which vocational skills are enhanced to impart relevant and latest training to improve the local employment opportunities and feed local industry with fresh talent. Training at these institutes is varied, ranging from entry level workers, such as plumbers and electricians, to specialised skills, such as beauticians and hair dressers.

There is a muchfelt need for the corporates to invest in skills of the people to fulfil the requirements at all levels of the organization by taking over and running it. Through this route, the twin objectives of empowerment of the underprivileged through education and subsequent employment and self-employment meet the growing needs of the industry.

While selecting technologies, enterprises are addressing efficiency and productivity, cleaner environment, orientation to employment generation, flexibility for further research.

In a conference on Inclusive Growth and Industry organised by CII (Confederation of Indian Industry) one of the industry leaders, Mr. Dhruv M. Sawhney, observed that corporate have a very important role to play in fostering inclusive growth and in keeping with the government's vision of India at 75. Indian industry had taken upon itself to impart vocational and educational training to 315 million people all over the country. The Director General of CII, commented that imparting training and skills was crucial to any inclusive growth initiative and CII has been working in this direction and has undertaken a number of projects on skill development.

In fact, each sector has immense potential in its respective field. The State can provide enabling environment and space; business sector can solve the financial problems for the government's agenda of development; and NGOs can also be involved to implement the development agenda of government more economically, efficiently and effectively at the grass roots level. The time has come to forge a greater interface between the public and the private sectors in a wide range of activities in the country. The Public-Private Partnership (PPP) for social development can be built on the strengths of these sectors.

Corporate Social Responsibility (CSR)

In broad terms, CSR relates to responsibilities that corporates (or businesses) have towards society within which they operate. In the past few years, as a consequence of rising globalisation and pressing ecological issues, the perception of the role of corporates in the broader societal context within which it operates, has been altered. Stakeholders (employees, community, suppliers and shareholders) today are redefining the role of corporates taking into account the broader responsibility towards the society and environment, beyond economic performance, and trying to ensure that they are conducting their role in an ethical and socially responsible manner. The new set of ethics for corporate decision making arises from the fact that a business enterprise derives several direct and indirect benefits from society. The Indian society which is divided into various segments by both economic and non-economic factors also requires the utmost attention of the corporates to grow as a whole towards inclusive growth. Accordingly, it has become mandatory for Indian enterprises to report on the achievements on CSR and its impact in the annual reports to the shareholders. It is increasingly noticed that Indian enterprises are beginning to set apart funds to the tune of up to 3 per cent of the profits generated during a year to be utilised for supporting the CSR activities.

Corporate social responsibility, as pointed out earlier, is not new to

Indian companies and several business houses have been spearheading community initiatives even before Independence. A simple Google search will show that some of India's finest business houses—the Tatas, the Birlas, ACC, Bajaj—were giving back to the community much before the term CSR found its way into boardroom lexicon. Philanthropy was the biggest driver of community programmes. The other reason companies would initiate welfare schemes was the publicity it attracted for their promoters. In the past two decades, however, the whole concept of giving back to the society has undergone a sea change, both in terms of the scope of activity and for different set of reasons that drive CSR. Companies are no longer doing it simply to grab headlines or for the "feel-good" factor, it is also because of the needs of globalisation. Today, social responsibility is more about how companies align their values and move towards a social cause taking into account the investors, suppliers, regulators, employees and the society as a whole. Simply put, CSR today is basically linked to the broader issue of total corporate governance.

There is no standard approach to social responsibility and the model a company adopts will depend largely on the kind of objectives it seeks to achieve. A company entering a new market, for instance, will regard CSR as an image-building strategy in its bid to minimise the risk associated with investing in a geography or product line, and to capture a big slice of the market. Often, it will include its CSR in its advertising and align it to its social marketing activities. Some businesses have even been known to collaborate with not-for-profit organizations to achieve the objects.

There are companies that are fairly well established, but for which long-term sustainability of business is the prime objective. Their chief concerns typically are sustainability of production, assured supply of inputs and stability of the socio-political environment. The second concern is accentuated if the company is operating in a new territory or country. An example of this brand of CSR is ITC Ltd.'s *e-choupal* initiative, which leverages information technology to empower the farmer, a critical link in the company's supply chain. In a sense, ITC's social initiatives in this area function both as a philosophy (for its ability to strengthen the hands of the cultivator) and as a strategy (to ensure long-term supply of inputs for its operations).

Another school of corporate thought believes that an enterprise does not exist merely for engaging in a profitable business, but also assumes the role of a public institution. The CSR thrust of such an entity is a high degree of accountability and transparency. It places special emphasis on social and environmental investment. The Tata Group is one such example. The business house is one of the few in the country to draw up a CSR budget every year and to prepare programmes, such as creating a safe haven for Siberian cranes, contributing to the arts and other things that have little to do with its business activities.

Clean Management Processes and Green Productivity

An enterprise basically strives to fulfil the requirements of its customers and, in turn, to satisfy the stakeholders and the society that surround it. In respect of its customers, the focus is to provide best of products and services at affordable prices, serviced through internal customers (employees) who would like to derive best satisfaction that they cherish and become responsible and proud members of the society and at the same time realise their hidden potentials. Shareholders expect reasonable returns, good image of corporate governance and recognition as a responsible corporate citizen, while suppliers and vendors ask for reasonable compensation within the promised time including continuous support in their development. The market and its players expect a constructive and cooperative competition (cooptation) to maintain market stability and growth. The society demand adequate attention to conservation, protection of environment, balanced regional development, preserving culture and tradition and in addition lending a helping hand in the developmental initiatives of government for inclusive growth.

The management processes that ensure the foregoing objects in an integrated way could be termed as Green Processes and the underlying concept as Green Productivity, ensuring sustainable development in totality. The Green Productivity primarily focuses on the triple bottom line aspects of productivity, first Profitability for the investors, second the People, represented by employees and the society at large demanding social fairness in terms of equitable sharing of the gains of development and growth with all the stakeholders of the enterprise, and lastly, the Planet, seeking protection of its ecology and environment for the societal sustenance. To achieve this, the management practices and techniques would attempt to minimize the adverse societal impact. The recognised standards are :

1. Customer feedback and education
2. ISO 9000/HACCP/TQM and Benchmarking
3. ISO 14000/GRI
4. SA 8000/OHSAS
5. Corporate Governance and Ethics/AA1000
6. Corporate Citizen/Corporate Social Responsibility/Global Compact/ISO 26000

These standards call for value-based management and human-centred management, sustainable development (conservation of scarce resources and cultures), R&D and design for excellence, inclusiveness, spiritual outlook to development and management.

All these practices form essentials of good management strategy that enables an enterprise to go GREEN. When these practices are seriously pursued to the core by the managements of the corporates, it is bound to ameliorate the intensity of the identified issues of concern.

International Standards

Unlike in the West, where it percolates down to the SME, in India, the CSR practices are confined to the larger companies. It is still generally equated with philanthropy at the level of the small business. At best, the small organizations use it as a standard mechanism for retaining jobs, trade and investment. This has provided fuel to the argument favouring to make CSR standards mandatory.

Considering the significance of the new concept, international bodies like UN, ISO and Accountability International, have evolved some guidelines and standards to facilitate managements to focus on the issues of environmental and social concerns. Four of such guideline-based standards are (i) United Nations Global Compact that encourages businesses worldwide to adopt sustainable and socially responsible policies, and to report on their implementation; (ii) ISO Global Social Responsibility Standard (ISO 26000) (this merges the earlier SA8000 Guidelines) the goal of which is to encourage organizations all over the world to change their operating practices to improve their environmental and social impacts; (iii) GRI, that produces one of the world's most prevalent standards for sustainability reporting—also known as ecological footprint guidelines; (iv) The AA1000 series are principle-based standards for helping organizations become more accountable, responsible and sustainable. They are for use by any type of organization from multinational businesses to SMEs, governments and civil society organisations. These standards are developed through multi-stakeholder consultation processes which ensure that they are written for those they impact, not just those who may gain from them.

Partnership Models for Promoting Inclusive Growth

The government provides a variety of concessions and incentives to attract industry to the backward and less-developed hinterland. In fact, this resulted in faster spread and growth of industry through establishing large number of industrial estates, industry clusters across the length and breadth of the country apart from locating large public sector and private enterprises evenly as a policy initiative for regional development—even at the cost of productivity and economies of scale. This, no doubt, brought development closer to the backward and rural areas. It is further compounded by the fact that industry and business adapted villages and blocks for infrastructure development, which has wide ranging impacts on individuals, households and communities both in terms of income and other quality of life indicators. Economic benefits, such as increased income, employment, productivity gains, better income distribution and opportunity for diversification are obvious. Social benefits include time savings, school enrolment levels, access to health services, environmental improvement, skill development, capacity building, improved information and gender impacts. The government has often performed poorly in providing and maintenance of infrastructure. Industrial enterprises and large business houses as well as public sector undertakings (PSUs) have been adopting villages in a big way. Even auto-ancillaries of Maruti and Hero Honda (at SME level) are found to take such initiatives *via* village level adaptations for development of infrastructure that would result in inclusive growth.

Through PPP, the advantages of the private sector—innovation, access to capital resources, knowledge of technologies, managerial efficiency, and entrepreneurial spirit—are combined with social responsibility, environmental awareness and local knowedge of the public sector.

The self-help groups guarantee microcredit for financial security. Finance being the backbone of an economic activity has been kept in focus through constant efforts made by the banking industry as a whole. All commercial banks, Regional Rural Banks (RRBs), State cooperative banks, central cooperative banks and primary agricultural cooperative societies participate in infrastructure development projects in the rural areas.

All these programmes are further reinforced by several poverty alleviation initiatives of government. They aim to improve the capacity and opportunities for the poor to achieve sustainable livelihoods.

Four Pillars of Social Development

There are four aspects to focus on, the first being social empowerment and institution building. This is to empower the poor by helping to organize themselves into Self-Help Groups (SHGs) and federate into higher levels of institutions, such as Village Development Committees (VDCs), cluster-level organizations, and producer collectives. The second is the livelihood investment support. This is to develop the capacity of SHGs to start livelihood initiatives and to strengthen their business operations through producer-based federations. Mechanisms to identify and support innovative approaches to help the rural poor to organize themselves around livelihood based businesses also support this component. The third aspect is the employment promotion support. The objective is to enable the project beneficiaries to capture new employment opportunities arising out of the overall growth of the Indian economy through the establishment of a structured mechanism for skill development and job creation. Finally, the fourth aspect is the implementation support from government as well as industry. This is to facilitate various measures of governance, implementation, coordination, learning, and quality enhancement for the holistic improvement in the standard of living of the poors. As mentioned earlier, public sector undertakings PSU are in the forefront to support the above strategies of inclusive growth embracing the rural poor or weaker sections of the society especially the deprived classes.

Business and Civii Society Partnership

NGOs help to support the industrial development by ensuring community participation in the developmental processes. The community today needs external agency intervention in the alleviation of many social problems like poverty, disease, unemployment, lack of community understanding and harmony, homelessness and eco-development programmes. By identifying the needs of the community, the NGOs are able to understand the social needs of the people and enable them to intervene in the prevailing social issues and finding solutions. Integrated community investment strategies align internal community-related issues and link business goals with community needs. The NGOs existing within an industrial location and closer to the community can better act as moderators and facilitators in the realisation of the social needs and better environmental protection. This has given birth to symbiotic sustainability model which is based on mutuality of interests between NGO and industry.

The current trend for the industry is to float an NGO or a foundation with the surpluses that can be earmarked or network with an ongoing NGO to undertake societal development activities under the broad umbrella of CSR and inclusive growth. Companies and NGOs are increasingly forming partnerships to address issues concerning the global society. Companies are partnering with NGOs to gain and build expertise in policy matters relating to the well-being of the society. NGO's engagement can help a company to tune in with and be responsive to societal and environmental issues and concerns. NGOs and corporations, as part of the growing movement, are forming strategic alliances at an unprecedented level.

Public-Private Partnership (PPP) describes a spectrum of possible relationships between public and private sectors, especially for cooperative development of infrastructure services. Private sector may include private businesses, NGOs and community-based organizations (CBOs). Through PPPs, the advantages of the private sector—innovation, access to finance, knowledge of technologies, managerial efficiency, and entrepreneurial spirit—are combined with social responsibility, environmental awareness and local knowledge of the public sector. These programmes involve a contract between a public sector authority and a private party, in which the private party provides a public service or project and assumes a substantial financial, technical and operational risk in the project. These moves have given impetus to new interactions and institutions, blurring old boundaries and creating new configurations of power and resistance.

Future Directions

An enterprise management having the right understanding of the delicate linkage between its behaviour with environmental components only can formulate and practise suitable management methods that would make it to be a useful and responsible corporate citizen or a Green Company in the eyes of the society. Apart from orienting the current generation of managers to these concepts and practices, it is essential to invest in the future managers by integrating the cleaner management technologies in the educational curricula of the management institutions world over with a view to proliferating these concepts and practices to ensure sustainable development.

The management education and management development activity at enterprise level should address these issues more seriously in their pursuit to catalyse the current and future managers to the emerging needs of total societal/stakeholder satisfaction through Green Management processes (and technologies) ultimately leading to balanced and inclusive developmental contribution by the enterprise.

REFERENCES

Asian Productivity Council, *Green Productivity Work Book* (March 2000).

Asian Productivity Council, *Proceedings Second APO World Conference on Green Productivity* (Manila, December 2002).

Dholakia, J.R., *Perspectives on Inclusive Growth in India.*

Felipe, Jesus, *Inclusive Growth, Full Employment and Structural Change: Implications and Policies for Developing Asia.*

Gandhi, P. Jegadish, *Inclusive Growth In Globalised India—Challenges and Options.*

Khader, S.A., *Developing a Green SME*, in *Yojana* December 2003, Planning Commission Publication, Government of India.

Lynn, Johannson, *Green Productivity (GP): An Approach to Sustainable Development.* APO document presented at World Summit on Sustainable Development, September 2002.

Majumdar, N.A., *Inclusive Growth-Development Prospectives in Indian Economy.*

Mahendra Dev and S. Mahendra Dev, *Inclusive Growth in India—Essays on Agriculture, Poverty, and Human Development.*

Mita, Prof. Kazutomi, *Eco-business Market Development in New Evaluation Methodology,* 2002.

Royston, Prof. Michael, *Pollution Prevention Pays* (PPP Approach to Environment Management), IMI Publication, Geneva, 1980.

Salim, Prof. Emil, *Asia—The Challenge of Sustainability;* (Keynote Address at APO World Conference, 2002).

Singh, Ram Uddeshya and Thakur, Anil Kumar, *Inclusive Growth In India.*

Thian Guan, Dr. Peck, *Green Productivity for SMEs—Singaporean Experience,* 2002.

UNEP, Paris, *Sustainable Consumption and Cleaner Production: Global Status,* 2002.

CHAPTER 20

Transformation of the Indian Economy from Captivity into Freedom

D.N. PATODIA

The Perspective of Restraints

India obtained political freedom in 1947 and the process of economic planning started in 1950. With the historic backdrop of exploitation by the former rulers and influenced by the Soviet Union, India, under the leadership of Jawaharlal Nehru, decided to adopt a socialist pattern of development heavily controlled by the State. And in the process of planning, measures were adopted from the very beginning to expand state control over various economic activities and to restrict the operations of free enterprise.

Under the Industrial Development and Regulation Act of 1951, setting up of a new industrial unit or even expansion of the existing ones was not permitted without obtaining a prior licence. After taking over the Aviation Sector, Life Insurance was nationalised in 1956. By relying more on self-reliance and import substitution, India kept herself away from international competition and remained completely cut off from technical progress in the rest of the world. On the pretext of developing heavy industries, agriculture was ignored and neglected. Food shortage and famines became the routine features necessitating import of foodgrains year after year. With a heavy strain on foreign exchange resources, import of all items other than food, fertilizers and petroleum, was severely restricted.

When Mrs. Indira Gandhi took over in 1965 as the Prime Minister, economic policies shifted further left causing severe bottlenecks to economic growth. More stringent measures were adopted. Banks were taken over in 1969. Many key sectors of the economy including Insurance and Mining, as also several major commodities of foreign trade were brought under state control. Private sector operations were further marginalised.

The period between 1965 and 1979 was marked by economic stagnation. Growth in GDP was confined to 3.4 per cent per annum and rising government expenses were financed through deficit financing. Import tariffs were raised to an average of around 100 per cent, in some cases going up to 200 per cent. Taxes on income and wealth were raised to such prohibitive levels that beyond a particular slab the consolidated personal tax payable exceeded the amount of total income.

It was an era of perennial shortages, most items of necessity were in short supply. Rice, wheat and sugar were rationed. So were cement, kerosene and petrol. A recommendation at governmental level was needed even to get a telephone connection or a two wheeler.

Food famines and hunger deaths were a common feature. Under the heavy pressure of growing food shortages, several reforms were introduced in agriculture, leading to the Green Revolution (1966-1980) which, fortunately, relieved the country from repeated food famines. Production of foodgrains increased from around 80 million tonnes to 120 million tonnes but the pace of growth tapered off after 1980.

In 1985, when Rajiv Gandhi took over as the Prime Minister, the economy was already in a poor shape. Some half-hearted measures were adopted but they failed to create any meaningful impact. While several other underdeveloped countries in Asia, including some in our neighbourhood, adopted market-led liberal policies and made phenomenal progress, India failed to make any substantial progress and was left behind.

The Crisis and Economic Reforms

By 1991, the economy deteriorated still further facing a deep crisis. In a space of two years prior to 1991, four governments changed hands. Inflation was soaring high at 18 per cent and foreign exchange reserves fell down to US$ 1.1 billion, enough only to meet about two weeks of country's exchange requirements. On the brink of default, India was compelled to mortgage her gold reserves in order to meet her international commitments. Under such a threat of economic collapse, Mr. P.V. Narasimha Rao took over as Prime Minister with Dr. Manmohan Singh as his Finance Minister. Facing the crisis, realising its gravity and the need for immediate action, they decided to act and they acted fast. Bold decisions were taken and major reforms were introduced.

- Industrial licensing was nearly scrapped.
- Several sectors earlier reserved for the state sector were thrown open to the private sector to compete.
- Tariffs and taxes were reduced.
- Procedures for conforming to regulations were simplified.
- International trade was liberalised.
- Rupee was devalued.

The results were instantaneous and magnetic. Economy responded fast with GDP growth increasing from 1.4 per cent to 5.4 per cent and within 20 months inflation was brought down to 7 per cent. Foreign exchange reserves rose to US$ 5 billion. In simple words, the crisis was successfully managed.

After reforms, India assumed a totally new concept of economic development. In the subsequent years, in spite of changes in the government, the process of liberalisation continued and many more economic reforms were introduced.

- Administered Price Mechanism (APM) was abolished.
- Basic reforms were introduced in the telecommunication and related sectors.
- Foreign investment was significantly liberalised and FERA (Foreign Exchange Regulation Act), a major irritant, was repealed.
- In a major departure from earlier policies, it was decided to start disinvestment in public sector enterprises.
- Fiscal Responsibility and Budget Management Act (FRBM) was introduced in 2003 and enacted in 2004 to bring fiscal discipline in the budget.
- Taxes were further brought down to the levels prevailing in other countries. Gift tax was abolished.
- VAT (Value Added Tax) was finally introduced to eliminate multiple taxes on goods and services.
- Major projects to promote infrastructure, particularly, construction of highways, rural roads and rural housing, were taken up on a higher level.
- Labour laws, for the first time, were marginally reformed. The need for downsizing the Government was recognised.
- With a view to promote the basic rights of the citizen, Right to Information Act and Employment Guarantee Act were adopted. It

was decided to include basic education in the list of fundamental rights.

A Wholesome Transformation

Pace of economic growth continued to rise and got further accelerated to 8.5 per cent in 2003-04. Production increased all-round. The earlier nightmare of shortages, plaguing the Indian economy for decades, finally disappeared yielding place to an economy of abundance. Basic services including telephones, airlines and banks improved, reducing cost and improving efficiency. Number of telephone connections increased from 15 million in 1996-97 to over 600 million today. In the telecommunication sector India has assumed an unique leadership in the world. Sale of television sets exceeded 1.2 million in 2008. Number of passengers travelling by airlines increased from 10 million in 2002 to 71 million today. As against a tiny production of nearly 40,000 passenger cars confined to only 3 producers in earlier years, India today is flooded with automobile giants from all over the world producing and selling over 1.4 million passenger cars every year. Production of two wheelers has, similarly, multiplied from 1.8 million in 1991 to 8.4 million now.

Facing the crisis, realising its gravity and the need for immediate action, they decided to act and they acted fast. Bold decisions were taken and major reforms were introduced. The results were instant and magnetic.

The Indian economy has, for the first time, crossed US$ 1 trillion mark contributing 12 per cent to the world's economic growth. Foreign trade registered an impressive growth with exports closing to US$ 200 billion and foreign exchange reserves exceeding US$ 250 billion. Savings and investments have shown a remarkable rise from around 23 per cent in 2001-02 to nearly 36 per cent in 2007-08. Capital market has been considerably strengthened and mutual fund concept has emerged as a major instrument of savings and investment managing assets worth Rs. 500,000 crore.

With rising income, India today is a robust market comprising 300 million middle income persons equal to the size of the population of the USA. At the growth rate of 8 per cent, India, now is the second fastest growing country in the world. Released from the shackles of the past and waking up in the new dawn of economic freedom, the Indian corporate sector has emerged as the prime engine of growth contributing extensively in the process of development. Growing domestically and bringing foreign investment in a big way, around US$ 25 billion in 2007-08, Indian enterprise has, at the same time, also been moving out and spreading around the world establishing new enterprises and participating in major global operations, as demonstrated by several mega deals successfully negotiated including that of the Tatas taking over Corus Steel and Jaguar Automobiles and the other in which L.N. Mittal took over Arcelor to become the largest producer of steel in the world.

And yet, regardless of all these achievements, impressive as they are, looking at the overall performance on a wider scale, it is quite disturbing to see that the growth has generally been urban-centric, lopsided, and confined to trade, industry and services. Agriculture and rural sectors which are the heartland and backbone of the India's strength have been ignored leading to still greater disparity between the urban and the rural India. While the urban sector has been immensely benefited, it is a poor reflection on India's performance that 60 years after Independence we still have 22 per cent of our population living below the poverty line and nearly 300 million of our people living in the rural areas remain isolated from the mainstream of development, deprived of even the elementary needs like education, healthcare and clean drinking water. They still have no access to expanding employment opportunities, growing services sector and to vocational training programmes.

Released from the shackles of the past and waking up in the new dawn of economic freedom, the Indian corporate sector has emerged as the prime engine of growth contributing extensively in the process of development.

This dichotomy of widening gulf between urban and the rural must end before it assumes a more alarming proportion. The unfinished agenda of economic reforms must now address these fundamental issues. The menace of poverty has to be removed to transform our vast land into a progressive and resourceful nation. With this objective in view, a few thoughts on unfinished agenda may now be delineated.

Agriculture and Rural Sectors

Agriculture is the main stay of the Indian economy. It supports 50 per cent of India's population and contributes 18.5 per cent of GDP. Some 52 per cent of workforce is employed in agriculture and allied activities. It is a major source for industrial inputs, as also a major consumer of industrial outputs. Yet, in the course of 60 years of planning, agriculture and rural development have been grossly neglected. Growth of agriculture declined from an average of 5 per cent around 1991-94 to 3.8 per cent in 2006-07 and further down to 2.7 per cent in 2007-08. Production of foodgrains has stagnated, for the last 10 years, at around 210 million tonnes. Per capita availability of foodgrains declined from 495 gm per day in 1995 to 420 gm per day in 2005. Productivity in India is amongst the worst in the world and is only half of that in China. India is the largest producer of vegetables and the second largest producer of fruits. Yet, nearly 40 per cent of fruits and vegetables produced here are destroyed for want of adequate transport and storage facilities. Other areas, related to rural development, particularly education, healthcare and employment opportunities, which are equally vital for development, have also been grossly neglected.

This dichotomy of widening gulf between urban and the rural must end before it assumes a more alarming proportion. The unfinished agenda of economic reforms must now address these fundamental issues.

Speaking in October 2007, Prime Minister Dr. Manmohan Singh confessed: "I admit that there was a relative neglect of investment in agriculture, education and healthcare. Agriculture and employment generation can be ignored at our own peril". After suffering near stagnation for such long period, agriculture has lost its dynamism. It now needs a second Green Revolution on a wider scale directed towards greater diversification, higher productivity and improved quality. It will have to be supported by adequate supply of power and irrigation and supplemented by post harvest infrastructure, particularly storage, transportation and marketing.

Other reforms needed for economic development, which have not so far been adequately addressed, but are vital, are physical and social infrastructures, power, irrigation, interlinkage of rivers and fiscal reforms.

Issues of Continuing Concerns

For development of the rural and the urban sectors alike, growth of infrastructure is indispensable. On this front, with the exception of construction of roadways and houses on a moderate scale, other areas including power and irrigation need greater attention.

Shortage of power is a perennial feature in India and at the existing generating capacity of around 134,000 MW the country has a huge deficit of 14.8 per cent at peak availability. The targets fixed are never achieved in time resulting into heavy time and cost overruns. Transmission losses are heavy. In the year 2006-07, losses in the State-owned units alone amounted to over Rs. 28,000 crore. On the front of social infrastructure such as education, healthcare and fresh drinking water, the condition of rural India could be termed pathetic. The schools are still

After suffering near stagnation for such long period agriculture has lost its dynamism. It now needs a second Green Revolution on a wider scale directed towards greater diversification, higher productivity and improved quality.

without teachers, healthcare centres without doctors and villages without safe drinking water. Resources are wasted. Teachers and doctors are not paid on time and many do not attend their work. Corruption is rampant.

Lack of adequate irrigation facilities is another major problem of agriculture in India. Against assessed potential of irrigation of about 140 million hectares, only 74 per cent has so far been utilised. It needs to be augmented by improving water management, creating storage facility for flood waters applying advanced technology and introducing inter-basin transfers.

Related to water management is also the issue of extensive damage caused to agriculture due to excessive floods, on the one hand, and frequent droughts, on the other. By adequate management of river waters, it will be possible to prevent floods and, at the same time, to create additional irrigation facilities for the drought-affected area. An earlier scheme prepared by the former government for interlinkage of rivers definitely needs a revival.

Another area of concern is the absence of any growth in the production of crude oil. In the last 18 years, whereas production of crude oil is stagnated around 32 million tonnes, demand has grown from 60 million tonnes in 1991 to 120 million in 2008, increasing India's dependence on import of oil to the extent of 80 per cent.

Fiscal Reforms

On fiscal front the most important hurdle in the process of growth has been the gross mismanagement of government finances and the growing burden of deficit financing. To bring fiscal discipline, Fiscal Responsibility and Budget Management (FRBM) Act was enacted in 2004 with the declared objective to eliminate revenue deficit by 2008 and to reduce fiscal deficit by 0.3 per cent every year. Unfortunately, the commitment has not been kept and the deadline is being extended year after year. It needs to be clearly realised that discipline in fiscal management is not possible without effective control on fiscal deficit. In a recent report prepared by the Ministry of Statistics in respect of 742 central projects, it has been pointed out that against the original cost of Rs. 77,118 crore, there has been a cost overrun of as much as Rs. 50,880 crore constituting nearly 66 per cent of the original cost.

It needs to be clearly realised that discipline in fiscal management is not possible without effective control on fiscal deficit.

Increasing element of subsidies in our fiscal system is a cause of great concern. All the major and minor subsidies, direct and indirect, allocated by the Centre and the States together constitute as high as nearly 15 per cent of the GDP. And poor delivery, widespread corruption and misutilisation of the funds have now assumed alarming proportions. According to a recent study conducted by the Planning Commission Programme Evaluation Division, more than 50 per cent of the allocated amounts meant for the persons below the poverty line did not reach them.

With a view to monitor, regulate and discipline such colossal waste of nation's resources, the Government is planning to set up a Central Plans Scheme Monitoring System (CPSMS) to keep a watch on performance of different projects. It is only a very small step and may not make any significant impact. To bring a lasting solution to this vexed problem, a Central Agency vested with judicial powers, with representatives from the Centre, the States and the Local Agencies, needs to be created and adequately authorised to take final decisions including those relating to Centre-State differences.

Employment and Labour Laws

Employment generation in India has been very disappointing. Between 1999 and 2004, whereas labour force increased by 2.8 per cent, growth in employment was restricted to only 2.6 per cent and the number of unemployed persons increased from 7.8 per cent to 8.3 per cent. Agricultural sector, due to lack of development, suffered the most.

Labour laws in India, mostly applicable to the organised sector, are too restrictive and unduly protective, designed to protect the interest of only the organised labour which constitutes merely 4 per cent of the total labour force at the cost of ignoring the remaining 96 per cent. The adverse impact of existing laws on employment generation has been eloquently expressed in the Government's Economic Survey of 2005-06 which reads as follows :

> "Various studies indicate that Indian labour laws are highly protective of labour, and labour markets are relatively inflexible. These laws apply only to the organised sector. Consequently these laws have restricted labour mobility, have led to capital-intensive methods in the organized sector and adversely affected the sector's long run demand for labour."

Present labour laws are mostly obsolete and out of place. They need to be totally replaced to 'make them promotive of employment'.

The Judiciary

The operation of the judiciary in India is also a matter of concern. The number of pending cases including those in the Lower Courts is around 3 crore. The system is corrupt and excessively time consuming, and beyond the reach of an honest litigant. Government departments are the biggest litigants constituting nearly 50 per cent of the total cases and in majority of the cases, government departments finally lose.

Conclusion

Taking an overall view, while India has made impressive advances in the course of last eighteen years of reforms, the process has largely been confined to the urban sector causing wider disparities and bringing greater discontent amongst the rural inhabitants. Minimum basic needs of life along with the minimum basic rights enshrined in the Constitution of India are still denied to large sections of the Indian society. In building a free and truly liberal democracy we still have a long way to go. A few thoughts discussed above are designed to demarcate the additional measures needed which will help this great country to emerge as an economically vibrant and progressive nation where every citizen will have ample opportunity to determine his future and every consumer will have ample freedom to make his choices. Built on strong foundations of democracy and freedom, it will be an equitable and a just society, progressive and vibrant, a nation of the dreams of great visionaries of the vision of Dr. L.M. Singhvi.

Module IV

Selected Thoughts and Concerns of Dr. L.M. Singhvi

CHAPTER 21

Innovative Approaches to World Peace Promoting A World Culture of Heart

The Basic Global Challenge

The object before us today is to proclaim our commitment and resolve for fostering Inter-religious Understanding and for promoting World Peace. For too long in human history have religions been like warring factions at loggerheads. In the name of religions, wars have been waged and battles have been fought and sanctified, hatred and prejudices have been and are being purveyed, mass executions and massacres have been perpetrated, brutality and inhumanity have been practised. Innumerable impediments and countless obstacles have been placed in the humanity's path to peace, progress and prosperity.

I recall C.C. Cotton's anguished observation: "Men will wrangle for religion; write for it; fight for it; anything but—live for it." Are we then prepared to abandon religious exclusivism and chauvinism and, the pride and prejudice of our own respective faiths as 'the best and the truest' and 'the only ones' for salvation, and to embrace and celebrate the fundamental unity of all religions and the diversities of manifold expressions and interpretations of quintessentially religious and ethical truths and experiences? Are we prepared to conclude a new and more promising Universal Covenant on Inter-religious Cooperation for World Peace for the relief of those in distress and deprivation and for the preservation of the ecology of Planet Earth? Are we prepared to form a Coalition of the World's Religions to meet human needs, secure human rights and fulfil human obligations, for ecology, distress relief, justice (social, economic and political), for economic amelioration, locally and globally, and for peace and good governance? Are we prepared to carry forward the message of Rio on Environment and of Vienna on Human Rights through our deliberations in this federal conclave? Above all, are we prepared to proclaim and abide by a Universal Declaration on Good and Humane Governance, on Non-violence? Are we prepared to redeem our pledges to ourselves in the spirit of the First Parliament of World's Religions and the Centennial Parliament in Chicago twelve years ago, and to enlarge them and carry them forward into a holistic secular-spiritual reality?

In this broader context of interrogatories may I make a statement of my hopes and aspirations and the vision and mission of Inter-religious Understanding and for all our federal and confederal Dialogues on Civilisations. My hopes and aspirations are rooted in our ability and the ability of humankind everywhere to mobilise the moral will of humankind, to marshal the consent, concurrence and consensus of "We the Peoples of the World" and their diverse religions and spiritual and social traditions, and to give a new sense of direction and purpose and a new momentum, to the concept of the inherent unity and togetherness of all religions and spiritual traditions in the common cause of building, in the third millennium of the Gregorian calendar, an enduring *Eternal Temple of True Togetherness of Humankind*, a *Temple of Peace and Multi-religious and Multicultural Harmony*, a *Temple of Tolerance and Understanding*, a *Temple of Humanity, Compassion, Justice, and Equity*, a *Temple of Freedom, Development and Dignity* for all, a *Temple of Non-violence and Truth* in all its dimensions, a *Temple of Cosmic Reciprocity and Interdependence*, a *Temple of Shared Concerns and Collaborative and Concrete Responses for the Relief and Amelioration of the Suffering Humanity* and for prohibition of cruelty and violence, a *Temple of Homage to Planet Earth in an integral relationship to inner and outer space for the preservation of human ecology* and global environment, for the promotion of sustainable and multi-splendoured development, and for preventing collective suicide by wilful ecocide, and a *Temple of Unity and Solidarity of All Religions* committed to Global Ethics. All these Universal Temples of the ennobled human spirit have to be built in the hearts, minds and souls of men, women and children, so that our world may be saved from the scourge of wars, violence, distrust, antagonism and insecurity, so that defences of peace and justice may be built on lasting foundations, and so that humankind may fulfil its positive civilisational tryst with destiny without the trivializing and narrow-minded impediments which have often eclipsed and hamstrung the age-old vision of 'The World As One Family" or "*Vasudhaiva Kutumbakam*", as the ancient Indian seers put it trackless centuries ago.

These Universal Temples of the ennobled human spirit have to be built in the hearts, minds and souls of men, women and children so that our world may be saved from the scourge of wars, violence, distrust, antagonism and insecurity.

If the pilgrim's progress is slow and our pilgrim in quest for peace continues to face inhuman impediments, the reason is that human societies locally, nationally and globally have not so far succeeded in establishing a culture of the heart in promoting interreligious understanding, amity and cooperation. To be frontal and frank, I am bound to recall what the great American philosopher Emerson recorded in 1868 in his Journal, "Culture is one thing, and varnish another." During the last few centuries, and especially in the 20th century we have had a lot of varnish but not enough of the culture of the heart and not enough of a true commitment of peace, understanding and amity. We have frequently deployed crass calculations of our national interest to the point of cut-throat competition. In the words of William Wordsworth, getting and spending, we tend to lay waste our power. We have been out complicating strategic planning and have been engaged in interminable intellectual exercises, but we have not given the human heart an opportunity to tackle the intractable problems and the chance to solve them in a simple and human manner. We have forgotten the wisdom of the proverb that "where hearts are true, few words will do." No wonder, we found ourselves in an unhappy impasse. In the words of Shakespeare, "Unhappy that I am, I cannot heave my heart into my mouth." to aim for understanding, amity and to negotiate peace. The brave impetuous heart yields everywhere to the subtle, contriving head. The contriving and calculating cunning of the self-centred individual and nations is unable to listen to the inner voice of righteousness and rectitude. Worse still, segments of humanity dressed in their brief authority and affluence can listen no more to the footsteps of the future. These make them increasingly selfish, self-seeking and self-serving. If only we could feel the depths of our hearts for the causes to which we pay lip service and if we could act without intellect to fulfil our noble mission and our inspiring vision and ideal, we would be achieving what Lord Buddha taught us to strive for, a reconciliation of Intellect and Compassion, *Prajnya* and *Karuna*.

Let us, therefore, review and revisit what has been achieved during the last two centuries, declare the norms of a universal moral code and create a cangenine ambience and institutional framework for preparing, projecting and implementing what we would call A New Global Charter, for *a New World Order*, a new and innovative blueprint for inter-faith togetherness and collaboration for the sake of our tomorrow. The radically innovative role of the Culture of the Heart, the Discipline of the Mind and the stirring of the Soul resonating with the inner voice alone can sustain the moral order promoting a global ethic and bridging all the divides which create hatreds, miseries, sufferings, rancour, alienation, distress and despair in the universe of interreligious coexistence.

Governance and India's Role

I have been asked to address you on the theme of "Global Governance and the Role of India" in the context of "the role of governance in promoting interreligious co-operation and for promoting a world culture of heart and developing innovating approaches to World Peace". I need hardly stress that peace, freedom, justice, dialogue and cooperation among religions would depend a great deal on governance which has a vital role and profound relevance to Peace, Justice and Freedom both locally and globally. I should also add that it is my conviction that Peace without Justice is an empty dream, not worth the candle, and that Peace, Justice and Freedom are indivisible and inextricably intertwined.

> ***The crises of Democratic Governance in India are many and diverse—economic, social, political and administrative.***

All governance is based on the philosophy of the state and the civil society. It has to be viewed as a people's mindset as a culture, as a structural arrangement, as an ideological framework of accountability, and as a functional process.

Governance is viewed differently and is variously defined. The blueprint and the manual of governance in India is constitutionally rooted in the philosophy of justice, social, economic and political; equality of status and opportunity, and liberty of thought, expression and worship. The philosophy of governance under the Constitution of India is thus based on the key concepts of Liberty, Equality, Fraternity and the Dignity of the individual but they are not borrowed from the French Revolution. They are culturally embedded in the values of *Vedanta*, commitment to Lord Buddha's compassion, and to the Vẹdic, Jain and Buddhist ideas of Non-violence and Peace.

The unique cluster of the concepts of interfaith amity, harmony, cooperation and protection of minorities is etched and writ large in the Constitution of India and are based on the constitutional concept of freedom of religion which is enshrined in the Constitution as an integral part of secularism. Indian secularism is not anti-religion but is based on the recognition of religion as a legitimate dimension of human life. The framework of the Constitution is fundamentally and democratically parliamentary, federal and citizen-oriented. Fundamental Rights and Fundamental Duties of citizens are enshrined in Part III and Part IV of the Constitution. The fundamental rights guaranteed in the Constitution are not mere pious platitudes but are enforceable through the Courts of Law which have a reputation of being impartial, independent and public interest-orientation. In sum, governance in India has democratic ethos, constitutional structure and operational systems. The textual manual of governance is, of course, necessarily conditioned and contextualised by the Indian society and its cultural heritage of values. The democratic form of governance and the preservation of human rights is vital in India because the founding fathers did not accept the facile aphorism that what is governed best is best, and that for the form of government let fools contest.

Governance obviously encompasses all the vital aspects of the life of a nation and impacts life globally. It refers essentially to the exercise of economic, political and administrative authority to manage a nation's affairs at all levels. It subsumes institutions, processes and choices of individuals.

According to the World Bank in 1994, the term governance describes conditions in a country as a whole and includes the following aspects :

(i) The form of political regime;
(ii) The process by which authority is exercised in the management of a country's economic and social resources for development; and
(iii) The capacity of governments to design, formulate and implement policies and discharge functions.

According to a UNESCO Report in 1997, governance refers to "a process whereby citizens' needs and interests are articulated for the positive social and economic development of the entire society and in the light of a perceived common good, since governance means more than government and refers to a political "process that encompasses the whole society and citizens active participants in the social contract that binds them together. At the heart of democratic governance in India is the core concept of "We the People". Similarly, the UN Charter was proclaimed in the name of "We the Peoples of the World". The word "We" in the Indian Constitution denotes identity and togetherness in collectivity. There is a mysterious authority in the plural We which no single name, individual or pronoun can acquire. That collective plural, "We, the People of India" is used in the Preamble and the Prologue of the Constitution of India to proclaim its democratic republican and secular credentials and to declare to the world our inclusive collective identity as a People and a Nation. Those words constitute in themselves a declaration of faith and have a unique resonance of India's civilisational antiquity and its unrivalled continuity, and as a new constitutional system. The words, "We the People of India", have for many of us the same evocative sanctity as the national flag and the national anthem.

Of the institutions of democratic governance based not on direct democracy but on representation of the people, the three estates, namely, the Executive, the Legislative and the Judiciary are the most noteworthy.

The media as the Fourth Estate in India and throughout the democratic world have become in recent years the host, the critic, the ally, the opponent and the interlocutor, and in a sense even the mentor. Obviously we cannot afford to reckon without the host. Freedom of expression in the media and through the media has become a powerful source and symbol of democratic governance.

So incremental and exponential is the Fourth Estate in the magnitude of power bearing on democratic governance that all three Estates especially, the Executive and the Legislature tend to be media-driven. Trial by the media also puts pressure on the judiciary. That was perhaps inevitable in the context of the logic of democratic pressures in the system of governance. People, their perceptions and predilections as well as the mysterious and unpredictable phenomenon, the public opinion, are crucial. That is why the media, in effect, operate the levers of power and more often than not determine the perceptions, predilections and the preferences of the people.

The media often claim evasively that they only reflect and mirror the situations as they are. That is obviously a gross understatement. In fact the media surveys, opinion polls, and exit polls are capable of queering the pitch one-way or the other because they have the power to lead or mislead, hide or seek, accentuate or underplay. The sovereign electorate is often mistakenly thought to be quite gullible. It is well to remember that the Indian electorate is not, however, an undifferentiated mass and that in fact there are many layers and segments of psychological response to the media. Many in the public may suffer from a "herd instinct" and might have a proneness to accept whatever the media purvey. The media avalanche may, once in a while, sweep the electorate off their feet and make them flow with the current subject to some exceptions. Sometimes, parties which use the media and whom the media use in turn can often be the victims of their own media blitz and traps. There is also a robust and recognizable resilience in certain segments of the Indian electorate, which react negatively to extravagant, partisan and unsubstantiated claims of political parties and leaders disregarding the media. The crux of the situation is that media has come to acquire a formidable power without a modicum of responsibility except in the limited terms of their own professional norms. Worse still, there are many instances when those who are supposed to watch and work for the media and whose duty is it to report, inform and educate, and to oversee and umpire actually themselves become political players in the game.

The media often claim evasively that they only reflect and mirror the situations as they are. That is obviously a gross understatement.

The role of the media in democratic governance is extremely complex and critical. The problem is one which essentially, the media itself have to address in all earnestness and with a full sense of detachment and responsibility and for the sake of safeguarding the principle of freedom of speech and expression. Equally challenging are the perils of populism which is a chronic and recurrent disease of every system of democratic governance which has an inbuilt tendency to over-reach and circumvent Rule of Law.

Universal Adult Franchise

When we adopted the fundamental functional principle of universal adult franchise for democratic governance in India, it was a sheer act of faith since it may be said, as many elitist thinkers believe, that India was not yet fully ready for universal adult franchise. I do not share that elitist view. It is true that illiteracy, poverty malnutrition and denial of human dignity and human rights were rampant in India when we decided to introduce democratic governance based on universal adult franchise. Had we, however, denied ourselves the salutary and revolutionary safeguard of universal adult franchise, we would have sown the seeds of democratic self-destruction and would help to perpetuate the injustices and the inequalities of the past. I believe that the universal adult franchise has over the years proved itself in many ordeals of fire in India. In my childhood it used to be said that the only way to learn to swim is to begin to swim and that is what India did when the republican Constitution launched the great experiment in democratic governance on the basis of universal adult franchise.

The first general elections were held in 1952. The 14th general election was held in 2004. All these elections define democratic governance in electoral terms and delineate India's arduous democratic pilgrimage. I shall refer to the elections to the 14th Lok Sabha because they are the most recent and also the most instructive for the understanding of democratic governance in India.

The 14th general election for the Lok Sabha was held during three weeks in four separate rounds. It was obviously an over-extended period. The total number of seats for which the election was held was 543; the total number of candidates at the election was 5398; the total votes polled were over 38 crore or 380 million, the number of registered voters were 675 million; the number of polling station were 7,000,000. In a constituency in Chennai South, in Tamil Naidu there were as many as 35 candidates in a single parliamentary constituency. The highest altitude polling booth in India was a village in Ladakh called Fastan some 26 km from the nearest road. Those figures give us an idea of the uniqueness and the incredible magnitude of

Indian elections. What baffles a student of Indian democracy most is that there were as many as 220 parties in the 14th Indian Parliamentary elections and yet there were as many as 2,369 independent candidates. The total cost of the elections is estimated to have been upwards of Rupees 100 million approximately. Notably India went electronic cent per cent. The tragic part of the huge electoral process, however, is that there were a number of deaths and there were many who were wounded in electoral violence. The proliferation of political parties, the huge multiplicity of candidates, the enormous extravagance of electoral expenditure, the perversion of the democratic discourse and the mammoth unmanageable constituencies breed many critical challenges in the democratic governance of India. In many ways, we have to face the stark reality of electoral process being polluted at the source and because of that pollution the people do not always get the government they deserve.

Indisputably, the general elections in India provide the most colourful grand spectacle of the festival of democracy, unequalled and unmatched anywhere else in the world. It is a tribute to Indian democracy and democratic governance in India that except for the aberration of the Emergency in the 1970s, elections have been held regularly, and in a manner which broadly reinforces and testifies to the high credibility of the electoral process and the democratic system in the world's largest democracy. In many ways, the system and the way it works is also bizarre and baffling but at the same time reassuring in a fundamental sense. The common man in India has by and large shown an exceptional measure of maturity. In electing and rejecting regimes, the electorate has shown that it is the master, thus enforcing the principle of the sovereignty of the electorate. The Election Commission as a constitutional authority has been the sentinel *qui vive* and the knight in shining armour for Rule of Law in electoral democracy.

One of the most important contributions of the electoral process in India is the high degree of political legitimacy it confers on democratic governance both in national self perception and in the eyes of the world at large, making India a globally acclaimed example of democracy especially in the so called third world. The other great benefit of democratic governance based on a broadly credible electoral system is that political succession becomes systematic, peaceful and routinised unlike many other countries where democracy has fallen by the wayside because the possibility of change of regime often causes violent tremors, upheavals, bloodshed and overthrow of legally constituted governments.

The problem of universal adult franchise in a country as diverse and heterogeneous as India is that caste and creed are accentuated at the cost of constituency cohesion and at the cost of national perspective. All electoral constituencies are demarcated territorially and geographically but caste equations often obliterate those demarcations. Though Islam does not accept the caste system, the Muslims too have become, as it were, one more caste. Castes and creeds are generally converted into vote banks. National parties and local parties regularly choose their candidates on the basis of caste configurations. The identities of caste and creed tend to eclipse issues of public importance. There are academic apologists who would provide a whole barrage of justifications for the emergence of castes and creeds as the key players in the electoral process. I for one find that the caste as a factor in electoral politics is fast turning the great Indian democracy into a virtual "confederation of castes," and that in my opinion is a crisis and a challenge. The vintage nationalism of Dadabhai Naoroji, Bal Gangadhar Tilak, Bankim Chandra Chatterji, Swami Vivekananda, Sri Aurobindo, Mahatma Gandhi, Jawaharlal Nehru, Sardar Patel, Subhash Chandra Bose and others who led us to freedom appears to have been jettisoned and the cobwebs of caste and creed have been substituted in the interior of our democracy. In my opinion, it is a malaise, which impairs the cohesion of the nation state and undermines, and corrodes the principle of merit in governance.

The crises of Democratic Governance in India are many and diverse. They are primarily economic, social, political and administrative. "We the People of India" have to introspect and ask ourselves as to how and why our high resolve for a tryst with a great and glorious destiny is underlined and how the national consensus enshrined in the Constitution may be derailed.

Limits to Tolerance

It is my view that every society and every system has a certain tolerance limit but it would be dangerous if democratic India were lulled into complacency and inertia because of India's traditionally high tolerance limits. Poverty, privation, hunger, lack of healthcare and unemployment are causing irreparable ruptures in the Indian society. We all know that suicides of farmers in Andhra Pradesh and Karnataka took a heavy retributive toll on the incumbent governments. The lesson is loud and clear. No democratic society can afford to turn a blind eye and a deaf ear to the woes and vagaries of livelihood for the sake of the long term benefits. As Lord Keynes said, in the long run we all die. The first and foremost thesis of Democratic Governance in India is that it has to reconcile the claims of the long term and the short term. I believe that nothing works unless it works for the well-being and comfort of most of the people, that is, *Bahujana Hitaya, Bahujana Sukhaya.* Nehruvian socialism had to retreat because it took its cue from the fast failing socialist model without compromising democratic norms but the procedural shackles of State Socialism did create all kind of constraints and innumerable forms of corruption. We now face the challenge of creating a new model of Globalisation and Development with a human face which would inspire confidence. Obviously the dogmatism of State Socialism is not an answer, nor is simple and naive populism an answer. Nor is West-dominated WTO globalism the answer.

The hallmark of governance in India is the vitality of civil society and the space it allocates for democratic pluralism and cultural diversity. Constitution of India protects pluralism, guarantees the cultural diversities of India. The Indian Society and its cultural tradition accord a place of pride to these cultural diversities which are guaranteed and safeguarded not only by the Constitution of India but by the social ethics and cultural heritage of India. India's civil society defends and articulate the culture of secularism which is rooted in the culture of affirmative acceptances of diversities.

Every society and every system has a certain tolerance limit but it would be dangerous if democratic India were lulled into complacency and inertia because of India's traditionally high tolerance limits.

Indian literatures in different languages of India and Indian arts have entrenched the culture of pluralism in the lotus heart of India and its philosophy and way of life. India's civil society is rich in its diversities and in its espousal of human and humanitarian causes which the civil society of India have often made an affair of the heart. There is a passion for peace and tolerance in the heart of India, which has evoked a culture of the heart by building bridges between past, present and the future.

Gurudev Rabindranath Tagore, the Poet Laureate gave eloquent expression to India's culture of the heart and value system when he sang in his famous offering of poems, *Gitanjali* :

Where the mind is without fear and
The head is held high
Where knowledge is free;
Where the world has not been broken up
Into fragments by narrow domestic walls;
Where words come out from the depth of truth;
Where tireless striving stretches
Its arms towards perfection;
Where the clear stream of reason
Has not lost its way

Into the dreary desert sand of dead habit;
Where the mind is led forward by Thee
Into ever-widening thought and action;
Into that heaven of freedom, my Father,
Let my country awake.

CHAPTER 22

Human Rights Revolution and Fundamental Duties

Concept of Citizenship

The concept of citizenship is obviously much more than a mere physical fact of certain individuals residing within certain territorial boundaries and obtaining identity cards and passports to facilitate their travel from one country to another. Citizenship postulates the relationship of belonging to a state by birth or choice and an intention to continue that relationship of belonging. There is something emotional and spiritual about that sense of belonging. In operative terms and in the vocabulary of rights, citizenship connotes a right and a duty to take part in the affairs of the civil society.

The hallmark of citizenship is the basic right to have rights and the basic duty to discharge duties. A citizen is an individual who is a member of a community or the state, although he may be a member of many other communities within the state or those transcending the state. Citizenship is a concept of political and jural allegiance and relates individuals to political and juristic entities known as states. Within a state a person can conceivably be a citizen of a country, of a state within a country or of a local or regional unit also. There are many jurisdictions which recognise dual citizenship in relation to different sovereign entities. We also speak occasionally of world citizenship which is not, in my opinion, a mere flourish of empty verbiage, although it is not a full-fledged jural concept.

There is a beautiful quotation from Mahatma Gandhi and it finds a place in the United Nations documents. Mahatma Gandhi in a message to Julian Huxley before his death wrote this, and these are words which should be heard, repeated and remembered everywhere in the world. He said: "The very right to live accrues to us only when we do the duty of the citizenship of the world." From this one fundamental statement, it is, perhaps, easy enough to define the duties of men and women and correlate every right to some corresponding duty to be first performed. Every other right can be shown to be usurpation hardly worth fighting for.

Human Rights Revolution

It was on the 4th of July, 1776 that the founding fathers of the American Revolution wrote a new chapter in the history of democratic institutions by proclaiming the Declaration of Independence in words which glow eternally on the conscience of mankind. 'We—and when they said 'we', it meant all generations of citizens everywhere—hold these truths to be self-evident, that all men are created equal, that they are endowed by their Creator with certain unalienable rights. Among these are life, liberty and the pursuit of happiness, that to secure these rights governments are instituted among men, deriving their just powers from the consent of the governed, that whenever any form of government becomes destructive of these ends, it is the right of the people to alter or to abolish it and to institute a new government, laying its foundations on such principles and organising its powers in such a form as would seem most likely to effect their safety and happiness. Eleven years after that Declaration, that is, on September 17, 1787, to be precise, the Constitution of the United States was made and their preamble in the Constitution of India has something strikingly in common.

The preamble of Constitution of India covers in its span the synthesis of four revolutions, the American Revolution, the French Revolution, the Russian Revolution and the *Gandhian Revolution.* The American Constitution's Preamble two hundred years ago said: "We the people of the United States," and we said exactly this, "we the people of India," in our Constitution's Preamble—"in order to form a more perfect union, establish justice, ensure domestic tranquillity, provide for the common defence, promote the general welfare and secure the blessings of liberty to ourselves and our posterity do ordain and establish this Constitution." I believe that the Preamble to the Constitution of India represents an eclectic, integrated and meaningful synthesis embodying the philosophies of the four great revolutions during the last two hundred years.

In the first half of the twentieth century, the Gandhian Revolution took place following the great October Revolution in Russia. Before that the Revolution in America and the Revolution in France had brought about an awareness of liberty. All these four

> ***The preamble of Constitution of India covers in its span the synthesis of four revolutions, the American Revolution, the French Revolution, the Russian Revolution and the Gandhian Revolution.***

Revolutions have culminated in what I call the "Human Rights Revolution" of the later part of the twentieth century. That ideology of human rights revolution is the sheet-anchor of our republican faith. It postulates human rights and subsumes and implies corresponding and inherent human duties and obligations. Therefore, when we mean the words 'human rights', we must necessarily imply human obligations. Indeed, that is what the United Nations Human Rights Sub-Commission has, in precise terms, prescribed.

Complementarity of Rights and Duties

Both rights and duties are mutually complementary and equally fundamental in the scheme of things. Indeed human rights and obligations are carefully formulated and evocatively enshrined on a global scale in the constitutions of the world, such as in ours, in the Universal Declaration of Human Rights and in the two great international covenants. But unless they are astir and alive in the hearts and minds of men and women, unless they become an integral part of the living culture of citizens, there is little hope for a new and more just and human order. That is why we need to stress the decisive significance of value-based, informed, constructive and enlightened citizenship, to strike a balance between rights and duties and to inculcate and disseminate a sense of pride in citizenship and a sense of civic duty among other citizens.

To my mind the crying need of the hour and the age is a broad-based national and worldwide citizens' movement for the full socialisation of the shared ideals and common goals, of the ideology of human rights and obligations, of faith in democracy and rule of law and of trust in peaceful and constitutional methods for achieving a just and humane order.

When we speak of citizenship we have, as our framework of reference, a civil society, conscious of its identity and composition and bound together by rights and responsibilities. The laws of the state may confer, recognise and regulate citizenship, but it is the citizens who constitute the civil society, and therefore, the status of a citizen and the dignity of a citizen as a constituent determinant of the state cannot be belittled.

Hierarchy of Norms

Suffice it to say then that the individual today is both a subject and an object of international law. This is a revolutionary change which has come about in the last thirty-five or forty years. He is a part of the fabric of a new and emerging international order in which human rights have come to have a pride of place. The concept of citizenship is based on a bundle of rights and duties, which every citizen has by virtue and in consequence of his being a citizen—nay, by virtue and in consequence of his being a human being. There are 'no doubt' conflicting claims on an individual in respect of rights and duties of citizenship in different situations of life. There is a seeming tension between individual and community perspectives in relation to those rights and duties. There may be an occasional divergence between moral, emotional, political and legal perspectives of citizenship and its rights and obligations. A value system provides, therefore, a citizen with a hierarchy of norms when there are competing claims on his or her allegiance in a profoundly pluralistic contemporary human set-up. It is that set of values which imparts coherence to citizenship.

The crying need of the hour and the age is a broad-based national and worldwide citizens' movement for the full socialisation of the shared ideals and common goals, of the ideology of human rights and obligations, of faith in democracy.

It is axiomatic that the quality of citizenship makes or mars a civil society. Many of the developed nations of the world have achieved, augmented and maintained their momentum of development and growth because of the exceptional inputs of citizenship. A high level of citizenship in England enabled it to make an outstanding contribution to democratic self-government, parliamentary institutions and rule of law. A sense of devoted citizenship, with particular emphasis on discipline and diligence, made the miracle of Japanese and German recovery after the Second World War possible, just as a misdirected and distorted kind of emotionally aggressive and chauvinistic sense of citizenship made Hitler's Germany and Tojo's Japan the scourge of the earth.

Need for Citizenship Development

Demonstrably, an inert and indifferent citizenship can impede and arrest or deflect and distort the progress of a nation, just as a dynamic, human and coherent citizenship can combine democracy and development in a purposeful and fruitful manner. I am indicating and vindicating when I say that citizenship is one of the most vital determinants of the direction that a country takes, the speed at which it travels and the magnitude and quality of what it achieves. It is the most important single human resource on which depends the future of a society. I regret to say that it is this most vital human resource which is being subjected to inexcusable neglect today, in the so-called developing countries of the world, the world which is our first world and not the third world as we slavishly call it sometimes, adopting the stock stereotypes of phraseology from elsewhere. I believe that without a high degree of citizenship development there is not much we can hope to achieve. With it, there is nothing that is desirable and yet beyond our reach. It is no exaggeration to say that the quality of citizenship is the measure of our deserving what we desire.

Citizenship may also be defined as the sum total of contributions made by citizens individually and collectively to achieve certain goals in a certain manner. Citizenship development, therefore, must outline those goals or ends as well as appropriate methods and means. The relationship between means and ends is particularly important in citizenship development because good citizenship *per se* does not countenance the pursuit of any end if the means are dubious and questionable. On the other hand a society has to be pragmatic, even result-oriented. An effort has to be made to evolve a workable concordance of means and ends.

Need for Saving the Indian Society from Erosion of Values

We have in our country a proneness to hypocrisy and a proclivity for didactic moralisation, which often revels in a 'holier than thou' attitude, making our systems of accountability unreal and impractical, creating a psychological hiatus which in turn brings our laws into disrepute. We have to establish a new ambience of integrity and efficiency for laying down the strategy of achieving our ends by appropriate, affordable and viable means. The task is at once most elementary and yet most complex.

An inert and indifferent citizenship can impede and arrest or deflect and distort the progress of a nation, just as a dynamic, human and coherent citizenship can combine democracy and development in a purposeful and fruitful manner.

I believe the time has come when we should all put our heads together to achieve a national consensus on what we can do to achieve greater pragmatism, increased productivity and accelerated pace of development. We must rivet our attention on achieving our targets for a minimum national programme in every walk of life. Our political discourse ought not to be allowed to distort it by endless recrimination or by rampant corruption or by acquiescence and indifference.

The question is: Is there anything, we, the people of India, can do to save our society from the erosion and decadence of values? Can we, the 'people of India', do anything to save our society from a creeping or galloping sense of disillusionment with the establishmentarian and even egalitarian apparatus of power wrapped in miles and miles of red tape, from the sordid sorrows of caste, poverty and insular injustices?

My answer is a hesitant 'yes' with an emphatic 'if' (hesitant because the task would require mobilisation of all our moral and material resources).

That is possible only if and that is why I said an emphatic if as we are prepared to redefine the whole concept of power and accountability in our society in a manner that the whole concept of fundamental, inalienable duties has to take the place of the concept of rights. That is no doubt a big 'if'. But without it we have no chance of survival with dignity, no chance of keeping our body and soul together, no chance of the sovereign, democratic, secular, socialist republic of India ushering in, or even approximating to a reasonable measure of justice, equality, liberty, freedom, fraternity, national unity or individual dignity. We cannot afford to bid farewell to these great aspirations and ideals, nor can we afford to wallow in our misery and melancholy. If there ever were a cure for the malady which afflicts our society, it is in vigorous citizenship development, it is in a sense of realisation of our basic obligations as citizens and as human beings and it is in a resurrection of that sense of dedication and inspiration which is our great legacy from our freedom struggle.

Is there anything, we, the people of India, can do to save our society from the erosion and decadence of values?

Ends and Means as Enshrined in the Constitution of India

By citizenship development I do not mean that the nation should become a vast and sprawling debating club, nor do I mean to suggest a change from this to that system, nor do I suggest a system of coercion or of regimentation. I would advocate a certain consensus of thought, a certain coherence of approach, a certain candour of communication, a certain framework of norms in conducting our public affairs, and, above all, I would advocate a sense of commitment to the community. I would advocate the discipline of democracy and democracy in laying down the norms of that discipline.

I believe these are the moral imperatives of Indian citizenship today. Fortunately for us, our Constitution embodies an excellent statement of ends and means and provides a detailed route map for achieving a high degree of means and ends concordance. I believe that the reason for our country's failing to achieve higher levels of effectiveness and excellence in implementing our constitutionally prescribed goals is the enthronement of the new found god of political power in our body politic and the failure of our citizenship; in other words, failure of leadership and failure of citizenship in an institutional as well as in an operational sense.

Institutionally, the failure of the party system in Indian politics is the most glaring shortcoming. Our party system is fractured and fragmented. It produces a very superficial and irresponsible attitude to political processes. Our Constitution is often hamstrung by the strange workings

Our party system is fractured and fragmented. It produces a very superficial and irresponsible attitude to political processes.

of our party system. There is too much shadow-boxing, too much vituperation and mud-slinging, too much hypocrisy and self-seeking favouritism, corruption and arbitrariness, too much prolixity of words and laxity of conduct to allow democracy and rule of law to work out an acceptable design of law and life. The malady and sickness of our party system is naturally transmitted to our public discourse and dilutes citizenship development. The situation appears to be beyond repair, redemption or redress. Most of the political parties in India have at one time or the other suffered popular retribution at the polls. But like the Bourbons, they tend to render little and to learn nothing. The result is that we do not have healthy party system in our country. Citizenship development perhaps has an important part to play in bringing about a change of climate and institutional restructuring in our country.

Citizenship and leadership are two sides of the same coin. Therefore, when I speak of the citizen, I speak not merely of the voter but of the citizen in every walk of life. Similarly, we must refer to leadership in every walk of life. We live in a pluralist society and voting and wielding political power is only one of the many segments of our life. The quality of citizenship and leadership in non-political situations is bound to have a vital bearing on the quality of our political processes also. That is why it is important to emphasise excellence in the fields of education, culture, arts, medical, legal, judicial and other professions, civil services, the press, trade union, agriculture and industry, which would have a cumulative multiplier effect. In each autonomous activity, trade or calling, we should design a basic citizenship code with a voter not merely as a voter but in every walk of life, so that everyone in his or her own station of life will strive to do the very best for the society as well as for himself or herself. That is as important as the task of educating our ultimate masters—the people, or our immediate masters—the legislators and the ministers. All these programmes should be designed to explain and expound the system, its basic postulates and its operational realities, and to project and evaluate role perceptions and role performance. This is very important because most of us do not seem to appreciate what the role of a particular institution is. When I was in Parliament I found that members were not interested so

We should design a basic citizenship code, with a voter not merely as a voter but in every walk of life. That is as important as the task of educating our ultimate masters—the people, or our immediate masters—the legislators and the ministers.

much in legislation or in policy-making but they were interested in other things which were not a part of their role. A minister is not so much interested in policy-making as perhaps in transfers. An administrator, perforce or by inclination, is more interested in policy-making. The whole situation of role performance and role perception, therefore, becomes extremely important in drawing a proper line.

Each trade, activity or calling, every family, locality and village must be provided with appropriate educational kits and audio-visual materials suitable for different age-groups, so as to bring about a proper role perception for every citizen or citizen representative or citizen leader in every walk of life.

Let me add that that alone will restore to ourselves the long talisman bequeathed to us by Gandhiji. Let me add that we cannot be oblivious of warring ideologies, conflicting interests and competing claims. We cannot afford to be naive nor can we afford to be cynical. We can never take leave of reality, nor can we allow ourselves to be obsessed by a single-track calculus of class hatreds and class conflicts. Citizenship development has to have its own teleology, its objectives and goals, but should not allow itself to be lost in the dreary desert sand of divisive and fissiparous forces.

Fundamental Duties

If I may invite your attention to Article 51A, which is what provides for Fundamental Duties in our Constitution, I should remind you that it is in the nature of a very broad charter, indicative and illustrative of what we the people expect from ourselves. When that Article of the Constitution was proposed by the Swaran Singh Committee, there was a provision for penalties. That provision was, however, dropped and, I think. rightly. Fundamental duties are formulated in the most general terms in Article 51A. Some of them call upon the citizen to inculcate certain values or to cultivate a certain kind of temperament. Even those duties which deal with specified areas and norms of behaviour are not so defined as to give rise to triable and prosecutable offences. It would have been incongruous and anomalous to enact Article 51A as a kind of an appendix to the Indian Penal Code, which is crafted and drafted in precise terms with clearly identifiable ingredients.

The approach of Article-51A of our Constitution, as it stands today, is not to criminalise or to intimidate the citizen but to remind him of his basic duties, to offer him a talisman and touchstone and to hold a constitutional mirror to him. It is somewhat like a prayer and a pledge in the forum of his conscience. Its strength lies not in its enforceability by the police and the Courts of law but in its appeal to the nature of man in respect of his conduct as an Indian citizen. It is a comprehensive citizenship code. It reminds him of the debt he owes to the society and of the individual civic duty he owes to himself. It is a constitutional IOU of a citizen, a citizen's promissory note. Its observance may be highly individualistic and equally communitarian. It is meant to equip the citizen with a compass to give him a sense of direction and involvement. It gives him an encapsulated agenda or a checklist, so that he may regulate and canalise his thoughts and deeds with a measure of enlightened and purposeful coherence. It also relates the constitutional charter of Fundamental Duties to Fundamental Rights and Directive Principles of State Policy. Fundamental Rights are in the nature of legally enforceable guarantees and the Directive Principles are in the nature of guidelines and assurances, both of them by the state to the citizens. On the other hand, Fundamental Duties embodied in Article 51A are moral assurances of citizens to citizens. They are not enforceable in Courts of law without the aid of relevant and specific legislation but they are equally vital and fundamental in their own way. I may add that fundamental duties may also be used as a tool of judicial interpretation of statutes just as Directive Principles of State Policy have been so used.

Article 51A may also be employed to carry out a social audit of the commissions and omissions of the executive and to give *locus standi* to a concerned citizen in matters connected with or having a bearing on fundamental duties. Earnest Marker, in his famous work *The Politics of Aristotle*, observed and I quote: "A citizen is one who permanently shares in the administration of justice and the holding of office" and that "citizens in the common sense of that term are all who share in the civic life of ruling and being ruled in turn".

A sociologist of eminence wrote four years ago a thought-provoking book, *The Reconstruction of Patriotism*, in which he has defined civic obligations as contributions and sacrifices a citizen makes to keep the political system alive. That is important for a political system which seems sometimes to be crumbling. We must address ourselves to the contributions and the sacrifices which we the people of India must make in order to keep our constitutional and political system alive, to make it grow and to ensure it serves the larger goals which we have proclaimed. That is the task for a mighty mass movement which, like a mighty river, might have a modest beginning. Such a mass movement cannot be an official and departmental undertaking. It cannot be a prodigy of the state and its media. It calls for the confluence of the entire body of citizens and all their avocations. It calls for the pooling of all the institutional and human resources of the state and the society. It calls for a missionary spirit and a crusading zeal. Such a mass movement has to be built on the core and centrality of voluntary work and grass roots awareness and dissemination from

Panchayat to Parliament. When I speak of *Panchayats* I must congratulate the Chief Minister of Karnataka for having given a new shot in the arm of the whole concept of *panchayati raj* movement, particularly in Karnataka.

We have also to think of an ungrudging and respectful recognition of the role that every patriotic Indian citizen has a right and a duty to play in building up a new and better India. Such a mass movement has to be built on the basis of a deep, abiding interest in critical, self-respecting and value-based patriotism and social sensitivity. I underline these words, *partriotism* and *social sensitivity.* We did develop a nationalist ideology during our freedom struggle. But there is very little left to its credit in the account of the general run of Indians. I do not and I cannot plead in our open and democratic society of today for proclaiming a simplistic version of conventional nationalism as a Charge of the Light Brigade, which said, "You are not to question why, you have only to do and die." Instead, I would plead for the resurrection, rehabilitation and reconstruction of nationalism and patriotism, for a self-critical and rational commitment to civic consciousness and civic obligations. That I think is the unfinished task of the Constitution which beckons us for a tryst with destiny.

I must add a concluding note that citizenship development is not, as it were, a ready panacea to be dispensed by a chemist somewhere around the corner. As a Chinese philosopher put it many thousand years ago: "It may not prevent birds of sorrow and adversity from flying over our heads, but it will perhaps enable us to prevent those birds of sorrow and adversity from building their nests into our hair." This is, indeed, what we need.

CHAPTER 23

Towards a Jurisprudence of Non-violence

Even as I incur a new debt today, I am happy to have the privilege and the opportunity of acknowledging my old debt by fulfilling, howsoever briefly and inadequately, the academic obligation of my honorary professorial function in this University by endeavouring to set forth a framework of ideas, principally Mahatma Gandhi's ideas, and propose a fragmentary introduction to what I would call, "A Jurisprudence of Non-violence". My attempt is to translate some of the basic Gandhian concepts into a more familiar jural vocabulary and to transpose those ideas into the precincts of jurisprudence from which they have been conventionally excluded, if not consciously ostracised. I confess I am unable to attempt or offer within the span of this lecture an entire blueprint or even an elaborate table of contents. What I hope to do is to scratch the surface and prepare a seed-bed for my ruminations and reflections on a complex and a seemingly esoteric subject.

Most scholars and writers of jurisprudence are generally quite unaware of non-violence as a possible source of jurisprudence, but if I have chosen the title *Towards A Jurisprudence of Non-violence* it is not because I have succumbed to the novelty and the temptation of a teasing title. Nor was it the fascination of a fanciful utopia which launched me on an excursion to what some startled fellow lawyers may regard as outer space. My choice of the subject for this discourse was prompted by the universal anguish and collective anxiety of our age and time, embattled by violence at every step, and my conviction that the philosophy of *ahimsa* translated in a somewhat limited way as non-violence and some of its ground norms have a vital contribution to make to the possibility of a more just, humane and compassionate world. Sustained by that conviction, I am not deterred by the fact that the theme remains to this day a stranger to the textbooks of jurisprudence. That in itself was a bit of an incentive and a challenge for me. It is my hope that the theme will sooner or later find a place in the textbooks of the future, for if Non-violence is or could be a philosophy of life, it has also to be able to provide an approach to the philosophy of law. My attempt this evening is not to advocate or expound the idea of a full-fledged non-violent society or state, nor to claim that the Gandhian jurisprudence is an instant panacea or a miracle medicine available around the corner. What I would like to offer, more modestly, is an alternative view, a glimpse of an alternative jurisprudence and its wide range of experimental ideas, and above all the spirit of the enterprise of non-violence, which is the most precious legacy of that simple but colossal human being, Mahatma Gandhi who was at once one of the greatest iconoclasts and one of the greatest architects in human history. And what could be more appropriate than that the first lecture I deliver as Mahatma Gandhi Professor of Law at Leicester University should be devoted to the jurisprudence of Non-violence.

Roots of Non-violence in India

To the world at large, Gandhi is to Non-violence what Jesus Christ is to Christianity. In a very real sense, Mahatma Gandhi gave to the ancient concept of Non-violence a new global outreach, but he certainly did not invent the concept. It has pedigreed roots both in the Vedic and the Sramana traditions, both of which go back to many millennia before the beginning of the Christian era. The concept of *ahimsa* was a part of Gandhiji's Indic inheritance in Saurashtra where Vaishnavism and Jainism had converged and were woven into the culture, outlook and daily life of the people. Historically, there were many Hindu, Jain and Buddhist rulers, kingdoms, thinkers, statesmen, saints and savants who had taught and inculcated the philosophy and ethics of Non-violence in their personal and social lives and the idea of non-violence had become "an essential part of the religion of the masses." The ideal of *ahimsa* which was the cardinal principle of Jain and Buddhist traditions was equally acknowledged as the supreme religion in the great Hindu epic, *Mahabharata*. Emperor Asoka's renunciation of war and violence during the battle of Kalinga was a part of India's historical memory. The ethos of non-violence was also reflected in many of the famous Asokan edicts inscribed on the rocks in the far-flung Indian empire.

Mahatma Gandhi rediscovered the philosophy of Non-violence as a grammar of daily life, broadened it, almost reinvented it in its manifold and myriad applications, and made it an all-pervasive moral principle for the individual and for societal institutions. In the Gandhian philosophy, *ahimsa* became universal and worldwide, confined to no particular nation, creed or religion.

Mahatma Gandhi made Truth and Non-violence the sheet-anchor of his teachings and his technique. Of the relationship of Truth and Non-violence in his thought processes, he said "As I proceed in my search for truth it grows upon me that truth comprehends everything. It is not in *Ahimsa*, but *Ahimsa* is in it... We have to live a life of *Ahimsa* in the midst of a world of *himsa*, and that is possible only if we cling to truth. That is how I deduce *Ahimsa* from truth. Out of truth emanate love, tenderness, humility. A votary of truth has to be humble as the dust. His humility increases with his observance of truth."

Describing, as it were, his own voyage of discovery, Gandhiji goes back to his Indic roots and says, "It appears that the impossibility of full realisation of truth in this mortal body led an ancient seeker after truth to the appreciation of *Ahimsa*". The question which confronted him was: "Shall I bear with those who created difficulties for me, or shall I destroy them?" The seeker realised that he who went on destroying others did not make headway, but simply stayed where he was, while the man who suffered those who created difficulties marched ahead, and at times even took the others with him... The more he took to violence, the more he receded from truth. For in fighting the imagined enemy without, he neglected the enemy within."

The Ethical and Human Approach

Mahatma Gandhi was a deeply religious man, but his sense of religion was essentially ethical, humanitarian and spiritual and had a universal, non-denominational quality. He says "To me religion means Truth and *Ahimsa* or rather Truth alone, because Truth includes *Ahimsa*, *Ahimsa* being the necessary and indispensable means for its discovery." As Gandhiji put it', "They are like two sides of a coin, or rather of a smooth unstamped metallic disc. Who can say, which is the obverse and which is reverse? Nevertheless *Ahimsa* is the means; truth is the end. Means to be means must always be within our reach, and so *Ahimsa* is our supreme duty. If we take care of the means, we are bound to reach the end sooner or later."

Gandhiji's religion was a religion of Truth, Non-violence, Love and Humanitarian Service. With Gujarati poet, saint Narsi Mehta, he defined, a Vaishnava (a man or woman of God or of true religion) as one who knows and shares the pain, sorrow and suffering of others. He used to say "truth is love" and to him, love meant compassion and service to all living beings. He said, *I cannot practise ahimsa without the religion of service and I cannot find the truth without practising the religion* of *ahimsa... I am striving for the kingdom of heaven, which is*

> ***Mahatma Gandhi was a deeply religious man, but his sense of religion was essentially ethical, humanitarian and spiritual and had a universal, non-denominational quality.***

spiritual deliverance. For me the road to salvation lies through incessant toil in the service of my country and of my humanity. I want to identify myself with everything that lives. In the language of the Gita, I want to live at peace with both friend and foe. My patriotism is for me a stage in my journey to the land of eternal freedom and peace. Thus it will be seen that for me there is no politics devoid of religion. They subserve religion. Politics bereft of religion is a death-trap because it kills the soul."

Gandhiji felt that the law of love which governed the family in the civilised world should also be the basis of relations between the peoples and nations of the world. Equally, he felt that the only possible rule of conduct in any civilised society, he called it the golden rule of conduct, was mutual tolerance which was to him an aspect of truth and non-violence. He said, *"Truth is absolute, knowledge relative. Truth, in itself one and entire is reflected diversely in a myriad of facets in the reasons of men… Pride then stops the process of search and discovery, of distinguishing the true from the false, by which knowledge grows, while we go about extirpating not error, which is always with us, but our opponents, who may be wiser than we."*

In another passage, Gandhiji said, *"Everybody is right from his own standpoint, but it is not impossible that everybody is wrong. Hence the necessity for tolerance, which does not mean indifference to one's own faith, but more intelligent and purer love for it. Tolerance gives us spiritual insight, which is far from fanaticism as the north pole from the south. I very much like the doctrine of the manyness of reality. It is this doctrine that has taught me to judge a Mussulman (Moslem) from his own standpoint and a Christian from his… My Anekantvada (Jain doctrine of the many aspects "not one"—of reality) is the result of the two doctrines of Satya and Ahimsa."*

Gandhiji felt that the law of love which governed the family in the civilised world should also be the basis of relations between the peoples and nations of the world.

In the ultimate analysis, Mahatma Gandhi's doctrine of non-violence, though inspired initially by his Vaishnava-Jaina ambience of Gujarat, belonged to all the faiths of the world and to none exclusively. He found his principle of non-violence as the golden thread in all faith traditions as he saw them; he did not make it dependent upon any of them. Gandhiji himself said in October 1916, *"though my views on ahimsa are a result of my study of most of the faiths of the world, they are now no longer dependent upon the authority of these works. They are a part of my life, and if I suddenly discovered that the religious books read by me bore a different interpretation from the one I had learnt to give them, I should still hold to the view of ahimsa."*

For Mahatma Gandhi, non-violence was his religion, his worldview and his way of life. He was not an academic philosopher; he was a man of action. He did not consciously systematise his ideas and did not care to cast them into a juristic mould, but he was constantly in the thick of the basic discourse of jurisprudence and contributed a whole new range of ideas of non-violence which was his philosophy of life in action. His Jurisprudence of Non-violence which was still in the process of evolving may superficially appear to be strewn with baffling contradictions, but it offers a profound critique of the grooves into which modern life and many prevailing schools of jurisprudence are entrapped. What the Gandhian experiments with truth and nonviolence offer to jurisprudence is not a readymade alternative nor a wholly coherent and consistent system but a new mindset, a new problem-solving technique and a new sense of humanity and spirituality which are exemplified, illustrated and enlivened by his philosophy of life in action comprising his teachings, writings and his approaches to issues and problems. That I believe is the stuff of an Alternative Jurisprudence.

In the ultimate analysis, Mahatma Gandhi's doctrine of non-violence, though inspired initially by his Vaishnava-Jaina ambience of Gujarat, belonged to all the faiths of the world and to none exclusively.

And that takes me to the question of defining jurisprudence and to the question whether I am justified in giving to the core cluster of Gandhian ideas the appellation of "A Jurisprudence of Non-violence."

Non-violence and Jurisprudence

Dicey, the high priest of English law in the nineteenth century, quite candidly said that *"jurisprudence is a word which stinks in the nostrils of the practising barrister."* He was not only referring to the native English nostrils but also to those of all practising lawyers who generally tend to be like the Moliere's character who discovered to his surprise that he had been speaking prose for more than forty years without knowing it, perhaps, with the only difference that the prose that he spoke all his life did not stink in the nostrils of Moliere's bourgeois gentleman. Jurisprudence is to all lawyers the underlying structure of the prose they speak all their lives, knowingly or otherwise. It is unavoidable and inescapable for lawyers who must inevitably think about what the law says, why it says what it says, what it does or does not do, and in what manner and to what purpose do the laws operate, for better or worse. Most lawyers also have had their moments of disillusionment and exasperation with law and might even have strong feelings about what is wrong with the law and the society. That is why Julius Stone described jurisprudence as *"the lawyer's extra-version"*. It is the lawyer's examination of precepts, ideals, and techniques of the law in the light derived from present knowledge in disciplines other than the law. *"My rudimentary attempt at constructing a* jurisprudence of Non-violence is shaped by the much needed extroversion (extra-version) of law looking outside its own narrow and rigid confines and interacting with the philosophy of life in action."

In its etymological sense, *jurisprudential* means only knowledge of law or skill in law, but its connotations and usage vary considerably. The word jurisprudence is often used in some countries to describe the legal connections and implications of a body of knowledge as well as to describe the legal postulates which orbit a central philosophical, moral, political or economic concept or an ideology or 'a period of history. A jurisprudence may be linked to the teleology of values in a legal system or to the organising power and the operational dynamics of a set of concepts and precepts running through a legal system. For instance, we may legitimately speak of the jurisprudence of liberty or the jurisprudence of equality or the jurisprudence of human rights. Equally, we are familiar with jurisprudence linked to different ideologies. References to Marxist, Capitalist or Socialist Jurisprudence are examples in point. Nor are we unfamiliar with associated or derivative descriptions such as Hindu, Christian, Jewish and Islamic jurisprudence. It is demonstrable that jurisprudence of Non-violence satisfies the established philosophical, ethical, ideological, ontological, teleological, preceptorial, expositorial, censorial and reformist credentials of jurisprudence.

Unrepentant adherents of the Benthamite-Austinean school of analytical jurisprudence might still persist in questioning what they are prone to dub as the jurisprudential pretensions of non-violence on the ground that jurisprudence must distinguish the law as it is and as it ought to be (expositorial and censorial jurisprudence) whereas non-violence is concerned only with ethical precepts. Firstly, Jurisprudence of Non-violence does not avoid the expositorial role of analysing the formal structures of law. It needs to do that in any case to perform its censorial and reformist role. Secondly, the concept of non-violence is an existential fact as well as a normative prescription. Thirdly, we might remind ourselves of Ulpian's remark in the *Digest* quoted as the opening of Justinian's Institutes, *"Jurisprudence is the concept* of *things divine and human knowledge of the just and the unjust."* The jurisprudence of non-violence is the concept of things divine and human and affords us human knowledge of the just and the unjust. Moreover, the cartography of law and the canvas and concerns of jurisprudence have changed substantially since the Austinean demarcation of its domain. Buckland in his *Reflections on Jurisprudence* tells us in words which are vivid, though excessively harsh, *"The analysis* of *legal concepts is what jurisprudence meant for the student in the days of my youth. In fact, it meant Austin. He was a religion; today he seems to be regarded rather as a disease."*

The Gandhian jurisprudence of non-violence can best be understood through and in terms of 'the moral discourse of Mahatma Gandhi's epic life. Every article or letter he wrote, every interview he gave, every meeting he addressed, every advice he gave, every movement he led, every programme he launched, every *ashram* or settlement he established, and finally his martyrdom itself was a Socratic dialogue and a Christ-like encounter with life and its battles and dilemmas. In every situation and to every problem, he strove to find as far as practicable a solution based on his evolving philosophy of non-violence initially inculcated in him by his mother, later reinforced in some measure by his Jain friend and mentor, Shrimad Rajchandra, and eventually transmuted by him with the leavening of the basic teachings of different faith traditions and certain ideas of Thoreau, Ruskin, Carlyle, Tolstoy and Emerson into an elaborate set of norms. Gandhiji would apply those norms not only to individuals but also to groups, associations, organizations, and to the State and to its institutions and instrumentalities.

Gandhian jurisprudence is holistic, and although it is evolving and experimental, it is quite integrated and consistent. It does not exempt any area of activity or authority from the "sovereignty" of non-violence, even though Gandhiji would prescribe variations of the same norm in different situations. His jurisprudence of truth, non-violence, love and compassion, though quiescent and peaceable was not meant to turn a blind eye or a deaf ear to injustice or authoritarian arrogance. He was committed resolutely to seek justice and humanity, to resist oppression and exploitation, to enhance human dignity and basic human equality, to conduct conflict with goodwill and equanimity and to seek a fair resolution of conflicts amicably and in a spirit of reconciliation.

The Gandhian philosophy is very much a philosophy of goals for individuals and societies, but the jurisprudence of non-violence based on Mahatma Gandhi's life and thought is pre-eminently and distinctively *a jurisprudence of the process* in achieving those goals. Gandhiji did not subscribe to the dichotomous divide between ends and means. He did not regard means as a mere device or an instrumental aid. He said in a prayer speech shortly before his assassination that he regarded means and ends as convertible terms. Krishnalal Shridharani puts it aptly when he describes the Gandhian conception of the means as "the end in process and the ideal in the making". In a quatrain inspired by a translation of Ferdinand Lassalle in Arthur Koestler's *Darkness at Noon*, Joan Bondurant, an American Gandhian scholar, put it eloquently :

> "Point not the goal until you plot the course
> For ends and means to man are tangled so

That different means quite different aims enforce
Conceive the means as end in embryo."

The Gandhian approach to the intimate intertwining of means and ends and his emphasis on what I may term in Indian philosophical parlance, the qualitative integrity of the means as of the being in the process of becoming defines and distinguishes jurisprudence of non-violence with particular reference to the processual technique of non-violence. With a few honourable exceptions, most Western intellectuals including teachers and exponents of jurisprudence have failed to understand the unique significance of non-violence as a processual catalyst in the civil society.

The State and Non-violence

A few political scientists, Western as well as Indian, found elements of philosophical anarchism in the Gandhian ideology and approach, particularly because of Gandhiji's opposition like that of Kropotkin to centralisation of industry and centralisation of political power. Like Gandhi, Tolstoy and other Christian anarchists had also enjoined non-co-operation and refusal to pay state dues, but with Tolstoy non-violence meant mere avoidance of all force whereas Gandhi's concept of *Satyagraha* had the dimension of creative engagement, constructive and positive mobilisation, and peaceable dialogue to arrive at a consensus or a compromise. More importantly, Gandhiji's concept of democracy did not quite reject the institution of state as an instrument of justice and as a vehicle of change. His concept of decentralisation based on a federation of village communities was cemented by a sense of social cohesion and mutuality but it is not quite a state of statelessness. Moreover, Gandhiji did not reject the idea of the institution of state as we know it but envisaged a processual transformation moving hand in hand with structural and functional changes. Indeed, he accepted that a degree of non-violent pressure in the society could take different forms and provide a source of moral suasion. He himself participated in the discussions on constitutional reforms from time to time.

Gandhiji was an individualist and a pluralist and did, therefore, oppose the absolute sovereignty of the state and the unbridled power of impersonal, bureaucratic hierarchies. That is why he was prepared to opt for "ordered anarchy", a somewhat cryptic Gandhian synonym for his utopia. He had a distrust of the state but was nevertheless prepared to advocate state action for the advancement of the welfare of the people. He did not believe in much state interference because he was a democrat and a liberal and apprehended the insidious and inevitable intrusion of violence and authoritarianism in a system in which State exercised more than minimal control Gandhiji thought that "power rightly exercised must sit light as a flower; no one should feel the weight of it." Basic to Mahatma Gandhi's jurisprudence of non-violence is his theory of accountability, humility, transparency and service orientation of power as a functional component in society. Power in the raw is anathema to the jurisprudence of non-violence. He said in 1935: *I look upon an increase of the power of the state with the greatest fear, because, while apparently doing good by minimising exploitation, it does the greatest harm to mankind by destroying individuality, which lies at the root of all progress."*

Though a radical and a revolutionary, Gandhiji was too predisposed to good order and too much of a conservative and a conservationist to be ideologically a wholehearted philosophical anarchist. He envisioned a civil society, albeit a different kind of civil society, but the hallmark of difference was his concept of non-violence, persuasion, negotiation, reconciliation and the ability to empathise, to suffer and sacrifice consciously, and to serve with love. Unlike the anarchists, he offered an alternative model, a parallel organization, and a far-reaching constructive programme. Even when he launched his massive programme of civil disobedience and non-cooperation, it was not his purpose to bid a farewell to the machinery of the state. The mainstay of the Gandhian state and society was the village community and its guiding norm was non-violence in all its aspects.

Gandhiji was an individualist and a pluralist and did, therefore, oppose the absolute sovereignty of the State and the unbridled power of impersonal, bureaucratic hierarchies.

According to Mahatma Gandhi, violence logically leads to centralisation of power and *vice versa*. In turn, they lead to an increasingly unacceptable measure of coercion, authoritarianism, abuse of power, inequitous inequalities and exploitation. As a result, democracy, freedom, equality and human dignity, which are basic to Gandhian philosophy, are undermined. Gandhian jurisprudence would, therefore, aim to minimise violence and achieve optimum non-violence. To achieve a high degree of non-violence in a society, Gandhiji counted first and foremost on morally enlightened and responsible individuals living a life of service in a decentralised society. He regarded decentralisation as the technique of non-violent democracy. He had no hesitation in rejecting the dictatorship of the proletariat and in declaring even in the heyday of centralised state systems: *"That state will be the best which is governed the least."*

Gandhiji's concept of *Swaraj* or Self-government postulated not merely the independence of India from British *raj* but also the concept of *Gram Swaraj* or *Village Self-Government subsuriled* within the larger concept of

Purna Swaraj or, what I would call, Freedom in its Fullness. The Gandhian concept of *Purna Swaraj* offers a new universal civilisational ideal of *Ram Rajya* or Kingdom of God on earth. In a statement on what he meant by Ram Rajya (published *inter alia* in *The Hindu* of June 22, 1945), Mahatma Gandhi said: *"It can be religiously translated as Kingdom of God on earth. Politically translated, it is perfect democracy in which, inequalities based on possession and non-possession, colour, race or creed or sex vanish. In it land and state belong to the people, justice is prompt, perfect and cheap and, therefore, there is freedom of worship, and of speech and the Press—all this because of the reign of the self-imposed law of moral restraint. Such a State must be based on truth and non-violence and must consist of prosperous, happy and self-contained villages and village communities."*

To achieve a high degree of non-violence in a society, Gandhiji counted first and foremost on morally enlightened and responsible individuals living a life of service in a decentralised society.

The Concept of Village Self-sufficiency

Gandhiji felt that the soul of India was in its villages, that India lived in the villages. He said, *"If the village perishes, India will perish too."* He said, *"Just as the universe is contained in the self, so is India contained in the villages."* But, Gandhiji's romantic "villagism" was not confined to India. It had its roots in his fear of all-powerful, mechanical and monolithic states and had a much wider application. Not for Gandhiji the Hegelian glorification of the state as an end in itself. To sing in praise of state power or to be in awe of any establishment was alien to the moral crucible of Gandhian non-violence based on a sturdy sense of democratic individualism.

Although Gandhiji might have drawn on the intellectual inputs of the historical jurisprudence of Vinogradoff, Maitland and Maine, and in particular Sir Henry Maine's thesis of ancient India consisting of a congeries of village republics, Gandhiji's village communities in his constitutional thought were not to be a replica of the village communities of yore. He told Louis Fischer in 1942, *"A system like the one I have outlined to you did exist, though undoubtedly it had its weakness; otherwise; it would not have succumbed before the Moguls and the British. I would like to think that parts of it have survived, and that the roots have survived, despite the ravages of the British rule. These roots and the stock are waiting to sprout if a few drops* of *rain fall. What the plant will be like I do not know."*

It is reasonable to assume that Gandhiji was influenced in his allegiance to the idea of village communities to a certain extent by the intellectual inputs of the great exponents of historical jurisprudence in the nineteenth century and by his own understanding of ancient Indian history. He might also have been aware of the Prussian Minister of Legislation Savigny's concept of *"Volksgeist"* as the manifestation of the spirit of the people or their common consciousness. Gandhiji did regard the village community as representing the *volksgeist* of India and non-violence as the essence and basic spirit of India's spiritual-moral heritage, but he gave them a new content, a new moral thrust and a new resilience.

To go back to the root idea of ancient Indian village communities, let us recall the well known work of Sir Henry Maine, *Village Communities in the East and West*, in which he demonstrated that the Indian village community was a living and not a dead institution and that the Indian and the ancient European systems of village communities were, in all essential particulars, identical. Vinogradoff's survey of village communities in Europe (until they were subverted and distorted by feudalism) provided testimony of harmonious and mutually supportive community life. A committee of the East India Company noted as early as 1812 that the inhabitants of India had lived in village communities from time immemorial. Sir Charles Trevellyn observed, *"One foreign conqueror after another has swept over India but the Village Municipalities have stuck to the soil like their own Kusha grass."* Sir Charles Metcalfe, the then Acting Governor-General of India wrote of India's ancient village communities in a famous minute in 1830: *"They seem to last where nothing else lasts... The union of the village communities, each one forming a separate little state in itself, has, I conceive, contributed more than any other cause to the preservation of the people of India through all revolutions and changes which they have suffered and it is in a high degree conducive to their happiness and to the enjoyment of a 'great portion of freedom and independence'. I wish, therefore, that the village constitutions may never be disturbed and I dread everything that has a tendency to break them up."*

In his monumental work, *Das Capital*, Karl Marx wrote of the Indian village republics in the same vein as Maine, Trevellyn and Metcalfe. He wrote: *"The small and extremely ancient Indian communities, which still exist to some extent, are based upon the communal ownership of the land, upon a direct linking up of manual agriculture and handicraft and upon a fixed form of the division of labour which is adopted as a cut-and-dried scheme whenever new communities are founded. They constitute self-sufficient productive entities, the area* of *land upon which production is carried on ranging from a hundred to several thousand acres. The greater part of the products is produced for the satisfaction of the immediate needs of the community, not as commodities; and production, itself is, therefore, independent of the division of labour which the exchange of commodities has brought about in Indian society as well. In different regions of India we find different forms of such communities. In the simplest form, the land is commonly tilled and its produce is divided among the members of the community, while every family carries on spinning, weaving, etc., as an accessory occupation. The simplicity of the productive organism in these self-sufficient communities... unlocks for us the mystery of the unchangeableness of Asiatic society, which contrasts so strongly with the perpetual dissolutions and reconstructions of Asiatic states, and with the unceasing changes of dynasties. The structure of the economic elements of the society remains unaffected by the storms in the political weather."*

The Object of Republican Democracy

Gandhiji found in the basic concept of the village community the institutional seed of non-violent republican democracy and an ideal society. At the heart of Gandhiji's conception of an ideal social order and an ideal polity was his jural concept of a moral community best represented by his ideal of self-governing village communities. That moral community, the model village of Mahatma Gandhi is able to differentiate between the complex and wasteful consumerism of an incremental materialistic 'standard of living' on the one hand and the eco-friendly limitation on the use of earth's finite resources represented in a higher spiritual 'standard of life' on the other. Gandhiji wrote in *Harijan* of September 1, 1946: *believe that Independent India can only discharge her duty towards a groaning world by adopting a simple but ennobled life by developing her thousands of cottages and living at peace with the world. High thinking is inconsistent with complicated material life based on high speed imposed on us by Mammon worship. All the graces of life are possible only when we learn the art of living nobly."*

On November 10, 1946, he wrote in *Harijan*, describing his dream villages. *"When our villages are fully developed, there will be no dearth in them of men with a high degree of skill and artistic talent. There will be village poets, village artists, village architects, linguists and research workers. In short, there will be nothing in life ... worth having which will not be had in the villages. Today the villages are dung heaps. Tomorrow they will be like tiny gardens of Eden where dwell highly intelligent folk whom no one can deceive or exploit."*

Gandhiji found in the basic concept of the village community the institutional seed of non-violent republican democracy and an ideal society.

Gandhiji's democratic polity was essentially a non-conventional federal structure of a vast congeries of autonomous village republics. In that structure, Gandhiji contemplated ever-widening but "never-ascending circles", and in which "life will not be a pyramid with the apex sustained by the bottom." As he put it, *"it will be an oceanic circle whose centre will be the individuals... the outermost circumference will not wield power to crush the inner circle, but will give strength to all within and derive its own strength from it."* (*Harijan*, 28 July, 1946).

Gandhiji had earlier explained that he envisaged that *"power concentrated now in New Delhi or in Calcutta and Bombay, in the big cities, would have to be distributed among the 700,000 villages of India; voluntary cooperation will produce real freedom and a new order."*

Gandhi and the Constitution of India

Gandhiji was still alive when the great exercise in the making of the Indian Constitution began. The founding fathers of the Constitution of India were not unfamiliar with the Gandhian vision and its jural and moral postulates. There was a wealth of Gandhian responses to the constitutional issues. Mr. Shriman Narayan had already published the *Gandhian Constitution for Free India* in 1946 on the eve of the commencement of the deliberations of India's Constituent Assembly. Mahatma Gandhi had written a foreword to that publication which he regarded as a thoughtful contribution, and an attempt to do "what for want of time I have failed to do." The Constituent Assembly of India and its founding fathers, however, did not have the strong inclination and clear commitment to work out a constitution for India based on Gandhian jurisprudence of non-violence and paid it little attention except in terms of the lip service of sanctimonious rhetoric. Most of the eminent leaders of India, at that time, did not think it practicable to fashion and give to the people of India a Constitution based on Gandhiji's vision. They revered Gandhiji but did not have the same faith in the efficacy of non-violence and the viability of the village communities.

When the final draft of the Constitution was adopted and enacted on 26 November, 1949, Gandhiji's basic concept of village communities found only an apologetic acceptance in a grudging and halting concession in the form of Article 40 of the Directive Principles of State Policy which provides that "The state shall take steps to organise village panchayats and endow them with such powers and authority as may be necessary to enable them to function as units of self-government." Article 40 was embodied in the Constitution of India as a fundamental principle of state policy which was not enforceable. When Article 40 came to be discussed and inserted somewhat belatedly on 22 November, 1948 as Article 31(A) in the Constitution of India (now renumbered as Article 40 in Chapter IV of the Constitution of India), the Chairman of the Drafting Committee, Dr. B.R. Ambedkar expressed the view that the village communities which had survived many vicissitudes were not fit to be units of self-government. On that issue, there was considerable furor and ferment among members of the Constituent Assembly. The President of the Constituent Assembly, Dr. Rajendra Prasad did express his personal view somewhat wistfully that the Constituent Assembly should have attempted to adopt village republics as the basis of the Constitution. The Constitutional Adviser, Sir Benegal Narsing Rau, however, said that it was too late to make an attempt to change the basis of the Constitution, the preparation of which had already progressed considerably.

Although during the debate in the Constituent Assembly on Article 40, there were echoes of the Gandhian concept of village self-government and its philosophy of grass roots democracy coupled with eloquent references to India's ancient republican and democratic traditions, the inescapable conclusion is that the prime movers in the making of the Constitution of India had developed a curious amnesia for Gandhian ideas in the midst of their post-partition preoccupations with the problems of governance. Ever since the Constitution of India came into force in 1950, the irony of relegating the basic Gandhian precept to oblivion substituted by an innocuous back-burner in the form of an "I owe you" contained in Article 40 flashed on India's constitutional conscience. A serious attempt was made to introduce Panchayati Raj Institutions on the 2nd October, 1959, the birth anniversary of Mahatma Gandhi. Pandit Jawaharlal Nehru described the new beginning as the most revolutionary and historical step in the context of new India. For a while, the idea did ride on the crest of a new wave of public enthusiasm and did seem to capture the public imagination, but its downhill decline began within less than a decade.

Most of the eminent leaders of India, at that time, did not think it practicable to fashion and give to the people of India a Constitution based on Gandhiji's vision.

As someone who has consistently crusaded for the revitalisation of Panchayati Raj Institutions for democracy and development, it was my privilege as Chairman of the Committee appointed by the Government of India to conceptualise local self-government as an autonomous constitutionally protected third tier of government, to propose a draft constitutional amendment bill, and to suggest a number of steps to attempt and fulfil what I have always regarded as the unfinished task of India's democratic republican Constitution. The recommendations contained in the Report of my Committee which was submitted on 28th November 1986 have now finally found their place in a chapter of the Constitution of India. That I believe to be only a modest beginning and a small first step in a long and arduous journey towards building up the village communities of India as repositories of India's democratic vitality and its culture of non-violence. Without the moral vision and the intrepid spirit and stamina of Mahatma Gandhi, the constitutional amendment may prove to be a mere cosmetic consolation, an exercise in futility, and a journey to nowhere in particular.

Village Community and Non-violence

The Gandhian village community of the future represents the microcosm of non-violence in all its ramifications. It also unfolds the serious operational limitations of the concept in the world in which we live, for the Gandhian village economics are constantly challenged by demands and pressures of industrialisation, economies of scale, demography, modern technology, management, marketing and globalisation. The General Agreement on Trade and Tariffs threatens to be the vanishing point of the village community and its economic autonomy and self-sufficiency. Can Gandhian economics, panchayati raj and the jurisprudence of non-violence survive those challenges?

In my opinion, we must at the threshold distinguish the basic Gandhian idea of the village community and the philosophy of non-violence from his particular prescriptions in given situations and for achieving certain goals at a particular time. Moreover, we must remember that he always looked at problems rationally and with an open mind and we should, therefore, approach the issues before us in the spirit of Gandhi and look up to Gandhiji as a physician rather than as a pharmacopoeia. The challenges which endanger the sense of community in the thick of global economic forces have to be faced in the context of the crucial Gandhian test based on non-violence, love, compassion, fellow-feeling, mutuality and the preservation of human individuality.

The Gandhian village community of the future represents the microcosm of non-violence in all its ramifications.

If industrialisation leads to concentration of wealth and gives rise to greater exploitation and impoverishment, it would have to be rejected or modified. If modern technology only breeds violence and warfare it would have to be stopped in its tracks. If the growing globalisation of economies cannot come to terms with the preservation of human individuality, creativity and the distinctive identity of communities, it would have to be questioned and corrected. The crux of the critical apparatus of Gandhian jurisprudence, therefore, does not lose its validity in the face of many economic, political and technological changes of great magnitude. The Gandhian approaches assume a different tenor and content in the face of the changing challenges but they remain profoundly and characteristically Gandhian.

It is interesting to recall Gandhiji's response to Ruskin's book *Unto This Last* which he found impossible to lay aside once he had begun it. It gripped him. He discovered some of his own convictions reflected in it. During his journey of 24 hours from Johannesburg to Durban, Ruskin's teachings had become a part of Gandhiji. Later in his life, he translated the book into his own language and called it *Sarvodaya.* His great disciple, Vinoba Bhave said that the appropriate rendering of *Unto This Last* would be *Antyodaya* or *Upliftment* of *the Last* rather than *Sarvodaya.* He then went on to explain that the concept of uplift of all included first and foremost the uplift of the last. The impact of the teachings of *Unto This Last* as Gandhiji understood them to be in his own words, are as follows:

1. That the good of the individual is contained in the good of all.
2. That a lawyer's work has the same value as the barber's, inasmuch as all have the same right of earning their livelihood from their work.
3. That a life of labour, that is, the life of the tiller of the soil and the handicraftsman is the life worth living.

The first of these I knew. The second I had dimly realised. The third had never occurred to me. *Unto This Last* made it as clear as daylight for me that the second and the third were contained in the first. I arose with the dawn, ready to reduce these principles to practice.

These precepts of Ruskin internalised by Gandhi were not like the laws of the Persians and the Medes. It is the spirit which marks the Gandhian approach to work and define his work ethic.

Abuse of Power and Non-violence

Gandhiji was not against machines or modern scientific inventions. His touchstone was non-violence. His yardstick was non-exploitation. His insistence was on the avoidance of concentration of power and abuse of power. His belief was for preserving and enhancing the creative capacities of human beings and for enlarging the spirit of sympathy, sharing and service. These were the ingredients of "happiness", the pursuit of which was the principle propelling force of Gandhian jurisprudence. It was in this context that his charismatic talisman and his theory of trusteeship have to be understood. Said Mahatma Gandhi in one of the greatest moral and spiritual edicts of all time: *"I will give you a talisman. Whenever you are in doubt or when the self becomes too much with you, apply the following test. Recall the face of the poorest and the weakest man whom you may have seen, and ask yourself if the step you contemplate is going to be of any use to him. Will he gain anything by it? Will it restore him to a control over his own life and destiny? In other words, will it lead to Swaraj for the hungry and spiritually starving millions? Then, you will find your doubt and your Self melting away."*

The Gandhian theory of trusteeship was based on Ruskin's critique of socialist violence. In his essay titled *Ad Valorem* in *Unto This Last,* Ruskin said: *"The socialist, seeing a strong man oppresses a weak one, cries out—break the man's arms; but I say 'teach him to use them to better purpose'. The fortitude and intelligence which acquire riches are intended, by the Giver of both, not to scatter, nor to give away, but to employ those riches in the service of mankind."*

Gandhiji was not against machines or modern scientific inventions. His touch stone was non-violence. His yardstick was non-exploitation.

Although Gandhiji did not share Ruskin's elitist paternalism, he developed his theory of trusteeship as a non-violent alternative to state ownership and expropriation. This was a concept of social control in pursuing which he was prepared to enact statutory trusteeship also. He admitted that absolute trusteeship is an abstraction like. Euclid's definition of a point, and was equally unattainable. But he felt that the theory of trusteeship offered a more civilised and non-violent alternative. He regarded the state as a soul-less machine and that is why he wanted to achieve the moral accountability of wealth through trusteeship. At the Round Table Conference in London, he once said that every vested interest must be subjected to scrutiny and confiscation ordered, if necessary, with or without compensation as the case demanded. In 1939, he wrote: *"My theory* of *trusteeship is no makeshift, certainly no camouflage. I am confident that it will survive all other theories. It has the sanction of all philosophy and religion behind it... No other theory is compatible with non-violence."*

The essence of his theory of trusteeship is that it was offered as a means of transforming the social order. It is based on the faith that human nature is never beyond redemption. It views property in its social and functional context. It resembles the Gandhian idea that everything belongs to God. More specifically, it means that through philanthropy, self-denial and detachment, those who follow the trusteeship principle could become exemplars to the society. Asked if any of his capitalist friends or followers had become a trustee, Gandhiji said that none had, the only exception being Jamnalal Bajaj who came 'near, but only near to it'. Asked what should be done to get them to follow the trusteeship idea, he replied that the sustained pressure of educated and organized public opinion, including a *satyagraha* was the best way.

Gandhian Concept of Trusteeship

Basic to the Gandhian idea of trusteeship, his consuming concern for the welfare of the poor and the downtrodden and his theory of trusteeship was his view of human nature and his steadfast allegiance to the central concept of *Dharma*.

Gandhiji's view of human nature is a peculiar mix of Hobbes, Rousseau and traditional Indian metaphysics and ethics. He said that we were perhaps all originally brutes and that we had become men by a slow process of evolution from the brute. Rousseau's noble savage is also visible in some of his writings. Gandhiji was always practising austerity and penance to achieve a spiritual sublimation.

Basic to the Gandhian idea of trusteeship, his consuming concern for the welfare of the poor and the downtrodden and his theory of trusteeship was his view of human nature and his steadfast allegiance to the central concept of Dharma.

He recognised that *"Everyone of us is a mixture* of *good and evil. Is there not plenty of evil in us?—There is enough in me, I always pray to God to purge me of it."* (*Harijan*, June 10, 1939). What made him an optimist in respect of human nature was his faith in the spiritual element in the true self of human personality. He claimed to be a vivisector of his failings and said that he had discovered that "man is superior to the system he propounds." He considered himself to be a practical idealist and believed that "non-violence is the law of our species and violence is the law of the brute." It was his conviction that the moment the man awakes to the spirit within he could not remain violent. He said that to be human is to be potentially and essentially divine. In the ultimate analysis, he took his position as a believer in *Advaita*, the Indian doctrine of monism which declares the essential unity of God and man and for that matter of all lives. His philosophy of *Advaita* was the source of his sense of universality. He would say, *"I am a part and parcel of the whole, and I cannot find Him apart from the rest of humanity."* His personal credo was *"...true individuality consists in reducing oneself to zero. The secret of life is selfless service. The highest ideal for us is to become* vitaraga *(free from attachment). Ethical rules, were framed by rishis (seers) on the basis of personal experience. A* rishi *is one who has realised for himself.* Sannyasa *in the* Gita *is renunciation of actions inspired by desire (kama). He is a man who is the ruler over his body."*

Gandhiji's approach to crime and punishment was compassionate, humane and reformist. Retribution did not play any part in Gandhian criminology and penology because he believed in correction and rehabilitation rather than condemnation and social alienation and exile. To a question about the treatment to be meted out to criminals in Free India in the light of his non-violence, he said in *Harijan* (28th April, 1946/5th May, 1946): *"In independent India of the non-violent type, there will be crime but no criminals. They will not be punished. Crime is a disease like any other malady and is a product of the prevalent social system. Therefore, all crimes including murder will be treated as a disease. Whether such an India will ever come into being is another question."*

In July-August 1947, he wrote in *Harijan* to sympathise with the movement for the abolition of capital punishment, and to endorse the idea of converting many of the prisons into hospitals and reformatories for the treatment of criminals as if they were diseased persons. He made his point of view on crime and punishment the point of departure with the severe penology of scriptural jurisprudence. He said, *"The upshot of all I want to convey is that every work labelled as scripture is not necessarily so. Moreover, a scripture to be scientific lends itself to mendations as the times may really require. They must progress with the times if they are to live in the lives of the people. The changeless and universal fundamentals are always very few. They do not require learned treatises to be described. The treatises are built upon these immovable rocks. Further, it is not everyone who is entitled to punish evil doers. In a decent society it is always reserved for the state. It enacts laws and appoints judges to judge in accordance with them. If such were not the case, we would all bid fair to become evil-doers.*

Gandhiji's approach to crime and punishment was compassionate, humane and reformist.

Human Rights and Humanism

Gandhiji's approach to human rights was deeply ethical, egalitarian and proactive. He believed in balancing human needs, human obligations and human rights. He regarded the sense of duty ingrained and inculcated in every human being as the true bastion of human rights. Reminding each one of us of our moral predicament, he noted in the daily diary for Anand T. Hingorani on 18th March, 1945, *"The pity is that even while knowing what our duty is, we fail to perform it! For this, let every man answer to himself"*. He said on 9th April, 1945, *"Performance of duty is the only thing that really matters,"* and on 10th June, 1946, *"No joy can compare with the joy of doing one's duty quietly."* Speaking in the language of his ethical jurisprudence, he said in a post-prayer speech, *"I venture to suggest that rights that do not flow directly from duty well performed are not worth having."* It is an object lesson for the world as a whole and for the jurisprudence of human rights that Mahatma Gandhi who pioneered and inspired the human rights revolution all over the world against apartheid, discrimination, intolerance, colonialism, untouchability, gender injustice and other violations rested his philosophy of rights on the moral imperative of responding to basic human needs and performing our primary human obligations.

Gandhian jurisprudence of human rights is not a jurisprudence of *status quo*, but a jurisprudence of changing jural relations within a dynamic and evolving normative order. What is more, the Gandhian jurisprudence goes far beyond Hohfeld's limited scheme of jural correlatives and jural opposites and constructs a jurisprudence not only of formal legal claims and liabilities but also of moral obligations and voluntary service and sacrifice in the spirit of humanity and prompted by fellow feeling.

Modern realists would have no difficulty in summarily rejecting Gandhian jurisprudence which looks at human needs, aspirations and behaviour in the larger context of human nature and human impulses because it cannot assist the realists in making prophecies of what the Courts will do in fact, and that is the end-all and be-all of jurisprudence for them. By that token, those drilled rigorously in the methods taught by modern realists have relatively little to offer in building up a new normative jurisprudence and a new morality of human obligations to satisfy human needs and human rights except to say pass most of the time in this game of bridge.

Gandhian jurisprudence of human rights is not a jurisprudence of* status quo*, but a jurisprudence of changing jural relations within a dynamic and evolving normative order.

The most luminous and revolutionary concept in the Gandhian constellation of ideas in the realm of what I have called the Jurisprudence of Non-violence. The concept of *Satyagraha*, is a technique Gandhiji evolved first in South Africa and then in India. It grew out of the concept of passive resistance and grew far beyond it. When Lord Hunter inquiring into the first nationwide *Satyagraha* movement in India asked Mahatma Gandhi to explain it to him, he said, *"It is a movement intended* to *replace methods of violence and a movement based entirely upon truth."* It means conceptually an insistence on truth which includes Love and Non-violence or firmness in the cause of truth. In other words, it means "Truth-Force".

To Joseph Doke, one of the earliest biographers, Gandhiji explained how one verse by a Gujarati poet, Shamal Bhat, had clung to him. That verse said, *"If* a *man gives you* a *drink* of *water and you give him a drink in return, that is nothing. Real beauty is in doing good against evil."* Gandhiji added, *'It was the New Testament which really awakened me to the rightness and value of 'passive resistance'*. When I read in the *Sermon on the Mount* such passages as *'Resist not him that is evil but whoever smiteth thee on thy cheek turn to him the other also'*, and *'Love your enemies and pray for them that persecute you, that ye may be sons of your Father which is in heaven.' "I was simply overjoyed when I found my own opinion confirmed where I least expected it. The Bhagavadgita deepened the impression, and Tolstoy's The Kingdom of God is Within You'* gave it a permanent form."

The exchange between Hunter Committee's counsel and Gandhiji gives us a fairly clear idea of the *Satyagraha* principles and technique:

"Your *satyagraha* doctrine, so far as I understand it, involves the

> pursuit of truth and in that pursuit you invite suffering on yourself and do not cause violence to anybody else.
> However, honestly a man may strive in his search for truth, his notions of truth may be different from the notion of others. Who then is to determine the truth?
> The individual himself would determine that.
> Different individuals would have different views as to truth. Would that not lead to confusion?
> I do no think so.
> Honestly striving after truth differs in every case.
> That is why the non-violence part was a necessary corollary. Without that there would be confusion and worse."

Writing in *Young India* in January 1921, Gandhiji stressed: "*It is a test of our sincerity. It requires solid and silent self-sacrifice. It challenges our honesty and our capacity for national work. It is a movement that aims at translating ideas into action. And the more we do, the more we find that much more must be done than we had expected. And this thought of our imperfection must make us humble.*"

Each *Satyagraha* movement launched by Mahatma Gandhi had its own contextual setting and its own lessons. I wish to refer only to two particular episodes, the one in 1919 in the wake of Rowlett Act and Jallianwala Bagh atrocities, and the other in 1922 in the wake of the incidents of violence in Bombay and Chauri Chaura. In both cases, even when the stakes were high, Mahatma Gandhi suspended the *Satyagraha* because agitating public had resorted to violence. Gandhiji's *Satyagraha* was a synonym for ethical humanism and an instrument of socio-political action. It was Non-violence in action. His non-violence was love and self-sacrifice. Nine fundamental rules of *Satyagraha* were evolved by him:

(1) Self-reliance at all times;
(2) Initiative in the hands of the *satyagrahis*;
(3) Propagation of the objectives, strategy and tactics of the campaign;
(4) Reduction of demands to a minimum consistent with truth;
(5) Progressive advancement of the movement through appropriate steps and stages;
(6) Examination of weaknesses;
(7) Persistent search for avenues of cooperation, with the adversary on honourable terms;
(8) Refusal to surrender essentials in negotiation;
(9) Insistence upon full agreement.

Gandhiji laid down the following nine-point code of discipline for volunteers in the 1930 *Satyagraha* movement:

(1) Harbour no anger but suffer the anger of the opponent. Refuse to return the assaults of the opponent.
(2) Do not submit to any order given in anger, even though severe punishment is threatened for disobeying.
(3) Refrain from insults and swearmg.
(4) Protect opponents from insult or attack, even at the risk of life.
(5) Do not resist arrest nor the attachment of property, unless holding property as a trustee.
(6) Refuse to surrender any property held in trust at the risk of life.
(7) If taken prisoner, behave in an exemplary manner.
(8) As a member of a *satyagraha* unit, obey the orders of *satyagraha* leaders, and resign from the unit in the event of serious disagreement.
(9) Do not expect guarantees for maintenance of dependents.

Among the steps in a *Satyagraha* campaign, Gandhiji's nine steps, applicable to a wide range of conflict situations, included negotiation and arbitration, preparation of the group for direct action, active campaign through demonstrations and mass meetings, a strong appeal to the authority for conflict resolution, economic boycott and forms of strike, non-cooperation through non-payment of taxes and other forms of boycott, civil disobedience in respect of carefully chosen laws which are either symbolic or central to the grievance (and not in respect of all laws), performance of the government functions and the establishment of a kind of parallel government.

The most important caveat for all *satyagrahis* is that they should dedicate themselves without ill-will or feeling of enmity to the use of Truth-force, suffer themselves rather than inflict any suffering, approach the opponents with love and ensure total observance of non-violence. Those norms are essential to save a *satyagraha* movement from being a tactic of *duragraha.* We must also understand clearly that *satyagraha* is a technique of Truth-force and not an opportunistic tactic of convenience and cowardice. As Romain Rolland said of Gandhiji, *"No one has a greater horror of passivity than this tireless fighter, who is one of the most heroic incarnations of a man who resists. The soul of his movement is the active force of love, faith and sacrifice."*

I quote Gandhiji's challenging words to describe the elemental force of *satyagraha*: *"We will match your capacity to inflict suffering with our capacity to endure suffering. We will meet your physical force with soul-force. We will not hate you, but we cannot, in all good conscience, obey your unjust laws. Do to us what you will and we will still love you. Bomb our homes and threaten our children; send your hooded perpetrators of violence into our communities and drag us out of some way side road, beating us and leaving us half-dead, and we will still love you. But we will soon wear you down by our capacity to suffer. And in winning our freedom we will so appeal to, your heart and conscience that we will win you in the process."*

Martin Luther King, Jr., called *satyagraha* his pilgrimage to Non-violence and Truth. He said, *"Non-violence* can *touch men where the law cannot reach them. When the law regulates behaviour it plays an indirect part in moulding public sentiment. The enforcement of the law is itself a form of peaceful persuasion. But the law needs help. The Courts can order desegregation* of *the public schools. But what* can *be done* to *mitigate the fears, to disperse the hatred, violence, and irrationality gathered around school integration,* to *take the initiative out* of *the hands* of *racial demagogues, to release respect for the law? In the end, for laws to be obeyed, men must believe they are right.*

The most important caveat for all satyagrahis is that they should dedicate themselves without ill-will or feeling of enmity to the use of Truth-force, suffer themselves rather than inflict any suffering, approach the opponents with love and ensure total observance of non-violence.

"Here non-violence comes in as the ultimate form of persuasion. It is the methods which seek to implement the just law by appealing to the conscience of the great decent majority who through blindness, fear, pride, or irrationality have allowed their conscience to sleep."

"The non-violent resisters can summarise their message in the following simple terms: We will take direct action against injustice without waiting for other agencies to act. We will not obey unjust laws or submit to unjust practices. We will do this peacefully, openly, cheerfully because our aim is to persuade. We adopt the means of non-violence because our end is a community at peace with itself. We will try to persuade with our words, but if our efforts fail, we will try to persuade with our acts. We will always be willing to talk and seek, fair compromise, but we are ready to suffer when necessary and even risk our lives to *become witnesses to the truth as we see it."*

Satyagraha as a Moral Weapon

Satyagraha stands out as a modern and civilised moral weapon and as a jural catalyst in the jurisprudence of freedom. It enables us to view the rule of law not as a static and moribund set of rilles but as a peaceful liberator of men, women and children from the shackles of injustice. It tells us of the moral nature of humankind, the needs, rights and obligations of all of us in society, and of the moral accountability of every authority.

In a prophetic vein, Victor Hugo had once said: *"I represent a party which does not yet exist, The party of revolution and civilization. This party will make the twentieth century"*. Gandhiji represented the party of revolution and civilisation in a unique way. He heralded the end of apartheid and became the harbinger not only of freedom from colonialism throughout the world but also freedom in its fullness and in human rights and obligations. He inspired the jurisprudence of protest and gave moral legitimacy, dignity and meaning to the conduct of conflicts. He also gave us techniques of conflict resolution without rancour and malice, methods of making treaties of peace without wars and waging wars without violence.

Gandhiji gave us a new dimension of the jurisprudence of natural law for our age and time. He reminded us of natural law as a dictate of right reason, revived and resurrected the finer traditions of that school of jurisprudence in Anglo-Saxon and Indian jurisprudence and created a reunion of law and justice. Unless I substituted the word "might" by Truth-Force or Voice of the State as the Inner Voice of Conscience, Gandhian jurisprudence of non-violence cannot be described in the language of Salmond "as the perfect union of right and might" and "as justice speaking to men by the voice of the state." I might, however, turn to Blackstone to describe Gandhian jurisprudence of the natural law of non-violence as "being coeval with mankind and dictated by God himself... (and) of course superior in obligation to any other. It is binding over all the globe, in all countries and at all times"; no human laws are of any validity, if contrary to this."

Gandhian jurisprudence is thus the jurisprudence of all our tomorrows even if it seems a distant goal or an impractical utopia to narrow proponents of realism and pessimism. The next millennium might hopefully belong to the prophet of non-violence.

Speaking of Mahatma Gandhi, Dr. S. Radhakrishnan described him in his Kamla Lectures (1942) as a flame from God whose *"suffering embodies the wounded pride of India, and in his satyagraha is reflected the eternal patience of her wisdom."* Referring to his superhuman passion for truth and justice, he acclaims what Gandhiji offers as *"the purest, the most elevating and the most inspiring ideal known to man. His is a spiritual influence, a cleansing, purifying flame, which has burned up much dross and revealed much pure gold. All his life has been one continuous fight against the unspiritual."*

Gandhian jurisprudence is thus the jurisprudence of all our tomorrows even if it seems a distant goal or an impractical utopia to narrow proponents of realism and prophets of pessimism. The next millennium might hopefully belong to the prophet of the jurisprudence of non-violence.

CHAPTER 24

Environment and the Ancient Indian Heritage

The Genesis

For several centuries running into many millennia, India has been a veritable cradle and a truly hospitable home of different schools of thought and religious traditions. Throughout those trackless centuries, India has provided an ample expanse of friendly space for an open and ongoing discourse of ideas marked by a quintessential spirit of inquiry and a sense of freedom, enlarging and reinforcing its multicultural vision, uphoiding values of affirmative tolerance and consistently seeking and evolving a sense of unity in diversity.

The Vedic hymns and the discourses and dialogues in the *Upanishads* as well as the teachings of the Jain and Buddhist traditions bear eloquent testimony to a remarkable continuity of an exceptionally free discourse of ideas. In that discourse, within the orbit of ancient Indic heritage, there were manifold diversities but there was always an over-arching as well as a subterranean sense of unity and coherence which gave the Indic civilisation some of its defining characteristics and the Indic culture its spiritual *base* and its humanitarian and ecological *ethos.* It is that *base* and that ethos which are coherently and consistently reflected in the Indic approach to environment. That approach is a part of the living legacy of India even today, although that legacy often seems to be embattled and imperilled all around. At the same time, we know that the ancient Indian legacy is endowed with an uncanny and time-tested resilience. In the resilience of that legacy, there is hope and promise for India and the rest of the world.

The Vedic Cosmic Vision

The *Vedas* enshrine a holistic and poetic cosmic vision. They represent the oldest, the most carefully nurtured, the most elaborately systematised and the most lovingly preserved oral tradition in the annals of the world. Unique in their perspective of time and space, the *Vedas* have a universal and timeless quality. The evocative poetry of joyous and spontaneous affirmation of life and nature, the unravelling exploration of the seers into the terrestrial and transcendental destiny of mankind, the pervasive immanence and the pristine omnipresence of primeval reality and primordial matter, and the wisdom and philosophy of Moral and Social Order in an harmonious equilibrium unfold the luminous realm of the spirit of the *Vedas.*

Unfortunately, the Western Vedic scholarship of the late eighteenth and the nineteenth century, which introduced the Vedic literature to the Western World, though erudite and even original, missed the depth and meaning of Vedic symbolism mainly because the Western discovery of the Vedic lore and literature came in an age when unrepentant colonialism and self-opinionated missionary activity were in the ascendant and the traditional repositories and exponents of the Vedic heritage in their own Indian homeland were in a state of intellectual decline and social disarray. During that period, there was little awareness in the West of the multi-splendoured Indic achievements in philosophy, mathematics, astronomy, medicine, chemistry, biology, botany, physics, metaphysics, arts, aesthetics and statecraft. In fact, there was a certain insidious lack of respect for the culture of the conquered country.

As I have endeavoured to explain in my Foreword to the recently published text and translation of the *Vedas* in 24 volumes, the Vedic vision was somewhat eclipsed for many centuries by an ethnic amnesia and by India's long and forced isolation and subjugation. There was an overpowering sense in the devastation of our Indic identity and dignity and a denuding loss of self-respect and self-confidence.

In that state of decay and disillusionment and of penury and paralysis of critical Indian scholarship, Swami Dayanand Saraswati's self-confident interpretation of the *Vedas* came as a breath of fresh air, creating a new ambience for understanding, a new striving of resurgence and a new equation of independence. Swami Dayananda naturally saw the *Vedas* as an Indian, steeped in that tradition, as a living and universal scripture of mankind containing "a plenary revelation of religious, ethical and scientific truth". Sri Aurobindo's poetic, philosophical, mystical and spiritual approach to *Vedas* represents the flowering of that renaissance. Western translators and commentators whose contribution of Vedic learning is, in a historical sense, monumental and memorable, however, lacked that temperamental empathy to enable them to identify themselves with Vedic culture which enabled Swami Dayanand and Sri Aurobindo to give an integrated interpretation of the social ethos, religious spirit and spiritual values of the *Vedas*. Sri Aurobindo put it in a fair and objective appraisal:

> "It was the curiosity of a foreign culture that broke after many centuries the seal of final authoritativeness which Sayana had fixed on the ritualistic interpretation of the *Veda*. The ancient scripture was delivered over to a scholarship laboriously bold in speculation, ingenious in its flights of fancy, conscientious according to its own lights, but ill-fitted to the method of understanding old mystic poets; for it was void of any sympathy with that ancient temperament, unprovided with any due in its own intellectual or spiritual environment to the ideas hidden in the Vedic figures and parables. The result has been of a double character, on the one side the beginning of a more minute, thorough, careful as well as a freer handling of the problems of *Vedic* interpretation, on the other hand, a final exaggeration of its apparent material sense and the complete obscuration of its true and inner secret."

It is true that there still remain many unanswered questions in Vedic scholarship and the history of the *Sramana* tradition before *Lord Mahavira*, the twenty-fourth *tirthankara* of Jains remains obscure. What we do know in our limited understanding of the Vedic and the *Sramanic* traditions is perhaps merely a fraction of the totality of the *Vedic-Sramanic* universe of ideas, values, institutions, culture and languages. What is, however, no longer unclear is that the subtle, sophisticated philosophical efflorescence of *Upanishads* and of Jaina and Buddhist philosophies were intimately intertwined with the Vedic roots. Obviously, as shown by Sri Aurobindo, such profound and ultimate thoughts, such systems of subtle and elaborate psychology as are found in the substance of the *Upanishads*, could not spring out of a previous void and that in the nature of things, the human mind in its progress marches from knowledge to knowledge, or it renews and enlarges previous knowledge that has been obscured and overlaid, or it seizes on old imperfect clues and is led by them to new discoveries. Demonstrably, the thought-streams of the *Upanishads*, and by the same token, the wealth of basic ideas in the Jaina and Buddhist traditions could only have followed great origins anterior to them and the anterior Vedic *Sramanic* culture had a rich ambience of knowledge, experiences and attainments, and a vision and a worldview

Swami Dayanand Saraswati's self-confident interpretation of the Vedas came as a breath of fresh air, creating a new ambience for understanding, a new striving of resurgence and a new equation of independence.

which had the spiritual *content* and the humanitarian and ecological ethos at its heart.

In the Indic tradition, it has always been thought that to commune with the *Vedas* is to share in a cosmic vision and a universal faith. There is permeating and pervasive awareness and acknowledgement of that Vedic-Upanishadic as well as Sramanic "anterior" throughout the history of Indian thought. Its radiant richness was, however, lost on those who saw the *Vedas* only as pristine pastoral poetry or as a source book of ritual incantation of elemental gods, or as folksongs of unlettered and primitive pantheistic animism. No wonder then that Jaina and Buddhist traditions also received a somewhat brusque reckoning in the West. For a long time, Lord Mahavira and Lord Buddha were thought by many Western scholars to be the same person and Jainism and Buddhism were occasionally described interchangeably. I hope that the world can open a new account of deeper and clearer understanding of the Indic and Asian traditions as we approach the threshold of the twenty-first century.

Sri Aurobindo's poetic, philosophical, mystical and spiritual approach to Vedas represents the flowering of that renaissance.

Vedic cosmology and cosmogony and the Vedic pantheon are deeply symbolic. According to Sri Aurobindo, the pioneer scholar, philosopher and visionary, who illumined the path of subtle, symbolic and spiritual interpretation of the *Vedas*, the Vedic seers "arranged the substance of their thought in a system of parallelism by which the same deities were at once internal and external powers of universal Nature, and they managed its expression through a system of double values by which the same language served for their worship in both aspects." The physical universe and the attributes of the external powers of universal Nature thus provided the metaphor for mapping the deeper ineffable psychological and spiritual universe of inner consciousness. Since the *Vedas* were primarily intended to serve for spiritual enlightenment and self-culture, says Sri Aurobindo, the psychological sense of *Vedas* was particularly predominant, pervasive, close-knit and coherent.

The central idea of the Vedic religion is the idea of the One Being with gods or the *devas* expressing the many facets of that Unity in numerous forms and names. The colourful diversities of Hindu polytheism and pantheism are thus resolved and reconciled through the supervening philosophy and doctrine of *Vedic* and *Upanishadic* monotheism.

There is a cosmic celebration of the divine genesis of the creation in the *Vedas* particularly in the famous Creation Hymn (*RV* 10th Mandala). It has an anthropomorphic macro-cosmic symbolism ascribing the birth of the universe to the One Being: the birth of Moon to the Mind; of the Sun to the Eyes; of Indra and Agni to the Mouth; of Air to the Breath; of Firmament to the Navel; of Heaven to the Head; of Earth to the Feet; and of Space to the Ears. In *Mundaka upanishad*, the same thought is expressed as follows:

> Fire is His Head; His eyes, the Moon and the Sun;
> The regions of space, his Ears;
> His voice, the revealed *Vedas*;
> Wind, His breath (*prana*);
> His heart, the whole world;
> Out of His feet, the earth;
> Truly, He is the Inner Soul (*Atman*) of all.
> (Translated by Robert Ernest Hume, 1921)

In the *Sandilya* section of the *Chandogya Upanishad* (3.14), all possible qualities are attributed to the One Being:

> "Verily this whole world is Brahma... He who consists of mind, whose body is life, whose form is light, whose conception is truth, whose soul (*atman*) is space, containing all works, containing all desires, containing all odours, containing all tastes, encompassing this whole world, the unspeaking, the unconcerned... Smaller than a grain of rice, or a barley-corn, or a mustard seed, or a grain of millet, or the kernel of a grain of millet... (yet) greater than the atmosphere, greater than the sky, greater than these worlds."

We find in these and other hymns of creative cosmic monotheism an imaginative sophisticated and functional pantheism and polytheism so that the physical universe is perceived as cluster of diverse and even contrary faculties subsumed within the divine One Being. Thus, the Indic tradition intuitively discovered the unity of all beings in the concept of *Brahma*, the Real of the real, the Soul from which come forth all vital energies, all intelligence, all worlds, all gods, all beings. This unity of all beings in One Being whose macrocosmic reach and embrace encompasses everything and everyone establishes a universal philosophy of environment on a profoundly spiritual, moral and humanitarian basis.

The Physical and Objective Universe

The Vedic seers speak of certain cosmic divisions which refer, on the one hand, to the physical and objective universe and, on the other, to the inner space of subjective consciousness. The heart-throb of that inner space is a unique Vedic discovery called the *soul* which soars beyond physical and mental consciousness and climbs beyond the earth of body and the heaven of mind by the ascending path of the Truth to find the Godhead seated in the triple Divine Principle and the source of Beatitude waiting for it, leaning down to it reaching out to it. The soul finds in the manifestations of the One Being "the Friend and Lover", "the pastoral Master of the Herds" and "the source and outpourer of the ambrosial Wine of divine delight" drawn from "the sevenfold waters of existence or pressed out from the luminous plant on the hill of Being and uplifted by its raptures."

The intimate eternal relationship of the soul and the Soul of all souls establishes bonds between all souls and indeed the entire creation. That relationship provides an enduring spiritual foundation for a universal ecological philosophy in the inner space of the subjective consciousness of all souls.

In the inner space of subjective consciousness, the indwelling Vedic gods represent spiritual capacities and potentialities. To give just one example, the flaming godhead, *Agni* or Fire, represents the Divine Will perfectly inspired by Divine Wisdom which awakens the consciousness to Immortality. It symbolises the potency of the "Truth-consciousness" and becomes the Divine Will-Force portrayed as "flaming upwards to heaven to meet the Divine Dawn" and reaching the Paradise of Light and Bliss which is its own native supreme home and where the shining immortals sit in celestial sessions and drink the Wine of the infinite beatitude. *Agni* is portrayed symbolically as a child of the universal parents, Heaven and Earth, Mind and Body, Soul and Material Nature, also described as a child of the seven Mothers or the seven Principles which constitute conscious existence. In these images, there are innumerable parables which envelop many meaningful and symbolic myths. It is clear that *Agni* is not merely a Sacrificial Fire, not simply a material flame or physical heat and light.

The symbolism of Fire, Light and Dawn, in the same way as the symbolism of different gods of the Vedic pantheon including Surya, Savitri, Varuna Mitra and many others, represents and reflects the larger cosmic truth of concordance between inner and outer space and a bridge between the spiritual and the ecological. That larger cosmic truth is encapsulated in a triple-term epigram *"Satyam Rtam Brhat"*, which tells us of the Truth of the cosmos embedded in the absolute order of harmony. In the *Prithvi Sukta* (in *Atharva Veda*), the axiom is *"Satyam Brhat Rtam Ugram"* which particularly stresses the severely exacting and rigorous nature of the discipline of truth, harmony and rectitude. It is this principle of harmony which is the "Truth of things" and which sustains the universe in a state of equipoise, facilitates the transition of the human soul from the state of death to the state of immortality, maintains the conjunction of planets and the combination of elements and when translated into *dharma*, it prescribes the fundamental principles of social ethics and ecological balance.

Environmental Invocation

The Vedic Hymn to the Earth, the *Prithvi Sukta* in *Atharva Veda* is unquestionably the oldest and the most sublime and evocative environmental invocation in the history of the world. In it, the Vedic seer solemnly declares the enduring filial allegiance of humankind to Mother Earth: *Mata Bhumih Putroham Prithivyah*—"Earth is my mother, I am her son." Mother Earth is celebrated for all her natural bounties and particularly for her gifts of herbs and vegetation. Her blessings are sought for prosperity in all endeavours and fulfilment of all righteous aspirations. A covenant is made that the humankind shall secure the Earth against all environmental trespasses and shall never let her be oppressed *(Asambadham Madhyato Manavanam)*. A soul-stirring prayer is sung in one of the hymns for the preservation and conservation of hills, snow-clad mountains, and all brown, black and red earth, unhurt, unsmitten, unwounded, unbroken and well defended by *Indra*.

The Vedic seers regarded the Earth as a sacred space for the consecrated endeavours and aspirations of humankind and for the practice of restraint and responsibility.

Says the Hymn to the Earth in a prayerful thanksgiving and homage which is eternally inspiring and edifying:

> Earth, in which lie the sea, the river and other waters,
> in which food and cornfields have come to be,
> in which lives all that breathes and that moves,
> May she confer on us the finest and that moves,
> Earth, in which the waters, common to all,
> moving on all sides, flow unfailingly, day and night,
> may she pour on us milk in many streams,
> and endow us with lustre.
>
> May those born of thee, O Earth,
> Be for our welfare, free from sickness and waste.
> Wakeful through a long life, we shall become
> bearers of tribute to thee
> Earth, my mother, set me securely with bliss
> in full accord with heaven,
> O wish one,
> Uphold me in grace and splendour.

The Vedic seers regarded the Earth as a sacred space for the consecrated endeavours and aspirations of humankind and for the practice of restraint and responsibility. It is this affirmative view of the inviolable sacred space in human consciousness which is integral to the *Vedas* and the *Upanishads* and on which rests the Vedic vision of a world filled with the purity of spiritual environment and the sanctity of environmental spirituality and morality. Such a world can only be sustained by *"Satyam Brhat Rtam Ugram"* the severely exacting discipline of Truth, Harmony and Rectitude, based on a conception of cosmic and comprehensive Peace as envisioned in the famous Vedic Hymn of Peace:

Om Dyuv Shantih, Antariksham shantih.
Prithvee shantih, Aapah shantih,
Oshadhayah shantih, Vanaspatyah shantih,
Vishvedevaah shantih, Brahma shantih,
Sarve shantih, Shantireva shantih,
Saa maa shantiredhi,
Om Shantih Shantih Shantih.

We invoke and imbibe *Aum*, the primordial sound of
Cosmic Harmony and Pray for;
Peace and Harmony in Heaven;
Peace and Harmony in the Sky and on the Earth;
Peace and Harmony in the Waters;
Peace and Harmony in the Herbs, the Vegetation and the Forests;
Peace and Harmony
Among the Peoples and the Rulers of the World;
Peace and Harmony in Spiritual Quest and Realisation;
Peace and Harmony for one and all;
Peace and Harmony Everywhere and in Everything;
Peace, True and Real Peace,
Let that Peace repose in my inner space
Peace of Peace, Everlasting Peace,
We pray for Peace.

Compatibility of Different Traditions

The *Vedas* and the *Upanishads* are often described as constituting the Brahmana branch of the Indic tradition whereas the Jaina and the Buddhist traditions are referred to as belonging to the *Sramana* branch. The two, though distinct and often portrayed as somewhat adversarial, are, in fact, intimately and inextricably intertwined. There was a great deal of interaction, overlapping and cultural, social and intellectual commingling between the two branches so that the philosophical divergences did not introduce rigid frontiers between them. Many of the Vedic and Upanishadic concepts are to be found in the Jaina and Buddhist literature and *vice versa.*

As we look at the ancient Indic tradition as a whole, the superficial adversarial appearances fall in place as features of an open and questioning society in a resurgent state of dialectical dynamism, and many of the opposing and mutually contradictory aspects are seen as complementary.

On the approach to environment, there is a high degree of compatibility, consonance and commonality between the Brahmana and Sramana traditions which were, after all, the two sides of the same coin. The main resonance of Vedas is poetic and spiritual. The *Upanishads* map philosophical routes of spiritual experience by employing a combination of intellectual and intuitive tools. The Jaina and Buddhist traditions excel in analytical realism and compassionate ethics.

The roots of the Indic *Sramana* tradition go back to prehistoric times. We must remind ourselves that Vardhamana, later hailed as Mahavira, Great Hero, and the final teacher of the current time cycle, was born in 599 BC in the kingdom of Vaisali in the Magadha region and he was not the first but the twenty-fourth *Tirthankara.* Parsva, the twenty-third *Tirthankara,* whose historicity has been verified, flourished in Varanasi in *circa* 850 BC, some 250 years before Vardhamana was born. Neroi is said to be the same as Arishtanemi of Vedic literature. Nemi, according to popular Jaina tradition, seems to have lived in Saurashtra and to have been a contemporary of *Kṛsna.* On the other hand, the first *Tirthankara* of Jaina, Adinath Rsabha, belongs to the oldest phases of human civilisation. He is believed to have been the founder of the new way of life based on *Asi* (weapons of defence), *Masi* (representing ink and pen, in other words, scripts, literature and paintings), and *Kṛshi* (agriculture and animal husbandry), and the fountainhead of all the sixty-four crafts and vocations.

Parsva had taught in the ninth century BC the system of the four-fold restraint, later elaborated and consolidated by Vardhamana Mahavira. Buddhist texts are replete with references to a large number of Nirgrantha (without ties of attachment) ascetics, as the Jaina monks were then known.

On the approach to environment, there is a high degree of compatibility, consonance and commonality between the Brahmana and Sramana traditions which were, after all, the two sides of the same coin.

Jina is a spiritual victor and a peaceful liberator. The Vedic concepts of Peace, Harmony and Rectitude are to be found at the heart of the Jaina tradition also. But the Jaina tradition did not implicitly accept the authority of the *Vedas* and the Vedic pantheon: it denied the efficacy of sacrifice which had assumed centrality in Vedic ritual. Jainas also rejected the supremacy of the Brahmanical priestocracy.

The Jaina Tradition

The essential concepts of the Jaina tradition are related to the seven categories of truth beginning from the existence of souls and culminating in the liberation from worldly bondage. Jaina theology does not posit a Creator. It postulates a beginningless and endless universe. It recognises two fundamentals of existence. As Dr. Nathmal Tatia explains, the first fundamental existence is the beginningless and interdependent and coexistence of physical and spiritual reality; the second is the inexorable law of cause and effect (through *Karma*) which drives the universe. These two fundamental principles of life, that of spiritual and physical symbiosis and that of cause and effect, have shaped the precepts and practice of the Jaina tradition.

In his Introduction to the *Jaina Book of Books*, the title of which means *That which is,* to which I was privileged to contribute my Foreword, Dr. Tatia explains the central themes of Non-violence, Non-absolutism and Non-possession in the Jaina tradition as follows: "Non-violence strengthens the autonomy of life of everything. Non-absolutism strengthens the autonomy of thought of every individual. Non-possession strengthens the inter-dependence of all existence. If you feel that every soul is autonomous, you will never trample on its right to live. If you feel every person is a thinking person, you will not trample on his or her thoughts. If you feel that you own nothing and no one, you will not trample on the planet."

The premise of the Jaina religion is that the goal of human life is liberation, which is defined as perfect knowledge, perfect intuition and eternal bliss. The path to liberation is paved by enlightened worldview, enlightened knowledge and enlightened conduct.

The Jaina theory of knowledge, which is the doctrine of manifold aspects, describes the world as a multifaceted, everchanging reality with an infinity of viewpoints depending on the time, place, nature and state of the one who is the viewer and that which is viewed. It is this doctrine and the discipline of non-violence which leads to the doctrine of *syadvada* or relativity, which states that truth is relative to different viewpoints *(nayas)*. What is true from one point of view is open to question from another. Absolute truth cannot be grasped from any particular viewpoint alone because absolute truth is the sum total of all the different viewpoints that make up the universe. Because it is rooted in the doctrines of *anekantavada* and *syadvada*, Jainism does not look upon the universe from an anthropocentric, ethnocentric or egocentric viewpoint. It takes into account the viewpoints of other species, other communities and nations and other human beings.

According to the Jaina tradition, maximum abstinence from violence is of pivotal value and is the foundation of all virtues. Self-restraint is the hallmark of non-violence. Compassion and reverence for life are the sheet anchor of the Jain quest for Peace, Harmony and Rectitude, based on spiritual and physical symbiosis and a sense of responsibility and restraint arising out of the ethical principle of cause and effect.

Although the term *'Ahimsa'* is stated in the negative (*a* = non, *himsa* = violence), it is rooted in a host of positive aims and actions which have great relevance to contemporary environmental concerns. Its one aspect is *daya* (compassion, empathy and charity), described by a great Jain teacher as "the beneficent mother of all beings and the elixir for those who wander in suffering through the ocean of successive rebirths." *Jiva-daya* means caring for and sharing with all living beings, tending, protecting and serving them. It entails universal friendliness *(maitri)*, universal forgiveness *(kshama)* and universal fearlessness *(abhaya)*. Jains, whether monks, nuns or normal citizens, therefore, affirm prayerfully and sincerely, that their hearts are filled with forgiveness for all living beings and that they have sought and received the forgiveness of all beings, that they crave the friendship of all beings, that all beings give them their friendship and that there is not the slightest feeling of alienation or enmity in their hearts for anyone or anything. They also pray that forgiveness and friendliness may reign throughout the world and that all living beings may cherish each other.

In simple words of great wisdom which have a profound contemporary relevance, Dr. Tatia says: "We face personality problems because of a distorted self-identity either as a purely spiritual or purely physical being. We face social disorder because individuals and nations do not see themselves as ultimately responsible for their actions. We face economic decline because we ignore the fact that it is the harmony of souls with each other and the physical world which is the source of all wealth. We face environmental problems because we do not recognise our own interdependence with the physical world, nor take responsibility for the violence we inflict upon it. The Jaina philosophy, so articulately expressed by Umasvati, establishes harmony between the religious and the scientific, between the spiritual and the physical, and between personal *independence* and social, economic and ecological *interdependence.*"

Spiritual Connect with Ecology

The ecological philosophy of Jainism which flows from its spiritual quest has always been central to its ethics, aesthetics, art, literature, economics and statecraft. It is remarkable that the Jaina tradition, as indeed the Vedic and Buddhist traditions, established the principles of ecological harmony centuries ago not because the world was perceived as heading for an imminent environmental disaster or destruction, nor because of any immediate utilitarian exigency, but because of its quest for spiritual and physical symbiosis, synthesized in a system of ethical awareness and moral responsibility.

Jaina ecological philosophy is virtually synonymous with the principle of *ahimsa* (non-violence) which runs through the Jaina tradition like a golden thread. Non-violence is the supreme religion and is the keynote of the Jaina tradition. Lord Mahavira threw new light on the perennial quest of the soul with the truth and discipline of *ahimsa* and said: "There is nothing so small and subtle as the atom, nor any element so vast as space. Similarly, there is no quality of soul more subtle than non-violence and no virtue of spirit greater than reverence for life." *Ahimsa* is a principle of compassion and responsibility. It should be practised not only towards human beings, but towards all animals and nature.

The Jaina scriptures tell us: "The *Arhats* (Venerable Ones) of the past, present and future discourse, counsel, proclaim, propound and prescribe thus in unison: Do not injure, abuse or press, enslave, insult, torment, torture and kill any creature or any living being." Suffused with the theory of *Karma* and transmigration of souls, Mahavira sums up the rationale of his philosophy of compassion and non-violence when he says: "You are that which you intend to hit, injure, insult, torment, persecute, torture, enslave or kill." It is the same sense of compassion and non-violence which is the basis of the ancient Jaina scriptural aphorism *Parasparopagraho Jivanam* (all life is bound together by mutual support of interdependence). Lord Mahavira proclaimed a profound ecological truth for all times to come when he said: "One who neglects or disregards the existence of earth, air, fire, water and vegetation disregards his own existence which is entwined with them".

Jainas do not acknowledge an intelligent first cause as the creator of the universe. The Jaina theory is that the universe has no beginning or end. It is traced to *jiva* and *ajiva*, the two everlasting, uncreated, independent and co-existing categories. Consciousness is *jiva;* that which has no consciousness is *ajiva.* There are five substances of *ajiva: Dhamta* (the medium of motion), *Adharma* (the medium of rest), *Akmha (space)*, *Pudgala (matter)* and *Kala (time)*.

The ecological philosophy of Jainism which flows from its spiritual quest has always been central to its ethics, aesthetics, art, literature, economics and statecraft.

Pudgala (matter) has form and consists of individual atoms (*paramanu*) and conglomerates of atoms *(skandha)*, which can be seen, heard, smelt, tasted and/or touched. According to Jains, energy, or the phenomena of sound, darkness, shade, heat, light and the like, is produced by conglomerates of atoms. The *Jiva* (soul) has no form but, during its worldly career, it is vested with a body and becomes subject to an inflow of *karmic* 'dust' (*asravas*). These are the subtle material particles that are drawn to a soul because of its worldly activities. The *asravas* bind the soul to the physical world until they have brought about the *karmic* result when they fall away 'like ripe fruit' by which time other actions have drawn more *asravas* to the soul.

With the exception of the *Arihantas* (the ever-perfect) and the *Siddhas* (the liberated), who have dispelled the passions which provide the 'glue' for the *asravas*, all souls are in *karmic* bondage to the universe. They go through a continuous cycle of death and rebirth in a personal evolution that can lead at last to *moksha* (eternal release). In this cycle, there are countless souls at different stages of their personal evolution: earthly bodies, water bodies, fire bodies, air bodies, vegetable bodies, and mobile bodies ranging from bacteria, insects, worms, birds and larger animals to human beings, infernal beings and celestial beings.

The Jain evolutionary theory is based on a grading of the physical bodies containing souls according to the degree of sensory perception. All souls are equal but are bound by varying amounts of *asravas* (*karmic* particles) which is reflected in the type of body they inhabit. The lowest form of physical body has only the sense of touch. Trees and vegetation have the sense of touch and are, therefore, able to experience pleasure and pain, and have souls. Mahavira taught that only the one who understood the grave demerit and detriment caused by destruction of plants and trees understood the meaning and merit of reverence for nature. Even metals and stones might have life in them and should not be dealt with recklessly.

Above the single sense *jivas* are microorganisms and small animals with two, three or four senses. Higher in the order are the *jivas* with five senses. The highest grade of animals and human beings also possess rationality and intuition *(manas)*. As a highly evolved form of life, human beings have a great moral responsibility in their mutual dealings and in their relationship with the rest of the universe. It is this conception of life and its eternal coherence, in which human beings have an inescapable ethical responsibility, that made the Jaina tradition a cradle for the creed of environmental protection and harmony.

The Jaina tradition lays great emphasis on an integrated code of conduct, austere and exacting for the monks (*Mahavratas)* but comparatively moderate and flexible for the householders *(Anuvratas)*. The five (vows) in the Jaina code of conduct are:

- non-violence in thought, word and deed,
- to seek and speak the truth,
- to behave honestly and never to take anything by force or theft,
- to practise restraint and chastity in thought, word and deed, and
- to practise non-acquisitiveness.

The vow of *ahimsa* is the first and pivotal vow. The other vows may be viewed as aspects of the larger concept of *ahimsa* which together form an integrated code of conduct in the individual's quest for equanimity and the three jewels *(ratnatraya)* of right faith, right knowledge and right conduct.

Underlying the Jain code of conduct is the emphatic assertion of individual responsibility towards one and all. Indeed, the entire universe is the forum of one's own conscience. The code is profoundly ecological in its secular thrust and its practical consequences. The transgressions against the vow of non-violence include all forms of cruelty to animals and human beings. Many centuries ago, Jains condemned as evil the common practice of animal sacrifice to the gods. It is generally forbidden to keep animals in captivity, to whip, mutilate or overload them or to deprive them of adequate food and drink. The injunction is modified in respect of domestic animals to the extent that they may be roped or even whipped occasionally but always mercifully with due consideration and without anger.

Except for allowing themselves a judicious use of one-sensed life in the form of vegetables, Jains would not consciously take any life for food or sport. As a community, they are strict lecto vegetarians, consuming neither meat, nor fish nor eggs.

By taking the basic vows, the Jain laity endeavour to live a life of moderation and restraint and to practise a measure of abstinence and austerity. They must not procreate indiscriminately lest they overburden the universe and its resources. Regular periods of fasting for self-purification are encouraged.

The entire universe is the forum of one's own conscience. The code is profoundly ecological in its secular thrust and its practical consequences. The transgressions against the vow of non-violence include all forms of cruelty to animals and human beings.

In their use of the earth's resources, Jains take their cue from "the bee that sucks honey in the blossom of tree without hurting the blossom and strengthens itself. Wants should be reduced, desires curbed and consumption levels kept within reasonable limits." Using any resource beyond one's needs and misuse of any part of nature is considered a form of theft. Indeed, the Jaina faith goes one radical step further and declares unequivocally that waste and creating pollution are acts of violence.

Accumulation of possessions and enjoyment for personal ends should be minimised. Wealth creation must have a philanthropic goal. Giving charitable donations and one's time for community projects generously is a part of a Jain householder's obligations. That explains why the Jain temples and pilgrimage centres are well-endowed and well-managed. It is this sense of social obligation born out of religious teachings that has led the Jains to found and maintain innumerable schools, colleges, hospitals, clinics, lodging house, hostels, orphanages, relief and rehabilitation camps for the handicapped, old, sick and disadvantaged as well as hospitals for ailing birds and animals. Wealthy individuals are 'advised to recognise that beyond a certain point their wealth is superfluous to their needs and that they should manage the surplus as trustees for social benefit'. The five fundamental teachings of Jainism and the five-fold Jaina code of conduct are deeply rooted in its living ethos in unbroken continuity across the centuries. They offer the world today a time-tested anchor of moral imperatives and a viable route plan for humanity's common pilgrimage for holistic environmental protection, peace and harmony in the universe.

It is a measure of the concurrence and commonality of the Brahmana and the Sramana branches of the Indic tradition that Hindus who broadly follow the Vedic-Upanishadic tradition as well as the Buddhists, who differed from Jainas in certain respects would readily endorse and approve of the Jaina code of conduct even though different sects and denominations of Hindus would differ in the degree of strict compliance with some of the norms, particularly in respect of the application of the principles of non-violence.

Austerity and Non-violence

Buddhism has much in common with Jainism. Both of them belong broadly to the Sramana branch of the Indic tradition.

Founded by Prince Siddhartha of the Sakya clan and known as Buddha Sakyamuni, or Gautama (Gotama) Buddha after he attained Enlightenment, Buddhism is pre-eminently a religion of compassion and virtue. As a Buddhist scripture says:

> *"Not to do evil,* to *bring about the excellence of virtue, completely to subdue the mind, this is the teaching of the Buddha."*

Prince Siddhartha was born in the second half of the sixth century and attained *Nirvana circa* 483 BCE Vardhamana Mahavira, the last of the twenty-four *tirthankaras* of the Jainas, was his senior contemporary. When Prince Siddhartha was born, Vedic, Upanishadic and Jaina teachings held sway in India. *Tirthankara Parsva* in the ninth century and Lord Mahavira in the sixth century had challenged some of the premises and practices of the Brahmanical priestocracy, and the Jaina ideology and Upanishadic reflections had engendered a new questioning climate. Sakyamuni Buddha and Lord Mahavira endowed the Indic tradition with a new vision and vitality. Interestingly, Sakyamuni Buddha himself came to be accepted as an *avatara* or incarnation of Vishnu in the Hindu pantheon. Compassion, non-violence, cultivation of virtue and leading a life of virtue, wisdom of the middle path and emancipation from the cycle of rebirth carried the gentle message of Lord Buddha to the classes and masses of Indian people. That message also promised to unshackle the Indian society from the hegemonial hold of the priestly class and from discrimination against women and the other castes, especially the castes belonging to the working classes which constituted what may be called "the internal proletariat" of the Indic society during that period.

Lord Buddha did not, however, wage a class war. His was an existential and experiential personal quest for answers to questions and issues which his sensitive mind and compassionate heart encountered. He gave up royal riches and renounced family bonds and worldly ties in order to seek the way of salvation. The legend has it that Prince Siddhartha was greatly troubled and deeply moved by witnessing an old man, a sick man, a dead man and a recluse successively. He saw misery in front of his eyes and decided to seek the Truth of Truths by practising severe austerity and penance somewhat in the manner of the Jaina *Tirthankaras* and *Nirgrantha* monks. He found that his extreme austerities only enfeebled and emaciated him, but did not pave the way to his enlightenment. He, therefore, decided to devote himself to deep meditation. In *Ariyapariyesanasutta*, it is noted that "Himself being subject to birth, old age, sickness, death, sorrow and impurity, and knowing his subjection to them to be evil, he sought the highest security *(Yogakshema)*, that is, *Niffana.*" He attained the insight into the reality of the world and succeeded in dissolving the bonds of rebirth.

Buddha's journey to emancipation and enlightenment was his own achievement based on his own exertion through his own inward light. He taught on the basis of his own spiritual experience that an individual can only be saved through his own power by seeking Truth within one's own self, thus obtaining freedom from the pain and suffering of the world.

Lord Buddha's Four Noble Truths, which became in due course the foundation of the Buddhist tradition, might appear to be tinged with a world-weary sense of pessimism but it was in reality, a charter for self-development and one's own responsibility for it. The Four Noble Truths are, suffering, its causes, its cessation and the path to *Niffana* (*Nirvana*). *Niffana* means peace or quiescence attained by Enlightenment. According to certain Buddhist schools of thought, the goal of Buddha was to seek liberation from the rounds of transmigration *(Samsara)* or the cycle of rebirth. Doctrinally, to end the twelve-fold causal nexus which begins with ignorance *(nescience)* and ends with old age and death, caused by *Karma* and *Klesha* (afflicters) and culminating in the reality of suffering and sorrow *(Dukha)*, it is necessary to cultivate and follow the Buddhist 'Law' *(The Way* or *Dhamma)*, the foundation of which is to be found in its philosophy of causation. According to Ven. Geshe Sopa and Ven. Elwin W. Jones who drew a portrait of Buddhism for *A Sourcebook for the Community of Religions* prepared for the Parliament of the World's Religions in 1993:

> "The single most important and fundamental notion underpinning Buddhist thought was the idea of 'contingent genesis' or "dependent origination" (*pratitya-amutpada*). Here the thought is that every birth or origination occurs in dependence on necessary causes and conditions; however, not everything so asserted can function as a cause—in particular, any kind of eternal or permanent whole. Consequently, the Buddhist idea of 'contingent genesis' came to be characterised by three salient features, that is, unpropelledness, impermanence and consistency. 'Unpropelledness' signifies that origination or genesis is not propelled by an universal design such as the thought or will of a creator. 'Impermanence' means that the cause of an effect is always something impermanent and never permanent. Finally, consistent with and not exceeding the creative power of the cause. For example, it is on the basis of the quality of consistency that the Buddhist denies that any kind of material body can provide a sufficient material cause for the production of a mind. Thus, on account of this primary philosophical underpinning of contingent genesis, Buddhism has produced a quite large etiological rather than theological literature."

Considering Buddhist philosophy of causation, I cannot but recall the conclusion of that great Western Buddhist scholar, Professor T.W. Rhys Davids in his Lectures on The Origin and Growth of Religion in which he has endeavoured to show with refreshing originality and an authentic insight into the original source material that the Buddhist conception of KClIUM is not based on the idea of transmigration of souls. He tells us that "the transmigration of souls, very commonly supposed to be a fundamental part of Buddhism has never been found mentioned at all, or even referred to, in the *Pali Pitakas*". He opines clearly:

> "I have no hesitation in maintaining, therefore, that Gotama did not teach the transmigration of souls. What he did teach would be better summarised, if we wish to retain the word transmigration, as the transmigration of character. But it would be more accurate to drop the word transmigration altogether when speaking of Buddhism, and to call its doctrine the doctrine of *karma*. Gotama held that after the death of any being, whether human or not, there survived nothing at all but that being's '*Karma*,' the result, that is of its mental and bodily actions. Every individual, whether human or divine, was the last inheritor and the last result of the *Karma* of a long series of past individuals—a series so long that its beginning is beyond the reach of calculation, and its end will be coincident with the destruction of the world. From this it would follow that each generation was the exact, inevitable and natural result of the generation that had preceded it, that generation of the former one, and so on in succession during a practically endless past."

Historically, Gotama Buddha had in fact challenged the basic premises of the discourse of eschatology current in his age. There are many scholars who believe that the Vedic Aryans did not originally subscribe to the doctrine of transmigration of souls but there is no doubt that the idea was rife and rampant in the age in which Lord Buddha lived and taught his *Dhamma.* He disregarded the eschatological preoccupations of the Brahmanical philosophical discourse, made that disregard his point of departure, and fashioned a different soul theory with emphasis on self-development 'here and now'. The Buddhist doctrine in the *Suttas* advises unambiguously:

> "Try to get as near to wisdom and goodness as you can in this life. Trouble not yourselves about the gods. Disturb yourself not by curiosities or desires about any future existence. Seek only after the fruit of the path of self-culture and of self-control!"

In the *Book of the Great Decease (Mahaparinirvana)*, the moral and rational message to the adherents of Lord Buddha's teachings is to be "full of confidence, modest in heart, ashamed of wrong, full of learning, strong in energy, active in mind, and full of wisdom"; they were to live in the practice, both in public and private, of those virtues which, when unbroken, intact, unspotted and unblemished, make men free, and which are untarnished by the belief in the efficacy of any outward acts of ritual or ceremony, by the hope of any kind of future life."

Buddhism made a mature, clear and considered ethical break from the doctrine of transmigration of souls and snapped the linkage between righteousness and its reward in the next life. Buddhist writers explain that the relationship of the one life to the next is merely like that borne by the flame of a lamp to the flame of another lamp lighted by it. When the *Arahan*, the man made perfect according to the Buddhist faith, ceases to live, no new lamp, no new sentient being, will be lighted by the flame of any weak or ignorant longing entertained by him.

I believe that the concept of *'Arahat'* is in many ways common and basic to the Upanishadic, Jaina and Buddhist thought-streams, although there are distinctive variations of the concept among them. Even within the fold of Buddhism which comprises the Great Vehicle (*The Mahayana*) and the Little Vehicle *(The Hinayana)*, we have apart from the concept of *Arhat*, the concept of *Bodhisattva.* If the concept of *Arhat* was the keynote of early Buddhism, the concept of *Bodhisattva* became the concept of the later school led by great Buddhist exponents such as Nagarjuna. A later school believed that the attainment of the status of *Bodhisattva* came from a desire to save all moving creatures in all the ages which are to follow rather than from the individual bliss of attaining *Arhathood* or *Nirvana* in one's life. Essentially, the two kindred concepts of *Arhat* and *Bodhisattva* are reconcilable if they are seen in their historical context, but it is possible to say that the *Bodhisattva* concept put on a higher pedestal redeeming the concept of *Sarva-mangalya* or universal well-being.

Buddha dismissed as delusion the idea that an abiding spirit or self inside the bodily form of beasts and homo sapiens survives the dissolution of the impermanent shell or sheath. A well known verse in Pali says:

> "How transient are all component things !
> Growth is their nature and decay :
> They are produced, they are dissolved again :
> *And then is best—when they have sunk to Rest !"*

The fundamental principle of transitory and transient nature of the component constituents of life leads Buddhism to minimise and generally transcend the accidental or phenomenal differences between gods, men, plants, animals and things, which may be described as a chemical and biological variant of universal, microcosmic pantheism of the *Vedas* and the *Upanishads.* Seen in the correct perspective, the principle is profoundly ethical, at the same time deeply spiritual.

The Buddhist vision (in somewhat the same way as the Jaina vision) cannot really be said to be agnostic or atheistic, merely because it did not accept a creator, anthropomorphic or otherwise, or because it did not subscribe to the other prevailing versions of the concept of transmigration of souls. Buddha gave his own interpretation of *karma* as a moral cause, the cessation of *karma* in the state of *"Arhathood"* (*Arihant* in Jain tradition) and the *Niffana* (*Nirvana*) which represents not death but immortality, a complete, blissful peace by the conquest and extinction of all lusts which are inimical to spiritual realisation. There is, in my view, a noble and lucid inter-generational spiritual-ethical-ecological concept in the interstices of the Buddhist exposition of *karma*. That concept may be said to be that what the good one does will survive but not for individual benefit in an after-life but as a boon and a legacy for the unborn posterity from those who have lived, struggled and suffered in the ages past.

In The Buddhist Declaration on Nature, The Venerable Lungrig Namgyal Rinpoche, the Abbot of Gyuto Tantrik University, quotes Lord Buddha Himself, who said: "Because the cause was there, the consequences followed; because the cause is there, effects will follow" and concludes that these few words present the interrelationship between cause and its effects and shows that happiness and suffering do not simply come about by chance or by irrelevant causes. The simple thesis is that a human undertaking motivated by a healthy positive attitude constitutes one of the most important causes of happiness and this positive human attitude is, in the final analysis, rooted in the genuine and unselfish compassion and loving kindness that seeks to bring about light and happiness for all sentient beings. It is for this noble perspective that we owe a homage to Lord Buddha whose vision and speech made him unexcelled as a sage and a teacher and as the Enlightened Being who saw the interdependence of nature and taught it to the world through his religion of love, understanding and compassion and through his commitment to the ideal of non-violence.

Buddhism and Jainism, perhaps as much if not more than any other tradition, rejected the notion of humankind as the exclusive centre of life and existence and repudiated the selfish anthropomorphic calculus of utility to human beings for the evolution of other forms of life. As the Venerable Abbot puts it, we should be wary of justifying the right of any species to survive solely on the basis of its usefulness to human beings. He explains his view of the Buddhist philosophical system as one which propagates the theory of rebirth and life after death, and shows that in the continuous birth and rebirth of sentient beings (not only on this planet but in the universe as a whole) each being is related to us ourselves, just as our own parents are related to us in this life. He points out that for all their limitations, our ancestors were aware of the need for harmony between human beings and nature; they loved their environment and revered it as a source of life and wellbeing in the world. He quotes the following words of His Holiness The Dalai Lama in *The Buddhist Declaration on Nature*, which breathe and pulsate with the ethical and ecological vision of Lord Buddha and which have a compelling relevance for our own age and time:

> "As we all know, disregard for the natural inheritance of human beings has brought about the danger that now threatens the peace of the world as well as the chance to the lives of endangered species. Such destruction of the environment and the life depending upon it is a result of ignorance, greed and disregard for the richness of all living things. This disregard is gaining great influence. If peace does not become a reality in the world, and if the destruction of the environment continues as it does today, there is no doubt that future generations will inherit a dead world.
>
> "Various crises face the international community. The mass starvation of human species may not have overshadowed the great achievements in science and technology, but they have assumed equal proportions. Side by side with the exploration of outer space, there is the continuing pollution of lakes, rivers and vast parts of the oceans, out of human ignorance and misunderstanding. There is a great danger that future generations will not know the natural habitat of animals; they may not know the forests and the animals which we of this generation know to be in danger of extinction. We are the generation with the awareness of a great danger. We are the ones with the responsibility and the ability to take steps of concrete action, before it is too late."

Indian Continuum on Environment

My broad survey of the Indic heritage comprising the Vedic, Upanishadic, Jain and Buddhist traditions shows that the spiritual, ethical, individual and collective dimensions of human life constitute a continuum. It is that continuum which encompasses the whole of the Indic heritage and transcends all segments and fragments. The Vedic, Upanishadic, Jain and Buddhist traditions perceived that continuum and together they built an enduring spiritual, intellectual and cultural foundation for an environment-friendly value system and a balanced life-style in the Indian society, generally recognising the respective claims of four *Purusharthas* (Endeavours): *Kama* (Desire and Aesthetics), *Artha* (Economics, Statecraft and other secular pursuits), *Dhaltma* (the Normative Moral and Legal Order conducive to Peace, Harmony and Rectitude) and *Moksha* or *Kaivalya* or *Nirvana* (Enlightenment and Emancipation).

Remarkably, that value system reflected in the noble Asokan edicts as well as in the life and message of Mahatma Gandhi and the provisions of the republican Constitution of India of 1950 derived its spiritual and moral inspiration from the composite Indic culture. The Indic value system was shared by different faith traditions and different faith communities in India through the ages and was often emulated and assimilated across the particular boundaries of religious affiliations. Folkways internalised that value system and made it a part of the living legacy of the Indic heritage for people at different levels. Not only is this value system reflected in the Vedic, Upanishadic, Jaina and Buddhist scriptural texts and other literature, it is a part of the social ethos of those traditions and other communities which trace their roots to them. The broad spectrum of a wide variety of sects and denominations which rose in India during the last two millennia has consistently dug and quarried from those Indic roots. The Sikh, Vaishnava and Bishnoi traditions and numerous other *Bhakti* denominations in medieval India which give spiritual joy, comfort and guidance to millions of people in India and abroad are the finest examples of the fecundity and fragrance as well as the everlasting truth, beauty and benevolence of the ancient Indic roots of civilisation and their ecological sap and flowering.

It is relevant to recall that, in the West, the term 'ecology' was coined only in the latter half of the nineteenth century from the Greek word meaning 'home', a place to which one returns, a science of habitat. Long before ecology became the refrain of the global song at Stockholm and Rio, the ancient Indic heritage had already provided a spacious spiritual home to environmental ethos by declaring that all aspects and phenomena of nature belong together and are bound in a physical as well as metaphysical relationship, and by its view of life as a gift of togetherness and of mutual accommodation and assistance in a universe teeming with interdependent constituents. It is with that sense of spirituality, morality and universality that Agenda 21 adopted at Rio has to be implemented if religion is to play a significant and soulful role in creating and sustaining a momentum for ecological conservation in the hearts and minds of men, women and children.

The soul of the Indic tradition is Peace and Harmony, *Dharma* and *Ṛta*, Restraint and Responsibility based on *ahimsa* (non-violence) and *karuna* (compassion). These ideas and precepts are the cardinal elements of the Indic heritage which have the capacity and potential to catalyse and enliven a deeper feeling of reverence for Life and Nature, and which will provide to the frightened and threatened humanity a sense of reassurance based on spiritual and moral vision of humankind as one family.

CHAPTER 25

Asian Civilisation
A Vision and the Promise

Civilisational Dialogue is what Sasakawa Peace Foundation, Indian Council of Cultural Relations, India International Centre, IGNCA, UNESCO and UNO have been engaged in promoting over the years. Indira Gandhi National Centre for the Arts and Indian Council of Cultural Relations are premier Indian institutions in the area of civilizational studies and intercultural exchanges. The Asia project of India International Centre deserves a very special mention in the present context. Particularly noteworthy is the substantial body of work done by The Asia Project of India International Centre and the outstanding work done by the Centre of Studies in Civilisations under the stewardship of my friend Professor D.P. Chattopadhyay.

The Dialogue for Peace Justice and Harmony

Our focus is frankly Asia without any apology and our theme is Civilisational Dialogue in all its dimensions and ramifications. We shall seek to understand the past of the Dialogue in every Asian civilization; we shall endeavour to understand the present and to shape the future. Of course, it is only a beginning. I have myself witnessed, as many of you must have, the incredible phenomenon of mighty rivers having modest origins. I believe that this modest beginning is potentially, a massive continental enterprise of the civil society in Asia. I personally believe it as an article of faith that the time of the idea of Civilisational Dialogue for Peace, Justice and Harmony has come and has come to stay. This Conference is a small and exploratory beginning but I believe that it has a vast potential.

If I may begin on a personal note as an humble protagonist of Civilizational Dialogue, the concept of the Asian Civilisational Conference grew for me out of my lifelong study of the *Vedas*, the *Vedanta*, the Jain and

The Asian Civilisational Dialogue is not an isolated island but is a continental particularization of the Dialogue Among Civilisations to which the UN and the UNESCO have made a large contribution.

Buddhist antiquity all which were founded on the culture and sanctity of the Dialogue. I see the Civilisations of the world as a great epic of Dialogue. I should also mention here the Dialogue-centred deliberations and events, conferences and meetings many of which I attended in the East as well as the West during the last two decades. My thoughts go back to the inspiring and uplifting. memories of Asian Relations Conference convened by Pandit Jawaharlal Nehru in New Delhi in 1946 even before the formal advent of our Independence. The event inspired me as a young man and captured the imagination of the youth of the country. We need many more such festivals to advance the cause of the Dialogue and to enhance its quality.

Years later, I chaired the Asian Festival of the Arts. I was particularly inspired by the deliberations of the Centennial Conference of the Parliament of World's Religions in Chicago twelve years ago when Swami Vivekananda's inspired words of wisdom infused in us a renewed resonance of civilizational values. We adopted, a declaratory document at Chicago and titled it 'Towards a Global Ethic'. I happened to be associated with the great philosopher Hans Kuhn who prepared the draft of the Declaration and was privileged to be one of the presidents of the Council of the Parliament of World's Religions in Chicago. Leading the official Indian delegation to the UN Conference on Human Rights in Vienna, I felt deeply that Democracy, Rule of Law, Human Rights and Responsibilities are the warp and woof of civilizations. The UNESCO Conference on Culture of Peace in Stockholm in 1998, when I had the honour to lead the Indian Delegation, was for me a milestone of the awareness of the fundamental imperatives of Civilizational Dialogue for the cause of peace. At the turn of the century, we had a Millennium Summit of Religious and Spiritual Leaders in New York under the auspices of the UN. I was entrusted with the task of preparing the draft of the Declaration for the UN Summit. At the London Peace Dialogue in September 2001, we discussed the basic dimensions of Civilisational Dialogue. In July 2003, the Government of India and the UNESCO jointly organized an inter-ministerial *World Conference on Dialogue among Civilisations* : *A Quest for New Perspectives.* I had the privilege of being the Chairman of the Steering Committee for the World Conference. At that Conference, the Declaration of New Delhi was adopted unanimously. That Declaration offers a roadmap and a blueprint for Civilisational Dialogue.

Out of my association with Sasakawa Peace Foundation with whom I had an interaction for this initiative during a brief visit to Tokyo, the idea of this Asian Dialogue began to take concrete shape. Ambassador Aftab Seth carefully and painstakingly fostered that dialogue. That is how India and Japan took the initiative to convene the Asian Civilizational Dialogue.

On the 11th of March, thanks to Mr. S.R. Bhatt and his colleagues in the Indian Council of Philosophical Research, we will be meeting at this very venue in a Conference to pay a commemorative homage, to the life and work of the late Professor Hazime Nakamura, a pilgrim of a new, more contemporary cultural silk route, a great world citizen, an extraordinary scholar and a veritable reincarnation of the two great Chinese pilgrims, Fa Hien and Hiuen-tsang whose legacy remains enshrined for ever in our memory.

The Asian Civilisational Dialogue is not an isolated island but is a continental particularization of the Dialogue among Civilizations to which the UN and the UNESCO have made a large contribution during the last two decades. We hope to sustain this Dialogue among Asian Civilizations and to extend it and to enlarge it. In due course, I hope we will have an Asia-Europe Dialogue, an Asia-Africa Dialogue and a Dialogue among Asian and Northern and Southern American Civilizations. We will have, I hope, Dialogues on Human Rights and Human Responsibilities, Democracy, Good Governance, Ecology, Faith Traditions, Cultures, Arts and Aesthetics.

The description of Asia as a continent may be open to question because geographically, Europe is itself an extension of the Asian continent and is a part of the Eurasian landmass, but Asia and Europe have long had their separate nomenclatures and identities. Asia was the Orient and the East, and the European Occident was the West. A sharp line of demarcation was habitually drawn in the West between Europe and Asia although many of the European faith traditions, languages and nations had Asian origins and were under the spell of Asian civilisational perspectives. Pax Romana itself gave way to Pax Christiana, and Christianity was regarded in its early years as an Asian civilisational force in Europe. During the colonial period, Asian countries and civilisations fell victims to imperial conquests and domination. Centuries after those conquests, we can safely assert that though Asian Civilizations have been deeply impacted by the West during the period of colonial dominance, they have survived and their civilizational identities have not been obliterated or eclipsed.

A sharp line of demarcation was habitually drawn in the West between Europe and Asia although many of the European faith traditions, languages and nations had Asian origins and were under the spell of Asian civilizational perspectives.

Indeed, the East and the West have encountered each other face to face in Asia and have often intermingled only to belie Rudyard Kipling's assertion which is generally quoted out of context:

Oh, East is East and West is West,
And never the twain shall meet,
Till Earth and Sky stand presently at God's
great Judgment seat.

To be fair to Rudyard Kipling and to contextualise his assertion, however, I must quote the two lines which follow the previous two lines. Says Kipling in his ballad of East and West:

But there is neither East nor West,
neither Border, nor Breed, nor Birth,
When two strong men stand face to face,
though they come from the ends of the earth !

At the present juncture, civilisations of Asian East and European West do stand face to face in a dialogue in which there is neither East nor West, neither border, nor breed, nor birth. I believe that Asian Civilisations have their own strength and resilience but then there has to be a level playing field culturally for a real dialogue.

East and West Not Antonyms

I submit that East and West are not civilisational antonyms and are not mutually exclusive, hostile or dichotomous. Of course, they have their own distinguishing characteristics and they have made their own unique contributions in the journey of humankind on planet earth. Often a few distinctive characteristics and contributions are chosen to define the East and the West and to draw stereotyped lines of demarcation in sweeping generalisations with only partial elements of historical and sociological truth. For instance Matthew Arnold drew a portrait when he wrote:

Centuries after those conquests, we can safely assert that though Asian Civilisations have been deeply impacted by the West during the period of colonial dominance, they have survived and their civilisational identities have not been obliterated or eclipsed.

The East bow'd low before the blast,
In patient, deep disdain.
She let the legions thunder past,
And plunged in thought again.

Another poet put it thus :

Men look to the East for the dawning things,
for the light of a rising sun
But they look to the West, to the crimson
West, for the things that are done, are done.

A Latin proverb says: "From the East comes light, from the West comes law (*ex oriente lux, ex occidente lex*). As a lawyer for more than half a century, I disagree. I am of the view that Law is a true manifestation of Light. I recall the words of an eminent English sergeant-at-law of many centuries ago, William Davy who said, "The farther I journey towards the West the more convinced I am that the wise men came from the East". William Davy did not ascribe the wisdom of the law exclusively to the West. Indeed, the moral vision of law is the quintessential wisdom of humankind and it emanated from the East as well as the West. That wisdom was the Civilisational Light of Asia of centuries ago in its Hindu, Buddhist, Zen, Dao, Shinto, Sikh, Confucian, Zoroastrian, Jewish, Christian, Islamic and Bahai visions and versions. And we must remember that each country, region and nation has put its own on those traditions.

At the present juncture, civilizations of Asian East and European West do stand face to face in a dialogue in which there is neither East nor West, neither border, nor breed, nor birth.

I am not prepared to subscribe to the overworked exclusive stereotype of the West as a colonial invader and conqueror and Asia invariably as the victim. The history of Asia and Europe bears testimony to many Asian conquests and invasions of Europe. Nor has Asia always been a zone of peace. Within Asia also there have been many conflicts and clashes and that potential persists even today. We need Dialogue within the universe of Asian Civilisations to avert future clashes and conflicts.

Civilizational Vision from the East

Colonial invasions of the West in Asia being proximate in point of time often appear larger than life. The point is that the vision of human life and the contemporary imperatives of the world have undergone a radical change. Chandragupta Maurya and the post-Kalinga Emperor Ashoka and Cyrus, the Great may be a acclaimed and extolled for their civilisational vision, but Alexander, Taimur, Kublai Khan, Changej Khan and Napoleon are no longer the world's role models for their wars and conquests. Colonialism and conquests are no longer legitimate. On the other hand,

Dialogue among Civilisations has an overriding legitimacy, for did we not express the resolve of world in the UN Charter to banish the ghosts of successive wars and did we not consecrate the new vision of peace, progress and prosperity as the new proclamation of the Charter of Humanity to outlaw wars and violence among nations?

The tragic truth is that during nearly 59 years which have elapsed after the United Nations Charter was promulgated, we have seen a succession of wars skirmishes, battles and turbulent episodes of violence, the worst forms of which have been ethnic cleansing, global terrorism and intolerant fanaticism. That is because the ghost of wars and violence still inhabits the minds of men, women and children and we have yet to build enduring defences of peace in the culture of human societies. It is in order to build a wholesome and salubrious climate of peace and to create conditions for peace and justice that we must work through a fair and meaningful dialogue among civilisations as well as among nations which alone can help to establish foundations of perpetual peace and cooperation. I do not wish to underestimate, overlook or minimize the central importance of sovereign nations and of diplomacy in the architecture of peace, but at the same time I cannot turn a blind eye and a deaf ear to the claims of the emerging civil society which in its inclusive definition must include established social, economic and political institutions of State and Society and which has much to contribute to peace and cooperation among the peoples of the world.

The ghost of wars and violence still inhabits the minds of men, women and children and we have yet to build enduring defences of peace in the culture of human societies.

A few years ago, I had occasion to explain my philosophy of Dialogue at the London Peace Conference, which I would like to share with you. First and foremost, let me suggest that we should not be prisoners of conventional semantics. We must give Civilisational Dialogue the largest and the most inclusive meaning in its widest amplitude. Civilisational Dialogue includes in my view cultural intellectual, literary, scientific, technological, educational, humanitarian, artistic, political and economic discourse.

Dialogue among civilisations is not necessarily a dialogue limited merely between any two civilizations or two points of view. It can also be a convocation and a colloquium of two or many more civilizations on many different issues and themes, a multi-logue and a poly-logue which ought not to be too adversarial and confrontationist. Dialogue has to be global both within and among civilisations and nations.

The spirit of the Dialogue is lost when it is pre-possessed by narrow chauvinistic prejudices and when it suffers from suspicion, mistrust and alienation. We must approach Dialogue with an open heart and an open mind. Asian Civilisational Dialogue should be a dialogue of an open society. Intolerance and prejudice are anathema to constructive Dialogue. Dialogue thrives in its larger sense of reciprocating and responsive communication among cultures and civilizations. Dialogue, I submit, is no longer an optional extra on the margins of our global agenda. Dialogue today is a sacred duty, a moral obligation. It is the only alternative to alienation and clashes of civilizations and cultures. It has to be mutually beneficial, multidimensional enriching and inspiring. A Dialogue of Civilizations must have the power and efficacy to reduce, defuse and avert clashes and conflicts of civilizations. Samuel Huntington to whom is attributed the theory of clashes of civilization, himself concedes at page 303 of his book, *The Clash of Civilizations and The Remaking of World Order*, "The overriding lesson of the history of civilizations, however, is that many things are probable but nothing is inevitable."

Dialogue is another name for friendly engagement. It has its own teleology, that is, its own design and purpose, it has its own ontology, its own physics, its own metaphysics, its own ethics and its own sociology, law and diplomacy. That is why I call Dialogue a discipline of many disciplines. The Dialogue has to take place not only between and among nations but also within nations and civilisations so that it may serve as an instrument of understanding and a vehicle of peace, amity and cooperation. Apart from certain eccentricities, angularities and omissions of academic speculation and theoretical discourse in his book, with which we need not agree, Samuel Huntington does conclude on a constructive note when he says at page 321 of his book,

> "The futures of both peace and civilization depend upon understanding and cooperation among the political, spiritual, and intellectual leaders of the world's major civilizations. In the clash of civilizations, Europe and America will hang together or hang separately. In the greater clash, the global "real clash," between Civilization and barbarism, the world's great civilizations, with their rich accomplishments in religion, art, literature, philosophy, science, technology, morality and compassion, will also hang together or hang separately. In the emerging era, clashes of civilizations are the greatest threat to world peace, and an international order based on civilizations is the surest safeguard against world war."

During the deliberations of the World Conference on Dialogue among Civilisations last year in New Delhi and during the Stockholm Conference on Culture and Peace, there was a consensus that the civil society has a very important role to play in furthering and enriching the Dialogue and in making Dialogue the foundation for culture, peace, harmony and reconciliation. This preliminary conference of Asian Civilisational Dialogue will perhaps be able to light a lamp and show the way. We plan to delve deeper into Asian civilisations, their concordances and disconcordances, contemporary issues and futuristic projects. The Asian Civilisational Dialogue is meant to be a contribution to the worldwide dialogue among civilisations. We wish to explore important, tangible and intangible heritage sites on the highway of harmony. The purpose is to provide a forum for unfolding the rich potential of Asian identity and solidarity in the cause of civilisational dialogue and in the cause of peace, progress and prosperity. We shall no doubt dwell on the roads and roots of history but as Mahatma Gandhi taught us, the past belongs to us, we do not belong to the past. We hope to take building blocks of history and the cement of a sensitive understanding of the contemporary human condition to build the future, for the power to shape the Future lies in our understanding of the past and the present and in the political will and resolve of the contemporary civil society. and that of the powers that be. We also hope to discover, redefine, reinforce and augment the sense of Asian togetherness in the global cause of peace and prosperity and contribute to the global framework of ideas and modalities of Civilisational Dialogue.

The Asian Civilizational Dialogue is meant to be a contribution to the worldwide dialogue among civilizations.

I submit that the uses and purposes of civilisational dialogue have to be seen in terms of better understanding, greater goodwill, enhanced amity and a more positive climate of cooperation. I would term those purposes as the prospectus and the promise of a substantial dividend of the Dialogue. After the end of the Cold War, the Peace Dividend was denied to the world by the powerful nations of the world but there will be a much larger Dialogue Dividend representing the true triumph of We the Peoples of the World. That Dividend, I am sure will not be a plaything of power politics and its vagaries. I hope that the Dialogue Dividend will not be in the power of the sovereign nations to withhold or to deny.

I shall conclude with an adoption of the immortal lines of the great poet, Rabindranath Tagore to state the promise, delineate the path and articulate the promise of Dialogue into a prayerful vision of an awakened and resurgent Asia.

> "Where the mind is without fear and
> The head is held high;
> Where knowledge is free;

Where the world has not been broken up
Into fragments by narrow domestic Walls;
Where words come out from the depth of truth;
Where tireless striving stretches
Its arms towards perfection;
Where the clear stream of reason
Has not lost its way
Into the dreary desert sand of dead habit;
Where the mind is led forward by Thee
Into ever-widening thought and action."

CHAPTER 26

Chinmaya Mission A Confluence of Jnana and Bhakti

The Spiritual Heritage of India

In the spiritual heritage of India, *Jnana* and *Bhakti* are, in the ultimate analysis, two sides of the *Jnana*. These are in the domain of *Rishi parampara* which is the philosophical tradition of seers and sages of self-realisation. *Bhakti* is the domain of saints and sages of devotion and emotive dedication. *Jnana* and *Bhakti* are not a compartmental dichotomy: they often coalesce. *Bhakti* gave rise to *sant parampara* in the quest of self-realization. Through great *Rishis* and great saints, the traditions of *Jnana* and *Bhakti* brought light and glory of fulfilment to the eternal quest of the human soul, particularly on the Indian soil. In that quest, *Jnana* is *Bhakti* and *Bhakti* is *Jnana*. There is *Sat, Chit* and *Anand* permeating *Jnana* as well as *Bhakti*. In my view of the panoramic perspective of Indian spirituality and ethics and the Hindu way of life, *Bhakti* is the *Upanishad* of perennial spirituality is commonly understood and accessible language of the people.

The saints of the *Bhakti* tradition experienced the blissful joy of *Jnana* and carried the common people with the uplifting spiritual thought and emotional experience and the seers of the *Jnana* tradition experienced that same blissful joy of Truth in pure consciousness. There is a profound subterranean unity of *Anubhuti* and *Ananda* in *Jnana* and *Bhakti* which are invisibly, intimately and inextricably intertwined. *Jnana* and *Bhakti* are both dimensions of inner experience. Bhakti represents the rich tapestry of that inner experience in which intellect and emotions are the warp and woof of divine presence in the inner and outer space so that the boundaries

Through great rishis and great saints, the traditions of Jnana and Bhakti brought light and glory of fulfilment to the eternal quest of the human soul.

of inner and outer space are obliterated and belong to the same divine domain that is spiritual *Advaita* at its sublime and lofty summit and in its oceanic depths to which great masters like Rama Krishna Paramhansa, Swami Vivekananda, Sri Aurobindo, Swami Chinmayananda and Swami Rangnathananda consecrated their lives of *sadhana* and self-realization.

The great *rishis* of our Vedic and Vedantic antiquity and Swami Vivekananda, Sri Aurobindo, Thakur Rabindranath, Paramacharya Chandrasekhar, Saraswati, Swami Chinmayanandji and Swami Ranganathanandaji constituted the pantheon galaxy of spiritual wisdom in the nineteenth and twentieth centuries. They created the confluence of *Jnana* and *Bhakti* in the Rig Veda-Saam Veda tradition which transforms sounds into words of divine devotion and words into celestial devotional poetry and music.

Jnana and Bhakti are both dimensions of inner experience. Bhakti represents the rich tapestry of that inner experience in which intellect and emotions are the warp and woof of divine presence in the inner and outer space.

We should recall the stirring and soul-searching words of Swamiji in his Bhakti Sandhya Message of 1988 in which he said that "*Bhakti* meant total surrender to the protector and sustainer of the Universe". He explained the process of sound with a meaning becoming words, and words becoming poetry, and poetry making up the cadence of music of Bhakti Sangeet Swamiji said:

> "When music is employed by a devoted heart of a saintly person, it lifts the listener's heart to new realms of Consciousness. To listen to music, adoring the Divine, with a worshipful heart, by a deeply devoted person of character and dedication is to transport all devoted hearts listening to it, most effortlessly, in a pleasant spontaneity, into an ecstasy of an inexplicable state of bliss and beatitude."

There is a moving message for us all from Swamiji on Bhakti poetry, *Bhakti Sangeet* and *Bhakti Pravaha* inspired by saints and seers of India's devotional transcendence and made fragrant by his own unique alchemy of the synthesis of *Jnana* and *Bhakti.* First and foremost, he asks us to listen to our saints who experienced the Truth and reached the innermost recesses of self-realization through singing their hearts to Him in *Bhakti* and who spread the quintessential message of *Jnana* through their *Bhakti* and their exploding (or imploding) music which was sung through them by the very angels of the Heaven. That is in my humble view the best approach to the understanding and interpretation of the confluence of

Chinmaya Mission proudly proclaims the beauty and grace of each stream and the depth of the great ocean. Each of those streams have a common Indian hallmark, no matter where it originates, where it flows, and where it joins the great ocean. That commonality defies chronology and transcends geography and linguistic diversities. It verily demonstrates the fundamental unity of India and its unity in all its diversities which we celebrate in our transparent sense of Indic unity, rooted in the *Vedas*, the *Vedanta*, *Sramana* and *Shaiva-Shaakta-Vaishnava* spirituality. I find the resonance and reverberations of Vedic hymns and *Vedanta* discourses watered, cultivated, nurtured and personalized through each saint poet and each *Nadopasaka* in the long panorama of *Bhakti* tradition.

Manikvacakar, Appar, Sundarar, Sambandar and Adi Shankaracharya (although Adi Shankaracharya, according to Kanchi tradition lived before the Christian era) gave expression to the fundamental Truth expounded in the Vedas and the *Upanishads*. Their *Tiruvacakam*, *thevaras* and lyrical compositions were remarkable for their insights and deep devotion and commanded universal respect and had household popularity and reverence. That was the period in and around the epoch of Adi Shankaracharya (if the routinely accepted date of birth and span of life are assumed to be correct) who was the fountainhead of Vedantic *Jnana* and the source of the most lyrical *Bhakti* poetry in Sanskrit.

That commonality defies chronology and transcends geography and linguistic diversities. It verily demonstrates the fundamental unity of India and its unity in all its diversities which we celebrate in our transparent sense of Indic unity.

So complete is Manikvacakar's surrender to Lord Shiva that he was able to say, as a true *Bhakta*, 'I am not afraid of being reborn, nor am I afraid of death. I seek no enjoyment in Paradise nor do I seek any of the good things below. May the glory of the Lord be the object of my contemplation and eternal inheritance." Asked to explain his philosophy and approach, Manikvacakar pointed to the Image of Chidambaram Nataraja and said: "The Deity is the object of my song, the source of my inspiration. He is my language and my *metre* and He is also the meaning of my Song." So saying, he merged with the Deity—*Jyoti in Jyoti*, quite like Meerabai in Dwarka. And his body could not be traced thereafter as in the case of Meerabai in Dwarka.

Gender and geography did not matter. It did not matter that Manikvacakar's *isht devata* was Lord Shiva and that of Meerabai was Lord Krishna. Although Appar who lived from 600 to 680 AD had adopted Jainism, he followed in the footsteps of Manikvacakar, and took a proactive initiative in restoring and rehabilitating the Shivalingam idols in Temples which had fallen prey to neglect, dereliction or royal wrath. He was a remarkable example of *Shaiva-Jaina* togetherness which takes us back to

Mount Kailash the seeds of which are found in Mohenjo-Daro and Harappa. Appar sings in total surrender and says in an ecstasy of devotion:

Lord Siva's praise—my wisdom and lore
Lord Siva's praise—the art I know
Lord Siva's praise—my tongue proclaims
Lord Siva's praise—the right way shows

Appar experienced the divine energy in his "fragile frame of flesh" and found Shiva standing like the celestial tree in his heart of hearts. His firm resolve was never to lose his hold of the Lord. Another Saint is South Indian, Tirujnana Sambandar to whom Adi Shankaracharya refers in his *"Saundarya Lahari"* was a great saint poet of Shaivism which was revitalised by his soulful devotional poetry and saintly life. As in the South so also in the North, the *Bhakti* movement had an upsurge under the impact of Adi Shankaracharya's revolutionary revival which embraced the whole of India from Kerala to Kashmir and from Dwarika to Jagannath Puri.

Remarkably common and comparable were the lives of the saint poets all over India.' They had a sense of *Vairagya* and were immersed in *Bhaktirasa.* They consecrated their lives to the pure truth and consciousness of Divine Bliss. Equally, their message and metaphor had the same yearning, the same striving, the same aspiration and the same heart frame of total surrender.

Andal and Meerabai and Lal Ded thus merge into one. Andal, Appar, Kabir and Lal Ded belong together; Hazrat Amir Khusrau, Baba Farid, and Rai Das (Ravi Das), Rahim, Raskhan, Tulsi, Meerabai, Appar, Andal and Bihari are not divided by caste or creed, or by north and south or by one century or other. Denominations cease to matter. They are united by their quest of the Divine and the disposition of spirituality. Time and space are thus bonded in their devotional spirituality. Through them there was true National Integration and Unity through *Bhakti* as the vehicle of Poetry, Music and Dance.

Kabir, Spirituality and Poetry

Kabir who had been brought up as a Muslim sought the blessings of Swami Ramanand as his Guru and felt fulfilled by the Guru's blessings. His poetry found a place of pride and permanence in *Guru Granth Sahib* as did Baba Farid's devotional poetry. The noble Gurus of the Sikh tradition and the *Bhakti* poetry was preserved and enshrined in *Guru Granth Sahib* through which Baba Farid, Kabir Sahib and Guru Ravidas acquired millions of additional followers and ardent admirers in all communities and in different parts of India in succeeding centuries. *Sabad Kirtan* and *Akhand Paath* of the Sikh tradition and the popular all night *kirtan* or *Ratjagaa* have filled the lives of Indians of all castes, creeds and classes with ethical purity and spiritual solace. Kabir's Rama was not the historical and legendary son of Dashrath, the King of Ayodhya and the hero of Valmiki's and Tulsi's *Ramayana*, but then he is the name and the symbol conjured and captured by Kabir sahib as the ultimate spiritual Reality. In every couplet and verse of Kabir and on every page of *Guru Granth Sahib Nirguna* Brahma is written large. There is in Kabir, Nanak and in *Guru Granth Sahib* a powerful restatement of the esoteric wisdom of Adi Shankara's *Advaita* in the most accessible and comprehensible way for the common folk. That is why I like to refer to Kabir's poetry and *Guru Granth Sahib* as *Loka-Veda*.

With the assistance of Acharya Hazari Prasad Dwivedi, Acharya Kshiti Mohan Sen, a colleague of Gurudev Tagore in Shanti Niketan and grandfather of Amartya Sen initiated Gurudev Rabindranath Tagore into the poetic world of Kabir. Gurudev was profoundly fascinated by Kabir. As a poet, he entered into the mystic spiritual world of Kabir and found the experience of transcreation of Kabir's poetic work deeply uplifting and fulfilling.

Kabir, the *Nirguna-Nirakar* philosopher of *Brahman* means by Rama the one who pervades and permeates the universe and not the one in physical frame.

> It is a question-mark,
> What we mean when we utter 'Rama '?
> Is it the Rama (son of Dashrath) who is known all over
> Or the Divine Lord who works miracles and charms?
> Says Kabir, you must repeat 'Rama '.
> But do it with understanding the name
> One Rama is He who pervades all over,
> The other is contained in his physical fame.

As my friend, the author and poet, Sardar Kartar Singh Duggal puts it "What we have in *Guru Granth Sahib* is Kabir unalloyed when a Sikh bows before the Holy Granth he pays respect as much to Kabir as to Guru Nanak" *Guru Granth Sahib* is an example of encyclopaedic sacred literature of epic proportions. The tenth Guru of the Sikh tradition enthroned it as the veritable Guru. The *Mool Mantra* and *Jap* with which the Holy *Guru Granth Sahib* opens is a statement of *Bhakti* in *Nirguna Brahma:*

> There is but one God.
> Truth incarnate.
> The Master Creator.

Unafraid.
Disdains none
Image Eternal.
Beyond incarnation.
Self-existent, True.
Realized through the grace of the Guru.

Guru Nanak, the great *Faquir* came to be accepted as Guru of the Hindus, and a *Pir* of the Muslims. He made religious issues a part of the great discourse of the Indian nation. He was the pioneering prophet of inter-faith amity and dialogue. His inter-faith tolerance and uncompromising quest of truth is beautifully expressed with piercing reason thus:

If Allah dwells in a mosque alone,
what about the rest of the space?
The Hindus believe He abides
In the image of the deity,
The truth is missed in
either case

Through his teachings of wisdom, Guru Nanak fostered a sense of *Karma-Yoga* and pragmatic work ethic. He says:

He who works hard and shares
He knows the path that leads there
and
One must mediate on the Lord;
but an active life is better
than a life of sheer contemplation

In Guru Nanak's *arati, Bhakti* reaches ecstatic depth of aesthetic grace and cosmic embrace, when he sings the Melody of His Name:

The sky is the platter,
The Sun and the Moon are the lights,
And stars the jewels,
Sandalwoods' fragrance is the incense,
The wind is the flywhisk,
And all the forests Your flowers.
What a wonderful *arati* it is!
Oh, You destroyer of life and death!
It's an unending strain—The melody of Your Name.

Guru Nanak, Guru Arjun Dev, Guru Teg Bahadur and Guru Gobind Singh enriched the treasure chest of socially enlightened and renascent *Nirguna Bhakti*. Guru Ravidas of Varanasi, born in family of tanners and cobblers was a contemporary of Kabir Sahib who was himself raised in a family of Muslim weavers. It is a triumph of *Jnana* and *Bhakti* that both Kabir and Ravidas think, teach and preach. Their *Jnana* and *Bhakti* are beyond the barriers of caste, creed and ritual. They sing the sacred song of the fundamental and intrinsic spiritual and secular unity of humankind united by divine presence in the deepest recesses of their consciousness. It is to them that India owes its deepest debt in the contemporary constitutional legacy of Justice, Equality, Liberty, Freedom, Secularism, Human Dignity and Fraternity.

Faquir came to be accepted as Guru of the Hindus, and a Pir of the Muslims. He made religious issues a part of the great discourse of the Indian nation. He was the pioneering prophet of inter-faith amity and dialogue.

Kabir's profound spirituality and saintliness made him free and fearless. He lived the austere life of a householder. The most powerful reformer among the saint poets, he was frontal, frank and outright in his unsparing critique and denunciation of hypocrisy, discrimination, priestocracy, and ritual worship lacking in spirituality. That poetry and saintliness could have such compelling power to transform society and to compel all sections of Indian people to introspect and reflect is a tribute to the glory, of *Bhakti* poetry of Kabir, Ravidas (Revidas), Dadu and a host of emancipated *dalit* poets who enthroned values of spirituality, ethics, justice, compassion, humanity, equality and philanthropy through their stirring and uplifting poetry of social and cultural awakening. We hear those voices continually through the corridors of centuries and in the forum of our conscience.

Kabir who had a long life span was raised in a Muslim family of weavers and yet he wore Tulsi beads round his neck, lived the *Vaishnava* way of life, rejected the Hindu-Muslim divide, faced imprisonment, persecution and torture for his love and understanding of Hindu thought. His legacy is the legacy of *Nirguna Rama Bhakti* and emancipated humanity. He was the down-to-earth human being and high as sky, Saint poet of Self-Realization. Says Kabir:

It is to them that India owes its deepest debt in the contemporary constitutional legacy of Justice, Equality, Liberty, Freedom, Secularism, Human Dignity and Fraternity.

> As the pupil is in the eye, the Lord is in the body.
> Fools do not know this and go out to search for him.

Kabir's metaphor is often earthy and mundane, but his communion with Rama is spiritual. The anticipation and joy of Kabir's Bhakti bursts forth in a bridal song like Guru Nanak's song of the cosmic *Aarti.* Says Kabir in his bridal song:

Sing, O bride, the benedictive bridal song!
To my house has come King Rama, my Lord.
Having fully dedicated my body, I will perform intercourse
With my mind. The five elements are his bridal guests.
Rama Deva has come to be my guest.
I am intoxicated with Youth.
I will make my body the lake and marriage altar.
Brahma will chant the Vedaas.
With Rama Deva I will make the marriage rounds.
Wonderful, wonderful is my lot!
The three and thirty million gods have come and the eighty
Six thousand sages.
Kabir says, I go now wedded with the Man, the One,
The Deathless.

Rich mystic symbolism and imaginary, Kabir's *Bhakti Rasa* is ageless and quenches the thirst of ages, obliterating lust, anger, greed, *Karma*, sin and agonies conferring on him the boon of immortality:

The unaging juice is trickling in the sky cave,
Where a jingle arises without an instrument.
This is understood when one meditates.
Where lotuses have bloomed without a pond.
The swam climbs on them and has fun.
Light is seen without the moon.
Here and there a swan comes into view.
The gaze is fixed on the tenth gate,
on which the Invincible man meditates.
Death, the fierce, does not come near,
Lust, anger and greed are burnt.
The thirst of ages and ages is quenched
Karma, confusion
Sin and agonies are disappearing.

Kabir says, "Listen, O fellow saints! Having become immortal, one never dies."

Ravidas, like Kabir was also a pupil of Swami Ramanand. He belonged to the community of cobblers and some of his verses were included in *Guru Granth Sahib.* He is the saint poet of humility, human dignity and equality in the spirituality of *Advaita*. Says Ravidas:

> Tohi Mohi, Mohi Tohi antar kaisa
> Between Thee and Me, between me and thee
> How can there be lack of likeness or difference?
> Likeness or difference as between gold
> And a bracelet made of it,
> As between water
> And the waves that move on its surface!
> Behind all the various manifestations there is one God;
> In the motion of every heart it is God that throbs.
> Ravidas, He is nearer to us than our hands and feet!
> As the Lord willeth, so all things come to pass!

The *Vaishnava* and *Shaiva* waves of renaissance won the hearts and minds of embattled and oppressed Indian humanity at large and appealed deeply to their sensitive and cultivated conscience. A new sense of unity was forged in *Bhakti* in both *Nirguna* and *Saguna* streams, and in the North and the South and in East and the West and among thoughtful Hindus and contemplative Muslims, especially the Sufis.

Hazrat Khusrau was steeped in Sufi mysticism and wrote of love and longing and of separation, yearning and communion under the inspiration of his mentor, the great Nizamuddin Aulia. Baba Farid who was a senior contemporary of Amir Khusrau (1235-1325 AD) was one of the earliest Sufi saints of Punjab. His verses were incorporated in *Guru Granth Sahib* In its extraordinary eclectic inclusiveness. Baba Farid's verses teach us humanity, equality, detachment and Sufi *Shakti* of True Love. Says Baba Farid:

> Farid, attach not thy heart to houses,
> Mansions and lofty places
> When heavy earth falleth on thee
> Thou shalt have no friend.

Comparing princes to paupers and treating Hindus and Muslims alike, Farid says "In the end they too find rest in the burning ground or are buried in the grave like the poor and the orphans".

The Bhakti Tradition

Around twelfth century, Jayadeva gave to *Bharat-Bhakti-Pravaha* the most lyrical legacy of *Bhakti sringar* in the tradition of Kalidasa and Adi Shankaracharya and introduced divine erotics through the metaphor of Radha, the *Jeevatma* longing for union with Krishna, the *Paramatma.*

Apart from Jayadeva, Mahaprabhu Vallabhacharya and Chaitanya Mahaprabhu were the two of the greatest saints in the *Bhakti* tradition. Their impact is etched indelibly on the *Vaishnava* tradition of *Krishna Bhakti*, overflowing with love, beauty, grace and joy in Krishna-consciousness.

Mahaprabhu Vallabhacharya the founder of the *Vaishnava Saguna Pushtimarg* came from Andhra to the North and rose to be the most sonorous melodious voice of *Bhakti* after Jayadeva and inspired millions of Indians to embrace the *Pushti Marg* of Vaishnavism which has its many seats of establishment especially in Braja, Rajasthan and Gujarat. The temple of Srinathji in Nathdwara (Rajasthan) is testimony to the grandeur of that tradition and a reminder of the fanaticism of Aurangzeb who rose as a fateful metor of despotic intolerance and religious bigotry.

Mahaprabhu Vallabhacharya's greatest legacy was to enliven Vaishnavism and the *Bhakti* movement through the charismatic and emotive image of Krishna, who survived miraculously the many devious and murderous onslaughts of the absolutism of Kamsa who left no stone unturned in oppressing and intimidating the people of Gokul eliminating Krishna's existence. Krishna uniquely mobilized the pastoral people of the Gokul region against the excesses and intrusions of Kamsa and his evil emissaries, and also saved the people of Gokul from the wrath of Nature in the form of Indra's cyclonic cloudburst by lifting the mountain Goverdhana on his little finger and making the mountain a canopy for the people of Gokul weeping in distress. This was people's power against the wrath of Indra, and Kansa the King, of Mathura a metaphor for the power of popular resistance.

Krishna in Mahaprabhu Vallabhacharya's vision was not only an apostle of divine power of the people but was also the fountainhead of the sweetest of sweet graces (*Madhurya*).

Mahaprabhu Vallabhacharya's *Madhurshtakam* has the celestial grace of heavenliness soaked in the *Bhakti rasa* of *Giridhar Gopal* and resonant with the sonorous grace of Jayadeva of Bengal of the twelfth century but without the *sringar* of Nayika Radha in Jayadeva who gave to *Bhakti* the metaphysical symbol of the soul in a state of love and longing. Jayadeva's influence on Chaitanya Mahaprabhu and his movement was seminal. Bhakti Vedanta or ISKON movement which captured the hearts of many in the East and West during the later part of the second half of the twentieth century draws its inspiration from Chaitanya Mahaprabhu as also Jaydeva.

The exquisite poetic quality of Jayadeva's composition in *Geet Govinda* and Vidyapati's padas in Maithili and Chandidas in Bangla. We find the love and longing of Radha and the affirmation of Radha's love for Krishna with all the erotic paraphernalia, metaphor and symbolism of *shringar* whereas Mahaprabhu Vallabhacharya's *Madhurashtakanis* and Narsi Mehta's *Saguna* celebration of Lord's Madhurya makes everything in the world charming and captivating—as he puts it *"Madhuradhipate Akhilam Madhuram"*. In Mahaprabhu Vallabhacharya's *Bhakti* poetry and the tradition of *Havali Sangeet*, grace and sovereignty are proclaimed and enthroned.

In Kabir, we experience the limpid flow of *Nirguna Rama Bhakti*. Lalleshwari or Lal Ded of Kashmir was a poetess who wrote in a *Nirguna* Sufi style, rejected idolatry and sought and achieved communion with Him. Rejecting the idols and temples, she said: The idol and the temple stone they are but stone and nothing more. O silly *Pandit*, when does thou worship. Unite thy mind and breath in Him alone. In Tulsi we enter the Vast *Saguna* universe of *Rama-Bhakti*, in Jayadeva, Vaidyapati, Chaitanya, Surdas and the other *Astchaap* Saint poets. Meerabai, Raskhan and the saint poets of Maharashtra, we find the profoundly loving worship of Krishna in which the lord is adored in his human form in an intensely human way.

Meerabai was by common consent the most celebrated poetess of *Bhakti* of her time. A Rajput princess of *Merta* (Marwar) and married with the royal family of Marwar, Meerabai travelled extensively in Rajasthan, Uttar Pradesh and Gujarat. Her poetry is exquisitely lyrical and autobiographical. Forsaking her royal abode, she wandered with holy men and incurred the wrath of her family. "Nothing is really mine except Gopal", says Mira. She drank with joy poison offered by Ranaji and found ecstasy because of her total surrender to God; a cobra was sent to her and she saw in it only Krishna. Says Mira:

> None but Girdhar is my Lord
> I have searched the entire universe,
> Forsaken my kin, my family, my friends,
> I have sat with the ascetics and
> Ignored what everybody said

Mirabai's life was vibrant with the joy of *Bhakti* in all adversities and remains an unforgettable legend like that of Andal and Lalleshwari in the *Bhakti* movement.

Swami Haridas, the mentor and preceptor of the legendary musical genius, Tansen and the South Indian trinity of Syama Sastri, Thyagaraja and Muthuswami Dikshitar were the greatest figures in the political and musical tradition of *Bhakti*. Swami Haridas who lived in the sixteenth century was a musical genius and a hermit poet who poured his heart in the *Bhakti* of Radha Krishna with Radha as the central figure of *Bhakti*. A great exponent *Dhrupad,* Swami Haridas taught Baiju. Legend has it that Emperor Akbar went in a disguise to Swami Haridas' heritage in Vrindaban. Though Tansen was preeminent, Swamiji's music was clearly and vastly superior. Asked by the Emperor, Tansen explained: "How can it be otherwise? For I sing to the Emperor of this kind, Swamiji sings only for the Emperor of the entire creation."

Syama Sastri was a Devi *Bhakta* and composed nine *Kritis* in praise of Meenakshi in the Tanjore temple. Thyagaraja was indisputably the greatest composer in the Karnataka tradition. He was a Rama *Bhakta* and glorified Rama as the incarnated nectar and essence of Nada and perceived *Raga* as Rama's bow and the *Swaras* as its giggling bells. Muthu Swami Dikshitar was blessed with the discovery of *Veena* in the flow of Ganges, with Rama inscribed on it. He had a wideranging repertoire of *Bhakti Sangeet* and poetry including a memorable *Kriti* in praise of Saraswati.

An account of Krishna *Bhakti* would be incomplete without a brief recapitulation of the *Bhakti* poetry of Mahatma Surdas and poet Raskhan A Muslim Sardar who was a devotee of Krishna. Both Surdas and Raskhan belonged to the *Pushtimarg Parampara* of Mahaprabhu Vallabhacharya.

Surdas sang of Krishna joyfully as a child and Yashoda as a doting mother. His songs have been the life breath of Bhakti and constitute the greatest treasury of *vatsalya* poetry. His song *"mero man anat kahan sukh pawe, jaise udi jahaj ko ponchi fir jahaz pai awe"* has a haunting quality for it declares that there is no shelter or retreat for the heart of a *Bhakta* except in the Sanctuary of the Lord.

Raskhan's *Bhakti* poetry matches with the longing in Mahatma Surdas' poetry for the Lord.

Raskhan says to the Lord: "If you are to give me an animal rebirth, let me be a cow grazing daily with the other cows of Nanda; if You are to transform me into a stone, may I become a part of the very hill *(Govardhana)* which You lifted by Your hand, as one would an umbrella, to teach a lesson to Indra.

In a bewitching nostalgic vein, he continues:

> If I am reborn as man, O Rashkhan,
> Let me be born as a native of Gokula
> If I am to be an animal,
> Let me be fortunate enough to be a cow
> In the herd of Hari
> If I am a stone
> Let me be a rock of the Govardhana Hill
> If a bird, may my nest be in a tree
> On the bank of Yamuna.

The remembrance and adoration of the Lord has reached unfathomable depths of tender human feeling and incredible heights of sublime thought and that is what makes *Bhakti* a path of total intensity and intimacy in human-divine encounters at the thresholds and climactic communion in the innermost sanctum.

THE EPILOGUE

Dr. L. M. Singhvi : A Profile

Dr. Laxmi Mall Singhvi, a multi-faced personality, was an eminent jurist, a leading constitutional expert, an acclaimed diplomat, a distinguished parliamentarian, a highly respected intellectual, a prominent exponent of human rights, a doyen of the Indian Bar, a citizen-statesman, an author, a poet, a linguist and litterateur, a public speaker in English and Hindi, a Sanskrit scholar, all rolled in one. He played a unique multidirectional leadership role in social, national, intellectual, professional and international institutions.

A. ON THE GLOBAL SCENE

Was U.N. Special Rapporteur on the Impartiality and Independence of the Judiciary, Jurors and Assessors and the Independence of Lawyers. His Report on the Independence of Justice and his Draft Universal Declaration on the Independence of Justice (1987) received worldwide acclaim in the fora of the United Nations and in the world of law. • Was Chairman of the Working Group on The Independence of Justice at Vienna 1984 and was instrumental in preparing Guidelines for the Independence of the Judiciary, adopted at Seventh UN Congress on Crime Prevention and Treatment of Offenders at Milan (1985), approved by the General Assembly of the UN later that year and styled globally and in the UN movement as the "Singhvi Principles". • Was Chairman of the Seminar on Asian Approaches to Human Rights organised by the UN University and UNESCO in New Delhi. • Associated with and consulted in the drafting of the constitutions of Bangladesh, Nepal and South Africa. • Appointed as the Commissioner of Inquiry into the Administration of Justice in Trinidad and Tobago. Was Invited by the German Parliament to discuss the issue of "Brain Drain to Brain Gain – The Diaspora as A Resource in Development Policy". • Was Leader of the Indian Delegation at the UN Human Rights Conference at Vienna in 1993. • Was Leader of the Indian Delegation to, the biggest ever inter-governmental conference on Culture and Development in Stockholm. • Was presented with Inter-Faith Gold Medallion in 1994 at the Lambeth Palace by the Archbishop of Canterbury on behalf of the International Council of Christians and Jews. A year later, was asked to give the Award to the Hon'ble Speaker of the House of Commons; The Rt. Hon. Betty Booth Royd at, the Palace of Westminster. • Was Member of the UNESCO's Executive Board (2002-2005). • As early as 1956, attended the International Legal Science Conference under the auspices of UNESCO in Barcelona, Spain, as a member of the four-member Indian delegation, led by Mr. Justice Patanjali Sastri (formerly Chief Justice of India) and included Mr. Justice Vivian Bose, a Judge of the Supreme Court of India and later President of the International Commission of Jurists. • Was Co-Chairman of the World Conference of Judges and Lawyers at Montreal in 1980, Chairman of International Conference on Legal Aid in 1969. Trustee of International Legal Centre in New York from 1967 to 1976. • Was Patron of Public Law Centre and Honorary Fellow of the Institute of Advanced Legal Studies in London. • Was Patron, The Hunger Project in London and Patron, Child In Need Institute (CINI) UK. • Served as Honorary Visiting Professor in many Indian and British Universities. • Elected as the Member from Asia to serve on the World Comparative Constitutional Studies Committee of the American Council of Learned Societies (ACLS). • Advised and participated in the celebrations for the Bicentennial of the US Constitution. • Was invited by the President of the Republic of France to join in commemorating the Bicentennial of the French Revolution. • Was Chairman, Rotary International's Jury on Award for Crusade Against Corruption. • Was Member, Institute for World Congress on Human Rights. • Dr. L.M. Singhvi Foundation established in London with the active patronage and association of The Rt. Hon. The Lord Chancellor, the Rt. Hon. The Speaker of the House of Commons, The Rt. Hon. The Lord Chief Justice, The Rt. Hon. the Master of the Rolls and the Rt. Hon. The Lord Templeman. The Foundation has established an exchange programme for Judges, Lawyers and MPs. • His Holiness The Dalai Lama delivered L. M. Singhvi-Temenos Interfaith Lecture in May 2004, the earlier lectures delivered by Dr. Singhvi himself, Seyyed Hossein Nasr, Dr. Richard Chartres, Bishop of London; Professor Suheil Bushrui, Dr. Kapila Vatsyayan; and Rabbi Dr. Jonathan Magonet. • Presided over the World Congress of Judges and Lawyers in Montreal in 1979. • Presided over World Congress on Human Rights in New Delhi in 1991. • Presided over the Inter Governmental Maritime Conference in 1994-95.

B. ON THE NATIONAL FRONT

Was Member of Lok Sabha (1962-1967), the Lower House and Rajya Sabha, the Upper House (1998-2004) of the Indian Parliament. •Was the recipient of 'Padma Bhushan' hnonour by the President of India. • A leading Senior Advocate of the Supreme Court of India heading for several years the Supreme Court Bar Association. • Crusaded for the Ombudsman system in India and coined the words "Lokpal"and "Lokayukt", now an acknowledged part of the legislative vocabulary of India. • Was Chairman of the Government of India Committee on Revitalization of Panchayati Raj Institutions in 1986. His recommendations and the draft amendments have been incorporated into the Constitution by a Constitutional Amendment. • Was Life Trustee and President of India International Centre. Delivered the C.D. Deshmukh Memorial Lecture on 'The Unfinished Tasks of Our Constitution' which led to the national debate for review and reform of the Constitution. • Served as President, Indira Gandhi National Centre for Arts (2000-2005). • Was High Commissioner for India in the UK (1991-1997) and served with rare distinction marked as the golden phase of Indo-British relationship. • Established the Nehru Centre in London. • On his recommendation as Chairman of Indian Diaspora, in the year 2003, the Government of India had announced January 9 to 10 as Pravasi Bharatiya Divas and started celebrating and honouring NRIs and PIOs with "Pravasi Bharatiya Samman Award" which has become an annual event in the government calendar. Was Chairman of Pravasi Bharatiya Divas 2003 and 2004. • Was also appointed Chairman of a National High Level Committee on Persons of Indian Origin and Non Resident Indians with the rank of Cabinet Minister in Central Government (August 2000). President, Vatsal Nidhi. • Honorary Patron, The Red Rose Society.

C. IN THE AREA OF LAW AND JURISPRUDENCE

Was Founder President of the Supreme Court Bar Association Trust and President of the Supreme Court Bar Association, on four occasions. • Founded Law Day, which is widely observed by the Bench and the Bar in India on November 26th each year. • Was elected Honorary Bencher and Master of the Middle Temple, one of the highest honours for Judges and lawyers in the UK. • Associated with the Indian Law Institute, in its formative phase which he directed and administered. • Was Member of Permanent Court of Arbitration at the Hague and Commission of Inquiry into Administration of Justice in Trinidad and Tobago (2000). • Member Board of Law, Ahera Human Rights (magazine). • Founded among others, The Institute of Constitutional and Parliamentary Studies, Human Rights Rectangle, Centre for Human Rights Education and Training, Centre for the Study of Law and Society, the Federalism Centre, the Centre for the Independence of Judges and Lawyers, Centre for Unity of India *(Rashtriya Ekta Dham).*

D. IN INSTITUTION BUILDING

Was Chairman, The Heritage Foundation. • Honoured as Patron, Veerayatan. • Was Honorary Patron Shri Shanmukhananda Fine Arts Sangeet Sabha, Mumbai (2003). • Nominated Honorary Patron of the Senior Citizen Forum and Bal Vikas Bhaarti, Patron, All India Philosophy Association Parzor Foundation for Preservation of Vulnerable Human Heritage. Honoured as Patron, Cine-Goers Council and Tamana Special School. Honorary Patron, Savera Association, and Patron, Bhogilal Leherchand Institute of Indology.

E. IN THE AREA OF SOCIAL UPLIFTMENT

Was elected Chairman, Bharatiya Ekta evam Vikas Pratishthan. • Was Chairman, Thrombosis Research Institute of India. • Served as Chairman, Universal Peace Foundation of India. • Was honoured as Patron, Foundation for Peace and Sustainable Development. • Was Patron, Anti-Corruption Council of India. • Was Chief Patron, Bharat Vikas Parishad. • Advocated and influenced the creation of the National Human Rights Commission in India. • Was Chairman, Ramayan Kendra (Bharat). • Served as Chairman, Shri Dashrathmal Singhvi Memorial Trust. • Was Chairman, The Veena Foundation. • Was Chairman, Dada Bhai Naoroji Foundation. • Nominated as Chairman, Shri Guru Teg Bahadur International Foundation. • Was President, Centre for Contemporary Culture. • Was Chairman, Advisory Board of Chinmaya Centre of World Understanding. • Was President, World Jain Confederation. • Served as Chancellor, Jain Vishwa Bharati University. • Invited to give the Inaugural address on the Indic Vision at the World Summit at Atami (Japan). • Delivered the Sir Francis Younghusband Lecture for 1993 under the auspices of the World Congress of Faiths. • Elected one of the Presidents of the Centennial Parliament of World's Religions held at Chicago in 1993 and delivered the Keynote Address.

F. IN THE AREA OF EDUCATION AND AS AUTHOR AND POET

Bachelor of Arts, Allahabad University (Gold Medalist). • Took LL.B and M.A. degrees from Jaipur University. • Was First Rotary School from Rajasthan to study at Harvard University for LL.M. and Cornell University USA for LL.D. • Appointed as Faculty at Berkeley, California, a career he cut short and returned to India in 1957 at his father's persuasion. • Also honoured with titles of *Nyayavachaspati, Sahityavachaspati, Vidya Martand,* LL.D. and. D.Litt. *(honoris causa)*, the highest honour of Gurukul Kangri Vishva Vidyalaya. • Honoured with doctorates by different universities in India (Rajasthan, Allahabad, Calcutta, Delhi, Osmania, Andhra, Tamil Nadu and Jabalpur Universities). • Elected Honorary Tagore Law Professor in 1973 by Calcutta University, one of the oldest and most highly regarded Chairs in the world in the field of Law. • Founder-President (later Honorary Patron) of the Commonwealth Legal Education Association, London. Delivered the first series of Jawaharlal Nehru Memorial Lectures on 'Secularism' in celebration of Diamond Jubilee of the Banaras Hindu University (1975-76). • Elected as Mahatma Gandhi Professor at Leicester University. Delivered a course of lectures on Jurisprudence of Non-Violence. • Appointed Co-Chairman, Bharatiya Vidya Bhavan International. • Was Chairman of Pravara Mandal Jamna Lal Bajaj Award. • Was Chairman of Pravara Mandal of Jnan Peeth award. • Elected in 1992 to the Rede Chair at Cambridge University. The Rede Chair was founded in 1524 and was named after Sir Robert Rede, Lord Chief Justice of England. (The Cambridge University Press has published Dr. Singhvi's lecture in the form of a book titled *A Tale of Three Cities)*. • Served as Member of the Court of Jawaharlal Nehru University. • Was Chairman, Advisory Board of Sanskrit Pratishthan. • Served as Chairman, Akhil Bharatiya Hindi Sanstha Sangh. • Was President, Sasta Sahitya Mandal. • Was President, Global Indian Education Foundation. • Nominated as Honorary President, World Academy of Vedic Mathematics and International Resource and Research Foundation for Indian Heritage. • Was President, All India Rajasthani Bhasha Samity. • Served as President, The Poetry Society (India) (2004). • Was honoured as Chief Patron, *Abhudaya* (magazine). • Named as Patron *Paryavaran Vimarsha* (magazine). • Served as Member Board of Governors, Shri Jai Narain Vyas Shikshan Sansthan. • Also nominated Member Governing Council, Makhanlal Chaturvedi National University of Journalism. • Authored or edited a large number of books. His books in English, *Freedom on Trial* and *A Tale of Three Cities* widely acclaimed. • Was President, Authors' Guild of India for nearly a decade. • *Punaschaya* (a collection of his selected Editorials from *Sahitya Amrit Magazine* of which he was Editor). • Was Chairman, Foundation for National Integration through the Arts and Culture. • Several academic Chairs established in his name in British Universities such as Universities of Hull, Oxford; Edinburgh, Wales; London, and Leicester.

G. RECIPIENT OF OTHER DISTINGUISHED HONOURS

Was Rotary International's first recipient of the Ambassador of Excellence Award as a scholar-statesman for his exceptional personal and professional accomplishments and humanitarian service which best exemplifies the standards of Rotary and represents ideas of international service and "service above self". • Ranked as one of the five most skillful, eloquent, persuasive and highly respected MPs in India by Mr. M.C. Chagla in his book *'The Roses'*. • Invited to plant a tree to mark the opening of the New Law Library in Cambridge University. • His Holiness The Pope received Dr. and Mrs. Singhvi at the Vatican. • Authored *A Diplomatic Sojourn* (2002); *Democracy & Rule of Law; Towards Global Togetherness* (2002); *Bharat Aur Hamara Samaya; A Tale of Three Cities; Freedom on Trial* (1991); *The Evening Sun; Poems in Hindi; Jain Temples In India and Around the World* (2002); *Punascha* (2007); *Bharat ki Azadi aur Sanskriti* (2008) and others.

H. THE FAMILY

Father: Late Shri Dashrath Mall Singhvi, a distinguished political leader and a leading lawyer. • **Wife:** Smt. Kamla Singhvi, a well-known Hindi writer. Has deep interest in and supporter of institutions engaged in social service, music, poetry, arts, performing arts, and handicrafts. Authored *Kuchch Sabda Kuchch Artha; Man Ka Mausam; Dampatya Ke Dayare; Sambandho Ke Ghere Men, Mehandi Lage Hain Mere Hath, Nari, Bheetar aur Bahar; Ek Tookra Dharati* (collection of stories), *Grihakala – Soojh Bhoojh* and *Stree Ka Akash.* • **Son:** Dr. Abhishek Singhvi, a leading intellectual and forceful speaker; Senior Advocate of the Supreme Court of India; National Congress Spokesperson and an active Member of the Indian Parliament; Chairman, Parliament's Select Committee on Law and Justice; Former Additional Solicitor General of India; and Vice Chairman of the Supreme Court Bar Association; Honoured as the 'Global Leader of Tomorrow' by World Economic Forum; a Columnist (Prime Minister of India wrote the Foreword for his collection of column writings); Chairman of Indo-US Forum of Parliamentarians; Delivered Lectures at Stanford, Yale, and MIT • **Daughter-in-law:** Smt. Anita Singhvi, an outstanding painter and an eminent ghazal singer: Performed in India and abroad. • **Daughter:** Ms. Abhilasha Singhvi, a qualified lawyer actively engaged in humanitarian service with total commitment and dedication, in particular providing limbs to the handicapped (number exceeds 20,000) for the last 20 years as the promoter and the Executive Trustee of Manav Seva Sannidhi.

75 Facets of a Kaleidoscopic Personality

(Each Facet based on Multiple Evidence Acknowledged by Men and Women of Eminence)

1. Acknowledged World Diplomat
2. Brilliant Social Scientist
3. Doctor of Laws and of Letters
4. Eminent Constitutional Expert
5. Eminent Educationist
6. Enlightened Parliamentarian
7. Erudite Editor
8. Exemplary Scholar
9. Founder of Novel Institutions
10. Goal-oriented Administrator
11. Honoured Litterateur
12. Internationally Recognized Jurist
13. Literary Figure of Fame
14. Master of Languages
15. Orator Par Excellence
16. Outstanding Sanskrit Scholar
17. Passionate Poet
18. Powerful Speaker
19. Profound Researcher
20. Prolific Writer
21. Sensitive Writer
22. Thought Leader
23. Conferred several Honorary Doctorates
24. Decorated 'Padmabhushan'
25. Achiever Par Excellence
26. Accredited Conflict Resolver
27. Aggressive Pacifist
28. Ardent Animal Lover
29. Committed Believer of Non-Violence

30. Bold Fighter of Social Causes
31. Champion of Human Rights
32. Citizen Statesman of Distinction
33. Committed Exponent of Religious Thoughts
34. Compassionate Leader
35. Dedicated Environmentalist
36. Deep Creative Thinker
37. Discriminating Art Connoisseur
38. Distinguished Professor
39. Dreamer of a New World Order
40. Enlightened Public Leader
41. Established Inter-faith Leader
42. Exponent of Indian Culture
43. Fighter for Equity and Social Justice
44. Forward-looking Organizer
45. Follower of High Social Values
46. Global Votary of Democracy
47. Highly Soft-spoken Person
48. Humane by Disposition
49. Impartial Mediator
50. Inspiring Team Builder
51. Innovator of New Ideas
52. Intellectual of Distinction
53. Intense Scholar of Philosophy
54. International Institution Builder
55. Intrinsically Spiritual
56. Knowledge Explorer
57. Leading Man of Letters
58. Man of Determination
59. Man of Integrity and Character
60. Path-breaking Visionary
61. Performing Performer
62. Promoter of World Fellowship
63. Propagator of Religious Faiths
64. Protector of Ethical Values
65. Religious by Faith
66. Respected Arbitrator of Disputes
67. Robust Value Creator
68. Role Model of Dignity
69. Secular by Conviction
70. Spokesman of Indian Heritage
71. Subtle Social Activist

72. Supporter of Weaker Sections
73. Undaunted Path-breaker
74. Unique Storehouse of Knowledge
75. Unrelenting Pursuer of Excellence.

Some Impressions on the Life and Work of Dr. L.M. Singhvi

Dr. Laxmi Mall Singhvi has rendered invaluable service in diverse fields of national reconstruction. His contributions in spheres of law and jurisprudence, literature, culture, social service, diplomacy, and in Parliament, have been manifold and significant. His great abilities as a thinker, speaker and writer are complemented by the endearing charm and warmth of his personality.

—Shankar Dayal Sharma, President of India

Dr. Singhvi is a multisplendoured personality. Dr. Singhvi is practically a role model for every aspiring young man in any walk of life.

—R. Venkataraman, Former President of India

Dr. Singhvi's writings and lectures reflect his brilliant synthesis of the global concerns of mankind. He deals in a masterly manner with the trinity of Environment, Human Rights and the Interfaith Movement, in his Dickensian "A Tale of Three Cities".

—K.R. Narayanan, Former President of India

I will never forget the Poetry evening at your residence. For years the poet within me expected and craved for a friendly caress. Little did I imagine that it would happen across the seas and thousands of miles away from India at the hands of a diplomat! But then you are not merely an ambassador. Yours is truly the articulate voice of India's identity; you are a vigilant representative of the national renaissance.

—Atal Behari Vajpayee, Later Prime Minister of India

I am glad to join in this birthday tribute to L.M. Singhvi—Scholar Statesman, Jurist, Diplomat and distinguished High Commissioner in

London, whose company and conversation are always a pleasure. He has notably enhanced the standing of India in Britain.

—The Rt. Hon. Douglas Hurd, CBE, Secretary of State for Foreign and Commonwealth Affairs

His legal distinction has been recognised in Britain by his election as an Honorary Bencher and Master of the Middle Temple. Dr. Singhvi has also been recognised by those of us in the British Parliament as a fellow parliamentarian of distinction, as well as a scholar and world figure.

—The Rt. Hon. Dr. Sir Rhodes Boyson, Member, House of Commons, UK

Good lawyers know how to work to a brief and to present a case to the best effect. But few of us have the chance to put those skills to work for our country. That is Dr. Singhvi's privilege. And he performs the job with unwavering goodwill.

—The Hon'ble Greville Janner, QC, Member of Parliament, UK

I am deeply impressed by the life and work of Dr. L.M. Singhvi. Eminent man of letters, diplomat, parliamentarian, jurist and humanist, he is an outstanding example of a son of India who does credit to his country and enriches the cultural heritage of humankind. He represents a deep-seated democratic tradition which transcends the East-west divide.

—Sir Sigmund Sternberg O, St. J., KCSG, JP, London

I was so delighted to see Singhviji bringing such dynamic changes and reforms in our London mission. Nehru Centre is one of his major achievements, but there are so many others that I have been hearing about. His wisdom, eloquence and charm wins over everyone. But what attracts me most is the Indian inherent quality that he has!

—Pandit Ravi Shankar, Sitar Maestro

Dr. L.M. Singhvi was a dear friend for four decades. We shared so many interests and so many platforms in India and around the world that people began referring to us as Lav and Kush! Dr. Singhvi was a man of immense talent, which was displayed in whichever field he entered. In law he rose to be a leading lawyer and jurist; in politics he was an outstanding parliamentarian; in diplomacy his long stint as High Commissioner to the United Kingdom will always be remembered for the multiple projects that he initiated to strengthen our links with that country; as an author he wrote fluently and his books and articles remain a source of inspiration to many; as an orator he was equally fluent and effective in English as in Hindi; in philosophy he was one of the few people I knew who had an equal grasp over the Vedic and Shramanik traditions; in the Interfaith movement he played a major role in India and abroad.

—Dr. Karan Singh, Deputy Leader of the Congress Party in Rajya Sabha

I am deeply honoured to be invited to deliver the first Dr. L.M. Singhvi Memorial Lecture, and delighted that my friend Dr. Karan Singh is presiding over it. I first met Lakshmi Malji when he took charge as India's High Commissioner to the UK. We shared many interests in common, and over time became very good friends. He was a fine classical scholar, a first rate constitutional lawyer, a distinguished diplomat, an astute statesman with a fine sense of history, a devoted family man, committed to the highest values of public life, and above all, one of the most generous and affectionate human beings.

—Lord Bhikhu Parekh, House of Lords, London

Dr. L.M. Singhvi, also an Independent Member of Parliament, was profoundly learned in constitutional law and parliamentary practices; his contributions to the debate were always weighty and useful.

—M.C. Chagla, Former Foreign Minister of India

LM is a great internationalist, who worked and contributed significantly to the furtherance of Commonwealth objectives, in particular the principles of democracy and a common humanity.

—Chief Emeka Anyaoku, Commonwealth Secretary General

Let me quote a line from Hamlet to project my vision of a great person in whose category Dr. Singhvi falls:

'What a piece of work is a man!
How noble in reason!'
How infinite in faculty!
In form, in moving,
How express and admirable!
In action how like an angel!
In apprehension how like a god!

—Mr. Justice V.R. Krishna Iyer, Former Judge, Supreme Court of India

Dr. Singhvi's great practical contribution to this country has surely been in the realm of culture. He has put into practice a belief I share with him that the treasures of the inner worlds—of the ever-living imagination —are not only more real and enduring, but also have more practical value than the politics of this world, in those exchanges between nations upon which the future of us all depends.

—Kathleen Raine, British poetess and an "Honorary Indian"

Dr. L.M. Singhvi stands in the long tradition of scholar-statesmen—or, in Plato's phrase, philosopher-kings—for which India is known and of which Dr. Sarvapalli Radhakrishnan was an outstanding example.

—Marcus Braybrooke, Chairman, World Congress of Faiths

I have rarely come across a person of Dr. Singhvi's charm, erudition and deep knowledge of India.

—Professor Subrata Mitra, Director, Centre for Indian Studies, The University of Hull

In India Dr. Singhvi has long been known as a champion of the arts and humanities. It is, however, as a legal expert with a profound belief in the independence of the judiciary and the protection of human rights that Dr. Singhvi is best known.

—John Hanson, CBE, Former Director General, The British Council

What can one say about a towering personality—a person who was a friend of friends, a person who was so erudite, intelligent, possessed a keen razor sharp intellect, a person whose interests ranged from the legal to political to art and "literature, in short—a person who defied being put into the usual worldly brackets! ... His book of poems *Sandhya ka Sooraj* opened the doors to his philosophical persona. They reflected his inner search for the meaning of life, existence and consciousness. ... Dr. Singhvi spread light and warmth. He never was known to curse the darkness. He was like the oyster that turned water into pearl and numerous ideas into gold.

—Shovana Narayan, A Leading Kathak Dancer

Dr. Shinghvi's own illustrious career illustrates many facets of the ties between our two countries. A distinguished writer has judged Dr. Singhvi to be amongst of his time. To this accolade I can only add my personal admiration and respect for a great figure in Anglo-Indian relations, and a major figure in international statesmanship.

—(Professor) Sir David Williams, Vice Chancellor, University of Cambridge

Dr. Singhvi has demonstrated that the real man of culture is at home in all cultures. There is a sense of gratitude that a man of this stature would make professional sacrifices to serve his country.

—Lord Swraj Paul, Chairman, Caparo Group, London

Dr. L.M. Singhvi, a person of great intellect and rare virtues, who made outstanding contribution in every sphere of public activity he visited during fifty years of his illustrious career. ... Shri M.C. Chagla placed him amongst the five most skillful and highly respected MPs in India.

—D.N. Patodia, A Leading Businessman

Bassie Anderson Stanley has said
That man is a success
Who has lived well, laughed often
and loved much;
Who has gained the respect of intelligent men
And the love of children;
Who has filled his niche
And accomplished his task;
Who leaves the world better than he found it
Whether by
A perfect poem
Or a rescued Soul
Who never lacked appreciation of
Earth's beauty
Who looked for the best in others
And gave the best he had.

It seems that Stanley composed these beautiful lines anticipating knowledge of Dr. Singhvi's life and work. If he did not, he could quote these in validation of his poetic thesis.

—from *Towards a New Global Order 1993*
Edited by Dr. S.R. Mohnot

Selected Gems of Caveats and Concerns on Contemporary Human Milieu

From Dr. L. M. Singhvi

- Never before in the history of civilization has there been such a diamond, bright promise and potential of amelioration of the human condition.
- At the threshold of the last decennial of the twentieth century, we find ourselves, at the global level, at new frontiers of freedom.
- Citizenship and leadership are two sides of the same coin.
- The chief among the myths that abound the parliamentary system of government is that legislation is the exclusive concern and prerogative of the legislature.
- The concept of independence of justice is as variegated as different legal systems and cultures and yet it is quintessentially universal.
- Rule of law postulates within the confines of public order... Rule of law is a synthesis of social discipline with human dignity.
- At its best, social legislation seeks to make the weak strong and the strong just.
- Secularism is a part of our on-going struggle for larger freedom and better life. It is at once an ideal and an aspiration, a goal as well as a striving, a product as well as a process.
- We know an animal farm model of a world in which some nations are for ever and inherently more equal than others.
- The litmus test for a civilized society is the measure of care and consideration it bestows on women, children and the handicapped.
- Democracy is a comprehensive and composite cluster of social, cultural, economic, institutional, jural and processual concepts in operation. It is a system of values and norms both theoretically and operationally.

The Contributors

Avul Pakir Jainulabdeen Abdul Kalam. Born on 15th October, 1931. Was the 11th President of India, serving from 2002 to 2007. Popularly known as the People's President. • Received honorary doctorates from about 30 universities globally. Conferred the *Padma Bhushan* in 1981, the *Padma Vibhushan* in 1990 and the *Bharat Ratna* in 1997. Graduated in Physics from St. Joseph's College, Tiruchirapalli, later awarded diploma by the Madras Institute of Technology specializing in Aeronautical Engineering. • As Project Director, was involved in the development of India's first indigenous Satellite Launch Vehicle (SLV-III). • As Chief Executive of Integrated Guided Missile Development Programme (IGMDP), played a major part in developing many missiles of India including *Agni* and *Prithvi*. • Was the Chief Scientific Adviser to Prime Minister and Secretary, Department of Defence Research & Development from July 1992 to December 1999. Pokhran-II nuclear tests were conducted during this period. • Is Chancellor of Indian Institute of Space, Science and Technology (Thiruvanthapuram), a professor at Anna University (Chennai) and adjunct/visiting faculty at many other academic and research institutions across India. • Produced *India 2020* which highlights an action plan that will help develop the country into a knowledge superpower by 2020. • After his tenure as the President of India is now a visiting guest professor at JSS University, Mysore.

Dr. Justice A.S. Anand. Born in 1936 in Jammu (Jammu and Kashmir). •Graduated from Jammu and Kashmir University in 1958. • Took LL.B. and Diploma in Labour Laws 1960 from Lucknow University. • Was awarded Ph.D. in Laws from the London University in 1963. • Awarded Doctor of Letters (*Honoris Causa*) by the Jammu

University in 1999. • Was conferred the Degree of LL.D. (*Honoris Causa*) by Lucknow University in 1996. • Called to the Bar from the Society of Inner Temple, London in 1964 and later elected as its Hony. Bencher. Practiced Law in Punjab & Haryana High Court. • At the age of 38, appointed as Additional Judge of Jammu & Kashmir High Court in 1975 and as a permanent Judge in 1976, Acting Chief Justice of Jammu & Kashmir High Court in 1984, and Chief Justice in 1985 and of the High Court at Madras in 1989. • Elevated to the Bench of the Hon'ble Supreme Court of India in 1991. • Served as Chief Justice of India (1998-2001). • Served as the Chairman of the Human Rights Commission of India. • Headed various Commissions of Enquiry and Investigation. • Participated in various national and international conferences such as the Appellate Judges Conference at Manila (1977); New Delhi (1984); Law Asia Conference (1984 and 1986) and SAARC Law Conference at New Delhi (1994); 2nd Worldwide Common Law Judiciary Conference at Washington (1997); SAARC Chief Justices' Conference at Colombo (1998). • Was elected as President of the International Institute of Human Rights Society. • Has authored *The Constitution of Jammu & Kashmir. Its Development & Comments.* • Awarded the Fellowship of the University College, London in 1997. • Is Patron-in-Chief of National Legal Services Authority (India) from 1998.

Rahul Bajaj. Chairman of the Bajaj Group, launched by Gandhiji's associate Jamnalal Bajaj and ranks among the top business houses in India. The Group developed diversified interests ranging from automobiles to home appliances and lighting products. In 1980s, Bajaj Auto was top scooter producer in India and its popular brand had a 10-year waiting period. • Was the head of the historic Bombay Club of business leaders. • Is a Member of Parliament (Rajya Sabha). • Was awarded *Padma Bhushan* in 2001 by the President. • Was honoured with the Man of the Year Award (1975); Businessman of the Year Award (1985); and Bombay Management Award (1990). • Was appointed Member, International Council of International Business by the Prince of Wales. • Internationally respected for his business acumen and entrepreneurial spirit. Listed twentieth on the Forbes India's Richest 40. • Has been Director of a large number of companies. Also served as the Chairman of Board of Directors of the public sector, Indian Airlines. • Was elected President of the Confederation of Indian Industry (CII, the apex organization of Indian Industry) besides Marhatta Chambers of Commerce and Industries, Association of Indian Automobile Manu-facturers. • Has served as the Chairman of Development Council for Automobiles and Allied Industries, and as Member of several advisory and counselling committees of the Government. Is a law graduate from the University of Bombay and an MBA from Harvard Business School.

Dr. P.C. Bansil. Born in 1919, heads the Techno Economic Research Institute, New Delhi, founded by him in 1984. • Belongs to the first batch of Indian Economic Service and has served as Senior Planning Adviser with the UN Food and Agricultural Organization (FAO) for about 15 years in several countries, Sri Lanka, Thailand, Zambia, Libya and at the Headquarters in Rome. Has authored 30 books, besides a large number of reports for various governments and research and professional institutions. Has produced over 400 papers in professional and technical journals. • Has done extensive research and applied work on the formulation, implementation and evaluation of regional plans of agriculture, statistics, marketing, livestock, irrigation, fisheries, forestry, wildlife, national parks, tourism, agro-industries and social sectors like demography, health, education and housing. Included is the work on project identification, formulation and evaluation. During his FAO assignments in the capacity of Senior Planning Adviser, undertook micro level studies on issues relating to water. • Was appointed by the Planning Commission as Chairman of the Tenth and Twelfth Plans Working Groups on Animal Husbandry, Economics and Statistics. Has just completed a study on *Livestock in India, 2000-2030,* sponsored by UN FAO.

Somnath Chatterjee. Born in 1929 in Tezpur, Assam. • Was the Speaker of the 14th Lok Sabha. His father, Nirmal Chandra Chatterjee, was President of the Akhil Bharatiya Hindu Mahasabha, a forerunner of today's Bharatiya Janta Party. Later he left Hindu Mahasabha to join left politics and was elected to the Parliament with the support of Communist Party of India. • Educated at Presidency College and the University of Calcutta. Also attended Cambridge University and awarded an Honorary Fellowship of Jesus College. • Was a litigating barrister at the Calcutta High Court before joining active politics. Began career as a lawyer being called to the Bar in England and joined Indian politics in 1968 at the national level. Became a member of the Communist Party of India (Marxist). In 1971, he was given a ticket to contest an election caused by the death of his father who was earlier elected from that constituency. • Became a Member of the Lok Sabha (Lower House of Parliament) in 1971 and was elected first time as an independent candidate supported by the CPI (M). • Since then, he has served as a member in all successive Lok Sabhas, except in 1984. • Was elected for the tenth time in 2004 as a member of the 14th Lok Sabha.

Professor Indra Nath Choudhuri. A distinguished administrator and cultural diplomat. Was Secretary to Sahitya Akademi and Minister (Culture), Indian High Commission, London and Director, The Nehru Centre, London. Was Member Secretary and Academic Director, Indira Gandhi National Centre for the Arts. • Was Chief Editor, Concise Hindi Encyclopaedia, Kendriya Hindi Sansthan, Ministry of HRD and also Chief Editor, revised version of the Encyclopadia, Sahitya Academi. • Was Member, Board of Languages and Translation, IGNOU and also the Academic Council, Mahatma Gandhi International Hindi University and Member, Executive Board, Netaji Subhas Open University, Kolkata. Now Member Secretary of Vatsal Nidhi and Member Secretary, Sasta Sahitya Mandal. • Is Fellow of Temenos Akademi, and Millennium Trust, Kent, UK. • Was a professor at the Delhi University, Uccha Siksha aur Sodh Sansthan, Hyderabad and University of Bucharest (as an ICCR Visiting Professor). Was also Visiting Professor in many other Universities including Central University, and CIEFL, Hyderabad, Jadavpur University and Jawaharlal Nehru University, Delhi. • Written books on comparative literature, poetics and aesthetics in Hindi, English and Bengali. *The Genesis of Imagination, Selected Essays on Literature, Theory, Religion and Culture, (Sterling 2001) and Sparks Fly Upward: Three Essays on Aesthetics* (Temenos, London 1999), *Comparative Literature: Some Perspectives* (Hindi, 2006), *Hinduism: Religion without Religion (in the press)*. Contributed more than 50 research papers which include about a dozen on Tagore. • Received many awards including prestigious Kendriya Hindi Sansthan, Ministry of Human Resource Development Ganga Sharan Singh Award from the President of India in 2007 and also Delhi Hindi Academy Award, 2009. • Participated in a number of international conferences at Paris, New York, Tokyo, London, Hawaii, Moscow, Singapore, Belgrade, Potsdam, Turino, Oslo, Washington.

Prof. Abid Hussain. Economist, administrator and diplomat. • Was India's Ambassador to the United States (1990-1992). Held several senior positions: Secretary, Department of Heavy Industries, Ministry of Commerce and Member, Planning Commission. • Is Member, UNESCO's International Panel on Democracy and Development and Professor Emeritus at the Indian Institute of Foreign Trade (IIFT). • Is a Member of the Academy of the Kingdom of Morocco, BP Koirala Foundation, Kathmandu and International Film and Television Research Centre of Asian Academy of Film Television, Prasar Bharti Board. • Was a Member of the Council on Foreign Relations and Asia Society, New York and Chairman of Research Council of National Institute of Science, Technology and Development Studies; Bharatiya Vidya Bhavan. • Was a Trustee of Indira Gandhi National Centre for the Arts Trust; President of Katha; Member of Nehru Memorial Fund; the Population Foundation of India; Foundation for Academic Excellence Access;

Administrative Staff College, Hyderabad; and Governing Council of Ranbaxy Science Foundation. • Is Vice Chairman, Rajiv Gandhi Foundation. Was the Chancellor of Central University, Hyderabad. Was Special Rapporteur on UN Freedom of Opinion and Expression. • Was Member of the Constitution Review Commission. • Was UN Adviser to Turkey on Community Development and Chief of Industrial, Technology, Human Settlements and Environment in the UN Regional Commission of ESCAP, Bangkok.

Dr. Bimal Jalan. A distinguished economist. • Was Governor of the Reserve Bank of India from 1997 to 2003. • Nominated to the Rajya Sabha, the Upper House of Parliament of India in 2003. • Held several high level positions in India and abroad. In India, served as Chief Economic Adviser to the Government, Banking Secretary, Finance Secretary, Member-Secretary of the Planning Commission, and Chairman of the Economic Advisory Council to the Prime Minister. • Represented India as Executive Director on Boards of International Monetary Fund and the World Bank during 1988-89 and 1993-96. Earlier, served as Director (Economic Affairs) of Commonwealth Secretariat in London. • Has been Chairman/President of a number of distinguished academic institutions, such as the Indian Statistical Institute, National Council of Applied Economic Research, Institute of Economic Growth. • Was educated at Presidency College, Calcutta and Cambridge and Oxford. • Written extensively on the Indian economy. Books include *India's Economic Crisis: The Way Ahead* (1991), *The Indian Economy: Problems and Prospects* (1993, 2004), *India's Economic Policy: Preparing for the 21st Century* (1997), and *India's Economy in the New Millennium—Selected Essays* (2002). • Other publications include *Problems and Policies in Small Economies* (1982) and *Essays in Development Policy* (1975). • The recent ones: *The Future of India: Politics, Economics and Governance* (2005), and its sequel *India's Politics: A View from the Backbench* (2007).

L.N. Jhunjhunwala. Born in 1928 at Mukundgarh in Rajasthan. • Received higher education at Scottish Church College, Calcutta. Graduated in Philosophy from the Calcutta University with Honours in Mathematics. Was awarded Gold Medal for having secured the first position. During his Master's studies, was a student of Satyen Bose, the eminent scientist. • Despite his earnestness to pursue education, started business under family pressures. • After a successful stint with trading, established Bhilwara Spinning and Weaving Company Limited, which became the flagship of the large business conglomerate, The Bhilwara Group and now styled as LNJ Bhilwara Group. The group expanded to other industries, such as graphite electrodes, sponge iron and power generation. Passed on the baton to his son Ravi Jhunjhunwala and son-in-law Shekhar Agarwal. • While continuing his strong links with the business world for over half a century, evinced immense interest in cultural activities with special interest in Ramakrishna Mission and Astronomy. Has been the Founder Member (1954) of the Bhartiya Sanskriti Sansad, Calcutta. Undertook study in original Bangla of the Ramakrishna-Vivekanand literature. • Learnt Drupad from Ustad Aminuddin. • Was Chairman of the Russian Academy which produced first three Indian Grandmasters of Chess. • Has widely travelled in the Himalayas with special interest in glaciers.

Dr. Subhash C. Kashyap. Political Scientist and Constitutional Law and Parliamentary Affairs specialist and counsellor. Was Secretary General, Lok Sabha (Lower House) of the Indian Parliament (1994-1999). • Served as Honorary Constitutional Adviser to Government of India on Panchayati Raj Institutions. • Was Associated with the Parliament for over 40 years. Author of many prestigious works on Constitutional Law and Practices and other subject of social and political interest. • Received higher education and professional training at Allahabad, New Delhi, Washington D.C., Dallas, London and Geneva. • An experienced administrator, widely travelled over the world, Served as Director of Institute of Constitutional and Parliamentary Studies and as an international civil servant, headed the C.I.D.P., International Parliamentary Union, Geneva. • Recipient of many distinctions and honours in and outside India. • Was U.S. Congressional Fellow of the A.P.S.A., UNDP Fellow, Fellow of the Academy of American and International Law. • Was awarded the Honorary title of Commander and degree of. H.O.A.S.F. (Honorary Order of the Academy of San Francisco). • Received the Motilal Nehru Award twice and several State Prizes for best works in law and political science. • Founded several organisations like Rashtriya Jagriti Sansthan. Organised a large number of national and international discourses • Authored over 300 research papers and articles and around 40 books. • Currently, Honorary Visiting Professor at the Centre for Policy Research and Honorary Editor, *South Asia Politics.*

S.A. Khader. Principal Consultant, SAK Consultants & Associates and a Visiting Professor. • Teaches Consultancy Management at International Management Institute (IMI), New Delhi. • Has lifetime association with Indian productivity movement having served in several positions including the Deputy Director General of the National Productivity Council. • Was instrumental in devising the National Productivity Award Scheme and Public Sector Performance Awards instituted by the Government of India. • Was invited to deliver the maiden Foundation Day Lecture on the 10th Anniversary of Nigerian Productivity Centre • Provides training and consulting services based on his copyrighted model of Self-Assessment Approach to Competitiveness Enhancement. Served as international chief resource person in Asia-Pacific region in enhancing enterprise level P&Q, besides other management techniques like, Lean Manufacturing and TQM Practice. • His E-learning lessons on TQM Implementation on Asian Productivity Council Website are globally accessed. • Is B. Tech (Mechanical Engg.) from IIT Madras. • Is a PG IE and PG in Production Management from West Germany, certified MTM Practitioner & ISO Lead Auditor. Is also a CMC accredited by IMCI. • Writes regularly for professional journals having made over 100 contributions.

Kashi Nath Memani. Chartered Accountant • Former Chairman and Country Managing Partner of Ernst & Young India, international consulting firm. Retired in 2004 • Specialises in Business and Corporate Advisory, Financial Consultancy. • Widely consulted on corporate matters by several leading domestic and foreign companies. • Helped several multinational companies in setting up businesses in India • Joined the boards of listed companies, such as DLF Ltd., ICICI Venture Funds Management Company Ltd., HT Media Ltd. Aegon Religare Insurance Company Ltd, Chambal Fertilisers & Chemicals Ltd. • Is a member of governing bodies of some business schools, social, educational and charitable organisations and foundations. • Has been a Member of the Managing Committees of Federation of Indian Chambers of Commerce and Industry, Indo-American Chamber of Commerce, American Chamber of Commerce, Associated Chamber of Commerce, PHD Chamber of Commerce, and others. • Was a Member of External Audit Committee of IMF, Washington DC in 1999 and its Chairman in 2000, the only Indian so far to sit on this committee.

Dr. S.R. Mohnot. Editor of the present volume. • Executive Chairman, Centre for Industrial and Economic Research (CIER) and Chairman and Managing Director, Industrial Techno-Economic Services (INTECOS), international industrial and management consultants. • Former Industrial Economist and Team Leader with United Nations Industrial Development Organization (UNIDO) and United Nations Development Programme. • Worked as International Consultant to Asian Development Bank (ADB). • President Emeritus, Indian Society of Training and Development (ISTD). Honoured as Fellow for life. Is a Member of the Executive Board of the National Academy of Training and Development (NATAD) and was Co-Chairman of the Academic Council. • Former Vice Chairman, Consultancy Development Centre. • Is Director of some 10 industrial and service companies in India and other countries • Was Vice President, Institute of Management Consultants of India (IMCI). Also honoured as Fellow. • Has delivered lectures and acted as Chairman of a large number of international professional and academic conferences.

• Has authored or edited some 20 widely acclaimed books and a large number of technical papers. • Path-breaking works: *Concentration of Economic Power* (1962); *Market Forecasts and Indicators* (1997-2007), latest version 2010-20; *Reinventing the Public Sector* (2002) and *The Emerging Public Sector: New Vision of a National Treasure* (2010); *Concise Encyclopaedia of Management and Economic Sciences (2007)*. • Has edited several books such as Towards a New Global Order (1993) to which the Foreword was written by the President of India. Is Ph.D. and Sahitya Ratna.

D.N. Patodia. Born in January 1928 in Calcutta. • Took his M.A. from Calcutta University in 1951. • Is a Former Member of Lok Sabha (Lower House of the Indian Parliament), 1967-1971, elected from Jalore in Rajasthan as Swatantra Party candidate. • Was President, Federation of Indian Chambers of Commerce & Industry, the apex Business Industry Association of India (1985-86), Economics and Scientific Research Foundation, All India Bank Depositors Association. • Associated, amongst others, with several institutions in different capacities: Bhartiya Kala Kendra; • Birla Institute of Technology and Science, Ranchi; Birla Institute of Technology, Pilani, Indian Council of World Affairs, New Delhi; Federation of Indo-German Societies in India; • National Council of Applied Economic Research, New Delhi. • Business activities, covered manufacturing of a wide range of non-ferrous pressure die casting products and trading on a wide scale in electrical and engineering products, tea and gunnies.

Sharu S. Rangnekar. Well-known Management Educator for decades. Is a Chemical Engineer with an MBA from the USA. • Carried out research work in Mathematical Economics at the Carnegie-Mellon University, Pittsburgh, USA. • Had management training with Imperial Chemical Industries, UK and computer training with IBM and Union Carbide Corporation, USA. • Started management career in 1951 as a Consultant with Ibcon and subsequently worked in several multinationals till he took early retirement from Searle (India) as the Managing Director at the end of 1978. • Taught as Visiting Faculty at Tata Institute of Social Sciences and Management Institutes attached to Bombay University from 1979 to 1986. • His lectures on management topics have been issued in audio-CD formats. Has featured in several management development video-CDs. • Authored many books: *In the Wonderland of Indian Manager* and *In the World of Corporate Managers* which have become management classics. • Has participated as a faculty in nearly 5000 management development programmes in India and abroad since 1966.

Lord Bhikhu Parekh. Born 1935 in Amalsad, Gujarat in India. • Entered University of Bombay at the age of 15, and secured Bachelor's degree in 1954 and Master's in 1956. Joined London School of Economics in 1959 and secured his Ph.D. in 1966. • Taught at the London School and the University of Glasgow before undertaking a long-term position at the University of Hull. Was Vice-Chancellor at the Maharaja Sayajirao University of Baroda in India (1981-1984). Held the Centennial Professorship at the Centre for the Study of Global Governance at the London School of Economics and Professorship of Political Philosophy at the University of Westminster. • Served as President of the Academy of Learned Societies in the Social Sciences (2002). • Became Fellow of the Royal Society of Arts in 1988, and of the Academy of Learned Societies in Social Sciences in 1999. Was appointed a life peer in 2000 as Baron Parekh of the Kingston upon Hull in the East Riding of Yorkshire. • Awarded Fellowship of the British Academy and Honorary Doctorate by the University of Essex. Also awarded *Padma Bhushan* by Government of India in 2007. • Has authored and edited several books: *Bentham's Political Thought* (1973); *Marx's Theory of Ideology* (1982); *Colonialism, Tradition and Reform: An Analysis of Gandhi's Political Discourse* (1989); *Gandhi's Political Philosophy* (1991); *The Future of Multi-Ethnic Britain: Report of the Commission on the Future of Multi-Ethnic Britain* (2000); *Rethinking Multiculturalism: Cultural Diversity and Political Theory* (2002); *A New Politics of Identity: Political Principles for an Interdependent World* (2008). • Edited: *Colour, Culture and Consciousness: Immigrant Intellectuals in Britain* (1974).

Justice P. Sathasivam. Born 1947 • Practiced at the Bombay High Court. • Appointed as an Additional Judge in 1991 and as a Permanent Judge of the Bombay High Court in 1993. • Appointed as a Judge of the Special Court (Trial of Offences Relating to Transactions in Securities) Act in 1999. During the period, decided important matters under PIL pertaining to CRZ, under RBI and Banking Regulation Act; the constitutional validity of the 74th Amendment Act of 1992 dealing with Municipalities; Smugglers and Foreign Exchange Manipulators (Forfeiture of Property) Act, 1976; Mergers and Acquisitions; Payment of Bonus Act; Industrial Disputes Act. In addition dealt with matters under the Income Tax Act; Accounting treatment given to Modvat Credit Convergence of Tax. • As a Judge presided over the Special Court dealt with civil and criminal matters including matters concerning the Reports submitted by RBI and JPC *vis-à-vis* Evidence Act. Also dealt with accounts and finances of banks and financial institutions and of the share and stock brokers. Framed investment schemes dealing with valuation and disposal of shares and distribution of assets of the Notified Parties under the Act. • Appointed as Chief Justice of the Uttaranchal High Court in August 2003. • Elevated to the Bench of the Supreme Court of India in December 2003. • Has keen interest in Economics, Public Finance, Theoretical Physics and Hindu and Buddhist philosophies.

Dr. Karan Singh. Born on March 9, 1931, in Cannes, France, to the last ruler of the princely state of Jammu and Kashmir, Maharaja Hari Singh and Maharani Tara Devi. • Was educated at Doon School, Dehra Dun, and graduated from Jammu and Kashmir University. Took his Masters in Political Science and doctorate from the Delhi University. • At the age of eighteen, he was appointed the Regent of Jammu and Kashmir state after his father stepped down as the Maharaja, following the state's accession to India. He served successively as Regent, Sadr-i-Riyasat and Governor of the State of Jammu and Kashmir (1965-1967). He served successively as Union Minister for Tourism and Civil Aviation from 1967 to 1973, Minister of Health and Family Planning from 1973 to 1977 and Minister of Education and Culture in 1979-1980. In 1990-1991, served as Indian Ambassador to the US. • From 1967 to 1980, and in 1990, was elected as MP in the Lok Sabha. Since 1996, has been an MP in the Rajya Sabha. • Served as Chancellor of Banaras Hindu University, Jammu and Kashmir University, and Jawaharlal Nehru University. Is an active member of several boards, organizations, and foundations, including the Author's Guild of India, the Indian Council for Cultural Relations (ICCR). The Auroville Foundation, the Indian Board of Wildlife, and several others. • Was conferred the prestigious *Padma Vibhushan* in 2005.

Dr. Abhishek Manu Singhvi. An eminent jurist, parliamentarian, media personality, well known columnist, author and commentator. • A Member of Parliament; the seniormost National Spokesperson of the Congress Party and a lead Speaker in Parliament. Senior Advocate, Supreme Court of India; former Additional Solicitor General of India (ASG) and former Vice President, Supreme Court Bar Association.• Was the youngest to be appointed/elected as Senior Advocate, as ASG and as Vice President of Supreme Court Bar Association . • Currently the Chairman of the AICC, India Law and Human Rights Department. • Awarded the Global Leader of Tomorrow Award by World Economic Forum, Davos. • Authored fortnightly column, *Candid Corner*, in India's second largest English daily and now writes a fortnightly column in India's largest English daily, the *Times of India.* Also an occasional columnist in the largest Hindi daily. • The Prime Minister of India wrote the Foreword to his book of columns. • Is a Member of several important Parliamentary Committees, including Priveleges, Law & Justice, Urban Affairs and Office of Profit. • Is Chairman, Indo-US Forum of Parliamentarians; Vice President, Indo Greek Parliamentary Forum; President, SAARC LAW and Member, Governing Body of National Law University. • Graduated from St. Stephen's College, University of Delhi, and received MA and Ph.D. from Trinity College, Cambridge, UK. • Taught at St. John's College, Cambridge and did a programme, PIL, from Harvard. Delivered lectures at Stanford, Harvard, Yale, Boston, MIT and George Washington Universities to NGOs and think tanks. Addressed several international conferences.

Dr. M. S. Valiathan. Pioneered biomedical research in the country. • Led a group which developed a tilting disc heart valve and other cardiovascular devices. Credited with the development of artificial heart valves, blood bags, oxygenerators, vascular grafts and others. • Received M.B.B.S. degree from Kerala University in 1956 and F.R.C.S. from the Royal College of Surgeons, Edinburgh in 1960. • Received Cardiac Surgical training in the John Hopkins and Georgetown University Hospitals, U.S. • Served as Professor of Cardiac Surgery at the Sri Chitra Tirunal Institute of Medical Sciences and Technology for 20 years. • Elected to many academies in India and abroad. Awarded the Hunterian Professorship of the Royal College of Surgeons of England. • Has published several outstanding research papers on Endomyocardial Fibrosis Cardiac Surgery, Bio Materials & Artificial Internal Organs, Health & Health Policy. • Has undertaken the monumental work bringing out the foundational text of Indian Medicine in Sanskrit, *Charaka Samhita.* • Has received many national and international honours including the prestigious *Padma Bhushan* from the Hon'ble President of India.

Index